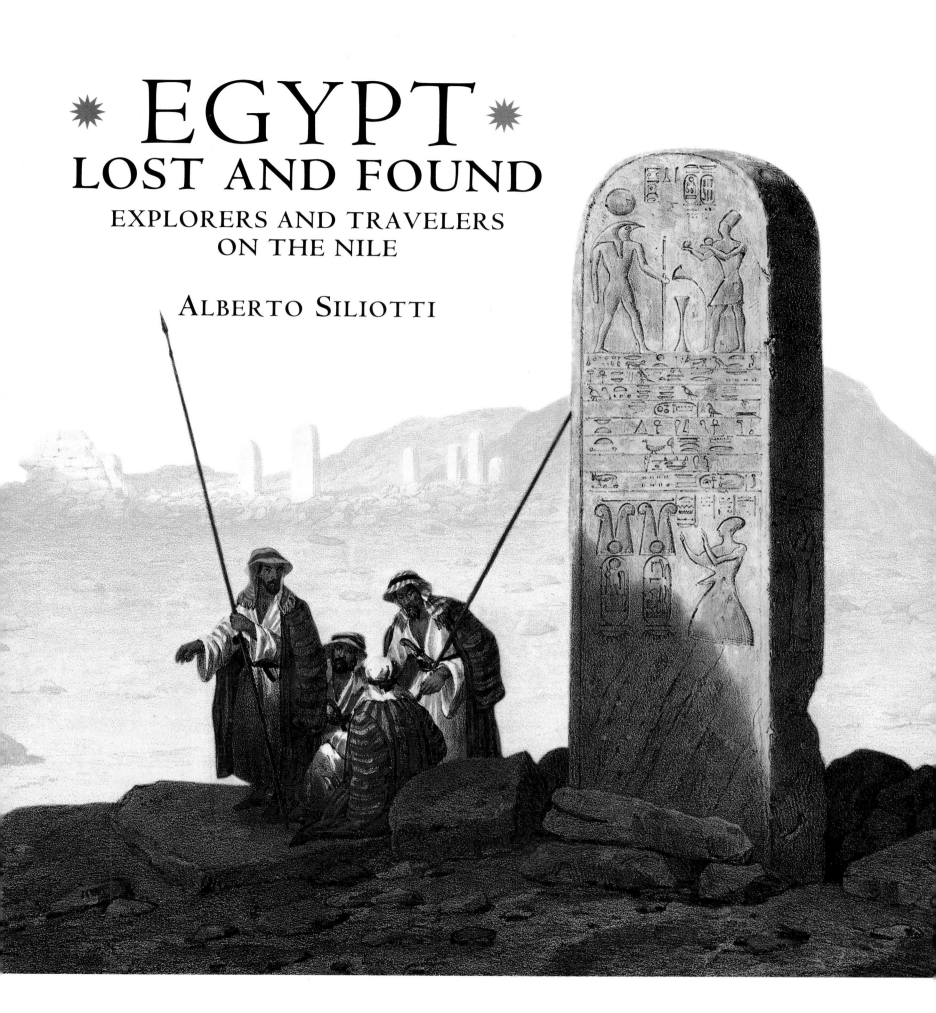

✹ EGYPT ✹
LOST AND FOUND
EXPLORERS AND TRAVELERS
ON THE NILE

ALBERTO SILIOTTI

Stewart, Tabori & Chang

NEW YORK

David Roberts R.A. Lithog. by

the Temple Edfou Upper Egypt Nov. 23rd 1838.

Text: ALBERTO SILIOTTI
Editorial production: MARCELLO BERTINETTI, VALERIA MANFERTO DE FABIANIS
Graphic design: PATRIZIA BALOCCO LOVISETTI

CONTENTS

Published in 1999 and distributed in the U.S. by Stewart, Tabori & Chang, a division of U.S.
Media Holdings, Inc., 115 West 18th Street, New York, New York, 10011

Library of Congress Catalog Card Number 98-87280

ISBN: 1–55670–876–9

Printed in Italy

10 9 8 7 6 5 4 3 2 1

(*Note: caption numbers refer to the pages on which the illustrations appear.*)

1 L.M.A. Linant de Bellefonds and Léon de Laborde were the first Europeans to draw the ruins of the ancient Egyptian temple of Serabit el-Khadim in the Sinai. The two travellers are depicted here in Arab costume at the site.

2–3 In this striking and very imaginative reconstruction of the great monuments of ancient Egypt, the French artist Louis François Cassas (1756–1827) has combined various architectural elements that in reality belong

to different periods. Towering over everything is a pyramid typical of the Old Kingdom; in front, a pylon and temple courtyard are in the Ptolemaic style; and a pair of obelisks date from the New Kingdom.

4–5 David Roberts (1796–1864) is one of the greatest and certainly the most famous of the artists who depicted the antiquities of ancient Egypt; his watercolours combine remarkable precision in the representation of detail with a high artistic standard. When he reached the site of Edfu in November 1838, the portico of the temple of Horus, dating from the Ptolemaic period, was still almost completely buried in sand.

6–7 Richard Lepsius (1810–84) reached Abu Simbel in 1843, at the head of the Prussian Expedition; in that year and the next he executed numerous drawings and carried out surveys of the Great Temple of Ramesses II. The expedition's artists tried to reproduce the original colours of the monument, as seen here. On the left is one of the colossi of the pharaoh as Osiris, appearing to hold up the ceiling of the first hypostyle hall. Above are four statues, representing, from left to right, the gods Ptah and Amun-Re, the deified Ramesses II and the god Re-Harakhty, which are situated in a niche at the back of the sanctuary of this temple.

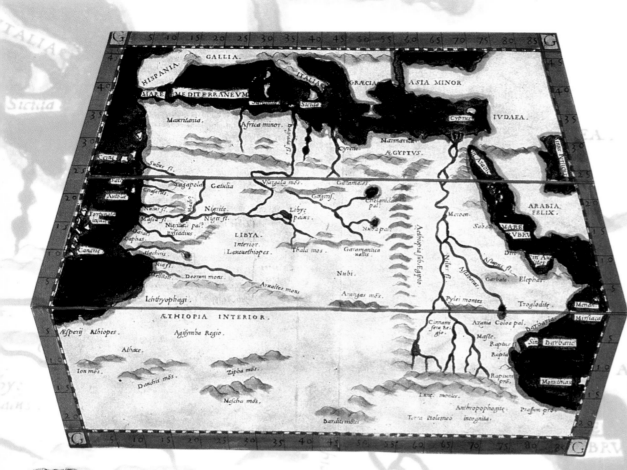

INTRODUCTION

I shall now speak of Egypt, because this country possesses many marvellous things and offers monuments that beggar description, being more magnificent than those of any other country.... The Egyptians, as a result of the climate, which in their country is different, and the river, which has characteristics that are different from those of other rivers, have customs and laws that are, in many respects, different from those of other peoples. In this country the women go to market and engage in trade while the men stay at home and weave ... the men carry loads on their heads while the women carry them on their backs.... In the other countries, the priests of the gods have long hair, in Egypt, on the contrary, they shave their heads. During periods of mourning, the men of other nations shave their heads, while, on such occasions, the Egyptians grow their hair and beards, although normally they shave them off.... (Herodotus, *History* II, 37).

This is how the Greek historian Herodotus, one of the most famous tourists of antiquity, begins his description of Egypt, displaying an evident sense of wonder and astonishment. He arrived in the country towards the middle of the fifth century BC, at a time when it was frequently visited by Greek merchants and sailors. Egypt was already considered an extremely fascinating land, arousing a great deal of interest, and it continued to exert such allure in the following centuries. After the country had been incorporated into the Roman Empire, it became a tourist destination that was visited not only by officials and ordinary citizens, but also by emperors such as Hadrian and Septimius Severus.

Egypt, with its long history and venerable religion, was the object of study of geographers such as Strabo, historians such as Diodorus Siculus and Plutarch, and naturalists such as Pliny the Elder. Precious building materials found there, such as the granite from Aswan and the porphyry from the mountains bordering the Red Sea coast, as well as numerous obelisks were transported to Rome to embellish the Forum; and one of the most popular cults of ancient Egypt – that of the goddess Isis – rapidly found favour in Rome and spread also to the provinces of the empire.

8

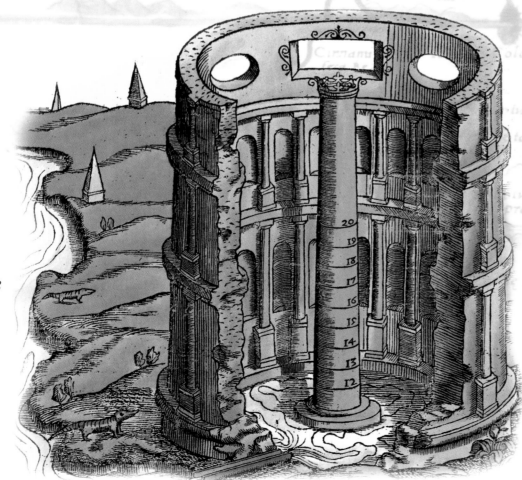

8 (opposite above) A map of Africa (Tabula Africa IIII) *by the second-century* AD *Alexandrian geographer Claudius Ptolemaeus, better known as Ptolemy, and drawn by the famous Venetian cartographer Jacopo Gastaldi in the sixteenth century. The course of the Nile is clearly visible, fed by springs flowing from the mythical Mountains of the Moon (Lunae Montes); two large tributaries, the* Astapus flumen *and* Astabora flumen, *join it from the Horn of Africa.*

8 (opposite below) In his Oedipus Aegyptiacus *the German Jesuit Athanasius Kircher (1602–80), one of the first scholars to attempt to decipher hieroglyphs, included this imaginary representation of what is described as the* Templum Isiacum. *In fact it seems to be a Nilometer.*

9 (above) The English antiquarian and traveller W.J. Bankes (1786–1855) visited Egypt and the Near East between 1815 and 1819. He commissioned this rather fanciful view of the pyramids of Giza and Saqqara on the west bank of the Nile: in the distance, on the east bank of the river, are the houses, mosques and churches of Cairo.

9 (right) The Frenchman Jean de Thevenot (1633–67), seen here examining a mummy contained in a sarcophagus that had just been opened in the necropolis of Saqqara, was one of the first to illustrate the published account of his travels with engravings, thus introducing Europeans to the antiquities of Egypt.

9

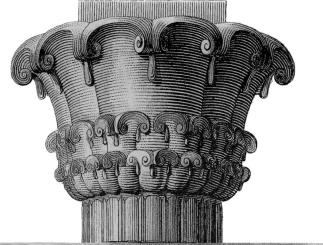

posts on the important trade routes linking equatorial Africa and the Orient to the Mediterranean basin, and resting-places for devotees of Christianity on their way to Jerusalem and the famous monastery of St Catherine's at Mount Sinai – continued to be thronged by merchants, crusaders and pilgrims. The interior of the country, however, was an area where no European dared to venture. Merchants from Venice, Provence and Marseille established trading centres called *fondachi* or *odkalli* (from the Arabic *wakala*, meaning 'caravanserai').

Mysteries, with Information regarding the Hiding Places and Finds and Treasures) – left no doubt as to its purpose. Mummies were also in great demand, soon becoming the object of a huge and lucrative trade. From the time of the Crusades it was widely believed in the West that mummy powder had remarkable therapeutic powers – an idea previously promoted by Arab physicians and writers – and the French king, Francis I, always carried a small quantity on his person.

Mummies, generally in pieces, were shipped from Alexandria to Europe, where they were reduced to powder with special grinders and distributed to the apothecaries of the day. The rare examples that remained in one piece took a different route, ending up, with other Egyptian objects such as statues and papyri, in the first cabinets of curiosities, such as those of the French antiquarian Nicolas Fabri de Peiresc or Cosimo I de'Medici in Florence, where all kinds of exotic, ancient or unusual objects were assembled.

In some respects the ancient world of the pharaohs had survived uninterrupted, and it was only the spread of Christianity – which, following the Edict of Milan in AD 313, became the official religion of the Roman Empire – that brought about its demise. Because they were now considered the work of the devil, the images of the ancient gods that had watched over the fortunes of Egypt for thousands of years were defaced or destroyed. Tombs were ransacked – their entire funerary furnishings burnt – to be used as dwellings by monks and hermits, while the closure of the Egyptian temples, the last bulwarks of a civilization that was now drawing to a close, meant that not only did age-old rites and traditions sink into oblivion, but also that knowledge of one of the most distinctive features of Egyptian culture, hieroglyphic writing, was soon forgotten.

The fall of the Eastern Roman Empire and the conquest of Egypt by the Arabs in AD 640 also contributed to this gradual loss of identity. Egypt was soon isolated from the rest of the world and Western travellers were barred from the country. Only Cairo and Alexandria – still essential staging

Defended by high walls, these were in effect urban fortresses that could accommodate entire caravans with their merchandise, as well as pilgrims and other travellers. In general, such visitors limited themselves to looking at sights in the two cities, especially places associated with the Holy Scriptures. They perhaps ventured as far as Giza to see the pyramids, which at this time were believed to be the 'granaries of Joseph' or the 'granaries of the pharaohs', or, alternatively, the ruins of the ancient city of Memphis.

In this period, the magnificent monuments of ancient Egypt were mainly used as quarries for building materials. Having withstood the ravages of time for over three thousand years, the splendid casing of white Tura limestone covering the pyramids of Giza was removed, while the archaeological sites, where it was believed extraordinary objects and immense riches were hidden, teemed with treasure-hunters. A manual was written for their benefit, and its title – *Livre des Perles enfouies et du Mystère précieux, au sujet des indications des cachettes des trouvailles et des trésors* (*Book of Hidden Pearls and Precious*

10 (opposite above) The great French draughtsman and antiquarian Dominique Vivant Denon (1747–1825), who, along with many other scholars and artists, participated in Napoleon's expedition to Egypt, was one of the first to focus on the architectural details of Egyptian temples. This is his drawing of the capital of a column of the Ptolemaic period.

10 (opposite centre) Louis François Cassas, a French artist whose work has only been rediscovered in recent years, drew many ancient Egyptian monuments, such as this temple from the Ptolemaic period. In an attempt to create a more vivid picture he embellished his drawings with elements that, on occasion, were rather romantic.

10–11 Frederik Ludwig Norden (1708–42), a Danish naval captain who went to Egypt on the orders of the king of Denmark, Christian VI, was the first person to make accurate drawings of the ancient monuments, such as the Great Sphinx at Giza, which at that time was still partially covered by desert sand.

11 (right) A detail of an anthropoid sarcophagus in a drawing by the Reverend Richard Pococke (1704–65), a British traveller and a contemporary of Norden.

12 (top) A drawing of a goddess from the tomb of Seti I by Alessandro Ricci (d. 1832), a physician from Sienna, Italy. The tomb was discovered in 1817 by the great explorer from Padua, Giovanni Battista Belzoni (1778–1823), who was also the first person to make plaster casts of the wall decorations of a tomb in the Valley of the Kings.

12 (above) The scholars and artists of Napoleon's expedition published the fruits of their labours in the monumental work entitled Description de l'Égypte. Such was its success that, in 1825, a second, cheaper, edition was published. Known as 'Panckoucke' (after its publisher), this lithograph appeared as the frontispiece.

12–13 (right) Prisse d'Avennes (1807–79), a French orientalist and architect, put his remarkable artistic talents at the service of Egyptology. His drawing of a scene from the Theban tomb of Huy, viceroy of Kush (Eighteenth Dynasty), depicts the procession of a Nubian princess, bringing gifts (gold in the form of ingots and dust) to Tutankhamun.

Such objects were the only examples of Egyptian antiquities in Europe, apart from the huge obelisks that the Popes, like the Roman emperors before them, had once more erected in Rome. In 1517 Egypt became part of the Ottoman Empire, controlled by the Sublime Porte (the Ottoman government), and began to be more accessible to Europeans. In 1589 an anonymous Venetian merchant was able to travel up the Nile as far as Luxor and the First Cataract.

Despite journeys undertaken in the seventeenth century by, for instance, a German Dominican friar, Jean Michel Vansleb, and a Parisian, Jean de Thevenot, who was one of the first to illustrate his

account with engravings, Egypt was still regarded as a land of fable, with arcane and esoteric associations. A good illustration of this attitude towards the country is to be found in the studies of a German Jesuit, Athanasius Kircher, and his attempts to decipher hieroglyphs.

The eighteenth century marked the beginning of the first journeys up the Nile as far as Upper Egypt. A French Jesuit, Claude Sicard (1677–1726), the first to identify the site of the ancient city of Thebes, the Reverend Richard Pococke and a Danish naval captain, Frederik Ludwig Norden, all illustrated their published travel journals with numerous accurate drawings, revealing the great archaeological sites and

monuments of ancient Egypt to European eyes. These were the beginnings of the rediscovery of Egypt that culminated in 1798 with the Napoleonic expedition.

Interest in this ancient civilization was further stimulated by the publication of two books. The first was *Voyage dans la Basse et la Haute Égypte* (*A Journey to Upper and Lower Egypt*) by Dominique Vivant Denon, an artist, man of letters and founding member of the Louvre, who travelled with the vanguard of the French army to Upper Egypt. This was followed by the *Description de l'Égypte*, a monumental account of the work of the scholars accompanying Napoleon's expeditionary force to Egypt. Suddenly there was a vogue

for all things Egyptian, and the governments of various Western nations charged their diplomatic representatives – the famous Consuls – with collecting antiquities, which were then shipped off to the leading museums of Europe.

The adventurers, travellers and explorers were soon joined by artists who, following in the footsteps of the pioneer, Vivant Denon, found a new source of inspiration in Egypt. The Frenchmen Louis François Cassas, Frédéric Cailliaud, Jean Jacques Rifaud, Nestor L'Hôte, Pascal Coste, Hector Horeau and Émile Prisse d'Avennes, the German Luigi Mayer, the Scotsmen David Roberts and Robert Hay, and the Englishmen George Hoskins and Owen Jones, were among the most important artists who drew and painted the recently rediscovered monuments and landscapes of the Nile Valley.

There was no lack of writers either: in 1806 François René Chateaubriand went to Egypt, following the example of his predecessor Claude Savary, author of the *Lettres sur Égypte* published in 1785. While Savary had created a mannered and sometimes fantastic image of Egypt, in his *Itinéraire de Paris à Jérusalem* Chateaubriand presented a more accurate and realistic picture, even though his is the pen of the literary man rather than that of the traveller. He was later emulated by other writers such as Gustave Flaubert, author of *Voyage en Orient* – who travelled in Egypt between 1849 and 1859 with the photographer Maxime Du Camp – William Henry Bartlett, Eugène Fromentin and Samuel Langhorne Clemens (better known as Mark Twain).

While the search for antiquities proceeded at fever pitch and excavations were underway all over Egypt a significant breakthrough took place far away in France. Thanks to the key provided by the Rosetta Stone – the basalt slab discovered by an officer in the Napoleonic army at Rosetta on the Nile Delta – Jean François Champollion was able to solve the greatest mystery of ancient Egypt: the enigma of hieroglyphs. Henceforth the monuments, temples and tombs – the walls of which were covered with inscriptions – acquired a new significance and began to reveal their history and that of their builders.

The adventurous explorations of the pioneers of the previous age were now replaced by the archaeological expeditions carried out using scientific methods by Champollion himself, the Englishman John Gardner Wilkinson and the Prussian Richard Lepsius. Thus, with the beginning of a new era in the rediscovery of Egypt, a new discipline was born: Egyptology.

14 (right) The bustling Khan el-Khalili bazaar in the centre of Cairo, with its numerous Islamic monuments, was one of the favourite subjects of nineteenth-century artists, such as the Maltese Amedeo Preziosi, whose drawing this is.

14–15 (far right) One of the most outstanding artists working in Egypt at the end of the eighteenth century was Luigi Mayer (1755–1803). A pupil of the famous Roman engraver Giovanni Battista Piranesi, Mayer produced a series of drawings that were published in the volume Views in Egypt, from which this splendid portrayal of a Mameluke horseman is taken.

14

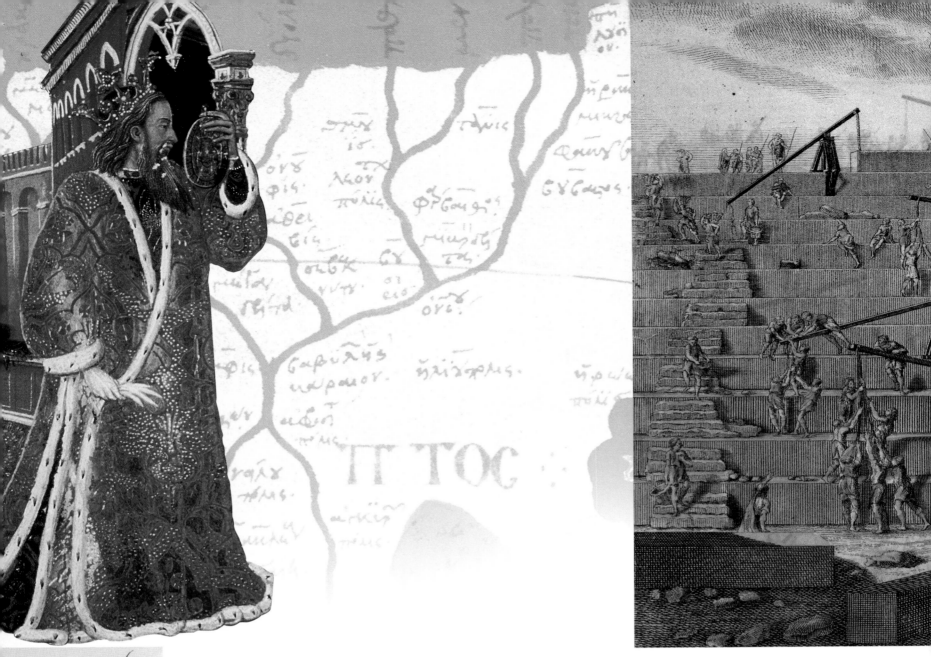

TOURISTS IN ANTIQUITY
GREEKS AND ROMANS IN THE LAND OF THE PHARAOHS

16 (top) Ptolemy, who lived in Alexandria in the second century AD, was the first great cartographer. In the codex of Cardinal Bessarion of Trebizond, which contains one of the earliest versions of Ptolemy's most important work, Geography, *the astronomer and geographer is shown holding an instrument for taking astronomical measurements. He has probably been confused with the Ptolemaic kings since he is also depicted with a royal crown.*

16 (left) In 332 BC Alexander the Great conquered Egypt, at that time under Persian domination, with comparative ease. The Macedonian general made a special journey to the oasis of Siwa, in the Libyan Desert, in order to consult a famous oracle to confirm his divine descent and thus legitimate his right to rule Egypt as the son of Amun. This is a detail from a mosaic depicting the Battle of Issus, from the House of the Faun, Pompeii.

Journeys undertaken by people simply wanting to see the great monuments of Egypt began very early. For instance, in the Third-Dynasty Step Pyramid complex of Djoser at Saqqara – more precisely in the small building east of the pyramid known as the 'House of the South' – traces of the first tourists dating from the New Kingdom can still be seen. These take the form of graffiti left by people who had visited the site, which at that time was already a respectable 1,200 years old, giving their names and their reasons for coming. For example one reads 'Ahmose, son of Iptah' who 'came to see the temple of Djoser'.

Phoenician travellers to the Great Temple of Ramesses II at Abu Simbel carved graffiti on the legs of the colossal statues of the pharaoh adorning the façade. Subsequently the Greeks, who in the seventh and sixth centuries BC had already set up a trading port at Naucratis in the Nile Delta and had settled at Elephantine in Upper Egypt, also left us reminders of their journeys on the Egyptian monuments, as well as important historical and geographical accounts of the country. Greek geographers of the sixth century BC, such as Anaximander and Hecataeus of Miletus, drew up maps and wrote descriptions of the known world, or

went on journeys of exploration, as did Scylax of Caryanda, admiral of the king of Persia, Darius I. Unfortunately these works have largely been lost, as have those of later geographers such as Artemidorus of Ephesus, who wrote a geography in eleven volumes, of which only a few fragments have survived.

The most famous Greek traveller, however, was the great historian Herodotus, who arrived in the Nile Valley in about 450 BC, when the country was under Persian rule. During his visit he collected a huge amount of important information regarding the civilization of Egypt, to which the second book of his monumental work, the *History*, was devoted.

After describing the landscape and geography of the Nile, Herodotus focused on the pyramids of Giza, recounting, in a rather fanciful manner, their history and the techniques used by the ancient Egyptians in their construction. Often he supplemented interesting and careful observations with fabulous or unfounded details. The deep-rooted but erroneous notion that the pyramids were built by thousands of slaves, for example, originated with Herodotus.

None the less, much of the information in the *History* that was once thought

16–17 and 17 *In his* History *Herodotus described both the historical aspects of Egypt and also the customs, habits and religious beliefs of its inhabitants. In particular he dwelt on the techniques used for building the pyramids of Giza. He asserted that the ancient labourers managed to hoist the massive limestone blocks forming the monument into place thanks to a system of machines built with 'short wooden beams'. A possible reconstruction of this method is shown in this lithograph, dated 1759, by a French artist about whom all we know is his surname: Gouget.*

18–19 (right) The Peutinger Table, named after one of its owners, the German humanist Konrad Peutinger, is a medieval copy of a Roman map dating from the third or fourth centuries AD, which in turn was probably based on one by Marcus Agrippa. Essentially a map of the road system of the empire, the distortion means that the course of the Nile is shown as parallel to the Mediterranean coast.

18 (below) The Roman penchant for exoticism is evident in this fresco representing a Nilotic scene, showing pygmies hunting wild animals. Originally adorning the walls of the House of the Physician at Pompeii, it is now in the Museo Archeologico Nazionale in Naples.

18

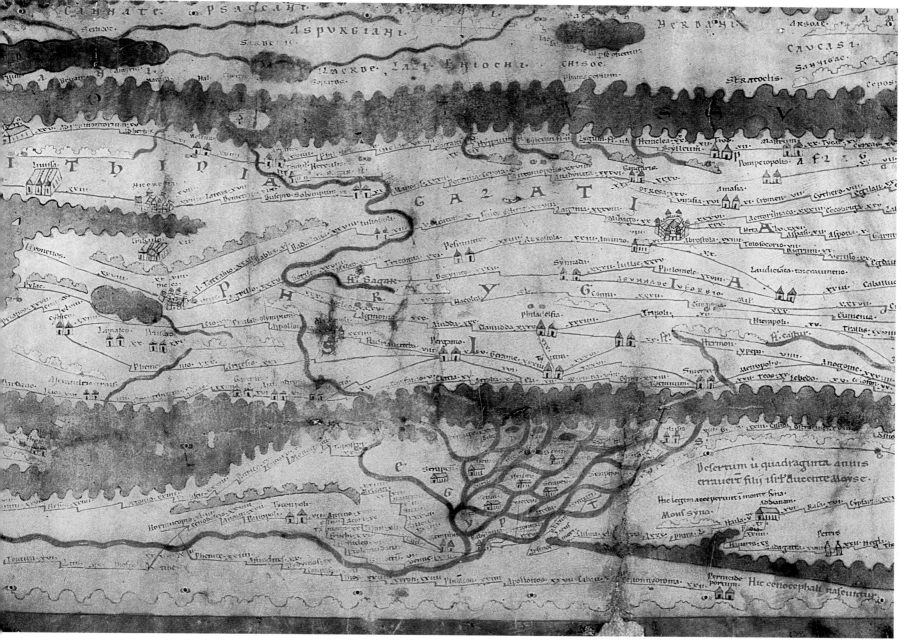

fantastic has, in fact, been shown by modern research to be accurate. Herodotus was not only interested in the historical aspects of Egyptian civilization, but he also described the inhabitants, their customs and practices, their religious beliefs, and the great sacred and popular festivals. He often drew comparisons between the Greek world and the Egyptian one – and highlighted the profound differences. For the Greek historian, everything was a source of wonder and amazement. It is thanks to Herodotus' work that we know the details of the daily lives of the Egyptians and the procedures used in what was, in the eyes of a Greek, one of the most surprising features of the Egyptian civilization – the embalming and mummification of the dead.

Herodotus visited Egypt during the reign of Nectanebo I, when the country was under Persian rule. Later, Egypt began once more to be ruled by a native dynasty and enjoyed a period of great splendour. New temples were constructed, old ones were enlarged and restored, the great religious festivals were once more celebrated with pomp and ceremony, and the influence of the priests increased.

Although the subsequent conquest of Egypt by Alexander the Great, in 332 BC, marked the end of the political independence of the country, it did not bring about a loss of its identity. Rather, it consolidated the power of the priestly class, on whom the new 'Lord of the world' relied to both legitimize his power and assert his divine descent. Alexander insisted on making the difficult journey to the oasis of Siwa in the Libyan Desert to consult the oracle of Jupiter Ammon and was rewarded by the oracle's reply, which sanctioned his rule. Following his example, the Ptolemies and the Romans continued the policy of presenting themselves as the successors to the pharaohs, becoming part of the theocratic system and building new temples and enlarging the existing ones. The persistence of Egyptian culture despite the loss of political independence is reflected in the work of the two leading post-Herodotean authors, Diodorus Siculus and the geographer Strabo. Fortunately, these have survived thanks to the patient work of copying by medieval monks.

Diodorus Siculus, who lived in the first century BC, travelled through Egypt and described all that he saw and was told in

19 A fresco from Herculaneum depicts a ceremony linked to the cult of Isis, which was very popular in Rome and the provinces of its empire.

19

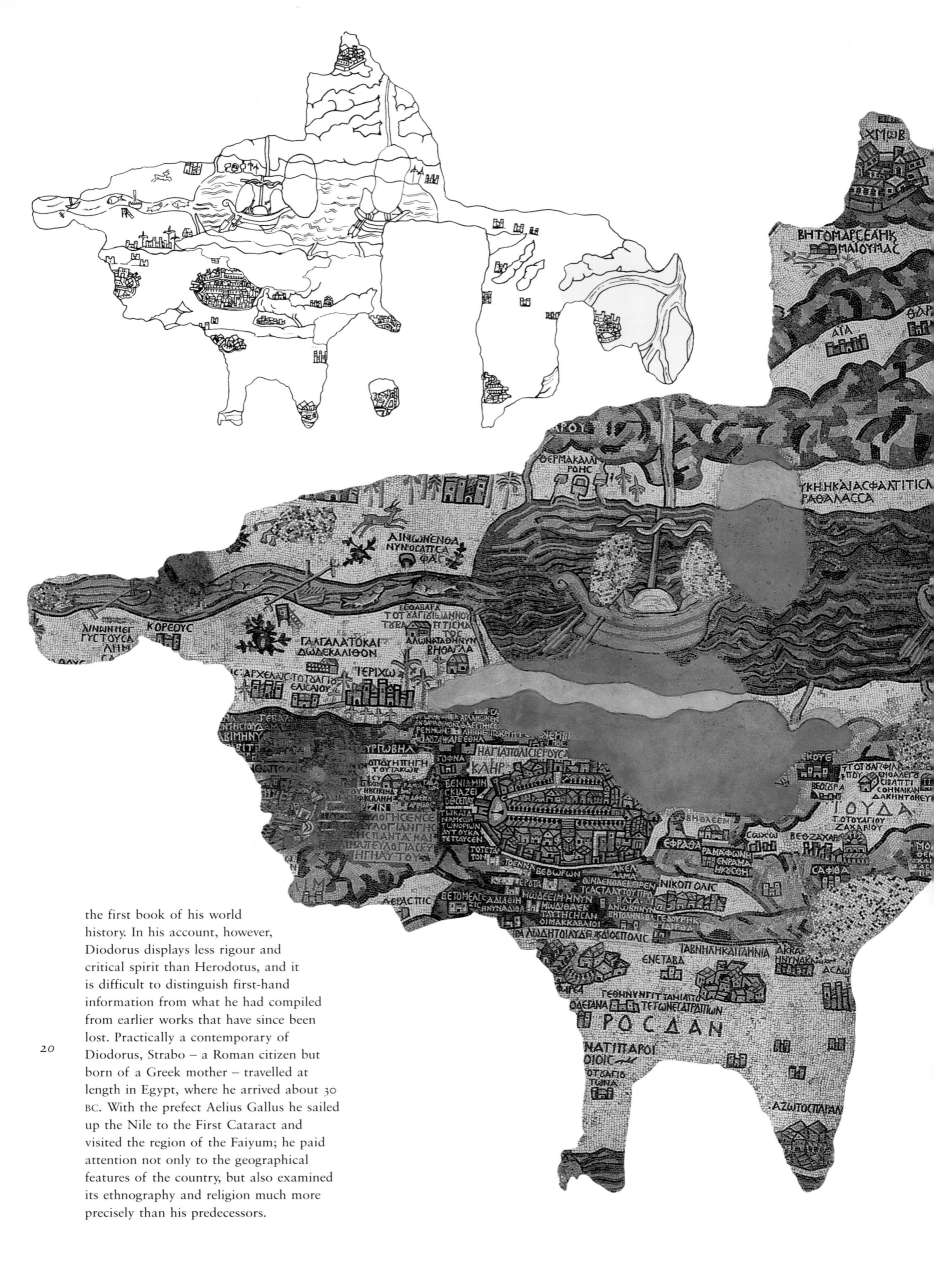

the first book of his world
history. In his account, however,
Diodorus displays less rigour and
critical spirit than Herodotus, and it
is difficult to distinguish first-hand
information from what he had compiled
from earlier works that have since been
lost. Practically a contemporary of
Diodorus, Strabo – a Roman citizen but
born of a Greek mother – travelled at
length in Egypt, where he arrived about 30
BC. With the prefect Aelius Gallus he sailed
up the Nile to the First Cataract and
visited the region of the Faiyum; he paid
attention not only to the geographical
features of the country, but also examined
its ethnography and religion much more
precisely than his predecessors.

After being revised and rearranged, Strabo's observations were included in the seventeenth volume of his *Geography*. This work was followed by that of the great naturalist, Pliny the Elder, who, in Books 6 and 33 of his monumental work, *Natural History*, described the Nile and Upper Egypt in great detail. The Roman biographer and philosopher Plutarch, who lived in the first century AD, also travelled to Egypt. He was especially interested in mythological questions, particularly the myth of Osiris, which he discussed in his treatise *de Iside et Osiride* (*On Isis and Osiris*).

A particular point of interest in Plutarch's work lies in the fact that he had probably been able to consult a copy of the writings of Manetho, an Egyptian high-priest and historian who lived in the third century BC. Manetho was the author of a monumental history of Egypt entitled *Aegyptiaca*, the original copy of which was lost in the destruction by fire of the Library of Alexandria, in which he set out the system of dividing the pharaohs of Egypt into dynasties.

Roman interest in Egyptian civilization is attested by the numerous mosaics inspired by Nilotic scenes and frescoes depicting the cult of the goddess Isis. Brought to Rome by the legionaries who had served in Egypt, this cult became extremely popular. In addition, the emperors of Rome not only transported the finest obelisks to the capital, but also built monuments in Egyptian style. In AD 19 Germanicus Julius Caesar, the adopted son of Tiberius, travelled to Egypt, for reasons of tourism as well as diplomacy. As Tacitus recounts in the second book of his *Annals*, Germanicus sailed up the Nile and visited Thebes and its temples, guided by an elderly priest who was able to read hieroglyphs. He reached 'Elephantine and Syene, the former borders of the Roman Empire, which now extends to the Red Sea' (*Annals* 2. 61, 2).

Just over a century later, in AD 130, the emperor Hadrian also set off on a journey to Egypt, lasting around ten months, during which he visited the famous Colossi of Memnon at Thebes. At that time the two colossal statues that originally stood at the entrance to the mortuary temple of Amenhotep III were thought to represent the hero Memnon, son of Eos and Tithonus. Following an earthquake in 27 BC one of the statues famously began to emit a sound at dawn (probably the effect of the rapid increase in the temperature of the rock as it was heated by the sun's rays). A tragic event occurred in Hadrian's journey, when his favourite, Antinous, drowned in the Nile. In his memory the emperor founded a city on the river bank, calling it Antinoöpolis.

Numerous travellers, either tourists or army officers stationed in Egypt, visited the country and its antiquities, often leaving graffiti, usually consisting simply of their names but sometimes with added comments. On the Colossi of Memnon 107 such inscriptions have been counted, and in the tombs of the Valley of the Kings – already a very popular tourist sight – there are no fewer than 2,100.

The Romans took a particular interest in the geography of their empire, and

Egypt was no exception. On the orders of the emperor Augustus, Marcus Agrippa made a large map of the empire, since lost, on which he indicated distances between places, as well as road and river routes, cities and ports. Agrippa's map was probably the source of the famous Peutinger Table, dating from the third or fourth centuries AD. This document, consisting of a roll of parchment on which a map of the Roman Empire was drawn with 534 illustrations, contains one of the oldest representations of the territory of Egypt.

Despite being annexed by Rome, Egypt retained its very distinctive identity, with its language, beliefs and rituals, although the fire of 47 BC that destroyed the famous Library at Alexandria – said to have contained over 700,000 volumes – deprived it of a large part of its historical memory. The world of the pharaohs finally came to an end later, with the spread of Christianity. Numerous monks and hermits settled in Egypt, often using tombs and ancient monuments as dwellings and setting up churches in the temples, which an edict issued by the emperor Theodosius I finally closed in AD 391.

Up to that time the temples had maintained their religious and cultural functions, and only the priests – the guardians of age-old traditions and knowledge accumulated over the centuries – were able to read and understand hieroglyphic writing, a skill that was soon lost. The last known hieroglyphic inscription, in the temple of Isis on Philae, dates from AD 394. When the priests who were able to read these signs passed away, a veil of silence was cast over the age-old civilization of the Nile – many centuries were to pass before it was again raised.

22–23 *Roman fascination with Egypt is evident in this marvellous mosaic depiction of the Nile Valley. From Palestrina (a small town near Rome, known as Praeneste), it has a surface area of over 20 square* *metres and probably dates from the mid-second century BC. It has recently been attributed to an Alexandrian artist, known as Demetrius the Topographer. In the foreground is the Delta region, with the imperial palace* *of Alexandria, while the upper reaches of the Nile and Nubia, teeming with African flora and fauna, are visible above; boats sail along the Nile, the banks of which are lined with temples and other buildings.*

In the seventh century AD, after the fall of the Eastern Roman Empire, Egypt became a province of the Arab khalifate and non-Muslims were barred from the country. The only exceptions were Cairo and Alexandria, which continued to have an important role as both ports during the Crusades or for pilgrimages to the Holy Land and Mount Sinai, and as centres for trade with the East. Spices, precious stones, perfumes and dyestuffs passed through them to reach the markets of Europe, carried by the merchant navy of Venice, the undisputed power in the eastern Mediterranean with a presence in all the ports of the Levant. At the beginning of the ninth century – probably in 829 – two Venetian merchants, Bruno di Malamocco and Rustico di Torcello, purchased in Egypt the mortal remains of a man they believed to be the Apostle Mark. They took the relics back to Venice, where the famous cathedral was then dedicated to the saint.

In the following centuries numerous travellers, mainly Crusaders and pilgrims, visited Egypt and wrote accounts of their journeys. One was a Venetian, Marin

EGYPTIAN TRAVELS FROM THE MIDDLE AGES TO MODERN TIMES
FOLLOWING IN THE FOOTSTEPS OF CRUSADERS, PILGRIMS AND ADVENTURERS

Sanudo the Elder, called Torsello (1274–1343), who in 1321 published the *Liber secretorum fidelium Crucis* (*Book of the Secrets of the Devotees of the Cross*), which included a description of the geography of Egypt and its main trade-routes. Another was Gabriele Capodilista (*c.* 1420–77) from Padua, who, in 1475, wrote *Itinerario di Terrasanta* (*Guide to the Holy Land*). The 'itinerari' – books containing practical information written by pilgrims who had made the journey to Jerusalem or Mount Sinai and wanted others to benefit from their experience – also include the *Libro d'Oltramare* (*Book on Overseas Countries*) by Niccolò da Poggibonsi; the *Viazo da Venetia al Sancto Jerusalem et al Monte Sinai* (*Journey from Venice to Holy Jerusalem and Mount Sinai*) by Giustiniano da Rubiera, which had about sixty editions; and the *Trattato di Terra Santa* (*Treatise on the Holy Land*)

24 (opposite, above left) Prosper Alpinus, a physician and naturalist, arrived in Egypt in 1582. He produced important studies of the flora and fauna of the country and the first precise measurements of the pyramids of Giza, especially Khufu's.

24 (opposite, above right) Jean de Thevenot visited Egypt in 1656 and it was through the illustrations in his book Voyage au Levant that many Europeans first encountered Egypt.

24 (opposite below) A detail from a medieval world map, of the 'T in O' type, so called because the space is divided into three parts resembling a T inside an O. This example was drawn between 1042 and 1072 by Gregorio di San Severo, a monk who copied a map dating from the eighth century in the 'Comment on the Apocalypse' by the Benedictine monk Beatus de Liebauz (or Lièbana). It is likely that this type of map was inspired by older Greek examples since lost.

25 (above) In the Middle Ages and the Renaissance the city of Cairo, shown here in an illustration from Giustiniano da Rubiera's work, was called the 'city of Babylon'. This was the name of the ancient Roman fortress – the remains of which are still visible today – which may have derived from an ancient Egyptian place-name.

25 (right, above) In 1589 an unknown traveller, referred to therefore as 'Anonimo Veneziano', was the first European to sail up the Nile to Thebes and Nubia. He described this remarkable venture in the manuscript entitled Viagio che ò fato l'anno 1589 dal Caiero in Ebrin navigando su per el Nillo (A Journey that I Made in the Year 1589 from Cairo to Ebrin Sailing up the Nile); Ebrin is the Nubian site now known as Qasr Ibrim.

25 (bottom) The pyramids of Giza as depicted in the mosaic decorations in St Mark's Cathedral in Venice (thirteenth century). In the Middle Ages the pyramids were thought to have a religious significance, since they were identified with the granaries where, according to the Bible, Joseph, son of Jacob, stored supplies to meet a period of famine after he had become the pharaoh's minister.

25

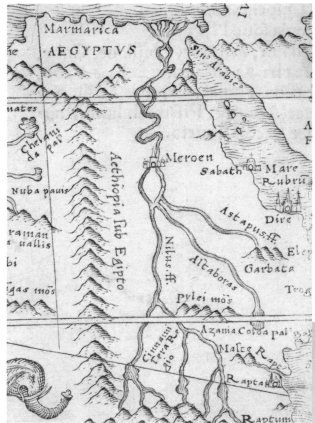

of Francesco Suriano (1450–1524). Less common were the scientists, such as Pierre Belon du Mans (1517–64), a French physician and naturalist who visited Egypt in 1547, and his Italian counterpart from Veneto, Prosper Alpinus (1553–1616), who wrote the first scientific study of the flora and fauna of Egypt. Alpinus, who arrived in Egypt in 1582, described the city of Cairo with its numerous mosques – in 1590 a French traveller, Jacques Sieur de Villamont, asserted that there were no fewer than 22,840 – and the pyramids of Giza, collecting his scientific observations in three important works entitled *Rerum Aegyptiarum Libri Quattuor* (*Four Books on Things Egyptian*); *De Medicina Aegyptiorum* (*On Egyptian Medicine*); and *De Plantis Aegypti* (*On Egyptian Plants*).

Egypt thus was identified with its two main cities and the few other places described in these accounts or in the reports of merchants and diplomats. No one dared to venture into the interior of the country, however. In fact, these works only rarely refer to the archaeological remains, except for those near Cairo, such

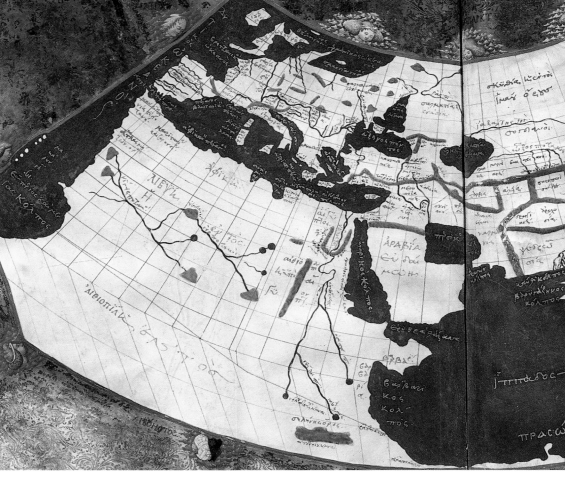

26 (top) Giovanni Battista Ramusio was a Venetian diplomat, a position which gave him access to the most recent geographical information contained not only in the accounts of the great voyages of exploration but also in official sources. In the first volume of his book Delle Navigationi et Viaggi, *published in 1550, he deals with Africa.*

26 (above and right) Ptolemy's Geography summed up the state of knowledge on this subject in Classical antiquity and survived in the form of Greek and Latin manuscripts. It was first printed in 1475, and over a period of twenty-five years another seven editions appeared. In 1548 a pocket edition was published, with maps engraved by Jacopo Gastaldi.

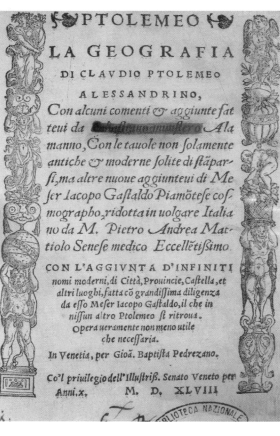

as the pyramids of Giza and the ruins of the old city of Memphis – the site of which was only identified precisely for the first time by Sieur de Villamont in 1590. The great cemeteries of Saqqara were another attraction, where the tourists of the day hunted for souvenirs, such as small antiquities and parts of mummies, finds that were also on sale in numerous bazaars in Cairo. There had been a thriving trade in mummies since the Middle Ages, due in particular to the widespread belief in Europe that powdered mummy had remarkable medicinal powers. As the demand for mummies increased, the shrewd merchants of Cairo had no scruples about making false ones.

The first report of a journey undertaken by a European to Upper Egypt simply as a 'tourist' dates from 1589. Driven by the desire to see the antiquities of the country, this traveller, whose name is unknown and who is usually therefore referred to as 'Anonimo Veneziano' (Anonymous Venetian), sailed up the Nile as far as Nubia and wrote a fascinating account of his adventures.

Just under a century later, in 1672, Jean Michel Vansleb, a Dominican friar, followed in the footsteps of Anonimo Veneziano. Vansleb went to Egypt on the orders of the chief minister to Louis XIV, Jean-Baptiste Colbert, to collect antiquities, and ventured as far as the city of Sohâg, about five hundred kilometres south of Cairo. He published his travel journals under the title *Nouvelle relation en forme*

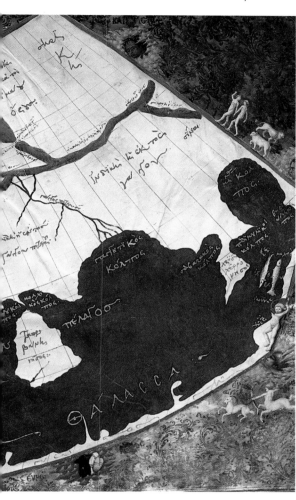

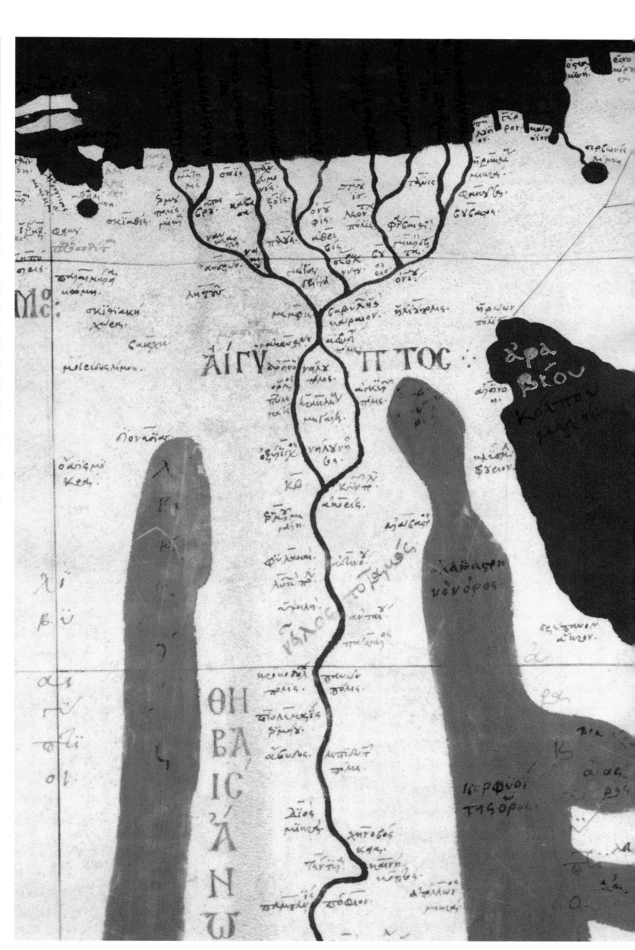

de journal d'un voyage fait en Égypte en 1672 & 1673 (New Account in the Form of a Travel Diary of a Journey in Egypt in 1672 and 1673).

One of the earliest travellers to present pictures of the Near East and Egypt to European eyes was a Parisian, Jean de Thevenot, who included engravings in his *Voyage au Levant*, published in 1664. A contemporary of Vansleb, de Thevenot made two long journeys in the Middle East, exploring both Persia and Egypt, although in the latter, like all the travellers of his day, he restricted himself to visiting Alexandria, Cairo and the pyramids of Giza and Saqqara.

This limited knowledge of the Egyptian interior – and of the African continent as a whole – is also reflected in the maps of the period. One of the first cartographers to map Egypt and the course of the Nile was the celebrated geographer Claudius Ptolemaeus, better known as Ptolemy, who

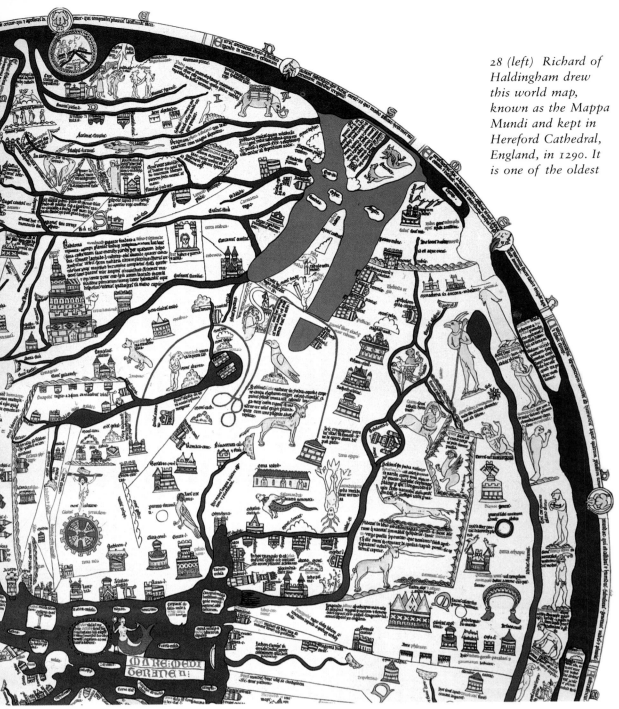

crucis by Sanudo the Elder, and a nautical atlas by a Venetian, Andrea Bianco, dating to 1436, also based on Ptolemy's maps.

As more great discoveries were made around the world, thanks to the voyages of Bartholomeu Dias, Vasco da Gama and Ferdinand Magellan, much information was added to that of Ptolemaic origin. A new generation of atlases appeared containing maps that were more faithful representations of the geography of the countries concerned. In the first volume of his book *Delle Navigationi et Viaggi* published in 1550, the Venetian diplomat Giovanni Battista Ramusio (1485–1557) drew not only on the published accounts of the voyages of exploration, but also on his own first-hand knowledge and other sources to which he had access in his capacity as an official of the Venetian Republic. In fact Venice at this time was one of the most important centres of map-making in the world, where all the most up-to-date information was available.

Ramusio's work allowed the cartographer Jacopo Gastaldi to produce

lived in Alexandria in the second century AD. One of his works, his *Geography*, achieved great fame and first appeared in a printed version in 1475. Ptolemy's map, which had a great influence over later cartographers, charts the outline of Africa fairly inaccurately, while the Nile is shown as flowing from a source in two large lakes situated near the *Lunae Montes* (the Mountains of the Moon). Another very early map is the Mappa Mundi, now kept in Hereford cathedral, England. Drawn in 1290, its representation of the course of the Nile is wholly fanciful.

The world map of the Camaldolese friar Fra Mauro, drawn in 1459 and now in the Marciana Library in Venice, was based on Ptolemaic concepts, but the territory of Egypt is shown in much greater detail and the most important sites are annotated by the cartographer. For example, he notes of the origins and function of the pyramids of Giza that: 'It is said that these pyramids were the granaries of the pharaohs'. Fra Mauro drew inspiration for his world map from two previous works, the planisphere drawn by a Genoese, Pietro Vesconte, in 1321 for the *Liber secretorum fidelium*

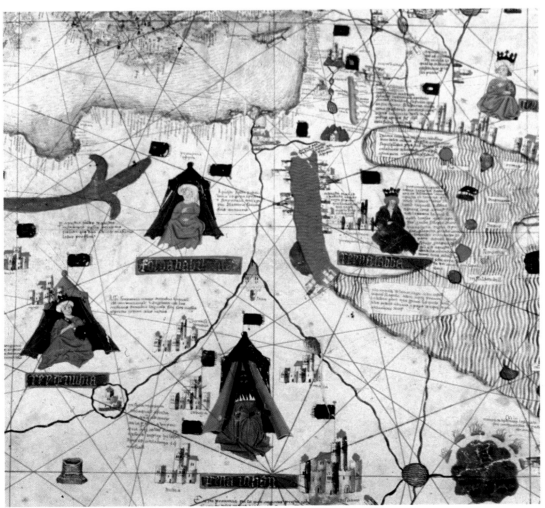

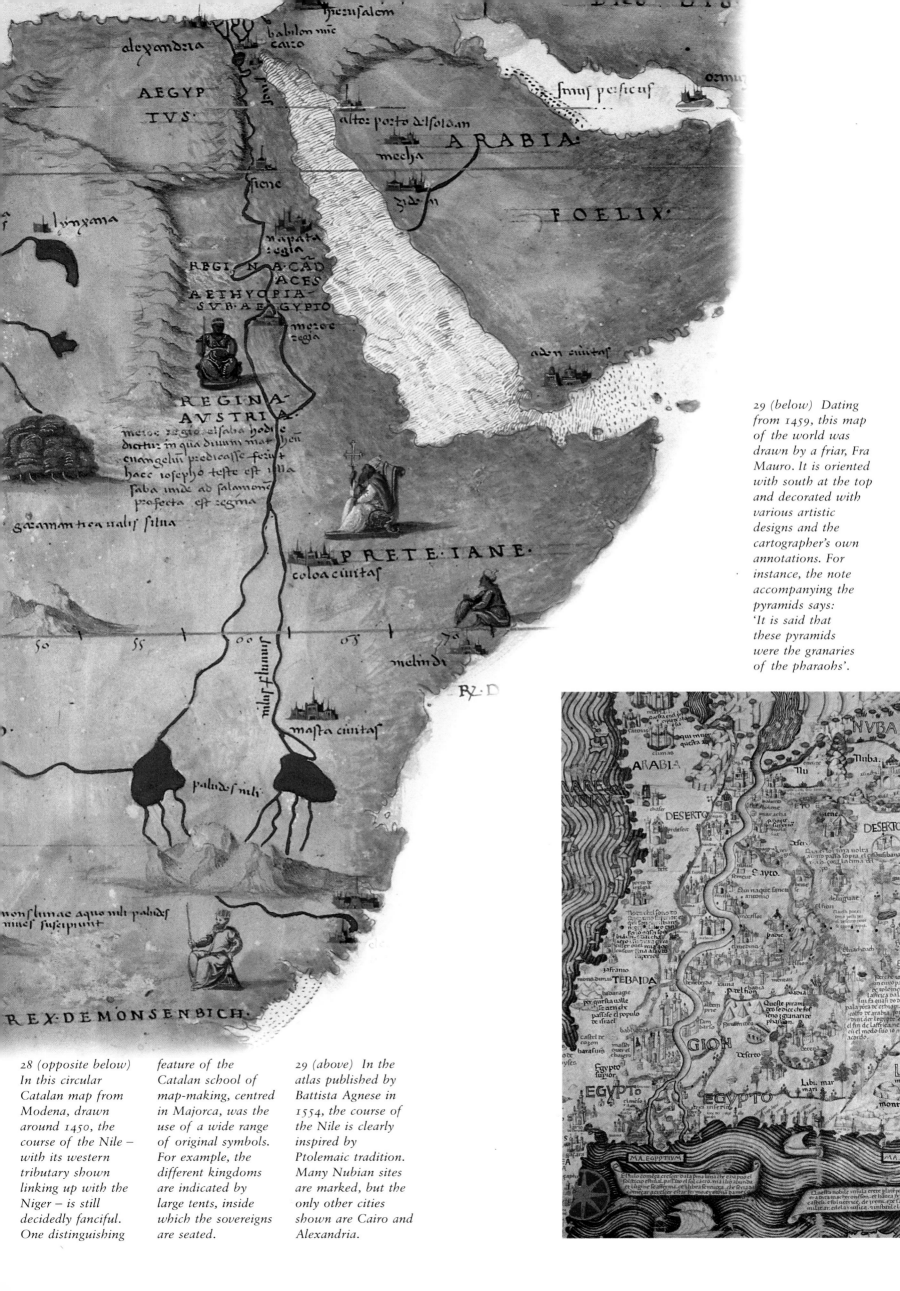

29 (below) Dating
from 1459, this map
of the world was
drawn by a friar, Fra
Mauro. It is oriented
with south at the top
and decorated with
various artistic
designs and the
cartographer's own
annotations. For
instance, the note
accompanying the
pyramids says:
'It is said that
these pyramids
were the granaries
of the pharaohs'.

28 (opposite below)
In this circular
Catalan map from
Modena, drawn
around 1450, the
course of the Nile –
with its western
tributary shown
linking up with the
Niger – is still
decidedly fanciful.
One distinguishing

feature of the
Catalan school of
map-making, centred
in Majorca, was the
use of a wide range
of original symbols.
For example, the
different kingdoms
are indicated by
large tents, inside
which the sovereigns
are seated.

29 (above) In the
atlas published by
Battista Agnese in
1554, the course of
the Nile is clearly
inspired by
Ptolemaic tradition.
Many Nubian sites
are marked, but the
only other cities
shown are Cairo and
Alexandria.

the first modern maps of Africa, and a general map of Egypt with details of the Nile Delta, in 1548, as part of a new edition of Ptolemy's *Geography*. Ramusio also inspired Battista Agnese, who published his nautical atlas in 1554. This contained two types of map, the *Tabulae antiquae*, drawing on the Classical tradition, and the *Tabulae novae*, based on new knowledge, since it was difficult – or impossible – to integrate the former, often wholly fantastic, works with the latter, which made use of more reliable information.

A great step forward was the map of Egypt drawn with impressive precision by Abraham Ortelius (1527–98) for his general world atlas entitled *Theatrum Orbis Terrarum*, first published in 1570. He was assisted in this task by a navigator and explorer, Filippo Pigafetta, a cousin of the more famous Antonio Pigafetta who took part in Magellan's expedition to the East Indies. Filippo was the author of a book entitled *Viaggio da Creta in Egitto e al Sinai 1576–1577* (*Journey from Crete to Egypt and the Sinai 1576–1577*); in 1591 he also drew a large map of the course of the Nile to illustrate another of his books, *Relazione del reame di Congo e delle circomvicine contrade* (*Account of the kingdom of Congo and the Surrounding Regions*).

In the early seventeenth century there were more interesting developments in maps and atlases. Two Dutchmen, Jan Blaeu and Olivier Dapper, and a Venetian, Vincenzo Maria Coronelli, who published maps in 1662, 1686 and 1692 respectively, were the most outstanding exponents of the new approach to cartography, and Egypt and the course of the Nile were now represented fairly precisely. It was, however, another half a century before the first modern map of Egypt was made by the French geographer Jean Baptiste Bourguignon d'Anville. Based on the journeys and studies of such great eighteenth-century explorers as the French Jesuit Claude Sicard, the Danish naval captain Frederik Ludwig Norden and the Reverend Richard Pococke, it was an essential source of information for travellers until the early nineteenth century.

During the Renaissance, Egypt was seen as a fabulous land and the source of all human knowledge and science. It fascinated scholars, who were attracted by

30 (opposite) The first modern map of Egypt was drawn in 1766 by the French geographer Jean Baptiste Bourguignon d'Anville, and was in use until the early nineteenth century. It was based on the journeys and accounts of the great explorers of the eighteenth century

31 In 1570, Abraham Ortelius, an outstanding cartographer from Antwerp, published his famous atlas entitled Theatrum Orbis Terrarum, *which included an impressively accurate map of Egypt. The 1592 edition is shown here.*

31

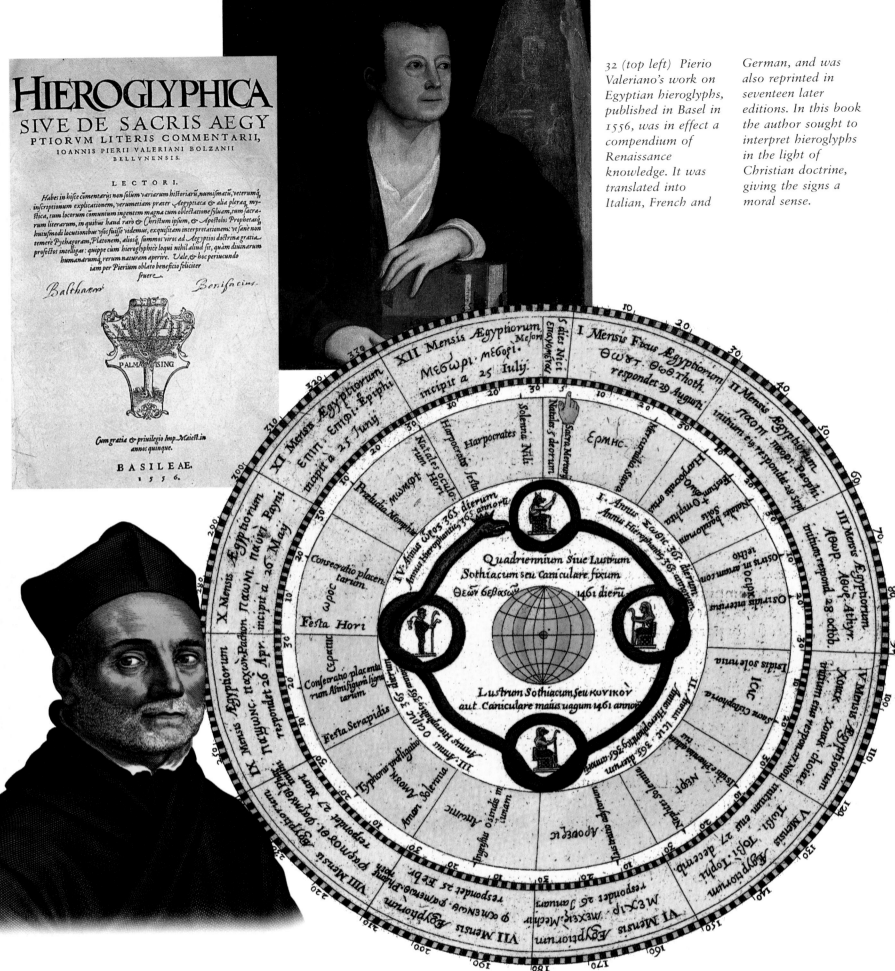

32 (top left) Pierio Valeriano's work on Egyptian hieroglyphs, published in Basel in 1556, was in effect a compendium of Renaissance knowledge. It was translated into Italian, French and German, and was also reprinted in seventeen later editions. In this book the author sought to interpret hieroglyphs in the light of Christian doctrine, giving the signs a moral sense.

the aura of mystery surrounding it – a mystery heightened by the fact that the secret of the meaning of hieroglyphic writing seemed impenetrable. The idea of hidden knowledge that was transmitted exclusively to initiates, often linked with the ancient tradition of alchemy, permeated the whole of the Renaissance world. Obelisks and other Egyptian artifacts inscribed with hieroglyphs, as well as objects of Roman origin – such as the *Mensa Isiaca*, a bronze tablet with silver inlays dating to the first century AD, now in the Museo Egizio, Turin – meant that

Egypt in general and hieroglyphs in particular were at the forefront of the attention of scholars in this period.

Interest in hieroglyphs – which were interpreted in a metaphorical sense, in the light of the conviction that they contained a profound mystical meaning – was revived by the discovery of two manuscripts. The first was found in Macedonia in 1647 and contained the so-called *Corpus hermeticum*. This was a collection of texts of a mystical and esoteric nature attributed to a fictitious author known as Hermes Trismegistus, who was considered by the

Neoplatonists to be the guardian of the ancient wisdom of Egypt. Hermes was the Greek god with whom the Egyptian god Thoth, the 'divine scribe', was identified, while the word Trismegistus – literally 'thrice-great' – was one of the epithets of Thoth himself. The work ascribed to this author – which was translated from Greek by the famous Neoplatonist Marsilio Ficino (1433–99) – contributed to the widespread conviction that hieroglyphs should be given a mystical interpretation.

The second manuscript was purchased in Greece by a Florentine monk at the

32 (opposite, above right) Pierio Valeriano, the pseudonym of Giovan Pietro Dalle Fosse, was born in Belluno, Italy, in 1477, and was one of the first humanists to attempt to decipher hieroglyphs.

32 (opposite, centre left) Athanasius Kircher, a German Jesuit, devoted himself to the study of hieroglyphs. His intuition that Coptic was the last stage in the development of the ancient Egyptian language contributed to the ultimate decipherment of hieroglyphs, though he attributed a symbolic meaning to them.

32 (opposite centre, right) Kircher sought to draw parallels between the calendar of the ancient Egyptians, the 360 degrees of the zodiac and the Gregorian calendar, devising a complex comparative system that he called Rota Chronica ex mente Aegyptorium (Chronological Disk according to the Custom of the Egyptians). In the centre a serpent surrounds the four gods of the Sothic cycle: Isis, Osiris, Horus and Sothis.

33 Kircher also studied the obelisks in Rome, vainly attempting to decipher the inscriptions on them. In particular, he looked at the obelisk of Domitian in the Piazza Navona and those in Piazza della Minerva, Piazza del Popolo and Piazza di Spagna (shown in the drawing), patiently copying the hieroglyphs on them with a fair degree of accuracy.

beginning of the fifteenth century and contained the work of Horapollo, an Alexandrine scholar of the fifth century AD. Entitled *Hyeroglyphica*, it was originally written in Coptic and later translated into Greek. Horapollo could translate and transcribe about thirty hieroglyphs, but had no knowledge of the syntax and grammar of hieroglyphic writing. None the less, when this work was published in 1505 it was so successful that thirty editions were subsequently printed, influencing numerous humanists – especially Pierio Valeriano and the more famous Athanasius Kircher – who, in their turn, attempted to decipher hieroglyphs.

Pierio Valeriano, whose real name was Giovan Pietro Dalle Fosse, was born in Belluno in 1477. He studied literature firstly in Venice, the home of his uncle, Fra Urbano Dalle Fosse, called Bolzanio – a famous humanist who had visited both Greece and Turkey – and then at the University of Padua. After living in Verona for about three years, Pierio Valeriano went to Rome to study the Classical world and the Latin and Greek authors. After living in Naples he returned to Rome, where he became the tutor of the nephews of Popes Clement VII and Paul III. Despite this prestigious post, Valeriano decided to leave Rome, and, after he had been ordained as a priest, he returned to his native town. He devoted many years to what is considered to be his principal work, *Hieroglyphica sive sacris Aegyptiorum literis commentarii* (*Hieroglyphics or Commentary on the*

Sacred Egyptian Writing). Dedicated to Cosimo de'Medici, it was published in 1556 in Basel and reprinted in seventeen later editions, and was also translated into Italian, French and German. In this book he sought to interpret hieroglyphs in the light of Christian moral teaching. With its numerous illustrations it was a compendium of Renaissance learning and for over a century was a reference work for scholars of ancient Egyptian writing and also had an important influence on European art.

The other great scholar of hieroglyphs in the seventeenth century was Athanasius Kircher, a German Jesuit born at Geisa in 1602. After teaching philosophy, science, mathematics and oriental languages at Würzburg, he was appointed professor of mathematics at the Collegio Romano in 1635. Kircher devoted the rest of his life to archaeology and the study of hieroglyphs and Coptic, the subject of his book *Prodromus Coptos sive Aegyptiacus* (*Introduction to Coptic, or rather Egyptian*). Kircher had previously contributed to the publication of an Arabic-Coptic dictionary, a work which had been purchased in the East by the traveller and humanist Pietro Della Valle, to which Kircher added a Latin translation. In 1643 Kircher published an essay entitled *Lingua Aegyptiaca restituta* (*The Egyptian Language Reconstructed*) in which he rightly recognized Coptic as the final stage in the development of the ancient Egyptian language, but he still attributed a purely

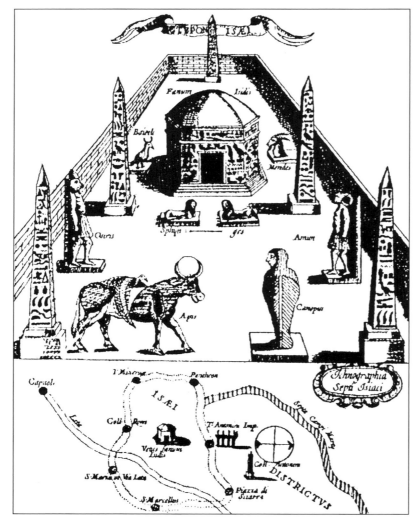

34 *In one of his last works, published in 1666, Kircher speculated on the original appearance of the Campus Martius in Rome, where the temple of Isis was situated.*

symbolic value to the hieroglyphs, believing them to have a hermetic, esoteric meaning.

While he continued his studies and, on the orders of Pope Alexander VII, attempted to translate the hieroglyphs on the obelisks in Rome – four of which had been erected by Sixtus V between 1586 and 1589 – Kircher also founded a museum at the Collegio Romano where numerous rare objects typifying the civilizations known at

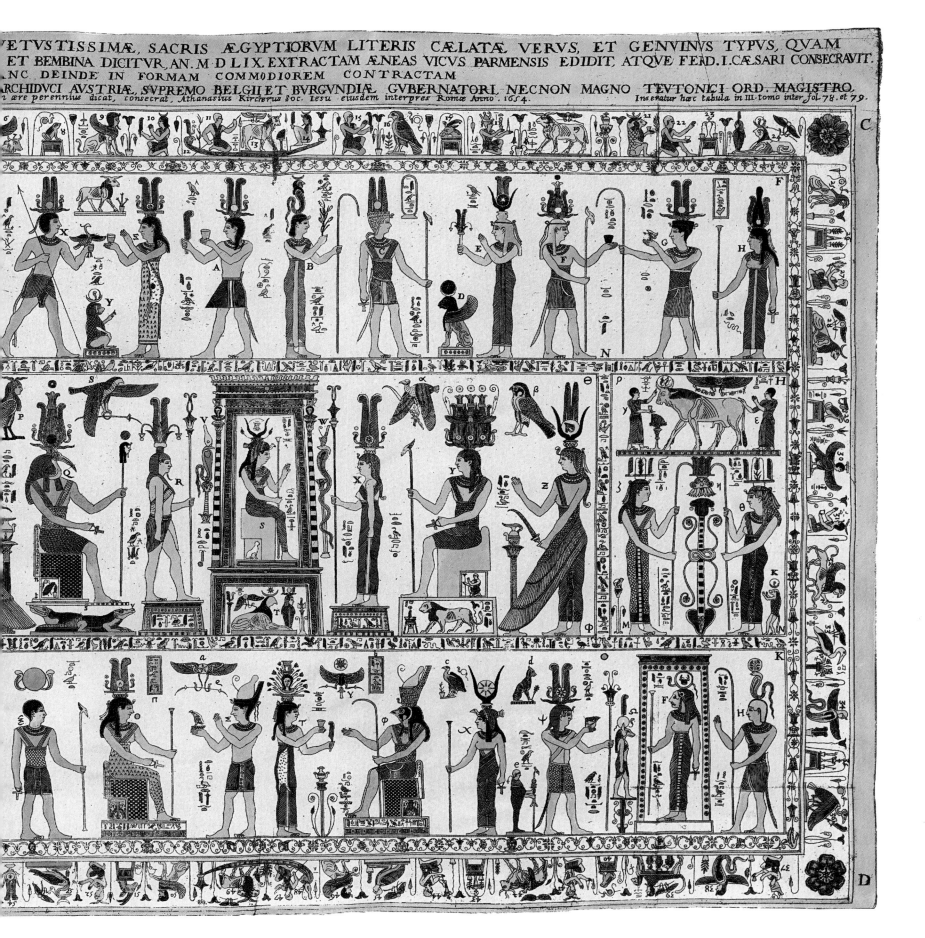

the time were displayed. Later called the Museo Kircheriano, it survived until the Papal States were absorbed by Italy. In 1652, the indefatigable Kircher published his famous *Oedipus Aegyptiacus* in four volumes, considered to be the work that made the greatest contribution to knowledge of ancient Egypt until the publication of Denon's *Voyage* and the *Description de l'Égypte*.

34–35 Kircher made a detailed study of the so-called Tabula Isiaca *or* Mensa Isiaca. *It was also known as the* Tabula Bembi, *after Cardinal Pietro Bembo, to whose collection this extraordinary artifact had at one time belonged. Discovered in Rome in 1525, the* Mensa Isiaca *is a bronze tablet on which are depicted numerous gods receiving or making offerings, accompanied by hieroglyphic texts. It was first studied in 1605 by Lorenzo Pignoria, a humanist from Padua.*

35

TRAVELLERS OF THE EIGHTEENTH CENTURY
THE REDISCOVERY OF AN ANCIENT CIVILIZATION

36 (left) A painting by Louis François Cassas of a tomb at Giza: at this time the ancient monuments of Egypt were used as a source of building materials or as dwellings.

36–37 (above) Claude Sicard, a French Jesuit, was one of the first to identify the ruins at Luxor and Karnak as the site of the ancient city of Thebes. He marked the location of the major sites of Egypt on his map of 1717.

36–37 (below) The Danish naval captain Frederik Norden was a skilled architect and draughtsman. He was the first to make careful drawings of the ancient Egyptian monuments, which illustrate his book Voyages d'Égypte et de Nubie, published after his death in 1755. His drawing of the Great Sphinx is well proportioned and gives an accurate impression of it – he was the first to portray it with the nose missing.

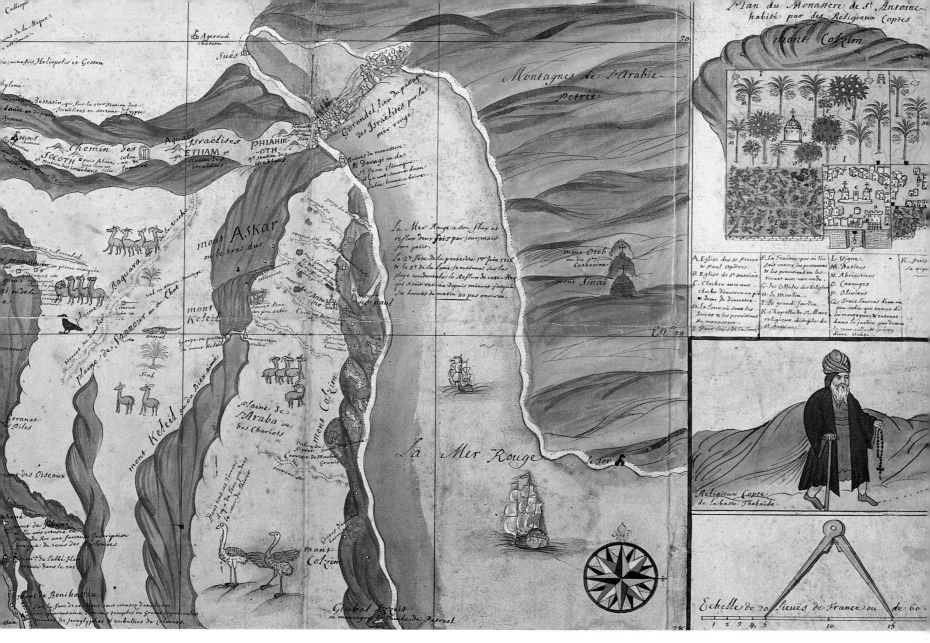

While in the sixteenth and seventeenth centuries Egypt was still a land of fable – half imaginary, half real – the eighteenth century marked the beginning of the first true scientific explorations. At its very threshold, Benoît de Maillet perfectly embodies the spirit of the new century. Born in Saint-Mihiel in Lorraine in 1656, in 1692 he was nominated Consul-General of the King of France in Egypt, where he lived for sixteen years, until 1708.

De Maillet to a certain extent prefigures the behaviour and outlook of the diplomats of the early nineteenth century: he was convinced of the need both to explore Upper Egypt and to study the ancient monuments systematically. He was also responsible for the publication of a cross-section of the pyramid of Khufu that was considerably more accurate, as far as its internal structure was concerned, than that published by John Greaves, an English astronomer, in his *Pyramidographia* of 1646. Like Sieur de Villamont, de Maillet identified the ruins near the present-day village of Mit Rahina, a few kilometres to the east of Saqqara, as the site of the ancient city of Memphis, the capital of Egypt during the Old Kingdom. One of his most ambitious plans was to transport the so-called Pompey's Pillar to France – among the most famous monuments of Alexandria, this is the only surviving

37

remnant of a temple of the third century BC dedicated to Serapis. De Maillet was also one of the first to gather together antiquities to send back to Europe to enlarge both the royal collections as well as those of the most famous collectors of the period, such as the antiquarian and traveller Anne Claude Philippe de Pestels de Lévis, better known as comte de Caylus, and comte Jérôme de Pontchartrain. After he had retired to Marseille, de Maillet dictated his memoirs to the abbot Le Mascrier, who published them in 1735, in the form of letters, entitled *Description de Égypte, contenant plusiers remarques curieuses sur la géographie anciennes de ces païs* (*Description of Egypt, Containing Many Curious Observations on the Ancient Geography of this Country*).

In 1699, during de Maillet's consulship, Paul Lucas, a merchant and antiquarian from Rouen, visited Egypt in the course of a long journey to the East. Although he did not manage to reach the First Cataract as he claimed in his book *Voyage au Levant*, he did travel up the Nile. Appointed royal antiquarian by Louis XIV, Lucas made a second journey to Egypt in 1714, and it is to him that we owe the first description of the temples of Armant and Dendera.

It is thanks to the work of Claude Sicard – a French Jesuit who arrived in Cairo in 1712, where he remained until his death in 1726 – that European knowledge of ancient Egypt made a notable leap forward. A competent speaker of Arabic, with a good understanding of astronomy and mathematics, and skilled at using the sextant, Sicard went on numerous journeys to Middle and Upper Egypt, the Faiyum, the Delta and the Sinai between 1714 and 1723. His main aim was to convert the Copts, but he also pursued the task, entrusted to him by Philip of Orleans, of drawing and studying the principal monuments of the country.

38 (top) Benoît de Maillet, who was made French Consul-General in Egypt in 1692, was convinced of the need to explore Upper Egypt systematically and to study the ancient monuments. He was one of the first to gather antiquities for both royal and private collections.

38–39 A detail of the map of Egypt drawn by the great cartographer from Antwerp, Abraham Ortelius, who published a famous atlas known as the Theatrum Orbis Terrarum (late sixteenth century).

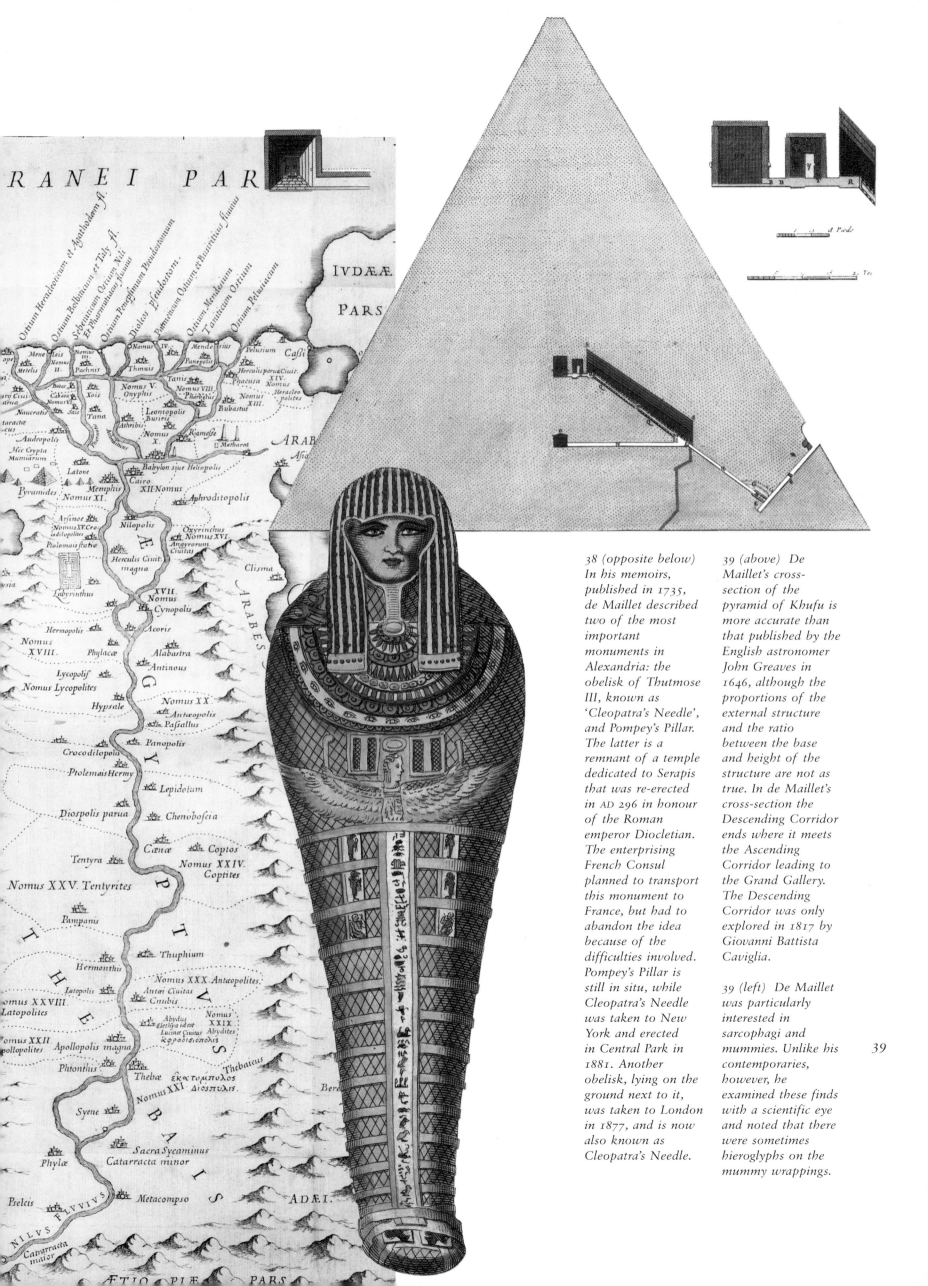

38 (opposite below) In his memoirs, published in 1735, de Maillet described two of the most important monuments in Alexandria: the obelisk of Thutmose III, known as 'Cleopatra's Needle', and Pompey's Pillar. The latter is a remnant of a temple dedicated to Serapis that was re-erected in AD 296 in honour of the Roman emperor Diocletian. The enterprising French Consul planned to transport this monument to France, but had to abandon the idea because of the difficulties involved. Pompey's Pillar is still in situ, while Cleopatra's Needle was taken to New York and erected in Central Park in 1881. Another obelisk, lying on the ground next to it, was taken to London in 1877, and is now also known as Cleopatra's Needle.

39 (above) De Maillet's cross-section of the pyramid of Khufu is more accurate than that published by the English astronomer John Greaves in 1646, although the proportions of the external structure and the ratio between the base and height of the structure are not as true. In de Maillet's cross-section the Descending Corridor ends where it meets the Ascending Corridor leading to the Grand Gallery. The Descending Corridor was only explored in 1817 by Giovanni Battista Caviglia.

39 (left) De Maillet was particularly interested in sarcophagi and mummies. Unlike his contemporaries, however, he examined these finds with a scientific eye and noted that there were sometimes hieroglyphs on the mummy wrappings.

39

During his journeys, Sicard managed to identify the site of the ancient city of Thebes, the exact position of which, it seems, was no longer known, although it was correctly shown on Abraham Ortelius's map of Egypt of 1570. Sicard also located the tombs of the Valley of the Kings and the sites of the main temples and religious centres of ancient Egypt mentioned by the Classical authors. He wrote accurate descriptions of twenty-four temples, more than fifty decorated tombs and twenty pyramids. In 1717 he drew the *Carte de la Basse Thébaïde* (*Map of the Lower Thebaïd*). This was followed in 1722 by a second, general, map of Egypt which can be seen as one of the first scholarly maps of the country and was the source of much of the information used by the geographer Jean Baptiste Bourguignon d'Anville to make his famous map of Egypt in 1766.

Some years after Sicard, in 1760, Vitaliano Donati, a professor of botany at the University of Turin who was originally from Padua in Italy, was charged by Carlo Emanuele III of Savoy to sail up the Nile beyond Aswan and the First Cataract. During this journey, Donati wrote a precious herbal, unfortunately now lost, and acquired three large diorite statues representing the lion-headed goddess Sekhmet, Ramesses II and Queen Tiye, the wife of Amenhotep III. He sent the statues back to Italy, where they were displayed at the Museo d'Antichità – later the Museo Egizio – in Turin.

40 (opposite, above left) Carlo Emanuele III of Savoy, king of Sardinia, promoted the development of the University of Turin and sought to enlarge his own collections by sending the Italian botanist Vitaliano Donati on a journey to Egypt and the East. Donati was instructed to collect specimens of the flora and fauna of the country, as well as antiquities, including mummies and manuscripts.

40 (opposite, above right) and 41 A very meticulous man, Donati kept a travel journal during the expedition; now in the Biblioteca Reale in Turin, it contains this delightful view of the pyramids of Egypt, the style of which is clearly inspired by the Classical world.

40 (opposite below) Donati sailed up the Nile as far as Nubia and during the voyage studied the flora of Egypt, writing a herbal that was later lost. He also acquired three large statues for the royal collections, now in the Museo Egizio in Turin.

42 *(left) Richard Pococke published this map in his book* Description of the East. *When the British clergyman arrived in Egypt in 1737, no precise maps of the country existed. Although the French Jesuit Claude Sicard had identified the position of the ancient city of Thebes and other major ancient Egyptian monuments, Jean Baptiste Bourguignon d'Anville had not yet drawn his more accurate map.*

Richard Pococke

The Reverend Richard Pococke (1704–65) can perhaps be regarded as the first true scholarly traveller in Egypt. Pococke was an unusual individual. Born in Southampton, he studied religion at Oxford, but in 1737 decided to set out on a long journey that would last three years and take him first to Egypt, where he sailed up the Nile as far as Aswan, then to Jerusalem in Palestine, Baalbek in Syria, Mesopotamia and finally the Sinai and Greece. He returned to England after travelling in Switzerland and Savoy, where he made one of the first crossings of the Mer de Glace, the huge glacier to the north of Mont Blanc, thus earning a reputation as a pioneer of Alpine exploration. He was later appointed Bishop of Ossory and subsequently of Meath.

His account of his journeys, published in two volumes in 1743 and 1745, was entitled *A Description of the East, and Some Other Countries*. The first volume was devoted to Egypt and the second to the other countries he visited – Palestine and Lebanon, Syria, Mesopotamia, Cyprus, Crete, Thrace, Greece and parts of western Europe. Exceptionally, his descriptions of the archaeological sites were both systematic and complete, and they were also accompanied by numerous drawings, maps and plans, giving the reader an overall picture of the monuments described. Pococke's work was so successful

42 (opposite, above right) Together with Claude Sicard and Frederik Norden, the Reverend Richard Pococke can be considered one of the first travellers in the eighteenth century to explore Egypt in a systematic manner. However, he believed that the pyramids of Giza had been constructed by covering natural hills with blocks of limestone and drew the Sphinx in an idealized manner – unlike Norden, he depicted it with its nose still in place.

42 (opposite below) At Luxor, Pococke drew the 'statues of Osymanduas', as he referred to the statues of Ramesses II. The name comes from Usermaatre, a forename of this pharaoh.

43 (below) In this illustration, entitled A View of Two Pyramides and Plans of two Catacombs at Saqqara, in addition to the pyramid of Djoser, Pococke has drawn a complex plan of the Serapeum – the enormous cemetery where the sacred Apis bulls were buried. This site was rediscovered and excavated by the great Egyptologist Auguste Mariette in 1850.

43 (right) Pococke also drew some antiquities that he had acquired for his collection, such as this block statue, which he believed was the goddess Isis.

The pictures reproduced in this section are taken from A Description of the East, and Some Other Countries, by Richard Pococke (London, 1743–45).

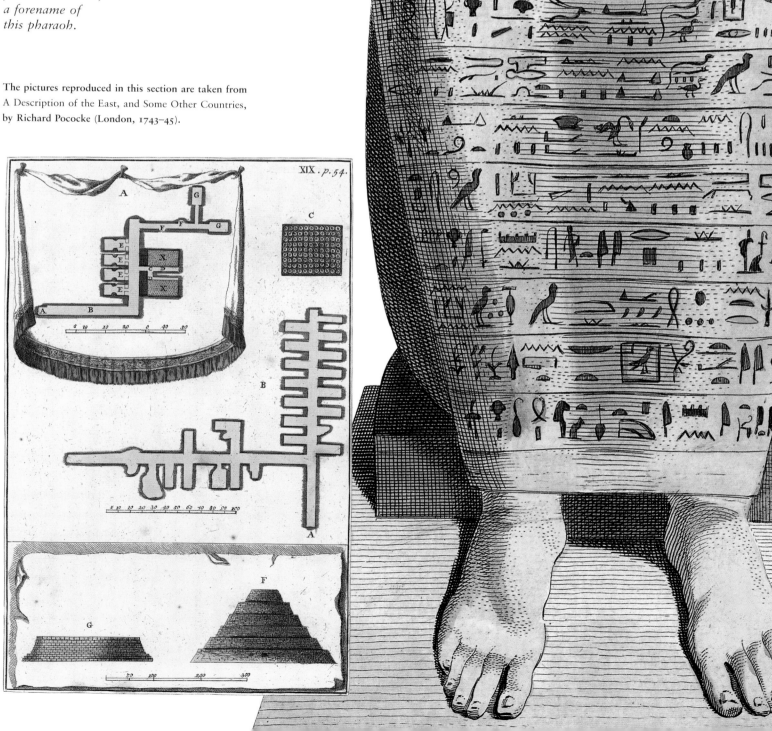

44 Pococke was the fourth European traveller to enter the Valley of the Kings in post-medieval times. In January 1738 the courageous clergyman visited the royal necropolis of Thebes, noting that there were eighteen tombs, nine of which were accessible. Pococke drew a plan of the tomb he managed to enter, and made the first known map of the site, which had been identified a few years previously by Sicard, although, oddly enough, it was clearly shown on an earlier map drawn by the Dutch cartographer Abraham Ortelius. In the background of Pococke's illustration the sacred peak of el-Qurn towers over the valley; its pyramidal form probably influenced the choice of this site as a royal cemetery.

45 (opposite above) At Saqqara Pococke acquired a wooden anthropoid coffin containing a mummy. He visited a number of underground tombs, as well as the catacombs in which the falcons and ibises, birds sacred to the gods Horus and Thoth, were buried.

45 (opposite below) Pococke also drew a general view of the desert cliffs at Thebes. In the foreground are the Colossi of Memnon; behind them, on the left, is the temple of Medinet Habu and, on the right, the Ramesseum, with the numerous rock-cut tombs forming the private necropolis in the background.

that it was immediately translated into French, German and Dutch. Its significance is all the greater because some of the monuments he described and drew were destroyed or severely damaged before the Napoleonic expedition, when Vivant Denon visited the country.

Although Pococke devoted several pages to the natural features of the areas he visited, as well as the customs and habits of the local population, he was mainly attracted by the monuments, especially those of ancient Egypt. In fact, rather than a travel diary, he conceived his book as a collection of observations on cities, places of interest and monuments, as well as the flora and fauna of the countries he visited.

Pococke sailed from Livorno, Italy, on 7 September 1737, reaching Alexandria on the twenty-ninth of that month. Of the inhabitants of this city he stated that they had 'a very bad character, especially the military men, and among them particularly the janizaries'. He visited the mosques, monasteries and churches, lingering over the 'very beautifully built' walls of the city and its monuments, and described what he saw: two obelisks, of which 'one is broke, and part of it lies on the ground' and

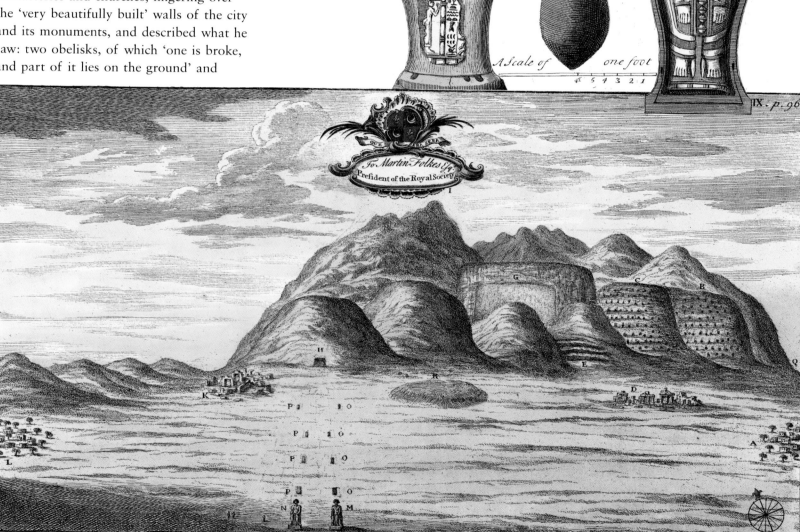

Pompey's Pillar, which 'may be supposed to have been erected after Strabo's time', around which were remains that 'some Arabian historians call...the palace of Julius Caesar', and the catacombs consisting of 'several apartments cut in the rock'. Pococke also visited the surrounding area, including Lake Mareotis, now Lake Maryût, the canal of Canopus 'which brings the water to Alexander', Aboukir,

Rosetta and Damietta. He then sailed up the Nile to Cairo, where he arrived on 11 November. In his diary Pococke noted:

The city of Cairo is situated about a mile from the river, and extends eastward near two miles to the mountain; it is about seven miles round, for I was something more than two hours and three quarters going round the city...computing that I went two miles and a half an hour.

Pococke described the city, beginning with the oldest part – called 'Old Cairo' – on the site of the Roman fortress of Babylon, part of the walls of which are still visible. He then continued with the modern city, 'New Cairo', with the river port of Bulaq, now a heavily populated district near the city centre but which at that time was 'about a mile from New Cairo' and was 'the port for all the boats

45

does not derive its name 'from the Patriarch Joseph but, as some authors observe, from a grand vizier of that name who had the care of this work under Sultan Mahomet, son of Calaun'.

Although he did not seem particularly interested in Islamic art, Pococke was greatly impressed by the mosques of the city – dubbed by medieval travellers 'devil's churches' – especially that of Sultan Hassan. He wrote:

There are several magnificent mosques in and about Cairo; but that which exceeds them all, both as to the solidity of its building, and a certain grandeur and magnificence that strikes in a very surprising manner, is the mosque of Sultan Hassan, built at the foot of the castle hill.

With great skill, Pococke also drew a map of Cairo, on which the various quarters of the city and the main monuments described in his account were clearly shown. He ended his description with some remarks about the inhabitants of the city who were 'a great mixture of people...the city being composed of original Egyptians, among whom are the Copti[c] Christians; of Arabians; of the people of Barbary, and the western parts of Africa; of the Berberines of the parts of Nubia, a great number of their men

47 (opposite) During his visit to Thebes Pococke spent about half a day in front of the Colossi of Memnon, drawing them and copying both the hieroglyphic inscriptions and the much more numerous graffiti from the Greek and Roman periods. The inhabitants sought in vain to prevent the dauntless clergyman from copying these inscriptions because they were convinced that they were the key to fabulous treasures.

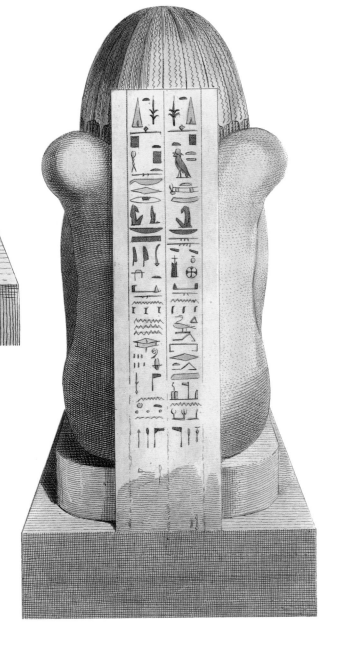

46 In addition to his 'statue of Isis', Pococke also acquired another statue of the same type from an Italian merchant in Cairo, which he believed represented Osiris. Amazed by the strange form of the statues, Pococke considered them to be 'very ancient'.

46

that come up the river from the parts of the Delta'.

After Pococke had described the two parts of the city, the Coptic churches, the synagogues, the aqueduct, the public baths, the caravanserai and the houses, he concentrated on the fortress, now known as the Citadel, 'situated on a rocky hill which seems to be separated by art from the hill or mountain Jebel Duise, which is the name of the east end of Jebel Mocattham. It is said this castle was built by Saladin'. Here there was also the famous Joseph's Well, which, as Pococke rightly observed, coming here to offer themselves as servants'. As far as the other peoples in Cairo were concerned, Pococke noted that there were also 'some Greeks, a few Armenians, and many Jews. Of the Europeans, there are settled here only the French, English, and some Italians from Venice and Leghorn'.

After completing his description of Cairo, Pococke then proceeded to discuss the antiquities in its environs – Giza and Saqqara – marvelling that 'the situation of Memphis should not be well known, which was so great and famous a city, and for so long a time the capital of Egypt'.

In his opinion, the lack of remains of this city was due to the fact that 'many of the best materials of it might be carried to Alexandria'. Pococke then described the great pyramids of Giza, giving the exact position of them with regard to Memphis, and he even climbed to the top of the pyramid of Khufu in order to draw a map of the area. Like the Scottish explorer James Bruce, he believed that the pyramids were simply small natural hills covered with dressed stone. As far as the interpretation of these monuments and the techniques used for their construction were concerned, Pococke followed Herodotus closely, displaying a thorough knowledge of

the second book of his *History*. He also explored the interior of the pyramid of Khufu, but did not carry out new measurements, giving those obtained by the astronomer John Greaves and Benoît de Maillet, and publishing the latter's drawing of the cross-section.

After Giza, Pococke turned his attention to Saqqara, where he drew a plan of the Serapeum – the enormous complex of underground galleries where the sacred Apis bulls were interred in huge granite sarcophagi – which was rediscovered a century later by Auguste Mariette. Pococke also visited Dahshur, site of the two large pyramids (the Bent Pyramid and the Red Pyramid) built by King Sneferu, founder of the Fourth Dynasty. He explored the fertile region of the Faiyum, where Lake Moeris (now Lake Qarun) is situated, as well as the remains of what some Classical authors referred to as the 'Egyptian Labyrinth', in fact the mortuary temple attached to the pyramid of Amenemhet III at Hawara.

Having completed his exploration of the Faiyum, the intrepid clergyman decided to leave for Upper Egypt. Having obtained from Sheikh Osman Bey an indispensable letter of introduction addressed to the authorities responsible for the regions he was to cross, he hired a small boat on

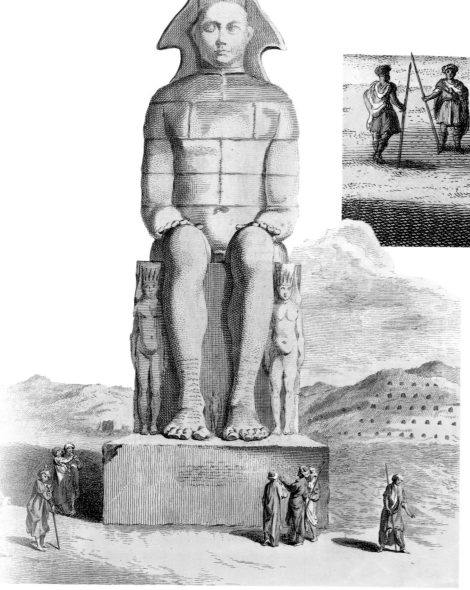

which he loaded provisions for himself and gifts (tobacco, rice, soap) for the important personages he was to meet. These proved to be very useful during his voyage.

On 6 December 1737 Pococke left Cairo for Upper Egypt accompanied by a servant and a dragoman (the name given to the guides and interpreters at the service of the European travellers). After passing the pyramid of Meidum, Pococke reached the monastery of St Anthony, where he stayed before starting out for Beni Suef. Continuing southwards, he visited the remains of Antinoöpolis, Hermopolis (modern Ashmunein), Lycopolis (Asyut), Panopolis (Akhmim) and Abydos, reaching the ruins of the ancient city of Tentyra (Dendera), where there were 'two gates and

48 (right) Pococke
drew a plan of the
Coptic monasteries
in the Arabian
Desert southeast of
Cairo dedicated to St
Paul and St Anthony.
The clergyman
stayed at them both
on his journey up
the Nile and on his
return voyage. The
monastery of St
Anthony was
surrounded by a high
wall built without
gates for reasons of
security. Visitors had
to be winched up to
an opening at a
considerable height
above the ground.

48 (below) and 49
Although ancient
Egyptian antiquities
were Pococke's main
interest, he also
made a number of
drawings of the
inhabitants of the
country, paying great
attention to the
details of their
costume. Here we
see a Copt and a
bey, a title given to
the country's
dignitaries in the
Ottoman period, as
well as a Muslim
holy man and a chief
of the guards, female
dancers and ordinary
women, a Coptic
priest and a woman
on a donkey.

48

four temples which seem to have relation to
one another'. Pococke was convinced that
the main temple was dedicated to the
goddess Isis, although it is dedicated to the
goddess Hathor. Here he admired the
columns, the capitals of which were
decorated on four sides with the image of
Hathor and are carved so finely that 'they
must have been executed by one of the best
Greek sculptors'. After passing the town of
Qift, formerly Coptos, the starting-point of
an important route linking the Nile to the
port of Berenice on the Red Sea – where he
saw remains of the ancient city that have
since disappeared – Pococke arrived at Qus,
formerly known as Apollinopolis Parva.

Pococke was given a friendly reception
by the sheikh and, after showing him his
letter of introduction, he presented him
with a pouch of tobacco, a bag of rice,
two bars of soap and a pair of red shoes.

In exchange the traveller received a sheep
and permission to visit Karnak, 'which is
part of the ancient Thebes, where there are
the ruins of a most magnificent temple'
and Luxor 'where are remains of another
grand building, which was probably the
temple or monument of Osymanduas'.

So it was that on 13 January 1738
Pococke arrived in Thebes – writing that
'the great and famous city of Thebes was
on both sides of the river; some say it was
built by Osiris'. However, the traveller was
somewhat puzzled because he could find
no trace of a city wall among the ruins,
though the city was known from Homer's
description as 'Thebes of the hundred
gates'. What Pococke failed to realize was
that the Greek word pilon had been
wrongly translated as 'gate' when in this
context it meant 'column'.

After spending some time admiring the

columns, sphinxes and obelisks of Karnak
and Luxor, Pococke crossed to the west
bank of the Nile. Here he was received by
the local sheikh, who accompanied him to
the village of Qurna and provided him
with guides and horses to take him to the
valley of Biban el-Muluk, where the
'sepulchres of the kings of Thebes' were
situated. Pococke described the access to
the Valley of the Kings, which must then
have looked much as it did in antiquity:
'We came to a part that is wider, being a
round opening, like an amphitheatre, and
ascended by a narrow steep passage about
ten feet high, which seems to have been
broke down thro' the rock....'

Pococke was the fourth European
traveller to enter this necropolis in post-
medieval times. The three who had
preceded him had also been clerics: Fathers
Protase and François in 1688, and the

French Jesuit Claude Sicard in 1708. Pococke drew the earliest known map of the royal cemetery – albeit with a certain amount of fantasy – indicating eighteen tombs, nine of which were sufficiently free of debris to allow him to enter. He also drew plans of the accessible tombs, but it is not always possible to ascertain which ones are represented. It is known, however, that he visited the tomb of Ramesses IV (KV2) and those of Ramesses VI (KV9), Amenemesses (KV10), Ramesses III (KV11), Tawosret and Setnakhte (KV14), Seti II (KV15) and Ramesses X (KV18) (using the standard numbering system).

After spending a couple of days exploring the Valley of the Kings, Pococke also visited a number of the so-called Tombs of the Nobles, in the sides of the Theban cliffs, and the Ramesseum, where 'there are ruins…of a very large colossal statue; it is broke off about the middle of the trunk, the head is six feet broad'. In the second courtyard of this temple Pococke also noted 'two statues of black granite; that to the west, which is sitting, measured from the hand to the elbow five feet', while, as regards the other statue on the east side, 'at a distance from it is the head with the cap'. The two statues were of Ramesses II – one still stands in the temple, while the other, the seated one that Pococke placed on the west side, fell down and broke a few years later at the time of the Napoleonic expedition, and its upper part was removed by Belzoni. Before returning to the east bank, Pococke also visited the temple of Medinet Habu, which he identified with the Memnonium of the Classical authors, and the Colossi of Memnon, the two enormous statues located in front of the few remains of the temple of Amenhotep III, of which he made splendid drawings.

Having paid another visit to the temple of Luxor, which he described as the 'Mausoleum of Osymanduas' because he believed it belonged to the 'King of Kings, Osymanduas', Pococke set off once more up the Nile, visiting Hermonthis (Armant), Esna, Edfu and Kom Ombo. On 21 January 1738 he reached Aswan – 'a poor small town, with a sort of fortress, or rather barrack for janizaries' – the final destination of his journey to Upper Egypt.

After visiting the ancient city of Syene, the granite quarries and the islands of Elephantine and Philae, Pococke began the return journey on 27 January. Helped by the favourable current and without the long stops of the outward journey, this was much speedier. On 20 February Pococke was already at Manfalût, and on the evening of 27 February he was in sight of Cairo, from where, shortly afterwards, he left for Jerusalem.

50 (left) Sphinxes, fantastic hieroglyphs and various statues decorate the opening of the section in Frederik Ludwig Norden's book dealing with the pyramids. He describes them as the 'monuments most worthy of the curiosity of those who travel in Egypt'.

Frederik Ludwig Norden

vant que d
rois me dif
gnes de la c
j'entends les
nombre des fept
encore aujourdhui,

Ces fuperbes Monumens ne fe trouvent qu'en Eg

Frederik Ludwig Norden, the son of an artillery officer, enlisted in the Danish navy at the age of fourteen. Like his four brothers, who had all followed military careers, Frederik had been prepared for this vocation by his education, with particular emphasis being placed on geography, foreign languages, history and mathematics. On becoming an officer, Norden soon distinguished himself due to his exceptional talents in mathematics and, above all, draughtsmanship and the art of navigation, so that he was given the task of correcting and remaking a series of plans and charts. As a result of his diligence and skill he was presented to King Christian VI in 1732; the king, an enlightened monarch who was particularly fond of art and literature, decided to give the cadet an opportunity to develop his gifts.

On the king's instructions, the admiralty made Norden a second lieutenant, granting him special status releasing him from the duties normally imposed on the other officers of this rank. Instead, he was under orders to devote himself to the study of naval architecture. In order to learn more about the subject, Norden went first to the Netherlands, then to France, to Marseille, and finally to Italy, where he stayed for three years. While there he came into contact with artists and historians and visited the first collections of antiquities in Rome and Florence, where he was made an associate member of the Accademia del Disegno. It was in Florence, in 1737, that Norden received orders from the king to go to Egypt and write a detailed report on the country and its monuments. His report was intended to be of use to the Danish navy if its operations were to increase in the eastern Mediterranean and, at the same time, provide further information about the art and history of a country that had now become celebrated.

Embarking at Livorno, Norden landed at Alexandria in June 1737, after a voyage of thirty days; he then continued on to Cairo, where he arrived on 7 July, four months before Richard Pococke, who at that time was probably unknown to him. The two travellers must have visited the same archaeological sites on numerous occasions without meeting. They were profoundly different both in character and

AU ROI.

SIRE,

'*Ouvrage du feu Capitaine Norden, que nous mettons aux pieds de* VOTRE MAJESTE, *a déjà l'avantage précieux de Lui appartenir. Non seulement c'étoit par ordre & sous*

a 2 *les*

50 (opposite centre) Norden was sent to Egypt in 1737 by King Christian VI of Denmark, with the task of writing a detailed report on the country. His skill as a draughtsman and his knowledge of mathematics and architecture allowed him to depict the Egyptian monuments with great precision. Norden stayed in Egypt for nearly a year and went up the Nile as far as the site

of el-Derr in Nubia. He was also one of the founders of the Egyptian Society, the first association for the promotion of studies of the country, set up in London in December 1741. Another member was Richard Pococke, although, curiously enough, the two travellers had visited the archaeological sites of Egypt in the same period without ever meeting.

50 (opposite below) In this view of the east side of the pyramids of Giza Norden displays his ability as a draughtsman. The pyramid on the left is one of the three secondary, or queens', pyramids belonging to Menkaure's pyramid.

51 Norden's travel diary, containing his drawings, plans and cross-sections, was only published in 1755 – 17 years after his return from Egypt and 13 years after his death. The work was dedicated to King Frederick V, Christian VI's successor.

The pictures reproduced in this section are taken from Voyages d'Egypte et de Nubie, by Frederik Ludwig Norden (Copenhagen, 1755).

Due to his authoritarian character and lack of understanding of the local people, Norden's journey to Upper Egypt was more eventful than Pococke's. At Luxor and Karnak, for example, he did not even manage to land on his outward journey. Pococke, in contrast, thanks to some small presents he had brought with him in case of need, was able visit the ruins undisturbed. It was only on the return journey that Norden visited the great Theban temples, albeit in haste. In order to avoid being pestered by the inhabitants, Norden was obliged to explore the temple of Luxor, of which he drew two splendid views, by moonlight.

background. Whereas Pococke was noted for his diplomacy, patience and ability to negotiate with local people and the authorities, enabling him to obtain many advantages and concessions, Norden, who was impulsive, courageous and enterprising, had a military mentality and did not hesitate to resort to the use of arms when he thought the situation warranted it.

Norden visited the pyramids of Giza, examining them very thoroughly, and drew the first fairly accurate map of the area. He also added a long commentary to the *Pyramidographia* by the English astronomer John Greaves. While in Cairo, however, Norden was obliged to interrupt his journey for over four months due to illness,

and it was only on 17 November that the young officer left for Upper Egypt. He was followed about twenty days later by Pococke, who had arrived in the country in the meantime, had visited Alexandria and the Delta, and was now in Cairo.

Norden reached Thebes on 11 December, and described his arrival in his travel diary:

At four o'clock in the afternoon I began to see an obelisk on the east side and, shortly afterwards, a large number of peristyles, various portals and some ancient buildings appeared, scattered higgledy-piggledy over the plain....

Unfortunately he was forced to observe these ruins – which were those of the temples of Karnak – from his boat because

53 (opposite above) After overcoming the captain's hostility, Norden managed to land on the west bank at Thebes and see, albeit rapidly and with his weapons at the ready, the Colossi of Memnon, Medinet Habu and the Ramesseum, which he described as the 'Palace of Memnon'. In his drawing of the second courtyard of the temple, seen from the east, are the remains of the second pylon and the Osirian colossi (E and D), and the colossus of Ramesses II, lying on the ground (G), which he wrongly believed emitted the groan mentioned by the Classical authors, confusing it with one of the Colossi of Memnon. In the courtyard, the head of Ramesses II is still visible, marked with the letter I, while H indicates the colossal statue of the pharaoh, at that time still intact. By the time Napoleon's experts drew it, it had already broken into two pieces: Belzoni managed to remove the bust, which was then transported to the British Museum.

the captain refused to set the passengers ashore. Pococke, on the other hand, who arrived about a month later, ingratiated himself with the local sheikh thanks to the small gifts that he had wisely brought with him for this purpose and was able to visit and study the ruins at his leisure. Only on the following day, and by resorting to threats, did Norden – who had now abandoned the idea of visiting Karnak and Luxor – manage to overcome the captain's hostility and land on the west bank. Here, his arms at the ready, he rapidly saw the main monuments: the Colossi of Memnon, the Ramesseum (described as the 'Palace of Memnon') and the ruins of Medinet Habu, although he had to forgo the exploration of the Valley of the Kings.

Determined to proceed up-river to visit Lower Nubia, Norden left Thebes on 13 December. After passing the temples of Esna, Edfu and Kom Ombo, he arrived at Aswan, where he visited the islands of Elephantine and Philae, describing the latter as the 'island of ell-Heiss'. After the First Cataract, Norden continued to ascend the Nile with the intention of reaching the Second Cataract. However, beyond the temples of Dabod and Kalabsha, where the inhabitants fired at his boat, he was only able to see the ruins of the temples of Dendur, el-Dakka, el-Maharraqa, el-Sebua, Korosko, Amada and el-Derr from the river before the captain refused to continue any further. Since Norden's promises and threats were to no avail, on 6 January 1738

he was obliged to begin the return journey. He was now able to take a closer look at some of the sites that he had seen so fleetingly on the outward voyage, and could add more detail to the drawings he had executed previously, as well as making new ones. On 3 February Norden was back at Thebes; Pococke had left the site of the ancient city a few days before, on 18 January, after staying there almost a week, and was now heading for Aswan.

On this occasion, despite further problems, Norden finally managed to visit – although rapidly and in difficult conditions – the ruins of Luxor and Karnak. In order to be able to wander undisturbed among the ruins of Luxor, the intrepid traveller decided to explore them

53 (centre) Norden drew the Colossi of Memnon without identifying the statues with those described by the Classical authors.

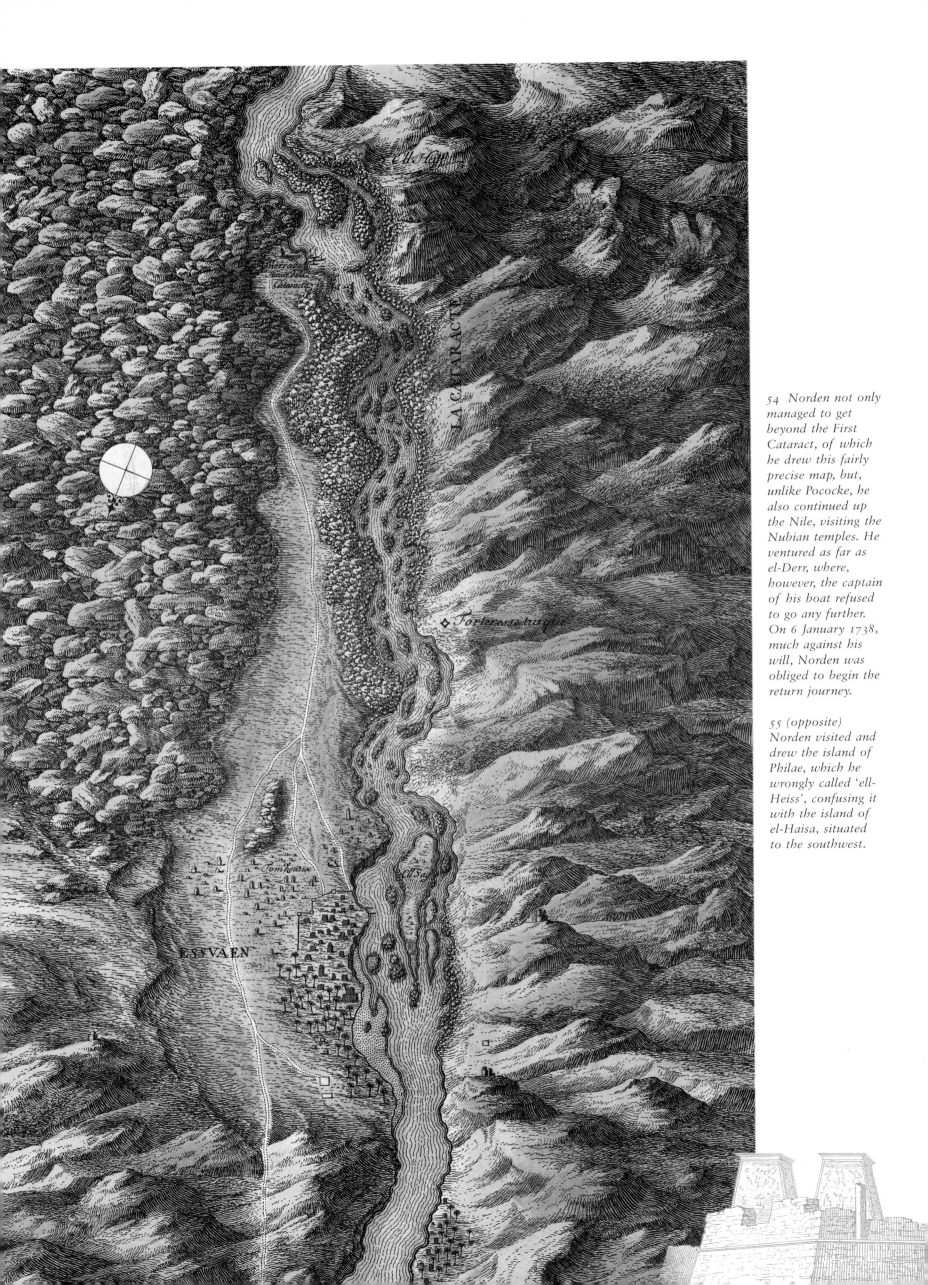

ell Heiss

Horrable Saut Philae Cataracte

LA CATARACTE

Forteresse turque

Pomheous

ell Saa

ESSVAEN

54 Norden not only
managed to get
beyond the First
Cataract, of which
he drew this fairly
precise map, but,
unlike Pococke, he
also continued up
the Nile, visiting the
Nubian temples. He
ventured as far as
el-Derr, where,
however, the captain
of his boat refused
to go any further.
On 6 January 1738,
much against his
will, Norden was
obliged to begin the
return journey.

55 (opposite)
Norden visited and
drew the island of
Philae, which he
wrongly called 'ell-
Heiss', confusing it
with the island of
el-Haisa, situated
to the southwest.

by night. His visit to Karnak was more eventful: surrounded by a hostile crowd of local people demanding money, the Danish officer was forced, once again, to resort to the threat of arms, and realizing it was no longer prudent to remain at the site, continued his descent of the Nile. Pococke, now on his way back from Aswan, reached Thebes the day after Norden's departure.

Having left Thebes on the evening of 4 February, Norden arrived in Cairo after a voyage of nineteen days. During his subsequent stay of three months in Cairo, he was able to explore Lower Egypt more thoroughly. At the end of May he set sail for Europe; in all, his journey had lasted a little over a year. While he was in Egypt,

and elevations – with great precision. The young traveller successfully presented the account of his journey, with its numerous illustrations, to the king, who, after promoting him to the rank of captain and commending him before the entire court, instructed him to prepare his material for publication. Thus Norden began to carry out a careful revision of all the drawings and give a final form to the account of his journey, in which he inserted the necessary references to the related drawings.

Unfortunately the process of revision was soon interrupted when Norden was seconded to the British navy to serve in the war against Spain. After having been at sea with the British navy for some time, taking

Norden remained in London until the summer of 1742, when his health began to deteriorate, perhaps due to an attack of tuberculosis. He decided to leave England and go to France to visit the ports and coasts of the country after a short stay in Paris. However, while he was in the French capital his health worsened and, on 22 September, Norden died at the age of just thirty-four. Before his death, he committed all the drawings and notes from his journey in Egypt to his friend Count Danneskiold, another captain in the Danish navy who had accompanied him to England.

When he was informed of Norden's untimely death, the king of Denmark ordered that the traveller's documents

the Danish traveller had collected a great deal of information, making a large number of drawings and observations, many of which, especially those concerning Lower Egypt, were written on loose sheets. His account relating to his three-month journey to Upper Egypt took the form of a journal, written in a bound notebook, in which Norden also drew a map of the course of the Nile that took up twenty-nine pages.

Norden's knowledge of mathematics and architecture, together with his excellent draughtsmanship, meant that he drew the monuments of Egypt – of which he also took the measurements and made plans

part in numerous engagements with the enemy, Norden returned to London, where he was made a member of the Royal Society and the Egyptian Society. The latter, founded in 1741 under the patronage of Lord Sandwich, was the first organization to promote research into the history and antiquities of ancient Egypt. Its members also included Richard Pococke. Norden read a report to the Society on the ruins of Thebes, taken from his travel diary, which was very well received and was later published with the title *Drawings of some Ruins and Colossal Statues at Thebes in Egypt with an Account of the Same in a Letter to the Royal Society*.

should be published and that the reproductions of his drawings be entrusted to the engraver Mark Tuscher of Nuremberg. One of the most famous artists of the day, Tuscher was a friend of Norden's and had already engraved two plates illustrating the report Norden had read to the Royal Society in 1741.

In 1755, Norden's work was finally published, during the reign of Frederick V, Christian VI's successor, thus doing justice to this great traveller to whom we owe the first accurate drawings of the monuments and the earliest relatively precise maps of the most important archaeological sites of Egypt.

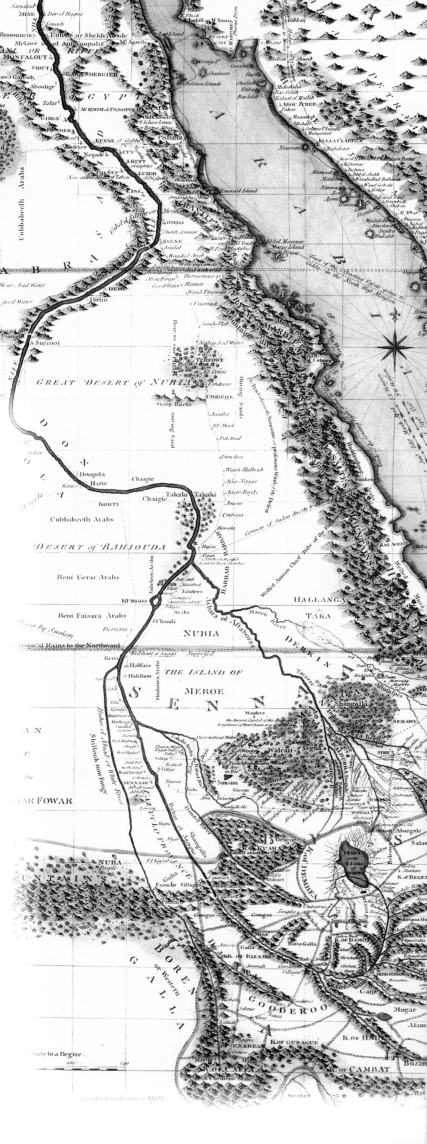

James Bruce

56 and 56–57 James Bruce of Kinnaird, a Scottish gentleman and diplomat, was a remarkable explorer of the Nile. In December 1768 he left Cairo, with his faithful secretary Luigi Balugani and Greek butler Strates, and, in the course of an adventurous journey, managed to travel beyond Lake Tana in Ethiopia and reach the source of the Blue Nile. In 1790, after returning to Britain, Bruce published his diary entitled Travels to Discover the Source of the Nile, *from which this portrait and the map of the itinerary of his journey are taken.*

A wealthy Scottish gentleman born at Kinnaird in 1730, James Bruce began his travels and voyages of exploration following the death of his beloved wife just a few months after their marriage, whom he had married at the age of twenty-four. In 1762 he was appointed British Consul in Algiers. This was a particularly difficult post because of the despotic character of the Bey (the title given by the Turks to the governor of a province of the Ottoman Empire), who appeared utterly to disregard diplomatic immunity and the normal rules applying to relations between civilized nations. None the less, Bruce managed to conclude his three-year term of office successfully, during which he also took an interest in the antiquities of the country. After leaving Algiers, Bruce travelled along the coast of North Africa to Tripoli and then visited Syria, Crete and Cyprus before arriving in Egypt in 1768.

In December of the same year, Bruce, together with his faithful secretary, Luigi Balugani, and his butler, a Greek called

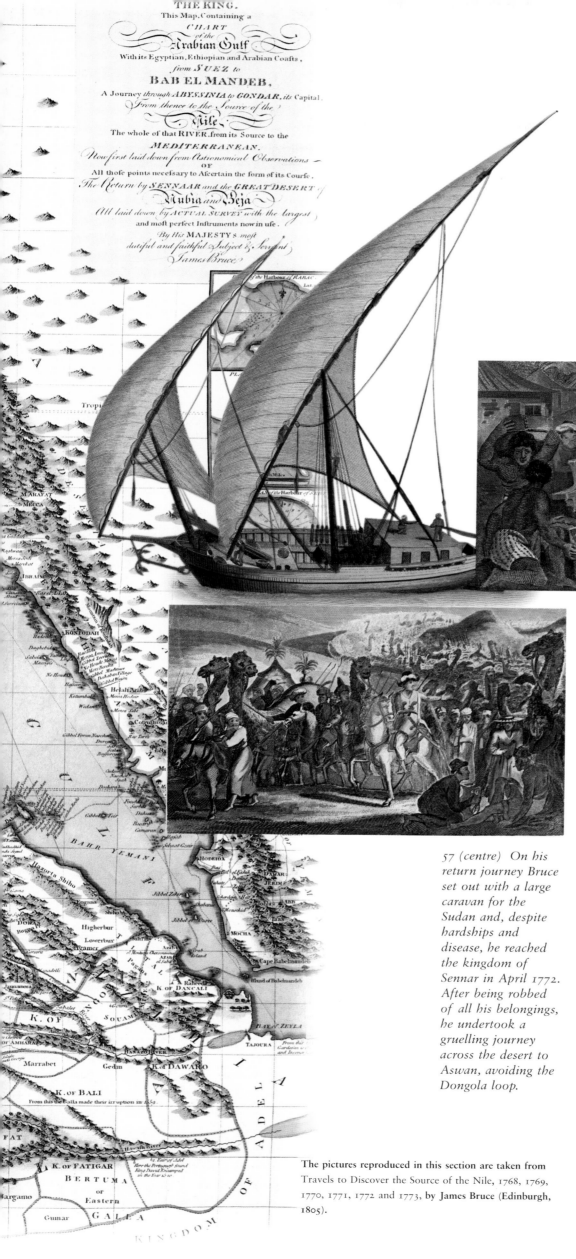

THE KING.
This Map, Containing a
CHART
of the
Arabian Gulf
With its Egyptian, Ethiopian and Arabian Coasts,
from SUEZ to
BAB EL MANDEB,
A Journey through ABYSSINIA to GONDAR, its Capital.
From thence to the Source of the
Nile,
The whole of that RIVER, from its Source to the
MEDITERRANEAN.
Now first laid down from Astronomical Observations —
or
All those points necessary to Ascertain the form of its Course.
The Return by SENNAAR and the GREAT DESERT of
Nubia and Beja
All laid down by ACTUAL SURVEY with the largest
and most perfect Instruments now in use.
By His MAJESTY's most
dutiful and faithful Subject & Servant
James Bruce

57 (above left) For his journey up the Nile, Bruce hired a type of local boat called a kanja, *with a capacious hull, rounded lines and a cabin towards the stern. These boats were rigged with two sails – a large spanker and a jib – which meant they could reach a reasonable speed.*

57 (below) Bruce sailed down the Red Sea from Quseir to Massawa, where he was received by the grandson of the governor of the city (seen here), who obliged him stay in an attempt to extort money from him. The explorer then continued to Gondar, capital of Abyssinia, where he stayed at the court of the king, Tecla Haimanout.

57 (centre) On his return journey Bruce set out with a large caravan for the Sudan and, despite hardships and disease, he reached the kingdom of Sennar in April 1772. After being robbed of all his belongings, he undertook a gruelling journey across the desert to Aswan, avoiding the Dongola loop.

The pictures reproduced in this section are taken from Travels to Discover the Source of the Nile, 1768, 1769, 1770, 1771, 1772 and 1773, by **James Bruce** (Edinburgh, 1805).

Strates, set off from Cairo on an expedition that would take him to the source of the Blue Nile. Bruce sailed up-river as far as Thebes, where he visited the temples of Luxor and Karnak, and the cemeteries on the west bank of the Nile. Overcoming the suspicion of the local guides, he managed to persuade them to take him to Biban el-Muluk, the Valley of the Kings. Here he entered a large tomb, where he was particularly fascinated by a large relief depicting two blind harpists. Thus he opened his notebook and made a drawing, albeit somewhat romantic, of the two figures. The tomb he had explored belonged to Ramesses III and its plan had been drawn just a few years previously by Pococke; but such was the sensation caused by Bruce's drawing, published some years later in his travel diary, that the tomb became universally known as the 'Harpers' Tomb' or simply 'Bruce's Tomb'.

Bruce then continued to Aswan, but, due to local disturbances, he had to retrace his steps and cross the Arabian Desert to the port of Quseir on the Red Sea. Here he hired a boat and, following the coast of Arabia, reached Massawa, from where, after innumerable difficulties and dangers, he set out for Aduwa, Aksum and Gondar, the capital of Abyssinia. Thanks to his knowledge of medicine and languages (before leaving Europe, Bruce had learnt Arabic and Ethiopian and the rudiments of medicine) he was received at the court of King Tecla Haimanout, where he managed to treat several members of the royal family for smallpox. Having thus found favour with the king, who even made him the governor of a province, Bruce obtained permission in 1780 to continue to Lake Tana, but his journey was interrupted by a revolt that obliged him to return to Gondar. From here he departed once more a few months later, still accompanied by his butler, Strates, managing this time to get beyond Lake Tana and finally reach the source of the Blue Nile. In fact, this had already been discovered and described more than a century earlier by Pedro Páez – whose account of the journey had been published in Latin by Athanasius Kircher – and Jeronimo Lobos. Bruce had studied the works of these two Portuguese Jesuits before he set out, but the fact that others had been there before him was evidently of little importance to the stubborn Scots explorer, who instead disparaged his predecessors, believing their exploits to have been fabricated.

After returning to Gondar, Bruce was forced to remain there for nearly a year until a bloody civil war had ended before he could begin the return to Cairo. He had to undertake this without his secretary, Balugani, who died, probably of malaria, in Gondar. On the way back, Bruce decided to descend the Nile through the Sudan, but while he was passing through the region of Sennar he was robbed of almost all his belongings. After passing Ed Damer, just before the confluence of the Nile with the Atbara, he left the river to

save time, avoiding the great curve it takes through Dongola. It took around twenty days to cross the Nubian Desert, and Bruce arrived directly at Aswan, from where he descended the Nile, reaching Cairo exhausted, in poor health and penniless.

Bruce had to stay in the Egyptian capital for four months before his strength returned sufficiently for him to set out on the return journey to Britain, where he arrived in 1773 after spending some time in Italy and France. Not only was his account of his remarkable journey and amazing adventures ridiculed, but it also aroused

58 (opposite right) and 59 (left) Bruce was taken to the Biban el-Muluk (the Arabic name for the Valley of the Kings), where he entered the tomb of Ramesses III. Here he was fascinated by reliefs depicting two blind harpists, which he reproduced, though somewhat romantically, in his notebook. It caused such a sensation when it was published some years later in his travel diary that the tomb became known as the 'Harpers' tomb' or 'Bruce's Tomb'.

59 (below) During his journey to Abyssinia, Bruce sailed down the Arabian coast of the Red Sea, staying at el-Laheia in Yemen, where he portrayed a woman wearing local costume.

controversy – and few believed the truth of his assertions, which were thought to be greatly exaggerated.

Having remarried, Bruce retired to his estate in Scotland, where he lived peacefully for a number of years. After the untimely death of his second wife in 1778, Bruce devoted himself to writing a detailed account of his travels. Published in 1790 in five volumes and entitled *Travels to Discover the Source of the Nile in the Years 1768, 1769, 1770, 1771, 1772 & 1773*, it was translated into French and German. Bruce died shortly afterwards, in 1794.

58 (opposite below) When he reached the kingdom of Sennar, Bruce paid homage to Ismail, the king of the region, and his favourite wife.

Louis François Cassas

60 and 61 (opposite left) While he was in Egypt, Louis François Cassas drew the antiquities of Alexandria, the pyramids of Giza and the mosques of Cairo. In Alexandria, Cassas, like all artists visiting Egypt, drew Cleopatra's Needle and Pompey's Pillar. Though unlike his predecessors, Cassas' drawing of Pompey's Pillar was not only artistic but it was also architecturally very precise.

61 (opposite right) Another important Alexandrian monument drawn by Cassas was the imposing fort of Qayt Bey. This was begun by the Mameluke sultan in 1480, at the entrance to the harbour. In ancient times the Pharos was situated here – a lofty tower on which a fire burned at night as a signal to warn approaching ships.

60

When Constantin-François Chasseboeuf set out for Egypt and Syria, with a haversack on his back and six thousand gold dinars in his money-belt, he was just twenty-five years old. He later became famous under the pseudonym of Volney – obtained by merging the name of Voltaire with that of Ferney, the village where the great writer eventually settled.

Volney landed in Alexandria in January 1783, remaining there for several weeks to visit the ancient monuments of the city and the Delta region. He then went up the Nile to Cairo, where he stayed until September, before returning to the Mediterranean and continuing his journey to Jaffa, Acre and Tyre. His next stop was Syria, where he visited numerous cities and archaeological sites, including Aleppo, Damascus, Latakia and the vast ruins of Palmyra.

In March 1785 Volney sailed, probably from Acre, first to Alexandria, and from there to France. In the final part of the voyage Volney met the painter Louis François Cassas, and he used a number of the artist's drawings to illustrate his travel diary, which was published in 1787 with the straightforward title *Voyage en Égypte et en Syrie*. The book was an immediate success, and was acclaimed for certain unusual features that distinguished it from all the other works written hitherto on the East. In fact it was regarded as 'one of the finest works of the eighteenth century and a masterpiece of its kind'. Despite the relative brevity of his journey – for which he had

61 (left) When Cassas arrived in Egypt, the country was dominated by the Mamelukes, emancipated slaves of Asiatic and Balkan origin, who, thanks to their military prowess, had seized power.

The pictures reproduced in this section are taken **from** Voyage Pittoresque de la Syrie, de la Phoenicie, de la Palestine et de la Basse Égypte, **by Louis François Cassas** (Paris, 1795).

meticulously prepared for a year, both by reading the most important books on the countries he was to visit and by training himself to bear the discomforts and fatigue that awaited him – Volney was able to make the most of the time he had available. He wrote a treatise on political geography, which included rigorous scientific observations of the socio-economic and political situations of the countries he travelled through. Surprisingly, perhaps, the detachment and precision with which Volney observed the countries he visited did not prevent his descriptions from being extremely poetic.

In fact, Volney's work provided cultural justification for Napoleon's expedition to Egypt, and his *Voyage* became the reference book for the commander of the French army and his generals. In some sense, perhaps, Volney foresaw, or even hoped for, the conquest – albeit peaceful and cultural – of Egypt by France, when he wrote:

If Egypt were possessed by a nation that loves the fine arts, we would have here an opportunity for discovering antiquities…

It was the curious fate of Louis François Cassas (1756–1827), the artist whom Volney met during his journey, to be almost

62–63 *The mosques of Cairo were one of the favourite subjects of Cassas, who drew them with remarkable accuracy, reproducing all the architectural details.*

On the left is the lofty portal of the mosque of Sultan Hassan, while on the right the artist has depicted a procession in front of the Al-Azhar mosque.

completely forgotten, despite his rare talents and great ability. Born at Azay-le-Ferron, Cassas studied art in Tours and Paris before travelling to Rome, where he was greatly impressed not only by the city's art but also by the obelisks erected by Pope Sixtus V. Cassas stayed in the city for three years, before, in 1784, he was invited to Constantinople by the French ambassador, Marie-Gabriel Florent Choiseul-Gouffier, a diplomat who was fond of the art of the past and a keen collector of antiquities.

Cassas then left the capital of the Ottoman Empire on a lengthy journey that took him to Syria, Palestine and Egypt. A skilled painter and draughtsman, he made numerous drawings – the best-known of which are of the ruins of Palmyra in Syria and of Baalbek in Lebanon – which were used to illustrate Volney's book. He remained in Egypt for only three months, from October to December 1785, but in this short space of time he produced a large number of magnificent drawings of the pyramids of Giza, the mosques of Cairo and the antiquities of Alexandria, before returning to Constantinople in 1786 and then, in 1787, to Italy, where he stayed another four years.

In 1791 Cassas went back to France where he mounted an exhibition of seventy-four models, made of terracotta or cork, representing many of the ancient Egyptian antiquities. Cassas later organized a public subscription – a common practice at the time – for the publication of his drawings, which were published in 1795 in Paris with the title *Voyage Pittoresque de la Syrie, de la Phoenicie, de la Palestine et de la Basse Égypte* (*A Picturesque Journey in Syria, Phoenicia, Palestine and Lower Egypt*). Comprising three folio volumes printed by the Imprimerie de la République, this contained only 175 plates, although as many as 330 had originally been planned.

Cassas, who was subsequently awarded the highest French distinction, the Légion d'honneur, died in Versailles in 1827.

63

64 (opposite) The Heliopolis obelisk was erected by Senwosret I before a temple dedicated to the sun god Re. At the time of Cassas' visit it was known as 'Matariyyah's Needle'. It is now in the centre of a densely populated district of Cairo.

65 Cassas' drawing of the pyramid of Khafre at Giza is fairly accurate. He shows the upper part still covered with limestone casing blocks, which had been removed lower down. His depiction of the mortuary temple, from which mysterious smoke is rising, is, on the other hand, a figment of the artist's imagination; in fact, he often combined real elements with imaginary ones.

66–67 A long procession winds past the so-called tombs of the Mamelukes in Cairo; at its head are dignitaries wearing turbans.

65

68 At the time of
Cassas' journey to
Egypt some of the
Old Kingdom tombs
at Giza and Saqqara
were used as houses
by local people.

69 (opposite)
Mysterious
ceremonies take
place in an
imaginary temple
in this drawing by
Cassas. A number
of the decorative
elements, such as the
winged solar disc on
the architrave above
the massive columns,
are fairly close to
reality, and the
architectural forms
recall, albeit with
a fair degree of
fantasy, those of
the Ptolemaic period.
The costumes worn
by the participants
are clearly inspired
by the Graeco-
Roman world.

70–71 Cassas not
only mixed reality
with fantasy, but he
also combined
architectural
elements from
different periods in
order to achieve the
desired effect: an
extravagant and
esoteric image of
Egypt, with
Renaissance
overtones. In this
illustration the large
pyramid of the
Fourth Dynasty –
inspired by either
Khufu's or Khafre's –
is fronted by a
temple built in
Ptolemaic style and
flanked by two
obelisks. In front is
an avenue of
sphinxes vaguely
recalling those of the
New Kingdom, while
the numerous figures
taking part in a
solemn procession
are wearing
classicizing tunics.

Richard Dalton

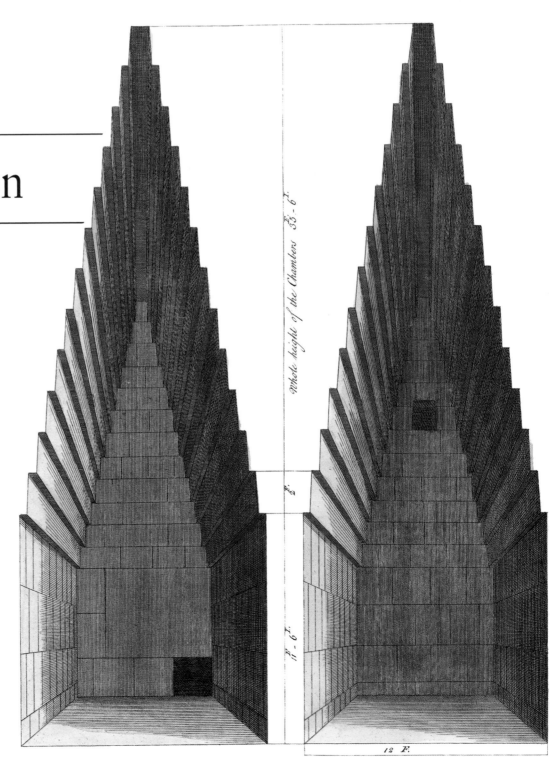

72 (above) Richard
Dalton (1715–91),
a remarkable artist,
man of letters and
traveller, arrived in
Egypt in 1749, twelve
years after Pococke
and Norden.
Although he did not
venture far beyond
Cairo and its
environs, he made
numerous useful
drawings during his
stay, which he
published in 1791.
Dalton's work is still
surprisingly little
known today, despite
its great scholarly
and artistic interest.
In this view of the
pyramids of Giza,
the artist, like
Pococke, depicts the
Sphinx with its nose
still intact.

72 (right) and 73
Dalton made a very
accurate drawing of
the second chamber
of the north pyramid
of Sneferu at
Dahshur, known as
the Red Pyramid,
(left) with its lofty
corbelled vault, and
also of the original
entrance to the
pyramid of Khufu
(right), which looks
much the same
today. Above the
opening leading to
the Descending
Corridor there is an
enormous monolithic
lintel surmounted by
a double pointed
vault, built to reduce
the weight pressing
down on the lintel
and so prevent it
from cracking.

The pictures reproduced in this section are taken from
Antiquities and Views in Greece and Egypt with the
Manners and Customs of the Inhabitants, by Richard
Dalton (London, 1791).

A few years after the journeys of Norden
and Pococke – followed also by that of
Charles Perry, an English doctor, who
reached Thebes in 1740 – in 1749 another
Englishman landed in Alexandria with the
aim of visiting Egypt. This was Richard
Dalton (1715–91), a librarian and
draughtsman born in Whitehaven in
northern England. After studying art and
literature in Rome, Dalton visited various
Mediterranean countries, including Greece
and Egypt.

Dalton's account of his travels, which
was only published in 1791, the year of his
death, entitled Antiquities and Views in
Greece and Egypt with the Manners and
Customs of the Inhabitants, was illustrated
with seventy-nine engravings based on the
drawings he had made on the spot.

Dalton's objectives were, however,
completely different from those of his
predecessors: he was not particularly
interested in the antiquities of ancient
Egypt, nor did he set out to provide a
complete account of the country, as he
explained in the introduction to the
marvellous plates illustrating his work:

*The Publisher of these Prints never had
the least intention of giving any description
of the country, either geographical or
historical; to perform which, a long
residence and proper assistants well versed
in various branches of knowledge, would
be required, to collect the material
necessary for such a purpose....*

An excellent draughtsman and an
observant traveller, Dalton's attention was,
in fact, mainly focused on the inhabitants

of the country, their dress, customs and
habits. Thus he did not attempt the long
and difficult journey that his predecessors
had undertaken to Upper Egypt, and his
drawings reveal an ethnographic rather
than an archaeological interest. Moreover,
his work – which is surprisingly still little
known today – does not overlap with those
of Norden, Pococke and Perry, but rather
complements them by describing aspects of
the population and their lifestyles that had
hitherto been relatively undocumented.

Dalton was one of the first visitors to
Egypt to describe and depict dress as a
reflection of the social position of the
wearer. He also made pictorial records of
the uniforms of the soldiers, horsemen and
officers, and the country's traditions and
religious ceremonies. Christians were

73

normally barred from these ceremonies, which included the 'procession of the sacred camel', when a camel crossed Cairo with a small tent on its back. Richly decorated with fabrics embroidered in gold with passages from the Koran, the tent contained precious cloths destined to adorn the sanctuaries of Mecca and Medina, the holy cities of Islam.

Dalton's detailed drawings also portrayed the pilgrims journeying to Mecca, including their costumes and the unusual way in which the elderly and the infirm were carried on special chairs slung from the side of a camel; the crowds of participants in the holy places; the composition and structure of the caravans; and the uniforms and arms of the different corps of horsemen who accompanied them.

Dalton also depicted the special costumes of the highest Mameluke dignitaries in Cairo – such as the Pasha, the Emir and the Bey – which they wore during their public appearances on horseback in the city and its environs, preceded or flanked by groups of servants who had to run to keep pace with their masters. Horses – especially their harnesses and decorations, and the techniques used for mounting them – were of great interest to Dalton, who represented them very faithfully with great plastic strength, stressing their movements and musculature.

In addition, Dalton also closely observed the merchants, dervishes, young female dancers and the poorest sector of the population who lived on the banks of the Nile, wearing rags or simply woven palm leaves. As he noted: 'the fatigue and poverty of these people is very great; who sometimes, when they are not strictly watchful, are devoured by the crocodiles. Those who survive, when they arrive at Bulack, sell their stores, which is divided amongst them, and work their passage back in boats, hired for Upper Egypt.'

Cairo's slave market was also described by Dalton. He noted that the Abyssinians arriving from Upper Egypt received 'far better treatment than most of those from other parts of Africa, with which the West India islands and part of the continent of America are stocked.'

74 (opposite left) Dalton's cross-section of the pyramid of Khufu was inspired by those by John Greaves and Benoît de Maillet, but appears to be more accurate – especially in the depiction of the ratio between the base and height of the superstructure and the details of the internal chambers. The Descending Corridor is shown terminating at the junction of the Ascending Corridor and the Grand Gallery.

74 (opposite right) In the so-called King's Chamber, seen here from the south side, is a large empty sarcophagus that must once have held the king's body.

75 (left) One of Dalton's most extraordinary drawings is that of the Grand Gallery in the pyramid of Khufu, which seems to have inspired subsequent drawings – for instance, a very similar one appears in the Description de l'Égypte, *published half a century later.*

75 (right) Dalton also made this drawing of the so-called Queen's Chamber, correctly depicting its pointed vault. The niche visible at the end of the chamber was probably intended to contain a statue of the royal ka.

Despite these distinctly ethnographic interests, Dalton also visited the ancient monuments situated in the environs of Cairo and Alexandria, following the same route taken by medieval travellers. His itinerary included Saqqara, the pyramids of Dahshur, described as the 'pyramids of Saqqara', and the 'Catacombs in which the Mummies are, which fall very short of those expectations we have been taught to form, from the false drawings of travellers'. He also made a number of accurate drawings of the pyramids of Giza, 'a number whereof being ruined, are become heaps of sand and pulverized stones...', paying particular attention to the pyramid of Khufu. In fact, his drawings of the Grand Gallery and the burial chamber were copied by many artists and draughtsmen in the nineteenth century.

76 and 77 With
almost ethnographic
precision, Dalton
drew the costumes
worn by the most
important Mameluke
dignitaries in their
public appearances
in Cairo, as well as
those of the city's
inhabitants. He also
depicted the different
turbans used by the
emir, *the* kyia-bey *(a
sort of secretary-
general), an ordinary*
man *(left) and the
imposing one of the
kadilisker (right), an
official sent from
Constantinople as an
inspector, who
remained in office
for a year.*

TRAVELS
IN
UPPER AND LOWER EGYPT:
UNDERTAKEN BY ORDER OF
THE OLD GOVERNMENT OF FRANCE;
BY
C. S. SONNINI,
THE FRENCH NAVY, AND MEMBER OF SEVERAL
NTIFIC AND LITERARY SOCIETIES.

Charles Nicolas Sonnini

78

Charles Nicolas Sigisbert Sonnini de Manoncour (1715–1812) was a contemporary of the philosopher and statesman Volney (Constantin François de Chasseboeuf). He spent three years exploring Egypt, between 1777 and 1780, ascending the Nile as far as Thebes, although in his written account he claimed to have reached Aswan. Born in 1751 in Lorraine – like Benoît de Maillet – Sonnini had a legal training; he quickly discovered, however, that his true vocation was not the law but rather travelling and observing the natural world. After becoming a naval officer, Sonnini first travelled to South America and Africa, and then prepared to set out for Egypt.

With his rigorously scientific mentality and profoundly anticlerical attitude, Sonnini was attracted by the philosophy of the Enlightenment, the natural sciences and medicine. A close friend of his was the celebrated naturalist comte de Buffon (Georges-Louis Leclerc), with whom he began to collaborate. On his return from Egypt in 1780, rather than immediately publishing an account of his journey – which was practically a requirement for every true traveller of the day – he devoted himself to writing entries on ornithology for the *Histoire naturelle*, the great work of his friend Buffon. He also edited a new edition of this work, in 128 volumes.

A series of financial difficulties due to family quarrels and the lack of government support for his exploration – for which he failed to obtain any financial assistance – delayed the publication of his book entitled *Voyage dans la Basse et la Haute Égypte*. However, in 1799, in the wake of the renewed interest in Egypt due to the Napoleonic expedition, it was brought out complete with an atlas containing forty plates. Unfortunately, the publication just three years later of Vivant Denon's book with the same title, meant that Sonnini's work was rapidly forgotten, despite its indisputable value. The French naturalist, in fact, managed to give a full and realistic

78 (above) *The traveller and naturalist Charles Nicolas Sigisbert Sonnini de Manoncour arrived in Egypt in June 1777. Having travelled up the Nile as far as Thebes he left to return to France. Sonnini's account, entitled* Voyage dans la Basse et Haute Égypte, *illustrated with forty plates, was published in 1799 and was translated into English immediately.*

78 (below) *Sonnini saw this statue, which came from the Theban area, in the house of an Italian cleric in Cairo. He believed it represented a priestess bearing the statues of Osiris and Isis; the hieroglyphic text is reproduced with a large degree of fantasy.*

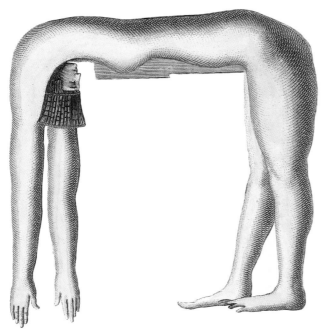

79 (left) This relief depicting the goddess Nut is from the ceiling of the atrium of the temple of Hathor at Dendera. Sonnini made a number of drawings of this temple.

79 (centre) Sonnini set out for Upper Egypt on 21 March 1778, with a letter of introduction from Murad Bey, a very important Mameluke leader. Egypt's splendid landscapes, rich in natural features, passed before him as he sailed up the Nile, and certainly interested him more than the ancient monuments.

79 (below) The monuments at Thebes did arouse Sonnini's enthusiasm, though the temple of Luxor was the only one that he drew. One reason for this was the conflict between the Mamelukes and factions hostile to them, which prevented him from prolonging his stay and obliged him to return to Cairo.

picture of the country, although his observations on the antiquities are neither of great interest nor particularly original.

Unlike other travellers, Sonnini was first and foremost a naturalist and for him the flora and fauna were certainly more captivating than archaeological remains and the lifestyles of the Arab world – but this is what makes his *Voyage* so fascinating.

The pictures reproduced in this section are taken from Travels in Upper and Lower Egypt, by Charles Nicolas Sonnini (London, 1799).

NAPOLEON AND THE EGYPTIAN EXPEDITION

80 (above) The Battle of the Pyramids took place on 21 July 1798 and was the first great victory achieved by Napoleon's army in Egypt. Dominique Vivant Denon, the most famous of the artists who accompanied the French expeditionary force, depicted the crucial phase of the battle, when the Mameluke cavalry launched an attack on the French divisions led by the generals Desaix, Dugua and Renier, who gave orders to use grapeshot. In the background is the city of Cairo.

On 19 May 1798 the French expeditionary force, commanded by Napoleon Bonaparte, left Toulon for Egypt, a country which still retained an air of mystery, despite the number of travellers who had visited it. Napoleon's force was enormous, comprising thirteen warships, six frigates, one corvette, thirty-five smaller ships and three hundred troop-ships carrying 10,000 sailors and 35,000 soldiers. Malta – vital for the control of the eastern Mediterranean – was conquered in just eight days. Eluding the British naval squadron commanded by Rear Admiral Horatio Nelson, whose military prowess was already legendary, the French fleet then set sail for Alexandria, where the soldiers disembarked on 2 July. Military intervention in Egypt had already been proposed during Louis XIV's reign, and was now supported by both the foreign minister of the Directory, Charles Maurice de Talleyrand, and by Napoleon – but each for personal reasons of their own, in which both foreign and internal policy played important roles.

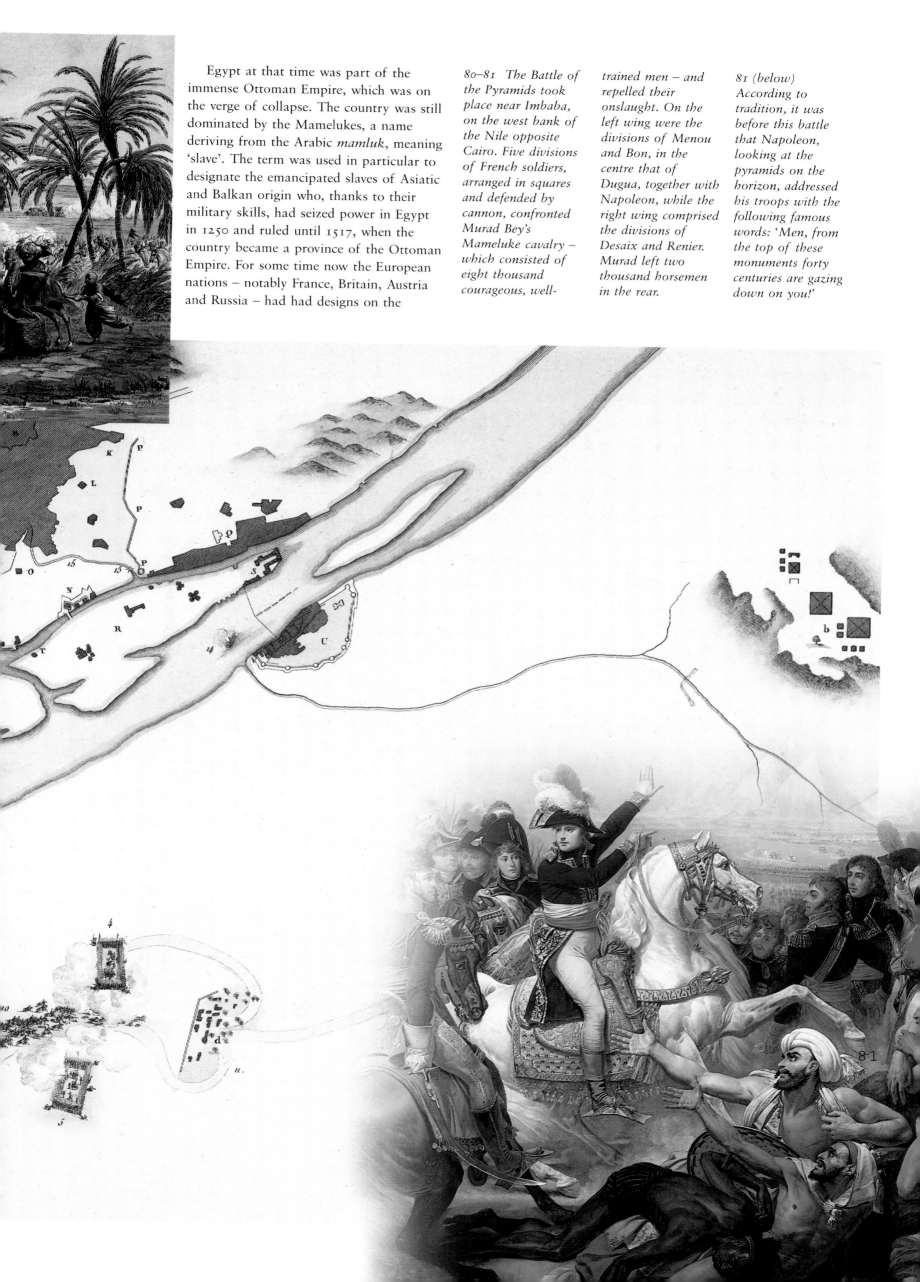

Egypt at that time was part of the immense Ottoman Empire, which was on the verge of collapse. The country was still dominated by the Mamelukes, a name deriving from the Arabic *mamluk*, meaning 'slave'. The term was used in particular to designate the emancipated slaves of Asiatic and Balkan origin who, thanks to their military skills, had seized power in Egypt in 1250 and ruled until 1517, when the country became a province of the Ottoman Empire. For some time now the European nations – notably France, Britain, Austria and Russia – had had designs on the

80–81 The Battle of the Pyramids took place near Imbaba, on the west bank of the Nile opposite Cairo. Five divisions of French soldiers, arranged in squares and defended by cannon, confronted Murad Bey's Mameluke cavalry – which consisted of eight thousand courageous, well-

trained men – and repelled their onslaught. On the left wing were the divisions of Menou and Bon, in the centre that of Dugua, together with Napoleon, while the right wing comprised the divisions of Desaix and Renier. Murad left two thousand horsemen in the rear.

81 (below) According to tradition, it was before this battle that Napoleon, looking at the pyramids on the horizon, addressed his troops with the following famous words: 'Men, from the top of these monuments forty centuries are gazing down on you!'

Balkans and the Ottoman territories in the eastern Mediterranean, especially Egypt, which occupied a strategic position on the Red Sea controlling the lucrative trade routes with the Indian Ocean. From the point of view of international politics, the time was ripe for the invasion of Egypt. After his epic campaign in Italy and the resulting Treaty of Campo Formio, signed in October 1797, Napoleon was the hero of the day in the eyes of the public, and French military power was at its height. Russia, Prussia and Austria had already carved up Poland, while Austria had been weakened by the wars with Turkey and France between 1787 and 1797.

Although these external considerations of a political character had led Talleyrand to support the invasion, there were others of an internal nature that encouraged Napoleon's interventionist stance. The Directory was favourable to taking direct military action against Britain; they were also aware that, if this were unsuccessful, it would help to cut the young general – now considered to be a potential danger to the Directory itself – down to size. Napoleon, however, believed a direct attack against France's traditional enemy would be too hazardous. At the same time, he had no wish to demobilize his troops and lose control of the Army of Italy, a powerful

82 (left) Murad Bey, one of the great Mameluke leaders, was the main adversary of the French army. Following his devastating defeat in the Battle of the Pyramids he fled to Upper Egypt with the remnants of his cavalry to organize resistance. The scar from a sabre wound received in the battle can be seen on his right cheek.

82 (opposite centre)
General Louis Charles
Antoine des Aix de
Veygoux, usually
called 'Desaix', was
just thirty years old
when he commanded
the vanguard of the
French army. His
orders were to pursue
and defeat Murad Bey
in Upper Egypt.

82 (opposite below)
Major-General Jean
Baptiste Kléber
became commander-
in-chief of the
expeditionary force
after Napoleon had
returned to France.
A man of culture
and a courageous
soldier, he was the
victor at the Battle
of Heliopolis on 20
March 1800 and
crushed the second
uprising in Cairo on
the following day; he
was assassinated by
a Syrian fanatic in
the same year.

82–83 Napoleon
offers a sword to the
military commander
of the city of
Alexandria.

83 (below)
Napoleon enters the
Great Mosque of
Cairo on horseback.
The mosque was
badly damaged
by French artillery
in the first Cairo
uprising of October
1798. Three hundred
French soldiers and
over three thousand
Egyptians were killed
in the revolt.

military force, which, although it was
trustworthy and had excellent morale,
needed to be employed in another military
campaign. Asserting that 'the road to
London passes through Egypt', Napoleon,
with the help of Talleyrand, managed to
persuade the Directory to organize the
expeditionary force and authorize the
Egyptian campaign. Egypt and the East,
moreover, exercised a particular fascination
over Napoleon, who wanted to follow –
metaphorically at least – in the footsteps
of Alexander the Great.

After the easy conquest of Alexandria,
Napoleon headed for Cairo to confront the
Mameluke troops commanded by Murad
Bey. On 21 July the French were victorious
at the Battle of the Pyramids, which took
place at Imbaba. Now a densely populated
district of Cairo, Imbaba is about ten
kilometres from the pyramids of Giza,
but their presence on the horizon had a
profoundly symbolic significance for the

general, as shown by his words when
addressing his troops before the battle:
'Men, from the top of these monuments
forty centuries are gazing down on you!'

While Murad Bey took refuge in Upper
Egypt and the other great Mameluke
leader, Ibrahim Bey, hastily left Cairo for
the Delta region, the French, after
overcoming the resistance of the Bedouins,
gained control of almost the entire
territory of Egypt. But this initial success
was shortlived: on 1 August 1798 the
English fleet under Nelson, which had
arrived off the Egyptian coast, managed to
destroy the French fleet, at anchor in
Aboukir Bay under the command of Vice
Admiral Brueys d'Aigailliers. Brueys was
killed in the battle, together with 1,500
sailors; his flagship, *L'Orient*, was sunk and
only four French ships managed to escape.
Napoleon's army was isolated, thus
becoming a prisoner in the country it had
just conquered.

Despite this serious defeat – which was later to be a decisive factor in the military failure of the entire campaign – Napoleon enthusiastically set about colonizing and modernizing Egypt, and also promoting the systematic study of the many fascinating aspects of the country. It was for this purpose that he had embarked, along with the military force, a group of 167 experts who formed part of the specially created Commission des Arts et des Sciences, continuing the tradition of the scholarly journeys of the eighteenth century.

Napoleon's commission was comprised of eminent specialists, forming a diverse group with different, but complementary, skills: thus there were geographers, architects, engineers, astronomers,

The officers and soldiers of the French army were somewhat bemused by these elegantly dressed, learned gentlemen who, during the fighting, heedless of the danger wandered around the monuments with pencil, paper and measuring instruments. In one memorable episode during a surprise attack by the Mamelukes, a French officer ordered his soldiers to form a square, adding: 'Donkeys and scholars in the middle'. In reality, the members of the Commission, who had to work in difficult and often perilous conditions, showed a combination of technical skill and notable courage: no fewer than thirty-two of them lost their lives, in combat or due to disease.

On 22 August 1798 Napoleon founded the Institut d'Égypte, an academy modelled

84 At ten o'clock in the evening of 1 August 1798, a decisive moment occurred in the Battle of Aboukir – also called the Battle of the Nile. The French flagship, L'Orient, which was on fire, exploded with a report so loud that it was said to have been heard as far away as Cairo. During the battle, the commander-in-chief of the French naval squadron, François Brueys

d'Aigailliers, was killed, while Horatio Nelson, who was on board the Vanguard, the flagship of the British fleet, was wounded on the temple by a piece of shrapnel.

physicians, economists, archaeologists, orientalists, mineralogists, chemists, naturalists, mathematicians, draughtsmen, artists and printers. They were mainly selected from the members of the Institut de France – for instance, the chemist Claude Louis Berthollet and the mathematician Gaspard Monge, who had accompanied Napoleon in his Italian campaign – although there were also academics from other great scientific institutions, such as the Jardin des Plantes and the Musée d'Histoire Naturelle, and the leading French schools such as the École Politéchnique and École des Arts et Métiers. Their average age was fairly young: the senior member, Jean Michel Venture de Paradis, was fifty-nine years old, while many prominent members, such as Prosper Jollois, Edmé François Jomard, René Edouard Villiers du Terrage and Michel-Ange Lancret, were aged between eighteen and twenty-five.

on the Institut de France. Divided into four sections (mathematics, physics, political economy, and literature and arts), it had thirty-six members, the élite of the Commission des Arts et des Sciences. The aims of the new institution, under its president Gaspard Monge, were, as article two of its charter stated, 'research, study and the publication of the natural, industrial and historical aspects of Egypt'.

Three days later, on 25 August 1798, General Louis Charles Antoine des Aix de Veygoux, known as Desaix, left Cairo for Upper Egypt with three thousand soldiers. His orders were to pursue Murad Bey and defeat him definitively. After he had sailed up the Nile as far as Sediman, on 7 October he confronted Murad Bey, who had around twelve thousand men, forcing him to retreat further south. On 22 January 1799 Desaix inflicted a second defeat on Murad Bey in the Battle of Samanud, a village to the south of Abydos,

which was followed by another Mameluke retreat.

While Desaix was pursuing Murad Bey and conquering Upper Egypt, Napoleon, dealt with Ibrahim Bey, the other great Mameluke leader, and began pacifying the country. In attempt to obtain the support of the local population he presented himself as the liberator of the nation from the Mamelukes and the champion of order, justice and human rights, with due respect for the Koran and Islam. However, the tensions caused by the clash of two cultures, two religions and two very different worlds, and the need to adopt a series of security measures that did not meet with the approval of the population, caused friction that, on 21 October 1798, culminated in the first Cairo uprising. Napoleon managed to crush this only by exhibiting the energy and determination that had played a fundamental role in his brilliant career.

84–85 *Late in the afternoon of 1 August 1798, the British fleet, with the flagship* Vanguard *in the centre, headed under full sail towards the French ships at anchor in a line across Aboukir Bay. The British divided into two wings to surround the French and opened fire from both sides. The manoeuvre was wholly successful: thirteen of sixteen French ships were destroyed, three thousand men died and the same number were taken prisoner.*

85 *Horatio Nelson, the hero of the first Battle of Aboukir: he utterly destroyed the French fleet under the command of Vice-Admiral Brueys, taking it by surprise in a bold manoeuvre that Brueys had thought impossible due to the shallow waters of the bay.*

Once he had obtained total victory, Napoleon was in a position to be able to show mercy towards those who chose to submit, while he ordered that those who refused to give in should be beheaded. Thus he earned the respect of the Egyptians, who, awestruck, dubbed him 'el-Sultan el-Khebir' (the great Sultan).

Meanwhile, the Ottoman Empire had formed an alliance with Britain and, after declaring war on France on 9 September 1798, the Sultan of Constantinople planned a military intervention to regain control of Egypt. Napoleon believed the best defence against this threat from the east was to occupy Palestine and Syria. On 10 February 1799, therefore, he left Cairo with twenty-five thousand men, taking the so-called Way of Horus, the ancient route used by the pharaohs during their campaigns in the Near East. The French army managed to conquer Gaza and Jaffa, but not the fortress of Acre, which withstood a siege for two months, during which an epidemic of plague broke out. When, on 14 June, Napoleon returned to Cairo, his army had been decimated; besides those who had fallen on the battlefield, many others had died from disease or the effects of the harsh climate. Thus his army had been reduced to only eighteen thousand men – about half the number who had landed in Alexandria less than a year earlier.

On 14 July an Anglo-Turkish fleet of 113 ships appeared off Aboukir, and eighteen thousand Turkish soldiers of Mustafa Pasha managed to land. Napoleon immediately arrived on the scene with eight thousand men, and without even waiting for the troops of General Kléber, second-in-command of the French army in Egypt, engaged the enemy in a bloody battle on 25 July 1799, known as the second Battle of Aboukir. Ten thousand men lost their lives but Napoleon won a famous victory.

Horatio Nelson

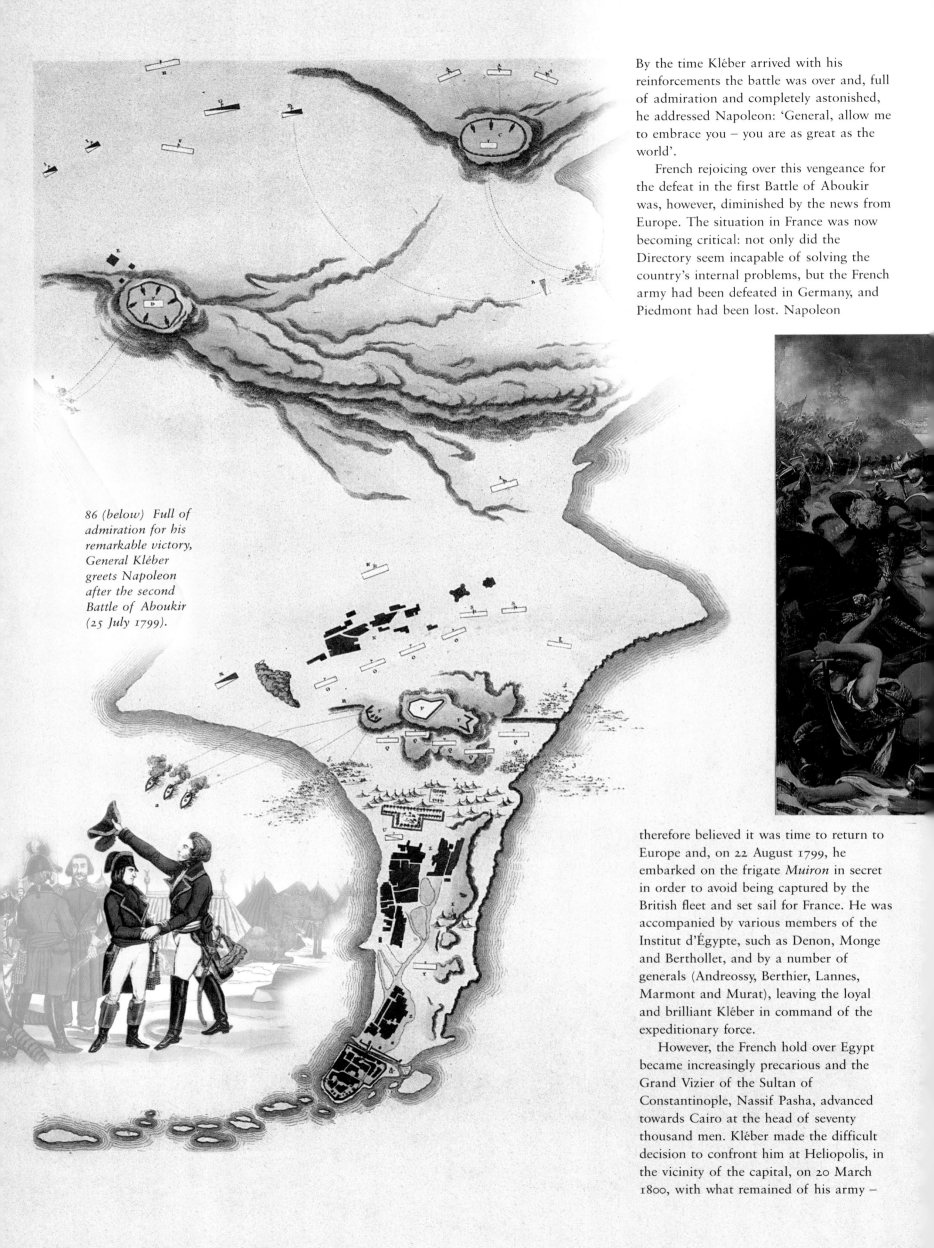

By the time Kléber arrived with his reinforcements the battle was over and, full of admiration and completely astonished, he addressed Napoleon: 'General, allow me to embrace you – you are as great as the world'.

French rejoicing over this vengeance for the defeat in the first Battle of Aboukir was, however, diminished by the news from Europe. The situation in France was now becoming critical: not only did the Directory seem incapable of solving the country's internal problems, but the French army had been defeated in Germany, and Piedmont had been lost. Napoleon

86 (below) Full of admiration for his remarkable victory, General Kléber greets Napoleon after the second Battle of Aboukir (25 July 1799).

therefore believed it was time to return to Europe and, on 22 August 1799, he embarked on the frigate *Muiron* in secret in order to avoid being captured by the British fleet and set sail for France. He was accompanied by various members of the Institut d'Égypte, such as Denon, Monge and Berthollet, and by a number of generals (Andreossy, Berthier, Lannes, Marmont and Murat), leaving the loyal and brilliant Kléber in command of the expeditionary force.

However, the French hold over Egypt became increasingly precarious and the Grand Vizier of the Sultan of Constantinople, Nassif Pasha, advanced towards Cairo at the head of seventy thousand men. Kléber made the difficult decision to confront him at Heliopolis, in the vicinity of the capital, on 20 March 1800, with what remained of his army –

a mere ten thousand men. After rousing his soldiers with a stirring speech, Kléber led the attack at the head of his troops, determined to risk everything and fight to the death. Against all expectations – and especially in view of the vastly superior numbers of the enemy – the valour of his men and his tactical skill won him an astonishing victory, enabling him to restore order. A new wave of discontent with the French, however, culminated in the second uprising in Cairo, on 21 March, the day after the Battle of Heliopolis, and Kléber only managed to crush it by bombarding and burning the quarter of Bulaq.

Perhaps the history of the Napoleonic expedition to Egypt would have been very different if, a few months later – on 14 June – Kléber had not been assassinated by a Syrian fanatic at the instigation of the emissaries of the Ottoman Empire and Britain. But with his death Napoleon's Egyptian adventure was drawing to a close. By a curious coincidence, on the very same day three thousand kilometres away in northern Italy, General Desaix – who had returned to France in May of that year – was killed in the Battle of Marengo.

Kléber's successor was Jacques-François de Bussay de Menou, an eccentric figure who had embraced the Muslim faith in order to marry an Egyptian woman, assuming the name of Menou Abdallah Pasha. He was not equal to the situation and matters rapidly reached crisis point. On 8 March 1801 the Anglo-Ottoman fleet,

commanded by Lord Keith, managed to land 17,500 men. There was now neither Napoleon nor Kléber to oppose them, and the few men under the command of General Friant, who had come from the nearby city of Alexandria, were powerless before such a huge and well-trained army.

On 21 March, Menou's army, comprising ten thousand soldiers and fifteen hundred cavalrymen, attempted to oppose the British troops under the command of Sir Ralph Abercromby between Aboukir and Alexandria in what is known as the Battle of Canopus. They suffered a catastrophic defeat, despite the support of the cavalry and the death of Abercromby. Menou's tactics were, in fact, disastrous, and four thousand French soldiers and no fewer than five generals lost their lives – including Major General Lanusse who, before dying, addressed the

following celebrated remark to Menou: 'A man like you should never have commanded the French army. You are not capable of running the kitchens of the Republic.'

A few months later, on 27 June 1801, General Belliard surrendered to Sir John Hutchinson, Abercromby's successor, obtaining permission for the repatriation of the French troops with their arms, animals and baggage. On 30 August, Menou, who was beleaguered in Alexandria, capitulated on the same honourable terms, but he was obliged to consign numerous archaeological finds to the British. Among the objects handed over was the Rosetta Stone, which had been discovered by the French near the town of that name and which later proved to be the key to deciphering hieroglyphs. Napoleon's campaign in Egypt was definitely over.

AN AVANT-GARDE ARTIST

Among the members of the Institut d'Égypte was a middle-aged gentleman: refined, handsome and of medium height, his name was Baron Dominique Vivant Denon. Born at Givry, a small village near Châlon-sur-Saône in 1747, Denon was a courtier during the reigns of Louis XV and Louis XVI, and a diplomat – he had held various posts in the French embassies in St Petersburg, then Stockholm and lastly in Naples, where he remained until 1785. He was also a man of letters, playwright, painter and draughtsman, and was perhaps the individual who made the greatest contribution to the academic success of the Egyptian campaign. A highly cultured man, endowed with considerable charm and an excellent conversationalist, he was at home in fashionable society and was at first considered too old to stand the fatigue and discomfort of the expedition. He was only able to depart for Egypt thanks to the insistence of his protectress, Joséphine de Beauharnais, Napoleon's future wife.

Despite his age, Denon proved to be indefatigable, as well as extremely courageous; he did not hesitate to set out with the vanguard of the French army commanded by General Desaix when the latter was ordered by Napoleon to pursue and defeat Murad Bey. Thus Denon was the first of the members of the Commission to visit the great monuments of Upper Egypt, of which he made countless drawings. The conditions in which the intrepid artist had to work, surrounded by the hostility of the local population and in the midst of armed clashes with the Mamelukes, were certainly not ideal for studying and drawing ancient monuments, but he nearly always managed to achieve his aims. As he wrote in his diary, replying to the questions of an imaginary interlocutor:

Here the pitiless reader, sitting quietly at his table with his map before him, will say to the poor, hungry, harassed traveller, exposed to all the trouble of war: 'I see no account of Aphroditopolis, Crocodilopolis, Ptolemais – what is become of all these towns? What had you to do there, if you could not give any account of them? Had you not a horse to carry you, an army to

88 (opposite left) Denon thought that Alexandria's most famous monument, called Cleopatra's Needle, together with the other obelisk lying on the ground nearby, 'might be conveyed to France without difficulty, and would there become a trophy of conquest'.

88–89 (centre) Perhaps one of the most beautiful and poetic of all Denon's drawings, this shows the artist at sunset as he prepares to draw the scant ruins of Hierakonpolis, south of Thebes between Esna and Edfu. In order to add interest to the scene Denon also included his servants, his horse and some camels.

89 (right) Pompey's Pillar was closely examined by Denon, who considered that its fame was not wholly justified and that it was, in fact, simply 'a beautiful column, but not a fine monument… a column is not a monument'.

88–89 (below) At Rosetta, Denon was fascinated by the rich mix of the population, which encompassed a wide variety of peoples and social classes, all recognizable by their dress: Coptic monks, officials, peasants, Jews and Greeks.

89 Denon – seen here as a young man – was the first of the members of the Commission des Arts et des Sciences to visit the monuments of Upper Egypt with General Desaix's army. His travel diary, Voyage dans la Basse et la Haute Égypte, published in 1802 and illustrated with numerous drawings, brought the great monuments of Egypt to the public's attention.

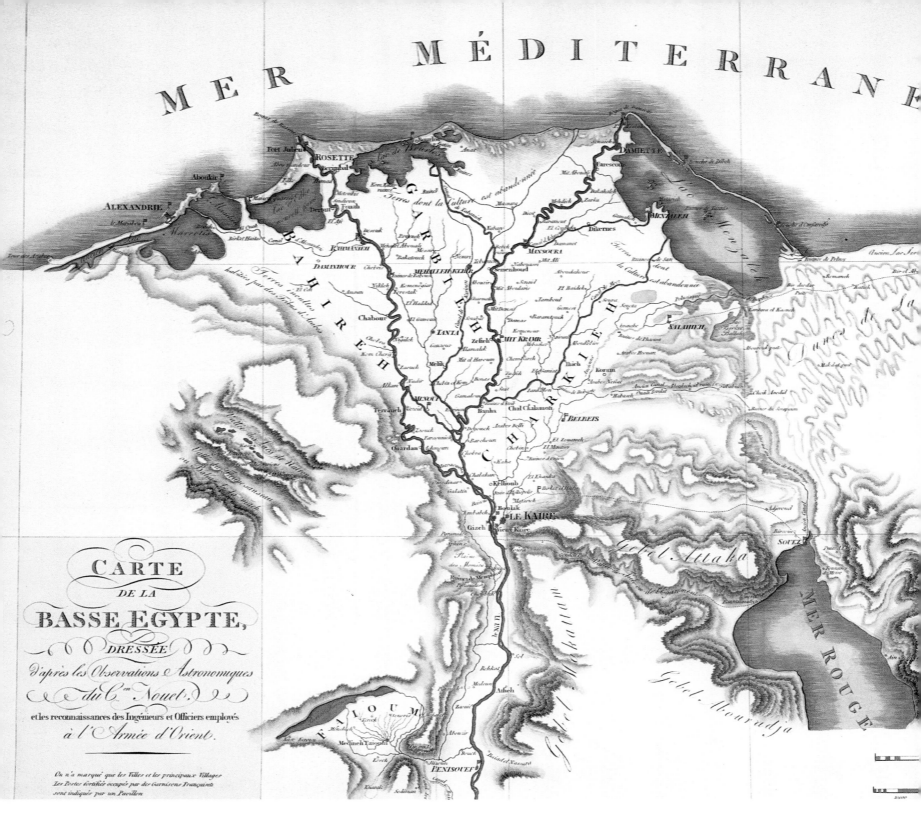

CARTE
DE LA
BASSE EGYPTE,
DRESSÉE
d'après les Observations Astronomiques
du C.ⁿ Nouet.
et les reconnaissances des Ingénieurs et Officiers employés
à l'Armée d'Orient.

On n'a marqué que les Villes et les principaux Villages
Les Postes fortifiés occupés par des Garnisons Françaises
sont indiqués par un Pavillon

protect you, and an interpreter to answer all your questions…?'. But, kind reader, please to recollect that we are surrounded with Arabs and Mamelukes, and that, in all probability, I should be made prisoner, pillaged, and very likely killed, if I had thought proper to venture only a hundred paces from the column to fetch some of the bricks of Aphroditopolis.

At Dendera, Denon was greatly impressed by the splendour of the temple of Hathor, as he wrote in his diary:

I wish I could here transfuse into the soul of my readers the sensation which I experienced. I was too much lost in astonishment to be capable of cool judgement; all that I had seen hitherto served here but to fix my admiration…. I could not expect to find any thing in Egypt

more compleat, more perfect than Tentrya [Dendera].

Two days later, on 26 January, in a state of great excitement, Denon came within sight of the ruins of Thebes, but his enthusiasm was dampened by the lack of time available for visiting its magnificent monuments. After examining the temple of Ramesses III at Medinet Habu, the Ramesseum and the Colossi of Memnon, Denon also attempted to explore the Theban necropolis and to enter the tombs in the side of the mountain, but the visit was far from being a relaxing experience, as he recounted:

I here entered on horseback, with Desaix, supposing that these gloomy retreats could only be the asylum of peace and silence; but scarcely were we immerged

in the obscurity of the galleries, than we were assailed with javelins and stones, by enemies whom we could not distinguish, and this put an end to our observations.

Although Desaix was a cultured man who was fond of the arts and archaeology, his needs were clearly at odds with those of Denon, who, naturally, had to bow to the necessities of war and forgo long visits to the archaeological sites since the pursuit of Murad Bey was the primary objective of the expedition. His sadness was, however, mitigated by the sight of the temples of Esna and Edfu (Apollinopolis Magna), and the ruins of ancient Syene (now Aswan), the capital of Upper Egypt, which Desaix's army reached on 2 February as Murad Bey retreated into the desert beyond the First Cataract.

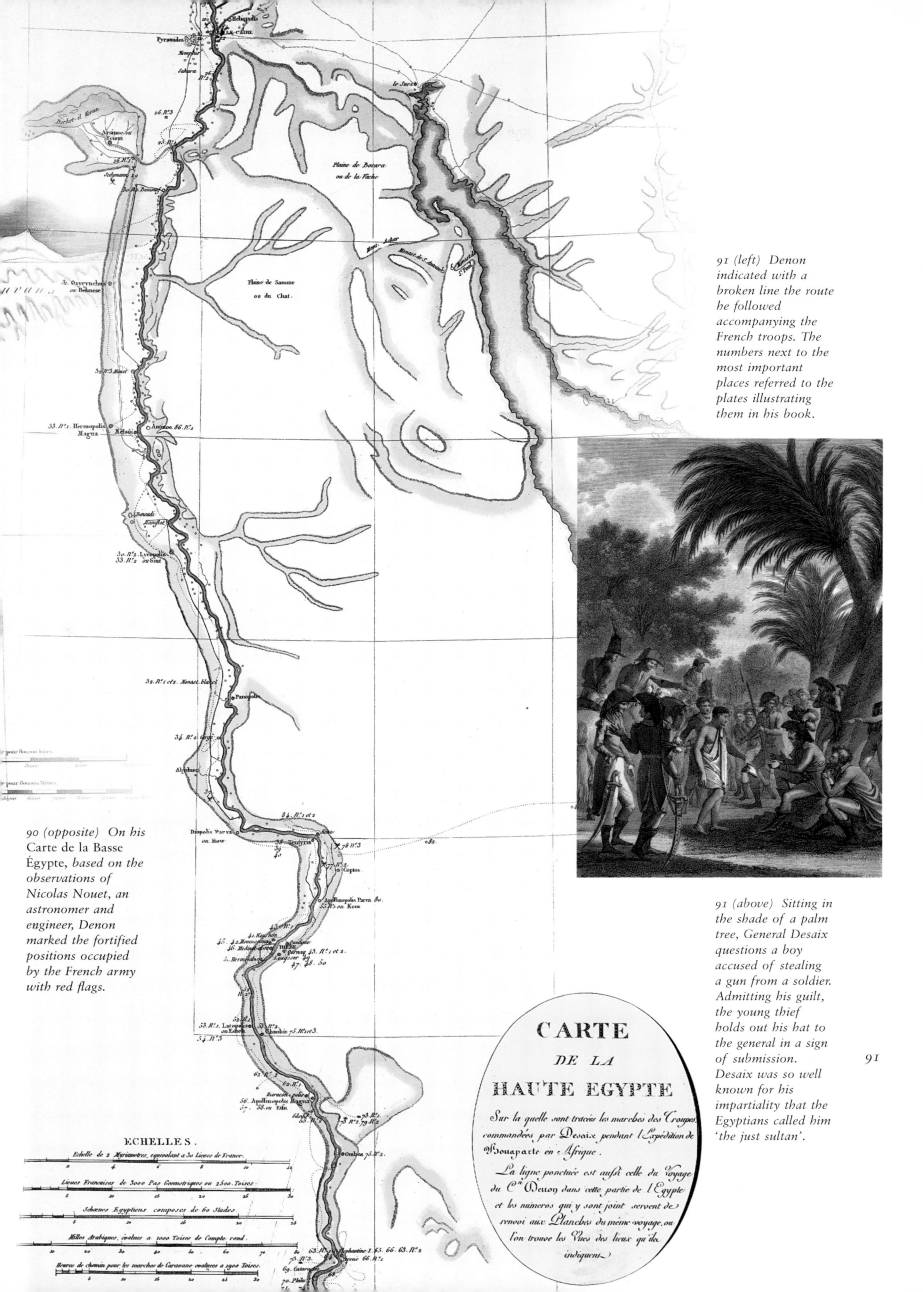

91 (left) Denon indicated with a broken line the route he followed accompanying the French troops. The numbers next to the most important places referred to the plates illustrating them in his book.

90 (opposite) On his Carte de la Basse Égypte, based on the observations of Nicolas Nouet, an astronomer and engineer, Denon marked the fortified positions occupied by the French army with red flags.

91 (above) Sitting in the shade of a palm tree, General Desaix questions a boy accused of stealing a gun from a soldier. Admitting his guilt, the young thief holds out his hat to the general in a sign of submission. Desaix was so well known for his impartiality that the Egyptians called him 'the just sultan'.

91

CARTE
DE LA
HAUTE EGYPTE

Sur la quelle sont tracées les marches des Troupes commandées par Desaix pendant l'Expédition de Bouaparte en Afrique.

La ligne ponctuée est aussi celle du Voyage du C.ⁿ Denon, dans cette partie de l'Égypte et les numéros qui y sont joint servent de renvoi aux Planches du même voyage, ou l'on trouve les Vues des lieux qu'ils indiquent.

ECHELLES.

92 (below) At the beginning of his journey to Upper Egypt, Denon passed near the pyramid of Meidum but could not get to it due to the Bahr Yussuf (Joseph's Canal), a tributary of the Nile linking the river to the Faiyum. Denon therefore had to content himself with drawing the monument as seen through a telescope. Unlike many of the other Egyptian pyramids, it has changed very little in appearance today.

92–93 (centre) While sailing on the Nile, Denon drew this splendid panorama of the pyramids in the Memphis area.

92 (left) Nothing remains today of the ruins of the temple of Hermopolis (Ashmunein), which Denon drew. He described them as colossal and his drawing successfully conveys an impression of their scale and magnitude.

At Aswan, Denon was enraptured by the magnificence of the island of Philae, dominated by the great temple of Isis. Here, for the first time, he was able to stay long enough – three weeks – to allow him to make numerous drawings of the monuments and to carry out a reasonably accurate survey of the whole island. An attack on the city of Qena by Arabs from Mecca who had landed at Quseir on the Red Sea, along with the threat from the Mameluke troops led by Hassan Bey, meant that the French army commanded by General Belliard – ordered by Desaix to garrison Aswan – had to leave. Very much against his will, Denon departed from Aswan on 24 February and sailed back down the Nile. On 7 March he reached Thebes and from there he continued to

Qus and Qift, villages built respectively on the sites of the ancient cities of Apollinopolis Parva and Coptos, the starting-point of the important route linking the Nile Valley to the Red Sea through the Wadi Hammamat.

In this area – at Benuth – on 8 March 1799, the French fought another, very fierce battle against the Mamelukes of Hassan Bey, who a few days previously had captured the boats of General Desaix's fleet transporting the wounded and munitions, slaughtering all five hundred members of the crew. After the bloody battle, which lasted three days and two nights and concluded with the massacre of over 1,200 Mamelukes, including Hassan Bey himself, Denon accompanied Belliard to Qena, a small town located some kilometres to the

north. Here they were joined by Desaix, who in the meantime had been pursuing Murad Bey, compelling him to take refuge in the Libyan Desert.

Desaix decided to garrison Bir Ambar, a strategic point controlling all the routes in the Arabian Desert, while Belliard was ordered to occupy the village of Nagadi (now Nag Hammadi), near Thebes. From here he then returned to Thebes itself, to the delight of Denon, who thus had another opportunity to visit the site and complete his drawings of Karnak and Luxor. Once more, however, the stay in Thebes was very brief because Belliard had to head south again towards Edfu, where there was another important route linking the Nile to the Red Sea, in order to pursue a group of Mamelukes. Denon barely had

93

94

time to draw the temples of Esna and
Edfu, where there was the 'sublime temple
of Apollinopolis, the most beautiful of all
Egypt, and, next to those of Thebes, the
largest. Being built at a period when the
arts and sciences had acquired all their
splendour', before he had to return to
Karnak and from there continue to Qena.
Here Belliard was obliged to stop to
prepare an expedition to Quseir, the most
important port on the Red Sea, towards
which some British ships were now sailing.

Denon availed himself of the stay at
Qena to pay another visit to the temple of
Dendera and see the remains of Coptos at
Qift. Meanwhile, Belliard had prepared the
caravan, consisting of 366 soldiers on
camels, and was about to leave for Quseir.
Denon, who now felt such an integral part
of Belliard's brigade that he shared 'their
successes, dangers, misfortunes and glory',
took part in the lightning expedition.
Belliard captured Quseir, where a white flag
had already been hoisted on the fort,
without firing a shot, on 29 May 1799. A
few days later the caravan returned to the
Nile, where they encountered a group of
eight scholars led by the engineer Pierre
Simon Girard, who were ascending the
river to carry out measurements of the
level of its waters. Thus Denon had yet
another chance to see Thebes, Esna and
Edfu; not only did he return to the sites
visited previously, but, for the first time, he
managed to enter the Valley of the Kings,
where he explored the tombs of Ramesses
III and Ramesses IV.

Denon's visit to Upper Egypt was now
drawing to a close, and on 3 August 1799
he began his journey back down the Nile,
stopping at the ruins of Antinoöpolis on
the east bank of the river south of the city

95 (right) Two obelisks stood before the pylon of the temple of Luxor, which Denon called 'the Entrance to the Village of Luxor'. Two colossal statues depicting Ramesses II were buried in sand almost up to the chest and the ground level was several metres higher than it is today. The western obelisk was given to France by Muhammad Ali; it was transported to Paris and erected in the Place de la Concorde in 1836.

95 (below) The temple of Luxor, seen from the Nile, glows golden in the sun, its ancient architecture punctuated by picturesque Arab buildings; this is the scene as recorded by Denon.

96–97 Denon was very impressed by the size and magnificence of the Ptolemaic temple dedicated to the falcon-god Horus at Edfu, the ancient city of Apollinopolis Magna. *Seen from the south (below), the temple appeared at that time to be almost completely submerged by the sand that invaded the first courtyard and the portico.*

of el-Minya. In Cairo he made a detailed report about everything he had seen to the members of the Institut d'Égypte and to Napoleon, who, fascinated by what he heard, on 14 August 1799, a few days before leaving Egypt, ordered the setting up of two new commissions. Directed by the mathematician Jean Baptiste Fourier and the engineer Louis Costaz, they were charged with following Denon's route to survey and draw all the monuments.

Denon returned to France with Napoleon, leaving his colleagues in the Commission the task of continuing the work that he had begun. He devoted himself to sorting out his travel notes and drawings, which were published shortly afterwards, in 1802, entitled *Voyage dans la Basse et la Haute Égypte pendant les campagnes du Général Bonaparte (A Journey to Upper and Lower Egypt during General Bonaparte's Campaigns)*. This was a work of great significance, due not only to the elegance of the text and splendour of the 141 plates that accompanied it, but, above all, because it was published seven years before the first volumes of the *Description d'Égypte* appeared. Denon dedicated the book to Napoleon, writing:

To combine the lustre of your Name with the splendour of the Monuments of Egypt, is to associate the glorious annals of our own age with the fabulous epocha of antiquity; and to reanimate the dust of Sesostris and Mendes, who like you were Conquerors, and like you benefactors. All Europe, by learning that I accompanied you in one of your most Memorable Expeditions, will receive my Work with eagerness and interest. I have neglected nothing in my power to render it worthy of the Hero to whom it is inscribed.

The book was an immense success, becoming a bestseller of the day; translated into English and German, it was printed in no fewer than forty editions and thousands of copies were sold. Denon's *Voyage* and the subsequent *Description de l'Égypte* were the only – albeit very important – fruit of the Egyptian expedition, which obtained neither political advantage for France nor works of art for its museums.

Many years later, after his exile on St Helena, Napoleon, writing his *Mémoires*, outlined the results of his Egyptian adventure in a few words: 'The glory of arms combined with artistic discovery – that is what the Egyptian expedition was.'

97 (above) Denon recounted that, while passing through the village of Qus, he saw the remains of a splendid large portal buried up to the lintel; this was 'the only element testifying to the fact that the site was that of the ancient city of Apollinopolis Parva'. The remains drawn by the artist belonged to a Ptolemaic temple dedicated to the gods Haroeris ('Horus the Elder') and Hekhet.

98 (centre) The picturesque island of Philae, dominated by the large Ptolemaic temple dedicated to Isis, was the only site where Denon managed to stay undisturbed for a number of days.

98 (below) In order to reach Philae Denon had to pass the First Cataract, and he described the rapids as: 'nothing more than a range of rocks, over which the river flows, forming in some places cascades a few inches in height; they are so insignificant, that they cannot be represented with any effect in a drawing'. However, he saw the cataract when the Nile was very low; others described it as a magnificent spectacle.

99 (opposite) Denon drew the first reasonably accurate plan of Philae, which he described as 'this enchanting island, where the monuments are only separated by groups of palm-trees'.

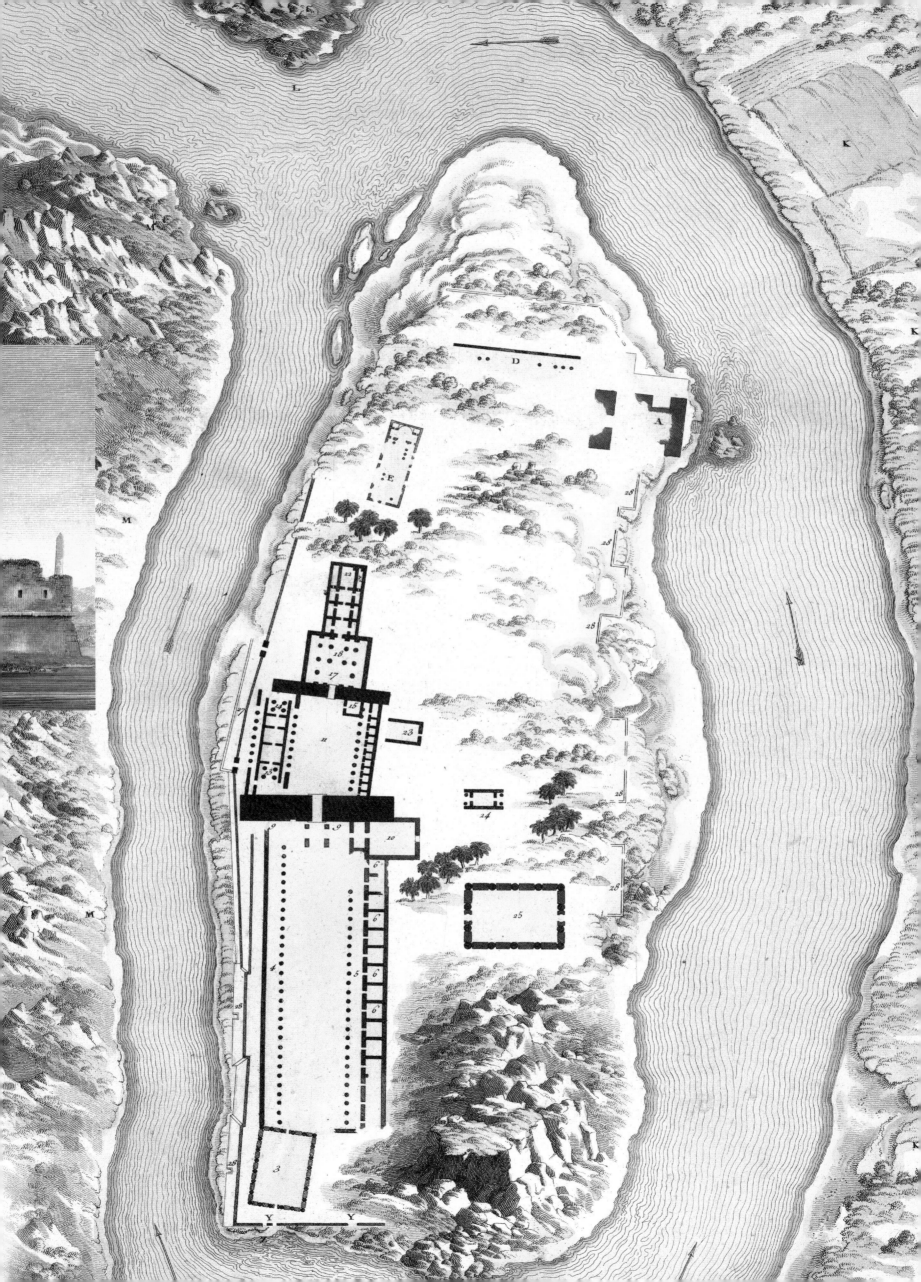

DESCRIPTION
DE L'ÉGYPTE
OU
RECUEIL
DES OBSERVATIONS ET DES RECHERCHES
QUI ONT ÉTÉ FAITES EN ÉGYPTE
PENDANT L'EXPÉDITION DE L'ARMÉE FRANÇAISE
SECONDE ÉDITION
DÉDIÉE AU ROI
PUBLIÉE PAR C. L. F. PANCKOUCKE
CHEVALIER DE LA LÉGION D'HONNEUR

ATLAS GÉOGRAPHIQUE

PARIS
IMPRIMERIE DE C. L. F. PANCKOUCKE
M D CCC XXVI.

Ordered by Napoleon to follow the army, the Commission des Arts et des Sciences travelled throughout Egypt drawing, cataloguing and recording all the ancient monuments in under three years. The efforts of its 167 members resulted in the publication of a prodigious work: printed in Paris over several years in a thousand copies, of which two hundred formed part of the so-called Imperial edition reserved for the crowned heads of Europe and the most important personages of the period, its full title was *Description de l'Égypte, ou Recueil des Observations et des Recherches qui ont été faites en Égypte pendant l'expédition de l'armée française, publié par les ordres de S.M. l'Empereur Napoléon* (Description of Egypt, or Collection of the Observations Made and Research

THE DESCRIPTION DE L'ÉGYPTE
A COLOSSAL WORK DOCUMENTS THE SPLENDOURS OF ANCIENT EGYPT

Undertaken in Egypt during the Campaign of the French Army, Published by Order of H.M. Emperor Napoleon). Comprising no fewer than nine folio volumes of text, with a total of over seven thousand pages, it was accompanied by ten volumes of large format plates (each measured 70 x 54 cm) and an atlas in three gigantic volumes that had the extraordinary dimensions of 108 x 70.2 cm. In order to print a work of this size it was necessary to create a new format for the paper and build a special printing press, designed for the purpose by Nicolas Jacques Conté.

The *Description* contained 897 plates, sixty of which were in colour, with a total of over three thousand drawings executed by two hundred artists.

ALEXANDRIE

CHOBRAKIS

PYRAMIDES

SALAHIEH

SEDMENT

EL-ARICH

GAZA

NAZARETH

MONT-TABOR

SYÈNE

THÈBES

ABOUKIR

N

Organized along scientific lines and constituting the first truly systematic study of Egyptian antiquity – with everything reproduced in glorious lithographs – the *Description* stimulated enormous public and academic interest. In effect, its publication was the only real success of Napoleon's venture in Egypt and it helped to distract the attention of the French public from the military and political failure of the campaign.

After the first edition rapidly sold out, the publisher Panckoucke brought out a second 'cheap' edition in twenty-seven volumes in a much smaller format. It was

102 (left) Among the members of the Commission des Arts et Sciences were prominent cultural figures and scientists of the day: (from the top) the chemist Claude Louis Berthollet; the mathematician Jean Baptiste Fourier; the artist Dominique Vivant Denon; the engineer and draughtsman François Charles Cécile; the mathematician and surveyor Gaspard Monge, the first president of the Institut d'Égypte; and André Dutertre, a draughtsman of the Commission and the artist responsible for these portraits.

102–103 (centre) The French scholars were required to hand over all the archaeological finds they had collected during the Egyptian campaign when the victorious British laid claim to them. It was only thanks to the determined stand of the naturalist Geoffroy Saint-Hilaire that they managed to keep their drawings and notes.

102 (opposite below) At el-Kab, the modern name of the ancient city of Nekheb, known in Graeco-Roman times as Eileithyiaspolis, the French scholars made a plan of the city and studied the decorations of the rock-cut tombs, such as this one belonging to Paheri, the mayor of the city at the beginning of the Eighteenth Dynasty.

accompanied also by a reprint of the plates, which made a great contribution to the work's huge popularity.

The vast size of the *Description* was the natural consequence of the incredible quantity of information gathered by Napoleon's experts, who not only drew the monuments but also studied them methodically and carefully measured them to obtain accurate plans and cross-sections. On occasion the engineers and topographers used large kites, for example to measure the exact height of Pompey's Pillar and Cleopatra's Needle in Alexandria. And the engineer Conté even designed a special probe to investigate structures still buried beneath the sand.

The French scientists' researches were not limited to archaeology, however: the naturalists examined the fauna of the country, catching and classifying the various species of fish in the Nile, and collecting samples of flowers, shrubs and other plants; while the geologists analysed the rocks and minerals.

103 (top) At Giza the scholars accompanying Napoleon's expedition to Egypt made very precise drawings of the pyramids and the Sphinx; they also carried out the first systematic survey of the archaeological area. Their plan remained the most accurate document recording the site for over a hundred and fifty years.

103 The members of the Commission des Arts et des Sciences who accompanied Napoleon's army are shown here gathered in the garden of the Institut d'Égypte in Cairo.

104–105 *During the annual inundation of the Nile, the Ezbekiya square in Cairo was submerged under water. This sight particularly fascinated artists and it was reproduced in the* Description. *To avoid the danger and inconvenience caused by the flooding, Muhammad Ali had the level of the ground raised.*

104 (opposite below)
The scholars of
Napoleon's
expedition took
an interest also in
contemporary Egypt,
and the customs and
dress of its people.

This drawing shows
the costumes of two
Mameluke officials:
an aga (a military
commander) on the
left and a sheikh (a
civilian authority) on
the right.

105 (top) Qasim
Bey's palace was one
of the many ancient
buildings in Cairo
used as residences by
the city's Mameluke
dignitaries.

105 (below left)
Murad Bey's splendid
palace at Giza, was
occupied by

Napoleon, who took
up residence there on
his arrival in Egypt.

105 (below right)
This lithograph,
taken from the
second volume
of the Description
depicts an
astronomer absorbed
in his work.

106–107 (above)
The Citadel, with its
massive walls, looms
over Cairo. Two
imposing towers
flank the gate known
as Bab el-Hazab –
the main entrance to
the fortress. In front
of it, caravans and
pilgrims preparing to
leave for Mecca
gathered in the huge
square known at the
time as Midan el-
Roumeyleh (now
Midan Salah el-Din).

106–107 (right)
At the time of
Napoleon's
expedition, Cairo
was a large city, with
over 260,000
inhabitants – a
sizeable population
for the period.

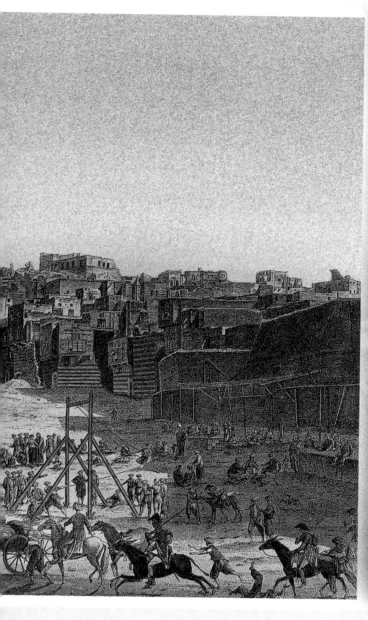

107 (above) Mustafa Pasha, depicted here in ceremonial costume, was the commander of the Ottoman troops defeated by Napoleon in the second Battle of Aboukir on 25 July 1799. Mustafa Pasha was himself wounded and taken prisoner by General Joachim Murat.

107

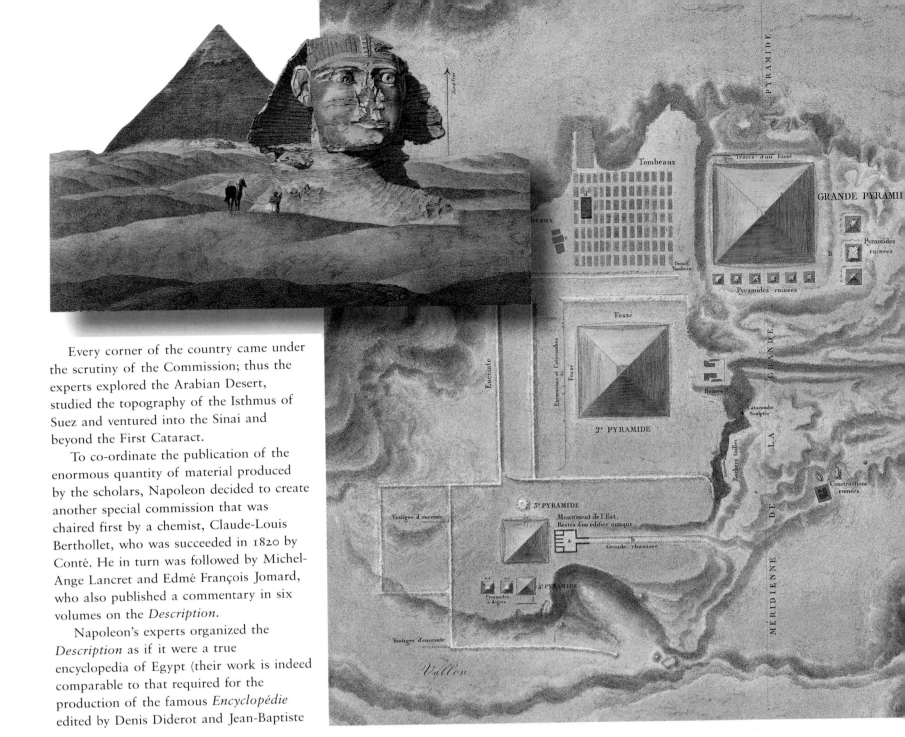

Every corner of the country came under the scrutiny of the Commission; thus the experts explored the Arabian Desert, studied the topography of the Isthmus of Suez and ventured into the Sinai and beyond the First Cataract.

To co-ordinate the publication of the enormous quantity of material produced by the scholars, Napoleon decided to create another special commission that was chaired first by a chemist, Claude-Louis Berthollet, who was succeeded in 1820 by Conté. He in turn was followed by Michel-Ange Lancret and Edmé François Jomard, who also published a commentary in six volumes on the *Description*.

Napoleon's experts organized the *Description* as if it were a true encyclopedia of Egypt (their work is indeed comparable to that required for the production of the famous *Encyclopédie* edited by Denis Diderot and Jean-Baptiste

le Rond d'Alembert). It was divided into three main sections. The first, and most important, was devoted to ancient Egypt; this alone constituted almost half the entire work, with four volumes of text and five of plates. The second and third parts of the *Description* dealt respectively with the modern state and the country's natural history; these two parts were composed of five volumes of text and five of plates.

The first volume of plates of the section devoted to ancient Egypt depicted the antiquities of Upper Egypt, in particular the temples on the islands of Philae and Elephantine at Aswan, and the temples of Kom Ombo, Edfu and Esna. It also included a map of the country based on the famous one published in 1766 by Jean Baptiste Bourguignon d'Anville. There were also drawings and plans of less important

108 (opposite, above left) Napoleon's artists depicted the Great Sphinx in an accurate manner – in fact this can be regarded as the first modern drawing of the monument, representing it realistically rather than interpreting it.

108–109 (above) This plan of the archaeological area of Giza shows the monuments with admirable precision and includes every detail visible at the time. In 1801, under the direction of Jean Marie Coutelle and Jean Baptiste Le Père, excavations were carried out in one of the secondary pyramids of Menkaure in an attempt to find its burial chamber, but

the search was abandoned due both to the difficulties encountered and the lack of time available.

108 (opposite below) This classic view of the pyramids of Giza, published in the Description, seems to have been inspired by the one painted several decades earlier by Frederik Norden.

109 At the time of the Egyptian campaign, the pyramid of Khufu was the only one that it was possible to enter. This famous drawing – very similar to the one drawn by Richard Dalton in 1749 – depicts the steep and spectacular Grand Gallery.

110 *While exploring the ruins of the ancient city of Memphis, a few miles south of Cairo, the scholars in Napoleon's expedition found a fragment of a colossal statue in pink granite representing Ramesses II. The draughtsmen made a preparatory watercolour painting (left) on which the illustration published in the* Description *was based (right).*

111 *(opposite) Murad Bey, after his defeat at the Battle of the Pyramids, took refuge in Upper Egypt where he was pursued by General Desaix. The French general reached Aswan, formerly known as Syene, on 2 February 1799. This ancient city was the most southerly point the French reached in their advance. When they stopped to rest, many of the troops carved their names on the ruins of a monument. The French artist Jean Charles Tardieu immortalized the scene in this oil painting, which was completed in 1812 and is now in the palace of Versailles.*

sites such as: Gebel Silsila; el-Kab, the ancient city of Nekheb, called Eileithyiaspolis by the Greeks; Tod on the east bank of the Nile north of Luxor, where a small temple was still visible; and Armant (Hermonthis in Greek) a town a few kilometres south of Luxor, on the west bank of the Nile, with ruins of a temple dedicated to the god Montu and a *mammisi* (a birth-house built to celebrate the mythological birth of the god to whom the main temple was dedicated) dating from Roman times. At the time the French studied this it was still in good condition, but in 1860 it was demolished to make way for a sugar factory.

The second volume of archaeology described the region of Thebes and all the monuments on the west bank of the Nile: the temple of Ramesses III at Medinet Habu; the Ramesseum; the temple of Deir el-Bahri; the Colossi of Memnon; the temple of Seti I; and, of course, the Valley of the Kings. An accurate map of the Valley was included, as were plans of numerous tombs, with reproductions of the wall decorations. In fact, in August 1799 in the West Valley the scholars on the expedition discovered a new tomb – that of Pharaoh Amenhotep III. A special section of the publication was devoted to reproductions of various objects found on the spot or purchased from the local inhabitants, including human and animal mummies, funerary furnishings, funerary statuettes (*ushabti*) and statuettes of divinities, vases and a number of papyri, some bearing passages from the Book of the Dead.

The third archaeological plate volume was entirely dedicated to the great temples of Luxor and Karnak, situated on the opposite bank of the Nile. This was the first time they were depicted in such detail.

The fourth volume described the area immediately to the south of the Theban region which included the ruins of Dendera (Tentyra to the Greeks); the temples of Abydos; the remains of the sanctuary of Qaw el-Kebir, totally destroyed during a flood of the Nile in 1821; the necropolis of Asyut (the Greek Lycopolis); and the ruins of Ashmunein (its Roman name, from the Greek, was Hermopolis Magna), which contained a large temple dedicated to the god Thoth, identified by the Greeks with Hermes (Mercury to the Romans).

At Dendera, the scholars studied and surveyed the large Ptolemaic temple dedicated to the goddess Hathor. They meticulously copied the numerous reliefs that decorated the walls and ceilings, including the famous zodiac that was taken

Route de Paris a Syene
Nº 1167....milles 340.....

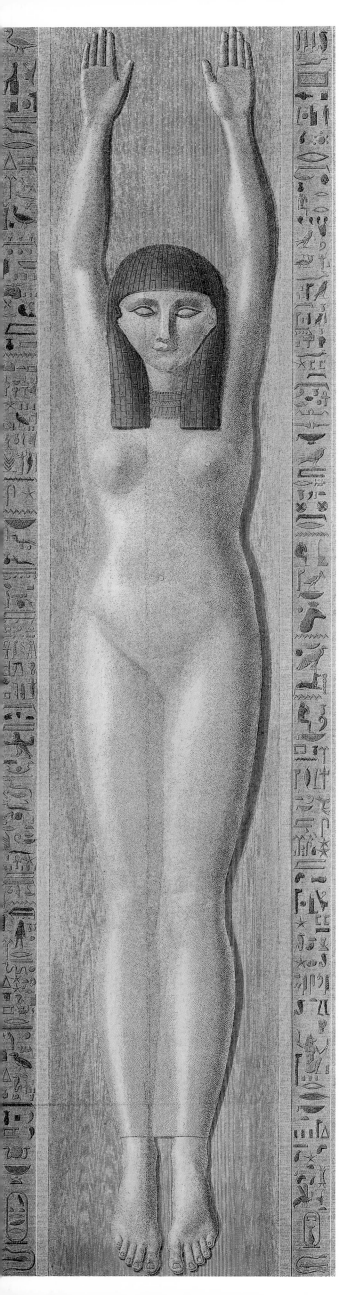

to the Louvre in 1821 (it has now been replaced by a copy at the site). Nearby was the *mammisi* built by Trajan, described by the scholars as a *typhonium* due to the fact that it was decorated with images of the god Bes, who was compared by the Greeks to Typhon, and a small temple dedicated to the goddess Isis. Abydos, once the centre of the cult of Osiris as the Lord of the Underworld because it was believed to be the location of one of his tombs, was the site of various important remains. These included the temple of Seti I, the Osireion – the strange cenotaph constructed by Seti I to symbolize the origin of the world from the primordial waters and the resurrection of Osiris – and the so-called *Shunet el-Zebib*, a name meaning 'raisin store', a funerary enclosure built of unfired bricks and dating to the Early Dynastic period.

In the second part of the fourth volume are descriptions of various sites: the ruins of Antinoöpolis, the city built by the emperor Hadrian in memory of his favourite, Antinous, who tragically drowned in the Nile, where Shiekh 'Ibada is now situated; the remains at Tell el-Amarna where the heretic pharaoh Amenhotep IV, who changed his name to Akhenaten, built his capital named Akhetaten; the Middle Kingdom necropolis of Beni Hasan; and the region of the Faiyum with Lake Qarun. Of the monuments of the Faiyum, those considered to be the most important are depicted, such as the Ptolemaic temple of Qasr Qarun, the obelisk of Abgig (dating from the reign of Senwosret I) and the pyramid of Amenemhet III at Hawara and that of Senwosret II at Illahun. This volume continues with a description of the pyramid of Meidum and the area of Dahshur, with the two important pyramids built by the pharaoh Sneferu – the Bent Pyramid and the Red Pyramid.

The fifth plate volume devoted to archaeology covers the region around Memphis, with the ruins of the ancient city and the great cemeteries at Saqqara and Giza. Particular attention is paid to the area around Giza with the major pyramids of Khufu, Khafre and Menkaure, and the Sphinx. The scholars accompanying Napoleon's expedition pitched their camp in front of this monument, which was still at that time almost entirely buried in sand.

112 (left) Nut, the sky-goddess, is one of the most frequently depicted divinities in the temple of Dendera; here she is shown by the French artists in a classicizing style.

112–113 (top) The
Ptolemaic temple of
Dendera, dedicated
to the goddess
Hathor, was much
admired for the
purity of its lines
and the elegance of
its well-preserved

decorations. In the
temple façade, as
seen in this drawing,
are six columns
surmounted by
elaborate capitals,
known as 'Hathoric'
because they are
decorated with

images of the
goddess. On the
terrace, some of the
French scholars are
examining the
structure, taking
measurements and
making drawings of
the columns.

112–113 (above) In
this side view of the
temple the structures
around the main
building are visible.
The temple's external
walls are covered
with reliefs and
inscriptions.

The scholars carefully measured and drew the pyramids of Giza, especially that of Khufu. At the time this was the only one that it was possible to enter, and the illustrations therefore reproduced details of its internal structure, including the famous Grand Gallery that had already astonished travellers in the eighteenth century. East and west of the Great Pyramid of Khufu the fields of mastaba-tombs were explored, and numerous drawings were made of their reliefs depicting funerary banquets and scenes of agriculture and everyday life.

The remainder of the fifth volume deals with Cairo, the Delta region, the Isthmus of Suez and the city of Alexandria. The ruins of the Roman area of Cairo, formerly known as the 'Babylon of Egypt', are recorded, as are those of Heliopolis. One of the main religious centres of ancient Egypt, Heliopolis was devoted to the cult of the sun god: the obelisk of Senwosret I still stands here today.

In the Delta several sites were studied, although incompletely: the ancient sites of Tanis (present-day San el-Hagar), the residence of the rulers of the Twenty-First and Twenty-Second Dynasties; Mendes (Tell el-Ruba); Bubastis (Tell Basta); and the Ptolemaic temple dedicated to Osiris and Isis at Bahbeit el-Haggar. In Alexandria the scholars drew the first accurate plan of the city, while the monuments that attracted their attention most were two obelisks dating from the reign of Thutmose III, commonly known as 'Cleopatra's Needles', and Pompey's Pillar, dating from the reign of the Roman

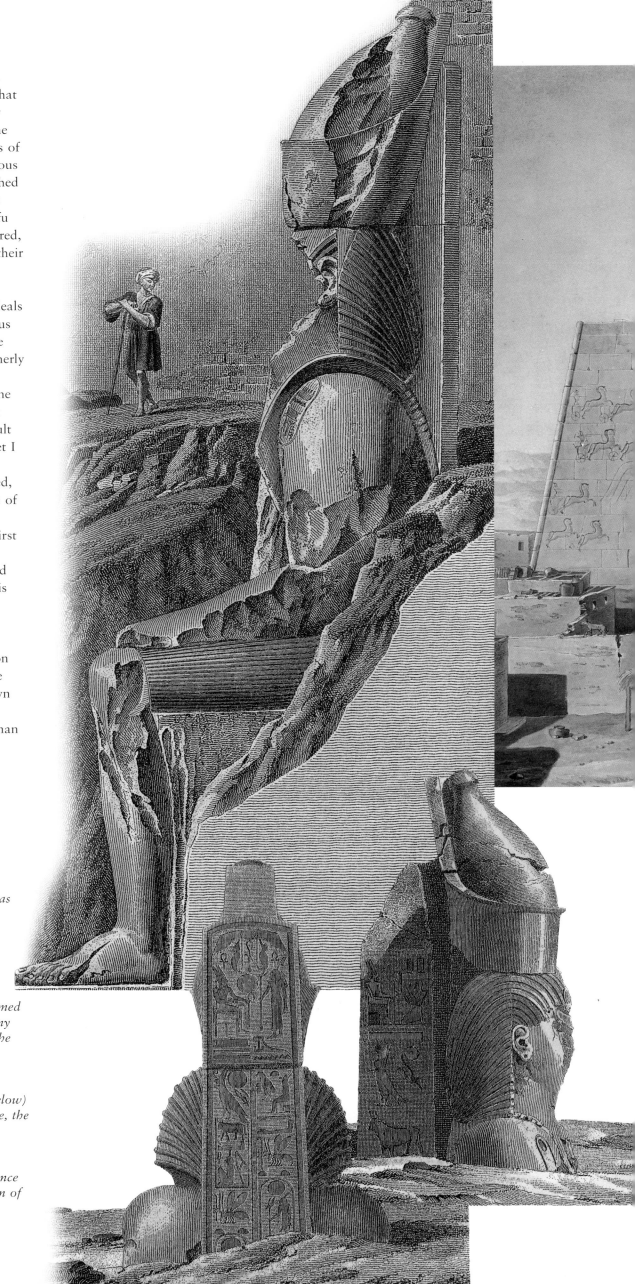

114 At the entrance to the temple of Luxor, the two colossal statues representing Ramesses II seated on a throne were still buried in sand up to the waist.

114–115 Until the middle of the nineteenth century the temple of Luxor was inhabited by the local people who built their mud-brick houses among the ruins, as well as a mosque, which still stands today. At that time the ground level

of the temple was some metres higher than it is at present. This watercolour is by François Charles Cécile, whose work formed the basis of many illustrations in the Description de l'Égypte.

115 (opposite below) For the first time, the French scholars attempted to reconstruct the original appearance of the first pylon of the temple at Luxor.

emperor Diocletian. Pompey's Pillar still stands in Alexandria today, while one of the obelisks was taken to London in 1878, and the other to New York in 1881. The scholars also took an interest in the later remains of the city, for instance the so-called 'Roman tower' – which was in fact part of the city walls built in the Byzantine period – and a number of Islamic buildings, including the mosque of 'Saint Athanasius'. The fountain of this mosque was made from the splendid sarcophagus of Nectanebo II, now in the British Museum.

Completing the section of the *Description* devoted to Alexandria and its antiquities is the Rosetta Stone, which was handed over to the British in 1801, and the ruins of Abusir, an ancient Ptolemaic city known to the Romans as Taposiris Magna. About forty kilometres west of Alexandria, on a narrow strip of land separating the Mediterranean from Lake Maryût, Abusir is the site of a temple dedicated to Osiris. It also contained a monument that, according to tradition, was a copy of one of the seven wonders of the ancient world: the *Pharos*, the lighthouse of Alexandria, the remains of which have recently been discovered beneath the sea near the port.

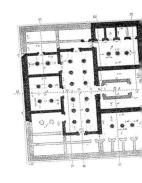

116 (left) The carved inscriptions on the pair of obelisks that stood in front of the first pylon of the temple of Luxor were copied with a surprising degree of accuracy, given the fact that at the time hieroglyphs had not yet been deciphered. Three sides of the eastern obelisk, which is still in its original position in the temple, are shown here.

116–117 (above) In this view of the temple of Luxor, the tops of the mud-brick buildings built by the local people are visible next to the courtyard of Amenhotep III, at the end of the great colonnade.

116–117 (below) Not only did the scholars make an exact plan of the temple, but they also drew a longitudinal section of it.

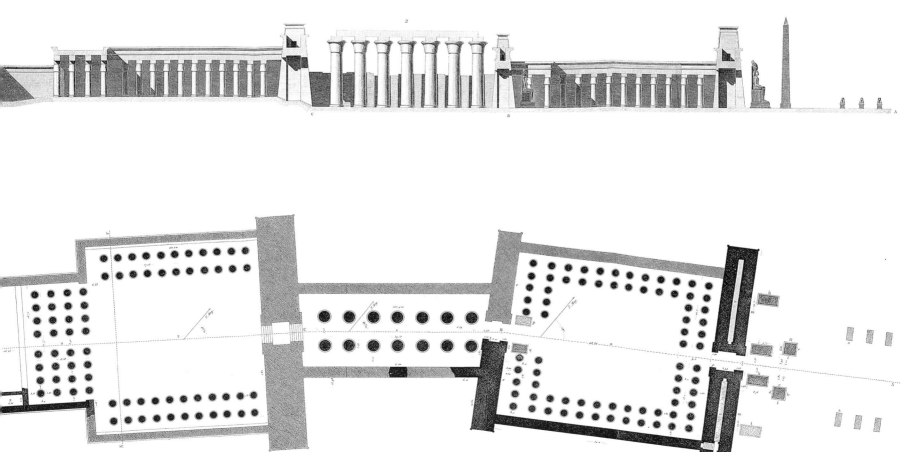

118 (left) Philip Arrhidaeus, successor to Alexander the Great, built a small sanctuary at Karnak. The reliefs depicted the ceremonies of purification and coronation of the king, and the procession of sacred barques of Amun, his wife Mut and their son Khonsu. The scholars in Napoleon's expedition were convinced that these were the decorative elements of a royal residence and not a religious building.

118–119 (centre)
The imposing ruins
of Karnak occupied
a large part of the
work of the French
scholars, and
numerous
illustrations in the
Description de
l'Égypte *were*
devoted to this

immense site. This
was the first time
Karnak had been
examined in such a
systematic manner –
previously it had
only been drawn and
described by the
Reverend Richard
Pococke, who visited
it in January 1738.

118–119 (below)
In this longitudinal
section of the central
colonnade of the
great temple of
Amun at Karnak,
the meticulous
attention to detail
that characterized
the approach taken
by the scholars of
Napoleon's
expedition is evident.
Vivant Denon's
paintings, on the
other hand, were
artistic rather
than scientific.

119 (right) As well
as architecture, the
illustrations in the
Description de
l'Égypte *devoted to*
Karnak also depicted
the numerous
sculptures found at
the site, such as this
colossal statue at
the entrance to the
hypostyle hall.

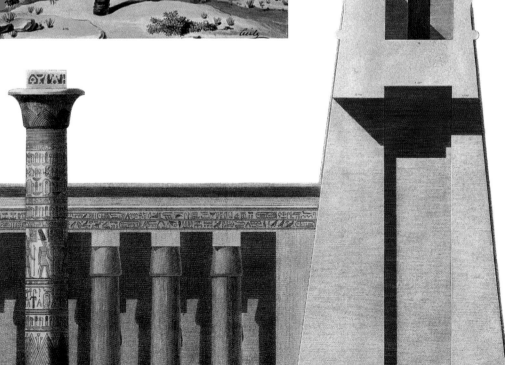

The fifth and last plate volume of the *Description* devoted to the antiquities of Egypt concluded with an epigraphic section, with reproductions of papyri, numerous hieroglyphic, Greek and Latin inscriptions, and a varied assortment of objects including statuettes of gods, amulets, *ushabti*, stelae and fragments of sarcophagi.

Still of fundamental importance for the study of Egyptology today, the *Description de l'Égypte* drew the attention of the world to Egypt and its fabulous past. It seemed, moreover, as if it was a land full of great art treasures that were at the disposal of whoever had the means and the desire to appropriate them. This was the beginning of a new chapter in the recent history of Egypt, which now became the theatre of a war waged between the leading nations not in order to secure political and territorial control over the Near East, but to acquire collections of antiquities that formed the basis of many of the great Egyptological museums of Europe.

121 The Colossi of Memnon originally stood in front of the mortuary temple of Amenhotep III, of which nothing remains today. In antiquity they were famous for the sound one of them emitted at dawn. The French scholars depicted the two statues fairly precisely, but in a style inspired by the Classical world.

120–121 (above) Napoleon's scholars were very active in western Thebes, where there are large royal and private cemeteries and the mortuary temples – known as the 'temples of millions of years' – of the pharaohs, intended for the cult of the divine king. This drawing depicts the temple of Ramesses III at Medinet Habu, from the south, with its distinctive tower, known as a migdol, inspired by the architecture of Asia Minor.

120 (opposite below) The walls of the temple of Medinet Habu were covered with brightly coloured reliefs which the scholars studied and faithfully copied. One of the colour plates in the Description de l'Égypte illustrates this scene from the triumphal procession of Ramesses III after his victory over the Sea Peoples; the king in his chariot presents the prisoners, standing between priests and officials, to Amun.

122 (centre)
Diodorus Siculus
called the
Ramesseum 'the
tomb of
Ozymandias', the
name also used by
the French scholars.
In this view of the
temple from the
northeast the tents
of the expedition
are visible.

122 (below) An
accurate plan was
made of the
Ramesseum, and a
longitudinal section.
The artists also drew
reconstructions of
the entrance leading
to the second
courtyard and the
hypostyle hall, based
on the description by
Diodorus Siculus.

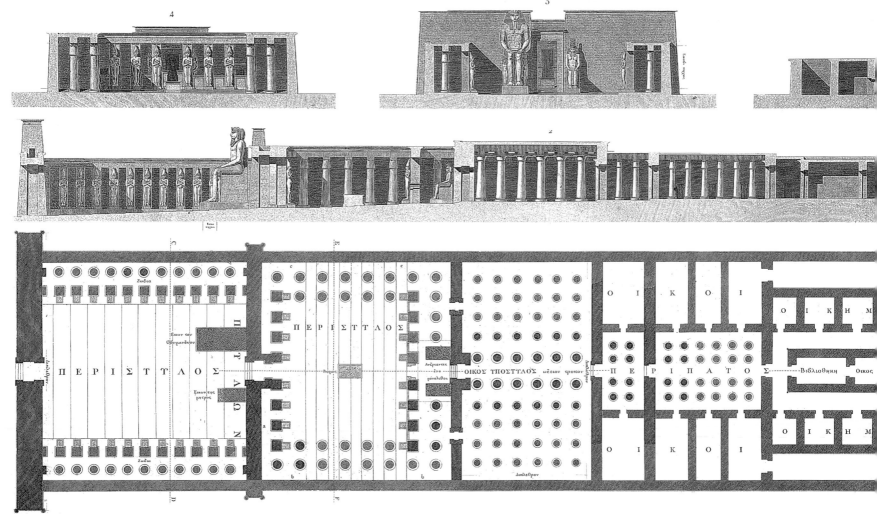

122–123 (above) The Ramesseum on the west bank at Thebes is the mortuary temple of Ramesses II. In this view (seen from the west), the colossal statue of Ramesses II, 'Sun of Rulers', is visible lying face up on the ground, as it still does today. The huge granite monolith may have been toppled deliberately by the hand of man, or possibly as a result of an earthquake.

123 (right) This colossal granite bust of Ramesses II was found by the French scholars lying in the second courtyard of the Ramesseum. They tried in vain to remove it, but it took the strength and ingenuity of the Paduan adventurer Giovanni Battista Belzoni to achieve this feat in 1816.

124–125 The huge Ptolemaic temple of Edfu, the site formerly known as Apollinopolis Magna, was dedicated to the falcon-god Horus and was in an almost perfect state of preservation, although local people had built their houses of mud-brick on the roof.

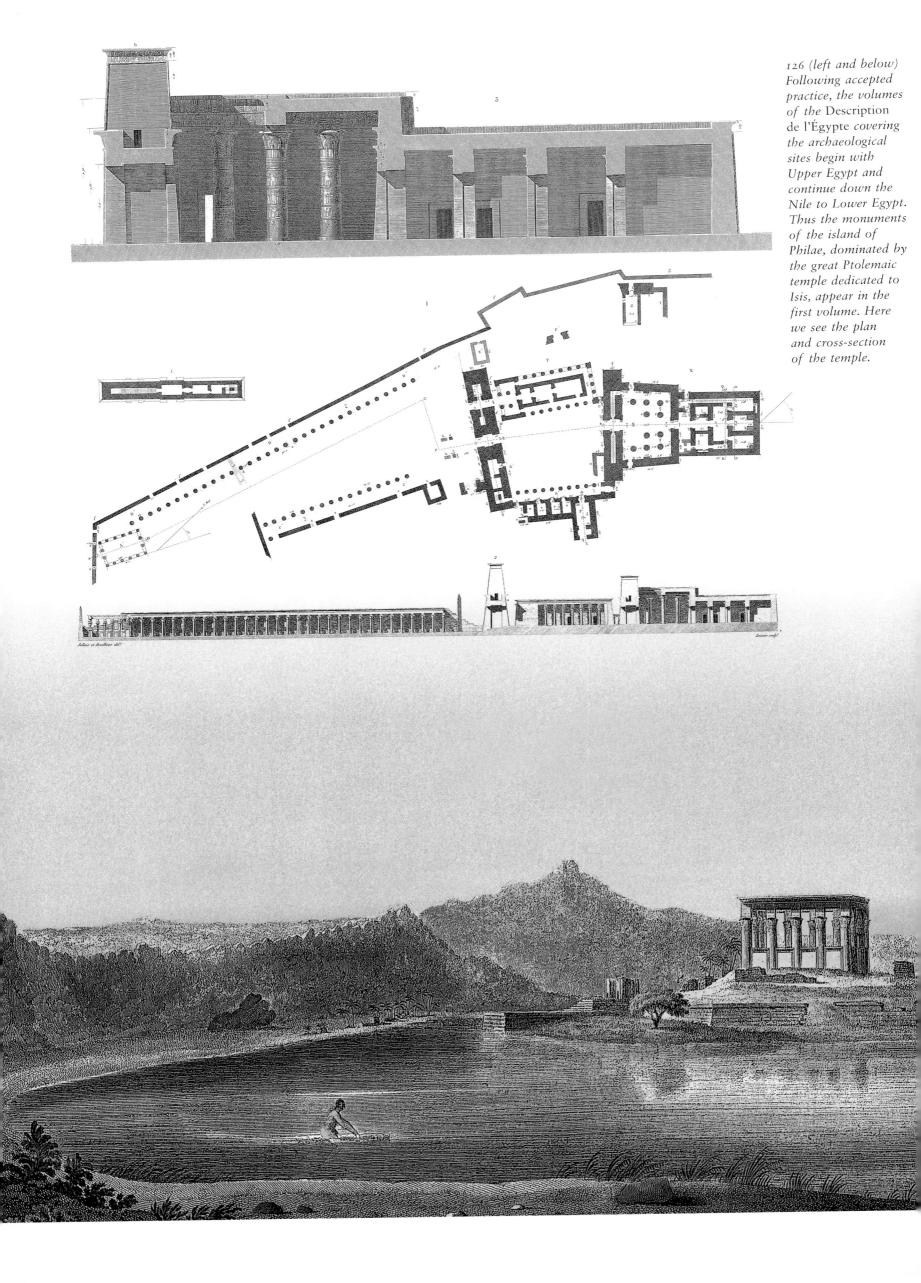

126 (left and below) Following accepted practice, the volumes of the Description de l'Égypte *covering the archaeological sites begin with Upper Egypt and continue down the Nile to Lower Egypt. Thus the monuments of the island of Philae, dominated by the great Ptolemaic temple dedicated to Isis, appear in the first volume. Here we see the plan and cross-section of the temple.*

126–127 (below) Situated in a picturesque landscape dominated by the granite rocks between which the waters of the Nile flow, the island of Philae held a particular fascination for the first visitors that is still felt today. It is located south of Aswan, the ancient city of Syene, and immediately upstream of the First Cataract.

127 (right) The elegant Kiosk of Trajan, often called 'pharaoh's bed', was originally used to house the sacred barque of Isis during the great religious processions.

128–129 One of the most splendid plates in the Description depicts the pronaos of the temple of Isis on Philae with its marvellous reliefs. At the time, the reliefs retained their original colours, but they have since disappeared. Following the construction of the first Aswan Dam in 1902, Philae, with its monuments, was submerged for several months each year, and after the High Dam was built the temples had to be moved to a completely new site.

THE 'WAR OF THE CONSULS'
ANTIQUARIANS AND ADVENTURERS IN SEARCH
OF PHARAONIC ANTIQUITIES

In the wake of Napoleon's Egyptian expedition, the publication of both Denon's *Voyage* and the *Description* brought a new world to the attention of Europeans and allowed them to rediscover a mysterious and fascinating lost civilization. In the early nineteenth century Egypt became one of the favourite destinations for travellers, explorers, adventurers and entrepreneurs eager not only to see the artistic marvels depicted in these books, but also – and perhaps above all – to create the earliest collections of antiquities. Europeans also came to set up the first factories and farms envisaged in the modernization programme of the Pasha, Muhammad Ali.

Muhammad Ali is the extraordinary figure who dominated Egypt for the whole of the first half of the nineteenth century. An obscure official born in 1769 at Kavalla in Macedonia, he established himself as the

champion of order in the country and, in 1805, was acclaimed Pasha of Egypt, a nomination confirmed later that year by the Sultan of Constantinople, since Egypt was still nominally part of the Ottoman Empire.

Small in stature, with a long beard and lively eyes, Muhammad Ali was gifted with a keen understanding of politics and remarkable courage. He was also ruthless – he eliminated all internal opposition by massacring the last Mameluke chiefs and their followers (about five hundred people) on 1 March 1811, after inviting them to his palace in the Citadel – the fortress that still dominates Cairo today – under the pretext of celebrating the appointment of his son Tussun as commander of the army. His active expansionist policy against neighbouring countries led, in 1812, to his conquest of Mecca and Medina, the most

sacred cities of Islam, and, subsequently, the Sudan – where he founded the city of Khartoum – as well as Syria. In 1841, as a reward for his services to the country, his family became the hereditary rulers of Egypt.

At home, Muhammad Ali embarked on a vast plan of reforms intended to turn Egypt into a modern nation. He was assisted in this ambitious undertaking by technicians, experts and counsellors, among whom one of the most important was the French Consul, Bernardino Drovetti. Thanks to his friendship with, and influence over, the Pasha, Drovetti obtained a special permit allowing him to excavate archaeological sites, thus enabling him to build up a collection of antiquities that he then sent back to France. Other European nations soon followed suit, giving their consuls – who at that time played a major

132–133 (below) Bernardino Drovetti, the French Consul-General, was portrayed at Thebes in 1818 by the traveller and antiquarian Louis Nicolas Philippe Auguste de Forbin. Drovetti stands in front of a fragment of a colossal statue, surrounded by his agents and assistants. On his left is Jean Jacques Rifaud, wearing a turban.

132–133 (above) De Forbin reached the ruins of the ancient city of Thebes on the evening of 28 January 1818. This was the site that he had most looked forward to visiting in Egypt. One of his first drawings was this side view of the great colonnade of the temple of Luxor. The columns are well preserved and are almost entirely free of sand.

Lith. de G. Engelmann.

role in conducting the foreign policy of their governments in the regions for which they were responsible – the task of collecting antiquities to send back to the museums in their own countries of origin. Thus began the systematic plunder of Egypt's archaeological heritage by the diplomats of various European nations and their agents, who engaged in an unprincipled, no-holds-barred struggle that was later described as the 'war of the consuls'.

Although this bitter struggle for the possession of archaeological treasures was dominated by Bernardino Drovetti and the British Consul, Henry Salt, others were also very active in building up collections

of antiquities, for instance the Austrian Consul Giuseppe Acerbi, and the Swedish and Norwegian one, Giovanni Anastasi. Giuseppe Acerbi, who was born in 1773 at Castelgoffredo, a small village near Mantua, in Italy, worked in Egypt from 1826 to 1834 and, in his capacity as Consul of Austria, acquired a small but interesting collection that is now displayed in the museum at the Palazzo Te in Mantua. On the other hand, the more substantial collection accumulated by Giovanni Anastasi was dispersed to various museums in London, Paris and Stockholm, and in the Netherlands. Above all, his name is associated with numerous important papyri now in the British Museum.

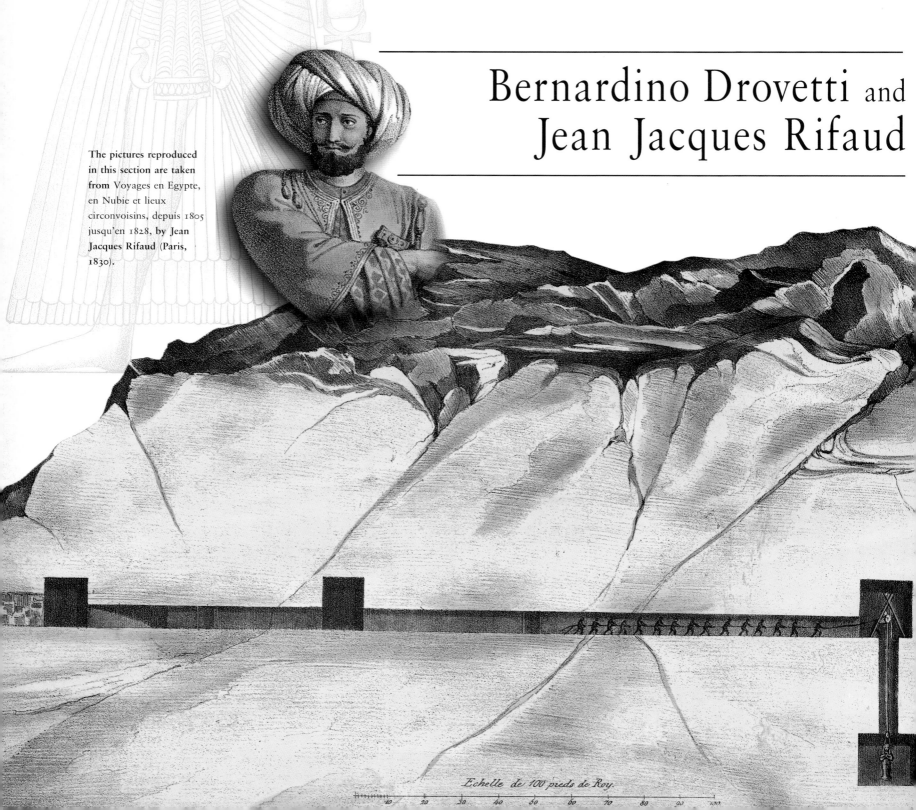

134 (centre) Jean
Jacques Rifaud,
a sculptor and
draughtsman, was
one of Drovetti's
main agents. Rifaud
worked in Egypt for
over forty years,
making more than
four thousand
drawings. He
excavated at Karnak
between 1817 and
1823, and discovered
no fewer than sixty-
six statues.

134 (below) In this
drawing Rifaud
demonstrates the
technique he used
for removing a
number of
sarcophagi from the
burial chamber of a
tomb in the Theban
necropolis.

135 (opposite)
Rifaud was not only
an able 'hunter of
antiquities' and a
skilled draughtsman,
but he was also an
excellent writer: in
1830 he published
a monumental
account of his work
in five volumes.

The pictures reproduced
in this section are taken
from Voyages en Egypte,
en Nubie et lieux
circonvoisins, depuis 1805
jusqu'en 1828, by Jean
Jacques Rifaud (Paris,
1830).

Of all the diplomats representing the
European powers, there is no doubt that
Bernardino Drovetti (1776–1852) was the
best-known and most distinctive. Born at
Barbania, in Piedmont (Italy), Drovetti
enlisted in the Napoleonic army during the
first Italian campaign. Thanks to his
remarkable personal qualities, his military
career was brilliant and he rose rapidly.
Within a few years he was promoted to the
rank of lieutenant, then captain and aide-
de-camp to Marshal Joachim Murat, and
finally he became a lieutenant-colonel. In
1803 Drovetti was sent to Egypt as a vice-
consul for France, and in 1801 he was
appointed Consul-General.

A careful observer gifted with notable
powers of intuition – and vigorous and
determined when the occasion demanded –
Drovetti was prepared to be quite

unscrupulous in order to achieve his
objectives. In the space of a few years he
became an expert on the Egyptian political
scene and the main characters figuring in it
in the early nineteenth century. This
familiarity proved providential when, a few
years later, in 1814, following Napoleon's
downfall, he was dismissed from his post.
He was reinstated in 1820 because it had
proved impossible to find a suitable
replacement for him in such a difficult and
delicate political situation.

In fact, Egypt in the early nineteenth
century was the centre of interest of
various European states vying for the role
of supreme power in the Near East. Their
representatives frequently found themselves
having to deal with the wily Muhammad
Ali, using all the diplomatic skills at their
disposal to obtain any results.

Bernardino Drovetti and Jean Jacques Rifaud

Echelle de 100 pieds de Roy.

VOYAGE
EN ÉGYPTE, EN NUBIE,
ET LIEUX CIRCONVOISINS,
depuis 1805 jusqu'en 1828;
PUBLIÉ
PAR M. Chevar. J. J. RIFAUD,

Chevalier de la Légion d'honneur, auteur d'un Tableau de l'Égypte, de la Nubie, et lieux circonvoisins et de plusieurs autres publications scientifiques; membre de l'Académie Royale de Marseille et de la Société statistique de la mém ville; membre adjoint du conseil de la Société de Géographie de Paris, de la Société asiatique de Paris; membre de la Société Royale des antiquaires de France; membre du Conseil de la Société statistique universelle de Paris; questeur de l'Académie de l'industrie agricole commerciale de Paris, et secrétaire du Comité des prix et des encouragements; membre de l'Institut historique de Paris, et de la Société pour l'émancipation intellectuelle de Paris, membre correspondant des Académies Royales de Bordeaux, d'Aix, Rouen, Nantes, Toulouse, et de la Société d'émulation d'Abbeville, membre correspondant de la Société Médico-Botanique de Londres, membre correspondant des antiquaires de Copenhague, de l'Académie des Sciences de Gothenbourg de la Société Royale de statistique de Dresde, membre honoraire et correspondant de la Société polytechnique (polytechnische Gesellschaft) de Leipzig, de cracavie de venise, etc. etc. etc.

OUVRAGE

Composé de trois cents planches et cinq volumes de Texte
représentant les Monumens de ces contrées, Costumes, Cérémonies, et l'histoire naturelle.

DÉDIÉ À S. M. L'EMPEREUR DE TOUTES LES RUSSIES.

And in this respect, too, Drovetti had an advantage over the other consuls. He provided Muhammad Ali with valuable aid in various fields, such as the organization of the army on a more modern basis; the improvement of agricultural methods and the development of irrigation systems on the cultivated land; the setting up of a textile industry in the country; and the fight against cholera. This meant that he was on very friendly personal terms with the Pasha, whom he sought to keep as far away as possible from British influence.

Drovetti's friendship with Muhammad Ali put him in a privileged position which allowed him to hold sway over the other Europeans living in the country, or even just visiting it, especially the archaeologists and antiquarians searching for ancient Egyptian artifacts. In this field Drovetti was himself indefatigable and, having a special permit from the Pasha that allowed him to work and travel as he wished, he hired numerous agents whom he sent to the most promising archaeological areas. The agents had instructions to buy archaeological finds or to excavate for them in order to build up Drovetti's personal collection. This rapidly grew to become the most important of all the many private collections that were being assembled in Egypt at the time. Among his agents were scientists such as Frédéric Cailliaud, a geologist and naturalist from Nantes; artists such as Jean Jacques Rifaud, a sculptor from Marseille; adventurers such as Antonio Lebolo; and also the so-called 'French Mamelukes', former soldiers in the Napoleonic army, many of them deserters, who had remained in Egypt, converting to Islam and assuming Arab names – for instance, Joseph Rosignani, called Yussef.

Often these agents clashed violently with their opposite numbers working for other consuls, and, on occasion, they resorted to the use of arms when they had to defend a find or an excavation, or when they wanted to prevent others from carrying out new excavations in an area thought to be promising. All this was recounted by Giovanni Battista Belzoni,

who had numerous skirmishes with Drovetti's agents; indeed, such was the bad feeling between them that Belzoni only referred to Drovetti by the first letter of his surname.

Drovetti did not confine himself to the collection of antiquities, but also took an active interest in the exploration of the areas of Egypt that were still little known. Thus in 1816 he went to Upper Egypt and surveyed the Nubian temples. He managed to get as far as Abu Simbel, where he attempted to enter the Great Temple of Ramesses II, but was unable to remove the sand blocking the entrance.

Three years later Drovetti began an exploration of the Libyan Desert, reaching the remote oasis of Siwa. He was accompanied by a physician from Sienna, Alessandro Ricci, and a draughtsman, Louis Maurice Adolphe Linant de Bellefonds. The results of this journey were subsequently published by François Jomard

136–137 (left) Rifaud accompanied Drovetti on his journey in 1816 as far as the Second Cataract. At Dendur he drew this temple which was built during the reign of the Emperor Augustus and was then situated between the temples of Kalabsha and el-Dakka. Threatened with submersion by the waters of the Nile after the construction of the Aswan High Dam, the temple was dismantled in 1963 and reassembled at the Metropolitan Museum of Art in New York.

137 (above) Nothing remains today of this temple drawn by Rifaud at the site known in antiquity as Contra Latopolis (now the village of el-Hella), on the east bank of the Nile, opposite Esna. In antiquity Esna was called Latopolis because it was the centre of worship of a species of fish known as lates, which includes the Nile perch.

137

in his book *Voyage à l'oasis de Syouah…* (*Journey to the Oasis of Siwah…*).

Drovetti continued in his diplomatic post until 1829, when he returned to Italy. He settled in Turin, where he lived until his death in 1852. His precious collection was turned down by the King of France, Louis XVIII, before it was acquired, in 1824, by the King of Sardinia, Carlo Felice, for the sum of 400,000 Piedmontese lire. In this way the original core of the Turin collection, later to form the Museo Egizio, was considerably enlarged. Under the king's encouragement, the collection was housed in the Palazzo dell'Accademia delle Scienze, designed by the famous architect Guarino Guarini. This, merely the first part of Drovetti's collection, comprised 169 papyri and manuscripts; 485 artifacts in iron, bronze and lead; over 2,400 scarabs and amulets; 102 mummies and other objects; 95 statues, including the famous one representing Ramesses II enthroned, which has practically become the symbol of the Turin museum; and 3,007 medals.

In addition to this the 'second Drovetti collection' included 3 sarcophagi, 10 stelae in granite, 60 stelae in limestone, 500 amulets, 30 manuscripts, 2 mummies and 80 gold objects. It was examined by Jean François Champollion, the 'father of Egyptology', at Livorno while it was being unloaded. It was then acquired by King Charles X of France, in 1827, and is now in the Louvre. On the recommendation of the famous Egyptologist Richard Lepsius, the third part of the collection was acquired by the Berlin Museum in 1836.

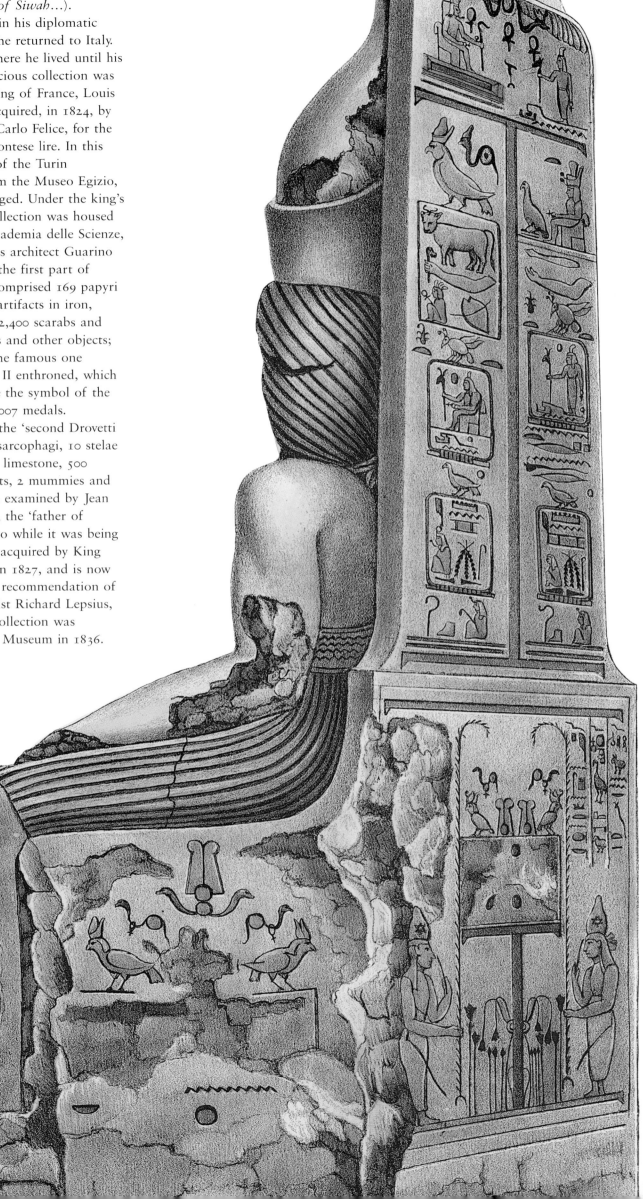

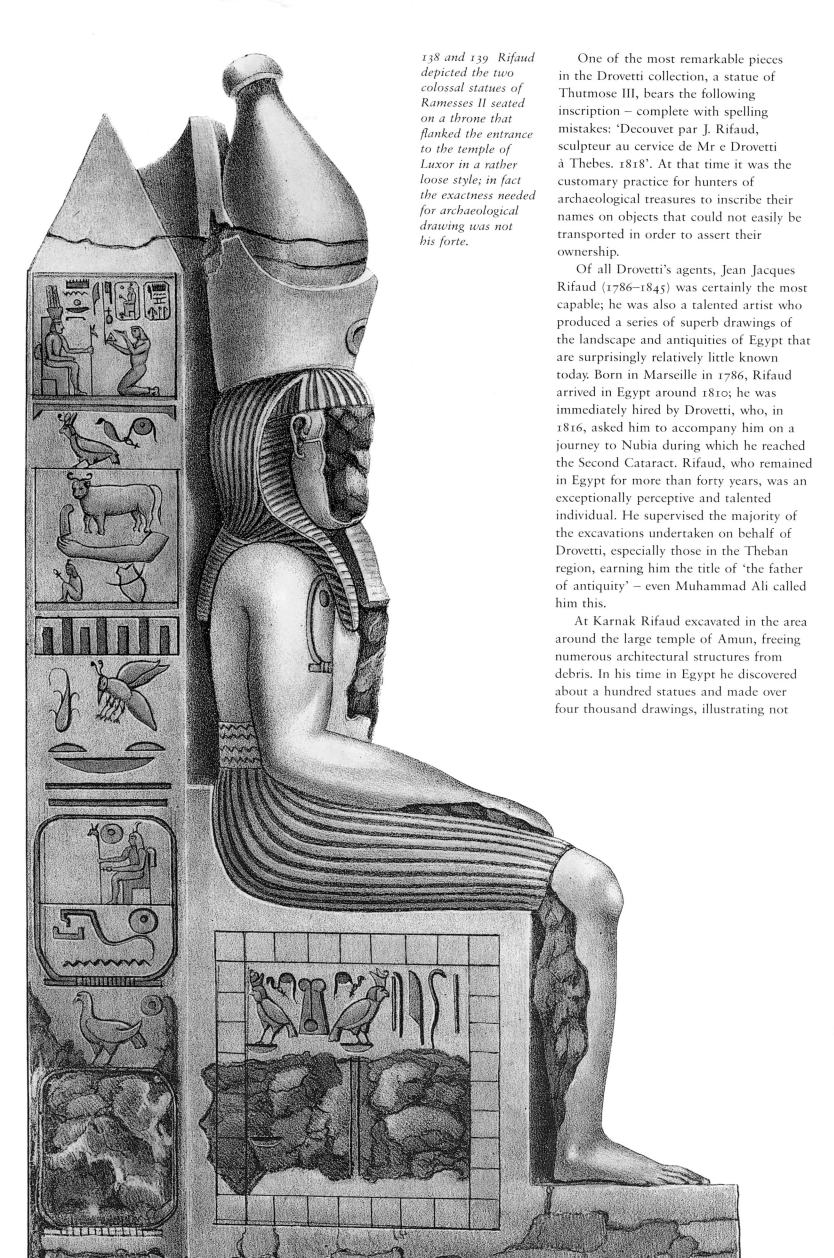

138 and 139 Rifaud
depicted the two
colossal statues of
Ramesses II seated
on a throne that
flanked the entrance
to the temple of
Luxor in a rather
loose style; in fact
the exactness needed
for archaeological
drawing was not
his forte.

One of the most remarkable pieces
in the Drovetti collection, a statue of
Thutmose III, bears the following
inscription – complete with spelling
mistakes: 'Decouvet par J. Rifaud,
sculpteur au cervice de Mr e Drovetti
à Thebes. 1818'. At that time it was the
customary practice for hunters of
archaeological treasures to inscribe their
names on objects that could not easily be
transported in order to assert their
ownership.

Of all Drovetti's agents, Jean Jacques
Rifaud (1786–1845) was certainly the most
capable; he was also a talented artist who
produced a series of superb drawings of
the landscape and antiquities of Egypt that
are surprisingly relatively little known
today. Born in Marseille in 1786, Rifaud
arrived in Egypt around 1810; he was
immediately hired by Drovetti, who, in
1816, asked him to accompany him on a
journey to Nubia during which he reached
the Second Cataract. Rifaud, who remained
in Egypt for more than forty years, was an
exceptionally perceptive and talented
individual. He supervised the majority of
the excavations undertaken on behalf of
Drovetti, especially those in the Theban
region, earning him the title of 'the father
of antiquity' – even Muhammad Ali called
him this.

At Karnak Rifaud excavated in the area
around the large temple of Amun, freeing
numerous architectural structures from
debris. In his time in Egypt he discovered
about a hundred statues and made over
four thousand drawings, illustrating not

140–141 *Rifaud's drawing of the temple of Luxor seen from the southeast shows it surrounded by the houses built by the local people using sun-dried bricks.*

140 *(below) In addition to collecting antiquities, Rifaud was also interested in the ethnographic aspects of the country, describing and drawing the* costumes and habits of the people. Here he portrays two Egyptian women carrying pitchers on their heads as they go to draw water from the Nile.*

only the country's antiquities but also aspects of life in Egypt at the time. Self-taught and possessing a strong artistic sensibility, Rifaud was also impulsive and lacked a scientific approach; thus he did not pay great attention to detail and his drawings – at least, those of an archaeological nature – are at times imprecise to the point of being unreliable.

Collecting and drawing Egyptian antiquities was but one of Rifaud's occupations, however, and besides being an artist he was also a writer. In 1830 he published a monumental work in five volumes in octavo entitled *Voyages en Égypte, en Nubie et lieux circonvoisins, depuis 1805 jusqu'en 1827* (*Journeys in Egypt, Nubia and Places in the Vicinity, from 1805 to 1827*) accompanied by a large-format volume of drawings. He also produced a guide for travellers of the period entitled *Tableau de l'Égypte, de la Nubie, et des lieux circonvoisins: ou l'itinéraire à l'usage des Voyageurs, etc.* (*Scenes of Egypt, Nubia and Places in the Vicinity: an Itinerary for the Use of Travellers, etc.*).

Rifaud died in 1845, and, although the antiquities he collected were mainly concentrated in the Drovetti collections in Turin and Paris, others were acquired by several leading European museums. His name will always be preserved for posterity because it is inscribed on four large statues, three of which are in the Museo Egizio in Turin, and one in the Staatliche Sammlung Ägyptischer Kunst in Munich.

140–141 (below) Rifaud's greatest skill as an artist was in depicting the landscapes and picturesque villages on the banks of the Nile, such as this one in Upper Egypt.

141 (below right) The flora and fauna of Egypt also attracted Rifaud's attention. His talent in this area is apparent in these drawings, one of an aquatic plant belonging to the family Liliaceae, and the other of a shrub, common in the Egyptian deserts.

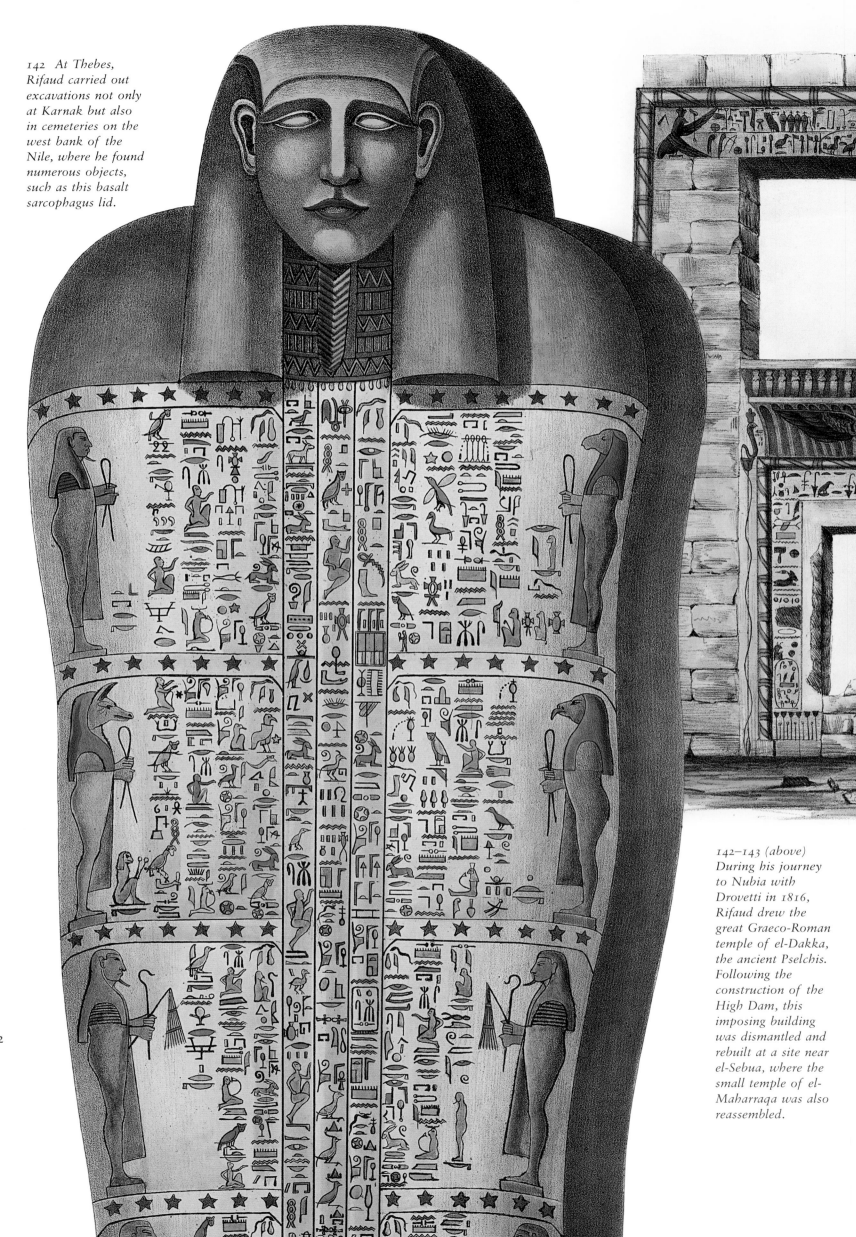

142 At Thebes, Rifaud carried out excavations not only at Karnak but also in cemeteries on the west bank of the Nile, where he found numerous objects, such as this basalt sarcophagus lid.

142–143 (above) During his journey to Nubia with Drovetti in 1816, Rifaud drew the great Graeco-Roman temple of el-Dakka, the ancient Pselchis. Following the construction of the High Dam, this imposing building was dismantled and rebuilt at a site near el-Sebua, where the small temple of el-Maharraqa was also reassembled.

143 (right) In the centre of this granite triad is Ramesses I, with the god Amun on the left and the goddess Mut on the right. It was discovered by Rifaud in the eastern part of the temple of Amun at Karnak. Rifaud found many magnificent statues at this site, in particular one of Ramesses II – now the most famous exhibit in the Museo Egizio in Turin.

144–145 *A view of the town of Tanta in the Delta, with its tower-houses dominated by two lofty minarets, as painted by Rifaud in his typical landscape style.*

144 (opposite below) and 145 (right) In his portraits of the people of Egypt, Rifaud reveals an almost ethnographic interest. Here an Arab woman sits under a tent and a boy crushes linseed.

144–145 (centre) The pyramid of Amenemhet III at Hawara in the Faiyum was only systematically explored in 1843

by the German archaeologist Richard Lepsius. Its enormous funerary temple was called 'the Labyrinth' by Classical authors.

Henry Salt

The pictures reproduced in this section are taken from Twenty-four Views Taken in St Helena, the Cape, India, Ceylon, Abyssinia and Egypt, by Henry Salt (London, 1809).

146 (left) Henry Salt, an artist, traveller and diplomat, portrayed here by J.J. Halls, was appointed British Consul-General in Egypt in 1816, with instructions to build up a collection of antiquities for the British Museum. Drovetti's main rival in the 'war of the consuls', Salt hired the Paduan adventurer Giovanni Battista Belzoni as his main agent, as well as a Greek, Giovanni d'Athanasi, known as Yanni.

Henry Salt (1780–1827) arrived in Egypt as British Consul-General in 1816; he had become a diplomat almost by chance at the age of thirty-six. Trained as a professional artist, he was appointed secretary to the English collector George Annesley, Earl of Mountnorris, Viscount Valentia, in 1802. He accompanied Valentia on two long journeys that took him to the Indies, Abyssinia and Egypt. Salt published a detailed description of these journeys, under the title *Account of a Voyage to Abyssinia and Travels into the Interior of the Country... in the Years 1809–1810*, and a collection of drawings entitled *Twenty-four Views Taken in St Helena, the Cape, India, Ceylon, Abyssinia and Egypt*.

On his appointment as Consul-General, Salt was instructed to assemble a collection of antiquities to send back to the British Museum. He devoted himself to this task with enormous zeal, although he was hindered in every possible way by Drovetti, who, having been dismissed from his official post, now had the time personally to supervise the search for antiquities around the country. Drovetti had great advantages over his British rival because of his thorough knowledge of Egypt, where he had been living for many years by this time, and also thanks to his close

friendship with the Pasha, Muhammad Ali. But Salt was not easily discouraged and, resorting to the same methods as his rival, he surrounded himself with agents who would stop at nothing. The year he arrived in Cairo he had the good fortune to meet both Giovanni Battista Belzoni, an extraordinary individual who immediately became his main agent, and Giovanni d'Athanasi, a Greek known as Yanni, who worked for him in the Thebes area from 1817 to 1827.

Thanks to his assistants, Salt was able to build up his first important collection in just two years. This was sold to the British Museum for the sum of two thousand pounds, and was then followed by another, more important, collection, accumulated between 1819 and 1824, comprising no fewer than 4,014 objects. After being rejected by the British Museum because it was considered too expensive, this second collection was sold to the King of France, Charles X, for ten thousand pounds, and helped to enlarge the impressive collections of the Louvre.

Salt also managed to assemble a third collection, containing 1,083 objects. It was sold by auction, largely to the British Museum, in 1835, eight years after his death near Alexandria in 1827.

146–147 (left) Before being appointed to his Egyptian post, Salt travelled to the East with Viscount Valentia, whose book Voyages and Travels to India Ceylon, the Red Sea, Abyssinia and Egypt in the Years 1802–1806 *he illustrated. His skill is evident in this view of the pyramids and the city of Cairo.*

146–147 (above) In this panoramic view, Salt depicted the mosques of Cairo, the architecture of which particularly fascinated him. In the foreground is the imposing mosque of Sultan Hassan; on the right stands the smaller mosque of al-Mahmudiyyah.

148 (below) The comte de Forbin was a talented artist, as seen in his illustrated account of his travels, to which was added a volume containing seventy-eight large-format plates. His drawings of the Holy Land and Egypt include many depictions of the way of the life of the inhabitants. Here, with fresh realism, the artist has portrayed a group of people at rest.

The story of William John Bankes (1786–1855) is closely linked to that of Henry Salt. A descendant of a rich aristocratic family, Bankes had a substantial personal fortune; he was also a friend of Lord Byron, aide-de-camp of the Duke of Wellington and a seasoned traveller. He was greatly attracted by the antiquities of Egypt and, in 1815, made his first journey to Nubia with Giovanni Finati. Finati was an adventurer from Ferrara, in Italy, who had enlisted in Muhammad Ali's army after deserting from the French, and now worked as a guide and interpreter for Western travellers.

It was during this first journey that Bankes discovered an important obelisk on the island of Philae. He later entrusted the

William John Bankes
and the comte Louis de Forbin

The pictures reproduced in this section are taken from Voyage dans le Levant en 1817 et 1818, by Louis de Forbin (Paris, 1819).

difficult task of removing it to the only person who was able to get the monolith past the First Cataract – Giovanni Battista Belzoni. Subsequently, in 1818 and 1819, Bankes returned to Nubia, this time with Henry Salt and Belzoni, staying for several months at Thebes with the artists Alessandro Ricci and Linant de Bellefonds.

148 (above) Seen here in Oriental dress in a portrait by Maxim Gauci, William John Bankes was a great traveller and antiquarian. He undertook two journeys to Upper Egypt and Nubia, during which he discovered the so-called Table of Kings in the temple of Ramesses II at Abydos. Bankes also entrusted Belzoni with the task of removing the obelisk that stood in front of the temple of Isis on the island of Philae. Belzoni achieved this difficult task and the monument was successfully re-erected on Bankes' estate at Kingston Lacy, in Dorset, England.

148–149 De Forbin wrote of the obelisk of Alexandria: 'The British have vainly attempted to remove the obelisk lying on the ground the base of which is visible next to the one still standing.'

149 (right) During his journey to Upper Egypt, de Forbin stopped at Beni Suef, where he admired the 'alma', the name given to the girls who performed in public, dancing or playing musical instruments.

Bankes was also responsible for the discovery of the famous Table of Kings in the temple of Ramesses II at Abydos (another similar list was found in the nearby temple of Seti I, also at Abydos) on which the names of the principal kings of Egypt were listed. It was later acquired for the collection of the French Consul, Jean François Mimaut, Drovetti's successor in Cairo, and was then sold to the British Museum, where it can still be seen today.

Bankes not only wrote two important essays entitled *Travels in the East* and *The Geometrical Elevation of an Obelisk... from the Island of Philae, ...First Discovered by W.J.B.*, but he also helped his friend and guide Finati to write his autobiography – *The Life and Adventures of Giovanni Finati* – which he published in London at his own expense in 1830.

Just as Bankes had been aided by Henry Salt in his search for antiquities, Louis Nicolas Philippe Auguste comte de Forbin (1777–1841) was helped by Bernardino Drovetti. De Forbin was an artist and great traveller. He was appointed director-general of the museums of France and in 1818 he arrived in Egypt, with the aim of obtaining antiquities for the Louvre.

In the course of his first journey – an account of which he published in a book, *Voyage dans le Levant en 1817 et 1818* (*Journey to the Levant in 1817 and 1818*), illustrated with his own splendid drawings

– de Forbin also visited Greece, Syria and Palestine, as he stated in the dedication of his book to the King of France:

Sire, Your Majesty has allowed me to visit the ruins of Athens, Syria, the cradle of the Christian religion, and Egypt.... Palestine preserves the memory of St Louis, and the name of your illustrious forefathers still protects Bethlehem, Mount Tabor and the Holy Sepulchre. Everywhere the traveller is reassured by the sight of the coat of arms with the fleurs-de-lis [the emblem of France] that recalls the noblest ideals of glory and justice. In the victors at Heliopolis, Egypt has recognized the sons of those Frenchmen who made the Sultans tremble.

De Forbin arrived in Egypt overland from Palestine and, after passing through northern Sinai, reached Damietta on the Nile Delta, where he boarded a boat heading for Cairo on 22 December 1817. During his stay in Cairo, de Forbin visited not only the Islamic monuments of the capital but also, like all the other visitors to Egypt, the pyramids of Giza, which made a deep impression on him.

On 13 January 1818 de Forbin left Cairo for Upper Egypt, arriving at Luxor on 28 January. He began systematically to explore the ruins of the ancient city of Thebes, meeting Henry Salt in the Valley of the Kings, where, a few months earlier, Belzoni had discovered the tombs of Ramesses I, Seti I and Prince Montuherkhepshef. De Forbin noted with a touch of envy that the British, Salt in particular, were now firmly established in the area. Indeed, as he wrote in his diary:

A number of presents, and a yet more profuse distribution of money had overpowered the barren affection of the Arabs and all [Salt's]

enterprises among them had succeeded in an amicable and wonderful manner.

De Forbin met the naturalist Frédéric Cailliaud at Thebes. Cailliaud was returning from an expedition to the Arabian Desert – where he claimed to have found the pharaohs' emerald mines and the ruins of the ancient city of Berenice. Also at Thebes were two of Drovetti's agents: Jean Jacques Rifaud, 'a Marseillais, small in stature, but bold, enterprising and choleric; occasionally beating the Arabs who had neither leisure nor taste to comprehend the Provençal tongue', and the French Mameluke called Yussef, alias Joseph Rosignani.

De Forbin had intended to sail further up the Nile to the First Cataract, but decided to abandon the idea and return to Cairo earlier than planned. He was greatly disconcerted by the presence of British travellers and tourists – particularly Lord Belmore, who had ventured as far as the Second Cataract and had accumulated a sizeable collection of antiquities – as well as by

'an English waiting-woman, in rose-coloured spencer, a parasol in her hand, crossing me, at almost every turn' as he wandered around the ruins of Luxor.

After visiting the temple of Dendera, de Forbin returned to Cairo, where he stayed for a few more days, managing to acquire a cross-section of the pyramid of Khafre, the entrance to which had only just been discovered by Belzoni. De Forbin was the first to publish this, before even Belzoni, thus arousing the Italian's anger. Belzoni accused him of wanting to take credit for the discovery, ignoring the fact that de Forbin had clearly written, in a note on the drawing, that he was simply publishing what Belzoni himself had discovered. From Cairo de Forbin sailed down the Nile to Alexandria, where he was a guest of Drovetti. Here he had the opportunity to admire what remained of the second collection (most of which had already been shipped to Europe), and was received a number of times by Muhammad Ali, of whom he made a portrait before leaving to return to France.

150

*150 (opposite above)
De Forbin was the
first to publish this
cross-section of the
pyramid of Khafre,
which was only
possible because
Belzoni had
discovered its
entrance. Belzoni,
then unjustly accused
the Frenchman of
taking credit for the
discovery. In reality,
de Forbin noted on
the drawing that it
was only thanks to
Belzoni's discovery
that he had been
able to publish it.*

*150 (opposite below)
Like many other
travellers in the
nineteenth century,
de Forbin called
the Ramesseum
the 'Memnonium',
describing it as
'a labyrinth of
courtyards,
sanctuaries and
columns'.*

*151 De Forbin's
drawing of Karnak
depicts the columns
of the hypostyle hall
and, in the
foreground, the
courtyard of the
third pylon with the
tall obelisk of
Thutmose I.*

CARTE
DE L'OASIS DE
et des Routes qui y con
Comprenant la Côte de la Méditerranée en
et la position de la Petite
Dressée d'après l'Itinéraire e
et d'après les relations et les observations de
PAR M. JOMARD membre a
Septembre 182

FRÉDÉRIC CAILLIAUD

IN SEARCH OF THE PHARAOHS' EMERALDS

152 (above) Frédéric Cailliaud was a naturalist, geologist and mineralogist. He was probably the most indefatigable of all the travellers in Egypt in the nineteenth century. Between 1816 and 1822 he undertook countless journeys up the Nile and he joined in Ismail Pasha's military expedition to the Sudan, during which he ascended the Blue Nile. On 25 April 1821, he discovered the remains of Meroë, the ancient capital of a vast Nubian empire. Cailliaud also explored both the Arabian and Libyan Deserts, venturing as far as the oasis of Siwa.

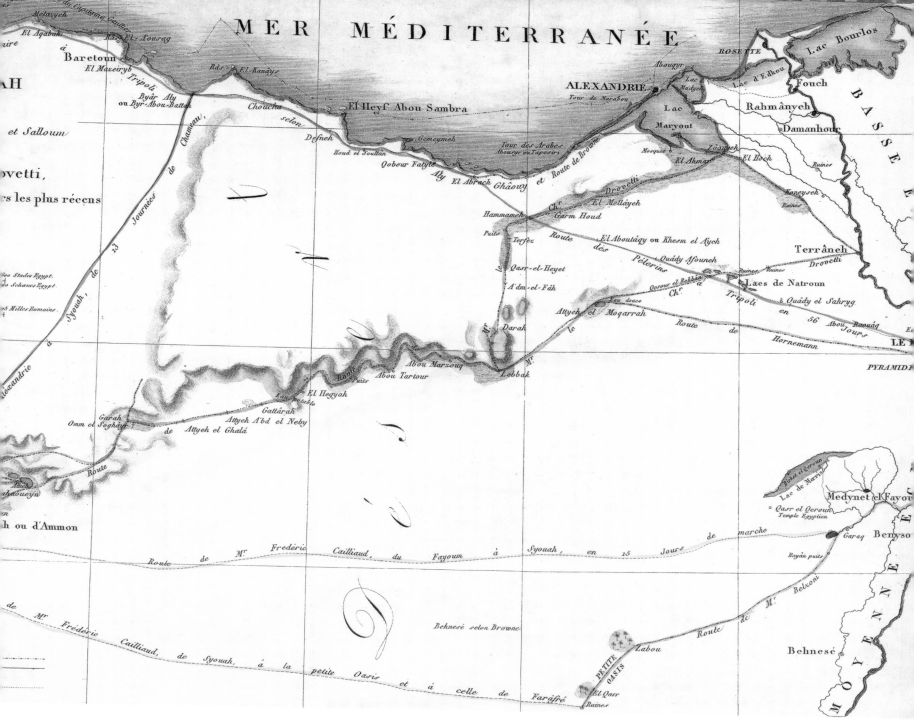

MER MÉDITERRANÉE

(map labels, partial): El Agabah · Baretoun · El Mazeiryb · Tripoli · Byâr Aly ou Byr Abou-Battas · Chouch selon · Choman · Journées de 13 · Syouah de 12 · El Heyf Abou Sambra · Defneh · Gemeymeh · Houd el Soultan · Qobour Fatyfe · Aly El Abrach Ghâovy · Hammameh · Chr. Garm Houd · Puits · Terfex · Route des Pélerins · El Aboutâgy ou Khesm el Aych · Quâdy Afouneh · Les Qasr-el-Heyet · A'dm-el-Fâh · Mr Darah · Abou Marzouq · Lebbak · Abou Tartour · Route Puits · Eau potable · El Hegyah · Gattârah · Attyeh A'bd el Neby · Attyeh el Ghalâ · Omm el Soghâyr · Garah · de · Route · ou d'Ammon · Route de Mr Frédéric Cailliaud, du Fayoum à Syouah, en 15 Jours de marche · Route de Mr Frédéric Cailliaud, de Syouah, à la petite Oasis et à celle de Farâfré · Behnesé selon Browne · PETITE OASIS · Labou · El Qasr · Ruines · ALEXANDRIE · Tour de Marabou · Aboukyr · Lac Madyeh · Lac Maryout · Tour des Arabes Aboukyr ou Taposiri · Mosquée · Zâouyeh · El Ahma · El Hoch · Drovetti · El Mellâyeh · El Aboutâgy · Qoseur el Rohbân · Chr. · Attyeh el Moqarrah · Eau douce · Tripoli · Route de Hornemann · ROSETTE · Lac Bourlos · Lac d'Edkou · Fouch · Rahmânyeh · Damanhour · Terrâneh · Drovetti · Koneysch · Ruines · Quâdy el Sahryg · en 56 Abou Raouâg Jours · Lacs de Natroun · BASSE · PYRAMIDE · Birket el Qeroun · Lac de Marxux · Qasr el Qeroun Temple Egyptien · Medynet el Fayou · Garaq · Benyso · Rayân puits · Belzoni · Behnesé · MOYENNE

At the end of August 1814, Frédéric Cailliaud (1787–1869) set sail from Sicily for Constantinople in a small boat, the *Esperance*, together with a former official in Murat's army. Cailliaud, a mineralogist born in Nantes, had left France for Italy with the intention of visiting Rome and Pompeii, and, above all, to study the rocks and minerals of Vesuvius and Etna. After staying there for more than a year, however, he decided to leave the country because the international situation meant it was no longer safe there for the French. After a difficult and eventful journey Cailliaud reached Constantinople, where he stayed for several months, managing to obtain a post at the Sultan's court as an expert in jewelry and precious stones.

During his stay in the capital of the Ottoman empire, Cailliaud decided to visit Egypt. He was attracted not only by the antiquities of the country, but also by the opportunity to find new rocks and minerals for his collection. In 1815 Cailliaud arrived in Alexandria, where he stayed for eight months, learning Arabic and studying the country's geography and history. Here he met Bernardino Drovetti,

152 (opposite below) Cailliaud was the fourth Western traveller to reach the oasis of Siwa. The previous one, Vincent Yves Boutin, had visited the oasis just a few months before Cailliaud, and had been robbed and imprisoned.

152–153 Cailliaud's journey to Siwa took place between November 1819 and March 1820, shortly before that of Drovetti, who accompanied the military expedition of Hassan Bey, which set out in February 1820. Cailliaud, who was accompanied by the midshipman Pierre Constant Letorzec, reached Siwa on 10 December 1819 from Beni Suef and the

Faiyum. On the return journey, the two Frenchmen also passed through the oases of Bahariya, Dakhla and Kharga, reaching the city of Asyut after a journey of about 1,800 kilometres.

153 (above) Cailliaud drew the remains of Graeco-Roman structures in the village of el-Qasr near the oasis of Bahariya, which was also known as the 'Small Oasis'.

153

who had been obliged to leave his post as the French Consul-General for political reasons, but who had maintained considerable power, had ample financial resources at his disposal and also continued to exercise a certain influence over Muhammad Ali.

After some initial suspicion, Drovetti proposed that he and Cailliaud should set out together on a journey to Upper Egypt, and the mineralogist agreed with enthusiasm. In late December 1815 Cailliaud arrived in Cairo, where Drovetti was making the necessary preparations for the expedition, and on 19 January 1816, the two Frenchmen began their journey up the Nile. The members of the expedition also included Drovetti's aide-de-campe, Joseph Rosignani who, together with Antonio Lebolo, another of the French consul's agents, had spent some time at Thebes searching for antiquities.

154–155 (above) The observations made by Cailliaud and Drovetti during their journeys in the Libyan Desert allowed Edmé François Jomard, the geographer and architect who had taken part in the Napoleonic expedition to Egypt and was co-ordinator of the Description de l'Égypte, to make an accurate map of the oasis of Kharga. This oasis was also known as 'the Oasis of Thebes' because it is located to the west of the ancient capital.

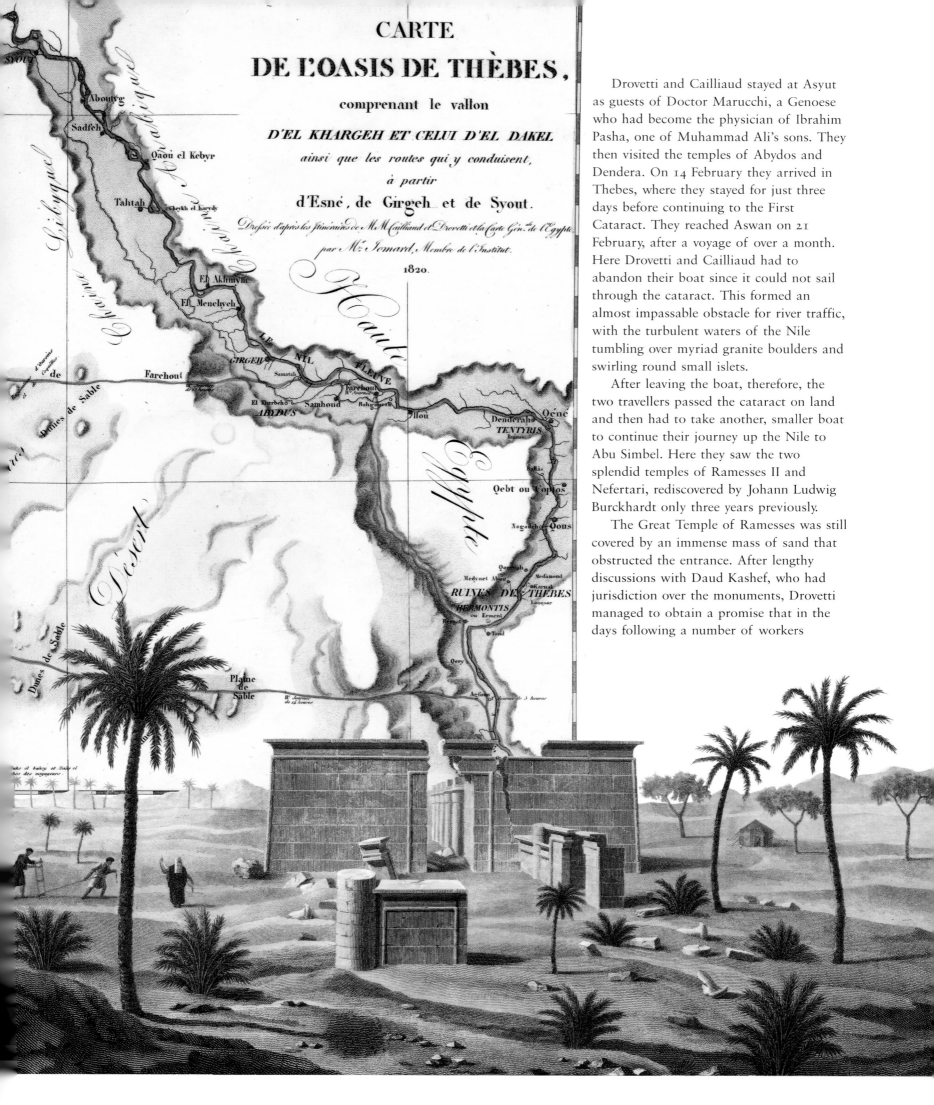

CARTE
DE L'OASIS DE THÈBES,
comprenant le vallon
D'EL KHARGEH ET CELUI D'EL DAKEL
ainsi que les routes qui y conduisent,
à partir
d'Esné, de Girgeh et de Syout.
Dressée d'après les itinéraires de MM. Cailliaud et Drovetti et la Carte Gén.le de l'Égypte,
par M.r Jomard, Membre de l'Institut.
1820.

Drovetti and Cailliaud stayed at Asyut as guests of Doctor Marucchi, a Genoese who had become the physician of Ibrahim Pasha, one of Muhammad Ali's sons. They then visited the temples of Abydos and Dendera. On 14 February they arrived in Thebes, where they stayed for just three days before continuing to the First Cataract. They reached Aswan on 21 February, after a voyage of over a month. Here Drovetti and Cailliaud had to abandon their boat since it could not sail through the cataract. This formed an almost impassable obstacle for river traffic, with the turbulent waters of the Nile tumbling over myriad granite boulders and swirling round small islets.

After leaving the boat, therefore, the two travellers passed the cataract on land and then had to take another, smaller boat to continue their journey up the Nile to Abu Simbel. Here they saw the two splendid temples of Ramesses II and Nefertari, rediscovered by Johann Ludwig Burckhardt only three years previously.

The Great Temple of Ramesses was still covered by an immense mass of sand that obstructed the entrance. After lengthy discussions with Daud Kashef, who had jurisdiction over the monuments, Drovetti managed to obtain a promise that in the days following a number of workers

154 (opposite below) The most important temple in the oasis of Kharga was that at Hibis, dedicated to Amun by the king of Persia, Darius I. Surrounded by a dense palm grove, it is still in a good state of preservation today. The Roman city of Hibis, from which the name of the temple was derived, was situated to the north. On his first journey, Cailliaud reached Kharga on 7 July 1818; he returned there again in March 1820, after visiting Siwa.

155 (above) The pylon of the temple of Hibis, which Cailliaud called 'the great temple of Kharga', was engulfed in sand, and a number of local people, visible on the left, are shown here attempting to remove it. On the right is the small tent used by the French traveller.

156 (top) In November 1816, during his first expedition to the Arabian Desert, Cailliaud discovered this rock-temple of Seti I on the track linking Edfu to the Red Sea, which he called the 'temple of Radasiyah'. When Belzoni visited it in September 1818, he called it 'the temple of Wadi el-Miah'.

156–157 (centre) Cailliaud published an account of his exploration of the Arabian Desert in his book Voyage à l'oasis de Thèbes... (Voyage to the Oasis of Thebes...), in which this, the first map of the region, appears.

sufficient for the task would be found to remove the sand blocking the temple's entrance.

Without waiting for the work to begin, Drovetti and Cailliaud decided to continue to Wadi Halfa, a few dozen miles further south near the Second Cataract. The journey lasted eight days, but, when the two travellers returned to Abu Simbel on 14 March, they were dismayed to find the temple exactly as they had left it the week before, with no sign of any attempt having been made to clear away the sand. Drovetti gave orders to begin the return journey, during which he stopped at all the temples

situated between Abu Simbel and the First Cataract, in many of which he engraved his name. After visiting the archaeological sites along the Nile and staying for a long period at Asyut, the two travellers arrived in Cairo in early August.

During this, his first journey, lasting nearly seven months, Cailliaud had learnt a great deal about the geography and monuments of Egypt. In addition, he had collected a large amount of scientific information concerning the rock formations of the regions crossed, and had made a considerable number of sketches and drawings, displaying admirable skill as

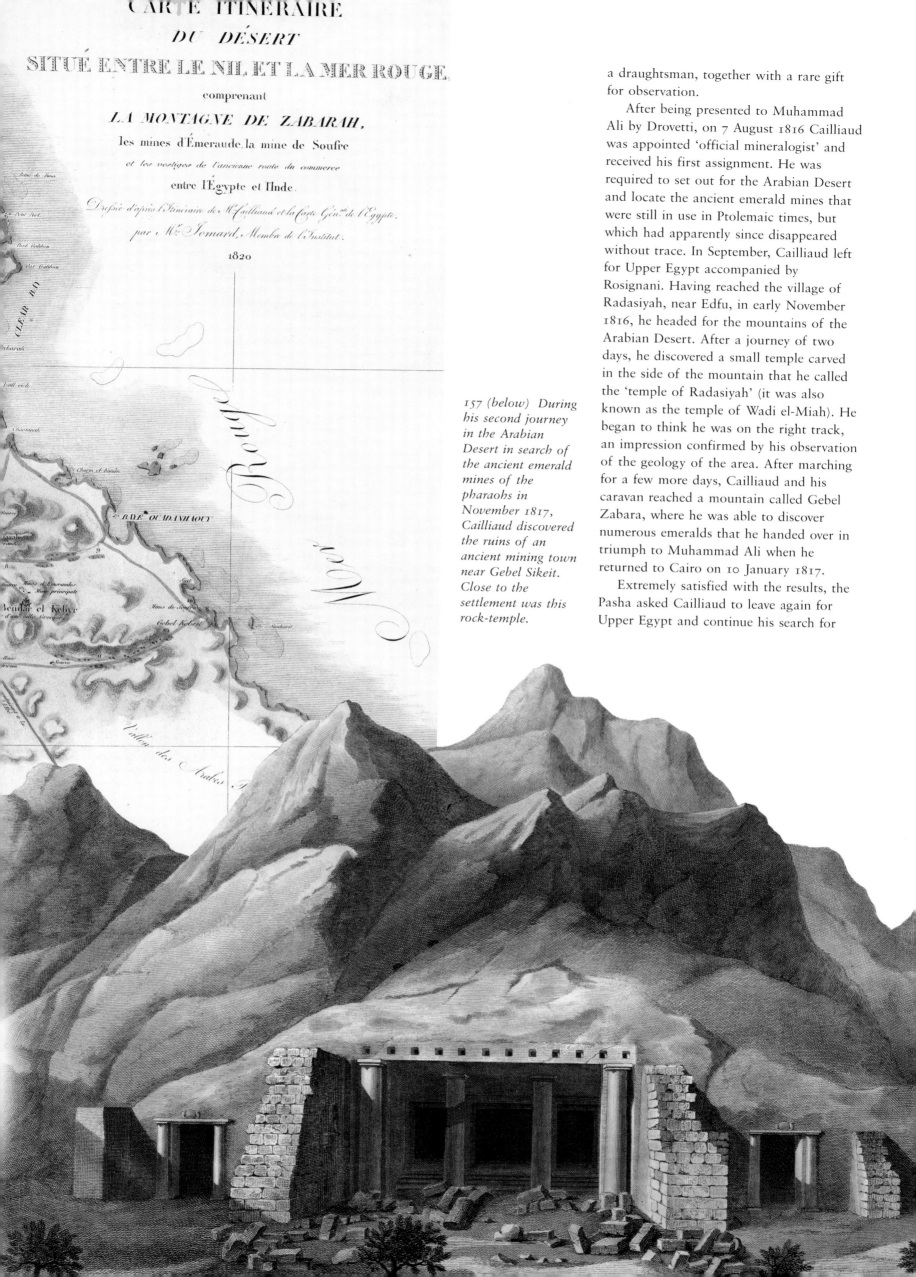

CARTE ITINÉRAIRE
DU DÉSERT
SITUÉ ENTRE LE NIL ET LA MER ROUGE,
comprenant
LA MONTAGNE DE ZABARAH,
les mines d'Émeraude, la mine de Soufre
et les vestiges de l'ancienne route du commerce
entre l'Égypte et l'Inde.

Dressée d'après l'Itinéraire de Mr Cailliaud et la Carte Génᵉ de l'Égypte,
par Mr Jomard, Membre de l'Institut.

1820

a draughtsman, together with a rare gift for observation.

After being presented to Muhammad Ali by Drovetti, on 7 August 1816 Cailliaud was appointed 'official mineralogist' and received his first assignment. He was required to set out for the Arabian Desert and locate the ancient emerald mines that were still in use in Ptolemaic times, but which had apparently since disappeared without trace. In September, Cailliaud left for Upper Egypt accompanied by Rosignani. Having reached the village of Radasiyah, near Edfu, in early November 1816, he headed for the mountains of the Arabian Desert. After a journey of two days, he discovered a small temple carved in the side of the mountain that he called the 'temple of Radasiyah' (it was also known as the temple of Wadi el-Miah). He began to think he was on the right track, an impression confirmed by his observation of the geology of the area. After marching for a few more days, Cailliaud and his caravan reached a mountain called Gebel Zabara, where he was able to discover numerous emeralds that he handed over in triumph to Muhammad Ali when he returned to Cairo on 10 January 1817.

Extremely satisfied with the results, the Pasha asked Cailliaud to leave again for Upper Egypt and continue his search for

157 (below) During his second journey in the Arabian Desert in search of the ancient emerald mines of the pharaohs in November 1817, Cailliaud discovered the ruins of an ancient mining town near Gebel Sikeit. Close to the settlement was this rock-temple.

archaeological remains and the emerald mines. Cailliaud was therefore obliged to undertake another journey, during which he revisited Middle Egypt and the Theban region to study the monuments and tombs he had seen all too briefly during the journey with Drovetti. He then left for a second – and much more important – expedition to the Arabian Desert, taking with him fifty miners and 120 camels.

In early November 1817 Cailliaud struck out into the desert, in the vicinity of Gebel Zabara, and arrived close to Gebel Sikeit. Here he discovered the ruins of a city 'as splendid as those of Pompeii', with numerous temples and over eight hundred dwellings, and, nearby, the most important of the ancient emerald mines.

In January 1818 Cailliaud returned to the Nile and reached Thebes, where he met various Europeans, including Belzoni, who had discovered the tombs of Ramesses I

and Seti I just a few months previously; de Forbin; the consul Henry Salt; and Lord and Lady Belmore, who were returning from a journey to the Second Cataract accompanied by Enegildo Frediani. Cailliaud was to meet the latter again a few years later, during Ismail Pasha's expedition to the Sudan.

A few days later, Cailliaud left for Cairo, and then continued down the Nile to Alexandria, where Muhammad Ali was resident at that time. He was able to hand over to the Pasha the numerous rough emeralds he had found during his mission and, what was much more important, to inform him of the discovery of the pharaoh's mines and the ruins of the ancient city of Sikeit, which he erroneously identified with the city of Berenice described by Classical authors.

In September of the same year, and following the same route, Belzoni

continued beyond Gebel Sikeit. He carried on in a southeasterly direction and reached the Red Sea coast near the promontory of Ras Banas, where he discovered the ruins of the Ptolemaic port and the true city of Berenice.

The indefatigable Frenchman set out once more shortly afterwards, on 26 March 1818, for Upper Egypt. He now intended to explore the Kharga Oasis, situated in the desert to the west of Thebes, which he reached on 8 April, after a gruelling march. In the following weeks Cailliaud visited the oasis and its numerous archaeological ruins, and, towards the middle of July returned to Esna, from where he descended the Nile to Cairo and Alexandria. Here he embarked on a ship sailing for France, after having organized all his notes, archaeological finds and natural history specimens intended for the museum in his native city of Nantes.

158 (left) In order to overcome the strong current at the southern end of the Second Cataract, Cailliaud's boat, which was about twenty metres long, had to be hauled up the river with ropes.

So perilous was this section of the Nile that Ismail Pasha's fleet, which had passed through the cataract two months previously, had lost about forty boats here. In the background, the ruins of the fortress of Semna East are visible; another fortress, Semna West (not visible in this drawing), stood on the west bank; both were built during the Middle Kingdom. The temple adjacent to the fortress of Semna East was built by Hatshepsut and Thutmose III; both it and the temple at Semna West were dismantled and were subsequently rebuilt at the museum in Khartoum.

159 (top) On 18 May 1822, after leaving Gebel Barkal, Cailliaud discovered this colossal granite statue, more than four metres high, at Tombos. Cailliaud has shown himself on the right, dressed in Oriental costume and wearing a large turban.

159 (centre) On 19 January 1821, during his journey up the Nile, Cailliaud reached the island of Argo, between the Third and Fourth Cataracts, where there were the remains of a temple built during the Twenty-Fifth Dynasty. Nearby there were two colossal granite statues, seven metres high, one of which, although complete, was broken into two parts.

159 (bottom) Towards the end of March 1822, Cailliaud visited the remains of Naqa, one of the settlements that grew up round Meroë. While he was there he made a plan of the site, as well as drawings of its principal monuments, such as the great east temple dedicated to Amun and the west temple, also known as 'the Lion Temple' because it was dedicated to the lion god Apedemak. Together with Amun, Apedemak was the main divinity in the Meroitic pantheon.

159

160–161 (top)
Cailliaud and
Letorzec left Cairo
for the Sudan on
3 October 1820 to
catch up with the
troops of Ismail
Pasha, who was
waging a campaign
to conquer that
country. The two
Frenchmen met up

with the Egyptian
army in February
1821, at the Fourth
Cataract near Nuri.
In April 1822, during
the return journey,
Cailliaud and
Letorzec, who were
travelling with
Linant de Bellefonds,
returned to the
vicinity of the

Fourth Cataract. At
the foot of Gebel
Barkal, the 'sacred
mountain', was
Napata, the principal
religious centre of
the Meroitic
kingdom. The two
Frenchmen studied
and drew the
numerous remains
of this site, with its

thirteen pyramids
and six temples,
including this one
dedicated to Hathor
and Bes, called the
Typhonium.
Cailliaud made
twenty-six drawings
of the monuments
of the region, where
he stayed for
seventeen days.

160 (above left) This
pyramid, drawn by
Cailliaud, was just to
the north of Meroë,
capital of the great
kingdom that, from
the fourth century BC
to the third century
AD, expanded to
cover the area
between the First
and Sixth Cataracts.

160 (above right)
At Gebel Barkal
the central temple
was dedicated to
the god Amun.

161 *During their journey up the Nile trying to catch up with Ismail's troops, Cailliaud and Letorzec reached the ruins of the temple of Amenhotep III at Soleb, downstream from the Third Cataract. Here they encountered numerous hippopotami.*

In Paris, where he arrived at the end of February 1819, Cailliaud was received with great ceremony. Edmé Jomard, the geographer and one of the members of the Commission des Arts et des Sciences accompanying Napoleon's expedition, declared 'What the scientists were unable to do in 1802, a young traveller managed to achieve fifteen years later…'.

Not content with this success, Cailliaud was already considering returning to Egypt, but this time on an official mission representing France. An opportunity arose quite soon and, on 15 September 1819, the mineralogist from Nantes, accompanied by his assistant, Pierre Constant Letorzec, was already on board a ship sailing for Egypt once more, but this time with excellent scientific equipment and adequate financial resources.

During his second visit to Egypt Cailliaud – who from then on was referred to in the official permits as Murad Effendi, while his assistant, Letorzec, was called Abdallah el–Faquir – concentrated above all on the exploration of the Libyan Desert. He set out on a long and difficult journey, from November 1819 to March 1820, that took him first of all to the oasis of Siwa. After overcoming the suspicion of the inhabitants, he managed to see – admittedly from a distance – the ruins of the temple of Jupiter Ammon. He then continued to the other oases in the Libyan Desert: Bahariya, Dakhla and Kharga, which he had already visited two years previously.

After returning to Cairo, Cailliaud participated in Ismail Pasha's expedition in the same year to the Sudan and Sennar, thwarting, thanks to the support of Muhammad Ali, a plot to exclude him, the nature of which has never been fully explained. The expedition, which included other Europeans such as Alessandro Ricci, Enegildo Frediani and Louis Linant de Bellefonds, was in the Dongola region, to the south of the Third Cataract, by the time Cailliaud and Letorzec were able to leave Cairo on 3 October.

During his journey up the Nile attempting to catch up with Ismail, Cailliaud visited the archaeological sites of Upper Nubia, including Gebel Barkal, between the Third and Fourth Cataracts. He was the first to identify the exact position of the ancient city of Meroë, with its numerous pyramids, which he reached on 25 April 1821.

On 27 September 1822, together with his travelling companion, Cailliaud returned to Cairo, from where he continued a few days later to Alexandria, the last stop on his long journey, before returning to France. After bidding farewell for the last time to Muhammad Ali and the French Consul Drovetti, who were both in this city at the time, Cailliaud set sail for France on 28 October, leaving Egypt for ever.

Cailliaud, who was then thirty-five years old, devoted the rest of his long life to the publication of his travel diaries and the study of the many finds that he had brought back with him. He took a special interest in the natural sciences and also in the museum of Nantes, of which he was appointed curator. He died in his native city in 1869.

The drawings reproduced in this section are from
Narrative of the Operations...in Egypt and Nubia...,
by Giovanni Battista Belzoni (London, 1820).

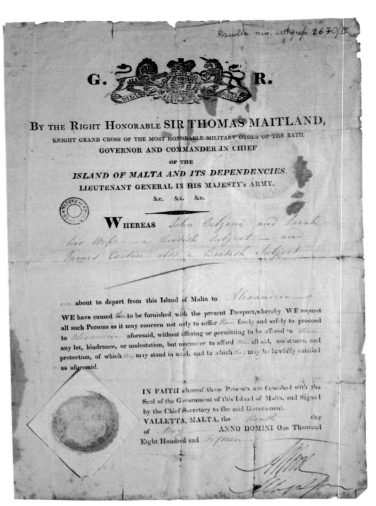

GIOVANNI BATTISTA BELZONI
THE GIANT OF THE NILE

162

*162 (top left)
In May 1815 the
governor of Malta,
Sir Thomas
Maitland, issued this
passport to Belzoni,
his wife Sarah and
their servant, James
Curtin. Belzoni
sailed from the
island to Alexandria,
where he landed on
9 June 1815.*

162 (opposite, above right) Giovanni Battista Belzoni was born in Padua, Italy, in 1778. When he was twenty-five years old he moved to England, where he lived until 1812. After visiting Spain, Portugal and Malta, he went to Egypt to demonstrate a hydraulic machine he had invented to the Pasha, Muhammad Ali. When his project was rejected, he devoted himself to the collection of antiquities in the service of the British Consul, Henry Salt. Among his many achievements are the clearing of the temple of Ramesses II at Abu Simbel, the discovery of the tombs of Ramesses I and Seti I in the Valley of the Kings, and the discovery of the entrance to the pyramid of Khafre at Giza.

In 1820, the famous London publisher John Murray brought out a book that was to cause a sensation. Entitled *Narrative of the Operations and Recent Discoveries within the Pyramids, Temples, Tombs, and Excavations in Egypt and Nubia; and of a Journey to the Coast of the Red Sea, in search of the Ancient Berenice; and another to the Oasis of Jupiter Ammon,* it was a quarto edition accompanied by an atlas containing forty-four watercolour drawings.

Immediately translated into several other languages, it was described a century later by Howard Carter, the discoverer of the tomb of Tutankhamun, as 'one of the most fascinating books in the whole of Egyptian literature'. In his own preface the author had to this say:

As I made my discoveries alone, I have been anxious to write my book by myself, though in so doing the reader will consider me, and with great propriety, guilty of temerity; but the public will perhaps gain in the fidelity of my narrative, what it loses in elegance. I am not an Englishman, but I prefer that my readers should receive from myself, as well as I am able to describe them, an account of my proceedings in Egypt, in Nubia, on the coast of the Red Sea, and in the Oasis; rather than run the risk of having my meaning misrepresented by another. If I am intelligible, it is all that I can expect. I shall state nothing but the plain matters of fact, as they occurred to me in those countries, in 1815-16-17-18 and 19. A description of the means I took in making my researches, the difficulties I had to encounter, and how I overcame them, will give a tolerably correct idea of the manners and customs of the people I had to deal with.

The author was Giovanni Battista Belzoni (1778–1823), whom George

162 (opposite below) An autograph letter by Belzoni.

162–163 Belzoni called the colossal bust of Ramesses II in the second courtyard of the Ramesseum at Thebes the 'Younger Memnon'. The recovery of this sculpture was the first difficult task he undertook in Egypt; it is now in the Egyptian sculpture gallery of the British Museum in London.

163

Bernard Depping, the translator of the French edition of the *Narrative*, described as 'a colossal man, built like Hercules, who touched the tops of doorways with his head'. Born in Padua, in northern Italy, on 5 November 1778, Giovanni Battista Bolzon – who later changed his name to Belzoni – began work as a barber in his father's shop. He soon realized he was not suited to this trade, and moved to Rome, then Paris and the Netherlands, apparently studying hydraulic mechanics along the way.

In 1803, together with his brother Francesco, he left for England, where he stayed for nine years, becoming a British citizen. In order to make a living he displayed the ornamental fountains he had invented at fairs, or, exploiting his magnificent physique, he participated in trials of strength at the Sadler's Wells Theatre, where he was known as the 'Patagonian Samson'. Belzoni's most

famous act was the 'human pyramid', in which the future explorer carried ten or more people round the stage. In this period he met and married a girl from Bristol, Sarah Banne.

While in Malta in 1815 he met up with Ishmael Gibraltar, an emissary of Muhammad Ali, who suggested that Belzoni should go to Egypt as an expert on hydraulics. At that time the Egyptian Pasha was carrying out a number of land-reclamation schemes and irrigation projects. After reaching Alexandria on 9 June, in the middle of an epidemic of plague, Belzoni had to spend a period in quarantine before he could hire a sailing boat to take him to Cairo. Here, after a long wait due to a number of tiresome setbacks, Belzoni was finally received by the Pasha, to whom he presented his project for a hydraulic machine which, he believed, could replace the traditional

water-wheel (called the *saqya*) for irrigating the fields. This immediately aroused the interest of Muhammad Ali, who ordered him to construct the machine and carry out a trial in his presence. Unfortunately, a minor accident – whether due to chance or design is uncertain – occurred during the demonstration and this, together with the unfavourable opinion of his counsellors, who were hostile to this innovation, persuaded Muhammad Ali to reject the offer of the new machine, leaving Belzoni without work.

Meanwhile, Belzoni had met many of the Europeans who thronged Cairo at the time, making friends with the famous Orientalist Ibrahim Ibn Abdallah, called 'the sheikh'. This was in fact Johann Ludwig Burckhardt, a Swiss from Lausanne, who had recently discovered the ruins of the city of Petra in present-day Jordan and the temples of Abu Simbel in

Nubia. Burckhardt put Belzoni in touch with Henry Salt, the new British Consul-General.

Burckhardt had previously attempted – without success – to transport a colossal granite bust to England. Weighing over seven tons, this fragmentary statue lay in a courtyard of the Memnonium (the name then given to the funerary temple of Ramesses II on the west bank at Thebes, known today as the Ramesseum). Belzoni declared that he was willing to recover the huge monolith; Salt accepted his offer, drawing up a formal contract, and also promised to purchase any antiquities that the Italian found.

On 30 June 1816 Belzoni, equipped with all the necessary permits, left for the ruins of the ancient city of Thebes, where the modern town of Luxor is now situated. He reached the site after a voyage of twenty-

164–165 Belzoni arrived at Abu Simbel for the first time in August 1816, shortly after Drovetti had visited the temples. As Drovetti had done before him, Belzoni also tried to remove the sand from the entrance, but was soon obliged to give up the attempt due to lack of time and shortage of food. It was only in following year, during his second journey, that Belzoni managed to complete the task and, on 1 August 1817, he entered the temple, where he was disappointed not to find any objects of interest.

165 (centre) Abu Simbel, known at the time as Ibsambul, had been discovered by the Swiss Orientalist Johann Ludwig Burckhardt on 22 March 1813. The second European traveller to visit the site was the English antiquarian William John Bankes, who arrived there in October 1815. This is Belzoni's drawing of the site.

165 (bottom) Belzoni's panoramic view of the ruins of the temple of Amun at Karnak may be regarded as one of his most outstanding drawings. He obtained this view by climbing on to the top of the first pylon. In the courtyard in front of the second pylon stands the large column that was part of a kiosk erected by Pharaoh Taharqa in the Twenty-Fifth Dynasty. Belzoni carried out excavations at Karnak, especially in the area of the temple of Mut, where he found numerous statues of the goddess Sekhmet.

two days and stayed on the west bank of the Nile, near the Ramesseum, firstly in a house in the nearby village of Qurna, then inside the temple itself. The colossal statue that he had committed himself to removing lay in the second courtyard. Given its size, it required several dozen men to move it, load it on to a sort of sledge and then push it as far as the river. Despite some problems in recruiting local labourers, Belzoni managed to muster about eighty men who, with great difficulty and despite the unbearable heat, managed in two weeks to get the bust as far as the river bank.

A suitable boat was not available, however, and so it was impossible to ship the statue immediately. Belzoni therefore decided to go on a journey to Nubia, as far as the Second Cataract. After visiting the temples of Esna, Edfu and Kom Ombo, the ruins of the ancient city of Syene at

Aswan and the island of Philae, Belzoni arrived at Abu Simbel. Three years earlier, his friend Burckhardt had discovered this site, with the stupendous rock-cut temple of Ramesses II, and the one dedicated to his principal queen, Nefertari, and the goddess Hathor next to it. Burckhardt had been unable to enter the monument because the façade, with the entrance in the centre, was half-buried by a great mound of sand and debris twenty metres high. Undaunted, Belzoni decided to attempt to remove this, but the task turned out to be more difficult than he had anticipated. A lack of time, food and money obliged Belzoni to give up the attempt after seven days of toil and return to Thebes, although before doing so he claimed possession, on the instructions of W.J. Bankes, of a perfectly preserved obelisk in front of the temple of Isis on the island of Philae. An inscription on this obelisk subsequently formed one of the

166

References.
1. 1st Tomb discovered.
2. 2nd do .... do .....
3. 3rd do .... do .....
4. 4th do .... do .....
5. 5th do .... do .....
6. Great Tomb of Samathis.
7. Two Mummy Pits discovered by G. Belzoni.
   All the others were never closed.
8. Tomb discovered by the French Scavans during their stay in Egypt.
The Six Tombs marked black were discovered & opened by G. Belzoni.

Valley of Biban Ell Malook

keys in the decipherment of hieroglyphs by Jean François Champollion.

At Thebes, while he was waiting for the colossal bust – known as the 'Younger Memnon' – to be loaded on to a boat, Belzoni began a number of excavations at the complex of Karnak in the area of the temple of Mut. He found no fewer than sixteen diorite statues representing the lion-headed goddess Sekhmet, six of which were complete, as well as a superb white quartzite statue of Seti II.

Belzoni also turned his attention to the Valley of the Kings and carried out a search in its western sector, known as the West Valley. Before long he discovered the tomb of Ay, the penultimate pharaoh of the Eighteenth Dynasty and Tutankhamun's successor. On the doorpost of its entrance he carved the inscription – now almost completely erased – 'Discovered by Belzoni - 1816'. Towards the middle of November Belzoni finally managed to load his precious finds on to a boat and he headed for Cairo. He did not remain in the city for long, however. In fact, he could not resist the urge to complete the task of clearing the sand from the façade of the Great Temple of Abu Simbel and enter its interior, and he left once more for Upper Egypt on 20 February 1817. After a long stay in Thebes – during which he managed to obtain more antiquities – Belzoni, accompanied by two British naval officers, Charles Irby and James Mangles, and a Ferrarese traveller, Giovanni Finati, reached Abu Simbel at the end of June. The work of removing the sand took the whole of July, and on this occasion, once again, the intense heat and the hired labourers caused great difficulties. But, on 1 August 1817, Belzoni finally entered the interior of the temple, where the temperature was around 44 degrees centigrade.

Although from an archaeological point of view the opening of the Abu Simbel temple was of immense significance, and certainly helped to increase Belzoni's

167 (left) This unpublished watercolour by Belzoni, painted on cardboard, formed part of the model of the tomb of Seti I and depicts one of the scenes on the walls of the burial chamber. The scene is of the second and third hours of the Book of Amduat.

167 (centre) Belzoni's preparatory drawing of a relief depicting a passage from the Book of Gates. It was in the hall of four pillars, which he called the antechamber, in the tomb of Seti I.

167 (below) This painting on cardboard was also part of the model of the tomb of Seti I. It is another scene in the hall of four pillars from the Book of Gates, and shows the nocturnal journey of the sun god Re on his celestial barque.

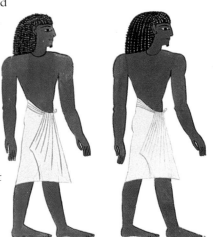

166 (opposite left) The alabaster sarcophagus of Seti I, empty and lacking its lid but in its original position, was the only valuable object that could be removed that Belzoni found in the king's tomb. The precious find, decorated with passages from the Book of Gates, was first offered to the British Museum, which turned it down because the price was too high. It was subsequently purchased for two thousand pounds by Sir John Soane, an architect and collector, who placed it in his house in London, now a museum, where it is still on display.

166–167 Belzoni drew a map of the Valley of the Kings, highlighting the tombs that he had discovered. The most important belong to: Ramesses I (KV16), Montuherkhepshef (KV19) and Ay (WV23), in the West Valley. Belzoni was also responsible for the discovery of another four tombs (KV21, KV30, KV31 and WV25) of lesser importance. The tomb of Seti I, still often known as 'Belzoni's tomb', was discovered on 18 October 1817.

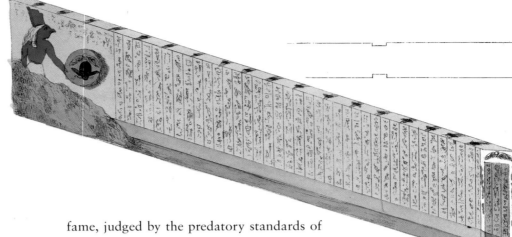

fame, judged by the predatory standards of the period it was somewhat disappointing. Despite the fabulous tales that were recounted locally about the magnificent treasures hidden away in its interior, in reality Belzoni found almost nothing that could be removed. He therefore decided to return to Thebes to continue his investigation of Biban el-Muluk, the Valley of the Kings.

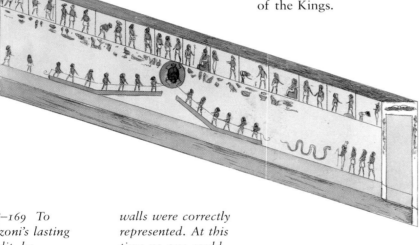

168–169 To Belzoni's lasting credit, he documented the tomb of Seti I meticulously. This was the first time a cross-section of a tomb had been made, in which the positions of all the reliefs decorating the

walls were correctly represented. At this time no one could read hieroglyphs and Belzoni, using the method proposed by the Englishman Thomas Young, attributed the tomb to a non-existent pharaoh called Psammis.

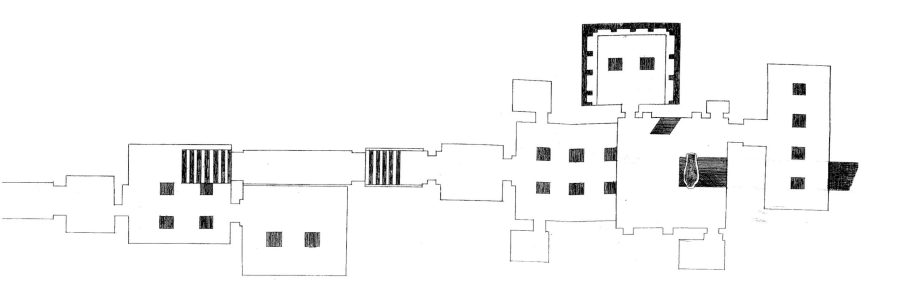

Belzoni's luck, and skill, held good and he first found the tomb of the prince Montuherkhepshef, followed by that of the pharaoh Ramesses I, and, a few days later, on 18 October 1817, he came across a new, extremely large tomb decorated with beautiful polychrome reliefs. Although the tomb had been completely despoiled – probably in antiquity like the other Theban royal tombs, with the exception of Tutankhamun's, found much later – a magnificent alabaster sarcophagus still stood in the burial chamber.

Champollion had not yet made his great breakthrough and no one could read hieroglyphs. Belzoni therefore attributed the tomb to a hypothetical pharaoh called Psammis or Psammuthis, although, in fact, it belonged to the pharaoh Seti I, father of Ramesses II. He completed the excavation of the tomb in about ten days (a task that would have taken years by modern techniques and standards) and, with the assistance of Alessandro Ricci, a physician and draughtsman from Sienna in Italy, Belzoni made over eight hundred casts of

169

170 A detail from one of Belzoni's drawings of the tomb of Seti I showing the vulture goddess Nekhbet with outspread wings. The royal cartouches are visible above the wings.

171 (opposite) In this splendid lithograph, Seti I is depicted before Hathor. The goddess holds the hand of the king in her left hand, while in her right hand she offers him a menat (a type of amulet). The relief was originally located on the right wall at the end of the staircase leading to the third corridor, while a similar relief was in the equivalent position on the left wall (see page 205). Both were removed by Champollion and Rosellini's Franco-Tuscan expedition in 1828–29, and are now in the Louvre and the Museo Archeologico in Florence.

170

the reliefs. Leaving Ricci in Thebes, Belzoni then returned to Cairo to dispatch some personal business. While there, he took the opportunity to pay another visit to the great pyramids of Giza, and decided to carry out excavations at the pyramid of Khafre, which, according to Herodotus, had no internal chambers.

A few days later, having hired a group of local workmen, Belzoni began his explorations. After an initial lack of success, on 2 March 1818 he discovered the entrance to the corridor leading into the interior of the pyramid, thus unlocking the mystery of the second pyramid of Giza. But to his great disappointment, when, after great effort, he finally managed to enter the burial chamber, an inscription in Arabic on one of the walls, probably

dating from the thirteenth century, revealed that the pyramid had already been violated six centuries previously. This previous event was completely undocumented, however, and Belzoni may rightly be considered the first true explorer of Khafre's pyramid. To commemorate the remarkable achievement, his admirers in Britain struck a medal bearing on one side the bust of Belzoni and on the other the pyramid of Khafre (called Chephren on the medal) and the inscription 'Opened by G. Belzoni March 2nd 1818'.

After returning to Thebes he completed the surveys and casts of the tomb of Seti I – later known also as 'Belzoni's tomb'. The Paduan adventurer then travelled to the Arabian Desert. His aim was now to search for emerald mines and the ruins of the

172 (centre) A drawing of the entrance discovered by Belzoni by which he gained access to the interior of the pyramid of Khafre. Inside, he came to the descending corridor leading from an upper entrance. The pyramid had two entrances placed one above the other, perhaps due to a modification of the original project: Belzoni used the upper one.

ancient city of Berenice, the port built by Ptolemy II Philadelphus, which Belzoni succeeded in discovering near the Ras Banas peninsula. After retrieving the obelisk of Philae, which he had laid claim to during his first journey, Belzoni left Thebes for the last time in January 1819, returning to Cairo with his precious treasures. But his Egyptian adventure was not yet over: a final journey awaited him. Leaving his wife in Cairo, he ventured into the Libyan

Desert – also known as the Western Desert – to seek the oasis of Siwa. Known in ancient times as the 'oasis of Jupiter Ammon', the oracle at the oasis had been consulted by Alexander the Great. Belzoni in fact reached the oasis of Bahariya, which no other Western traveller had yet visited. On his return from this journey, Belzoni and his wife embarked for Europe, leaving Egypt for good.

Belzoni's first stopover was Padua, where he paid his respects to his native city and offered the municipality – which had struck a medal to mark the occasion – two splendid diorite statues of the goddess Sekhmet, which are now displayed at the Museo degli Eremitani there.

172–173 When Belzoni entered it, the burial chamber of the pyramid of Khafre contained nothing but an empty sarcophagus with a few cattle bones, perhaps an offering. An inscription in Arabic revealed that the pyramid had been opened in the thirteenth century AD. On one of the walls Belzoni wrote his name and the date, 2 March 1818, still visible today.

172 (opposite below) Belzoni drew the first cross-section of the pyramid of Khafre, but was only able to publish it after his return to Europe in *1820. Meanwhile, the comte de Forbin included the drawing in his book Voyage dans le Levant, published in 1819, arousing the Italian's* *anger, despite the fact that the Frenchman had specifically stated that all the credit for the discovery should be given to Belzoni.*

173 (top) A medal was struck in Britain in Belzoni's honour to commemorate the feat of the opening of the pyramid of Khafre.

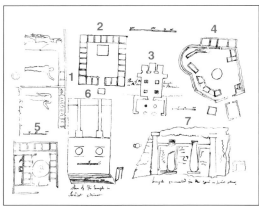

174 (left and below) Belzoni made these sketches during his expedition to the Arabian Desert in September and October 1818, recording those monuments that particularly attracted his attention: 1 reliefs in the temple at Berenice; 2 a plan of a caravanserai on the track to Berenice; 3 a plan of the temple of Wadi el-Miah on the route linking Edfu to the Red Sea; 4 a small Graeco-Roman fort on the road to Berenice; 5 a plan of the station of Bir Samut; 6 a plan of the rock-temple found at Wadi Sikeit; 7 a drawing of the façade of the rock-temple of Sikeit.

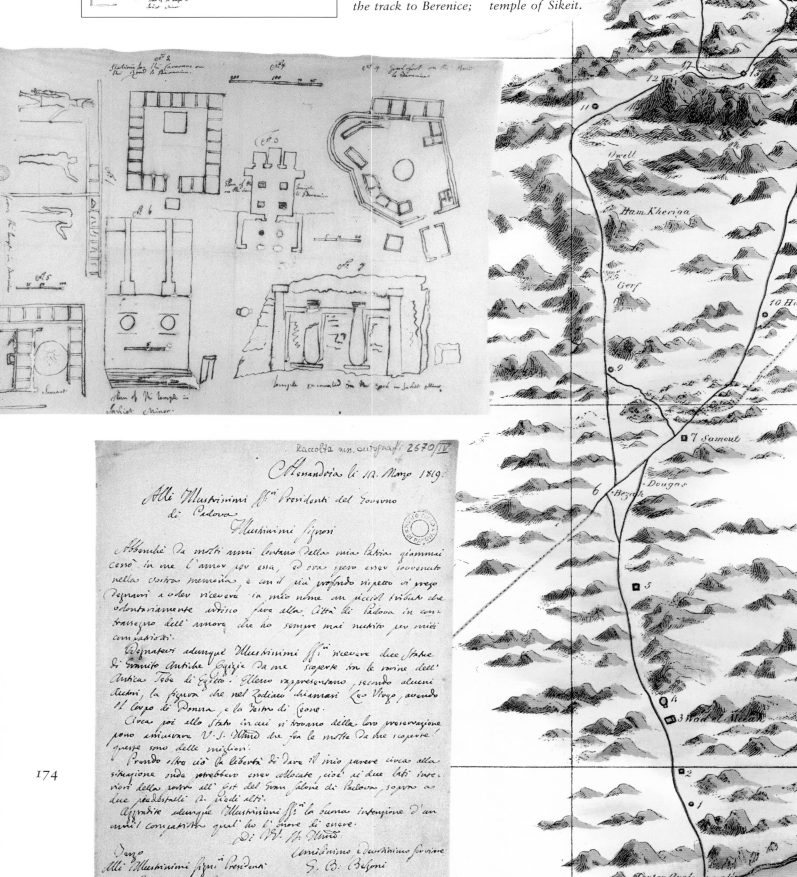

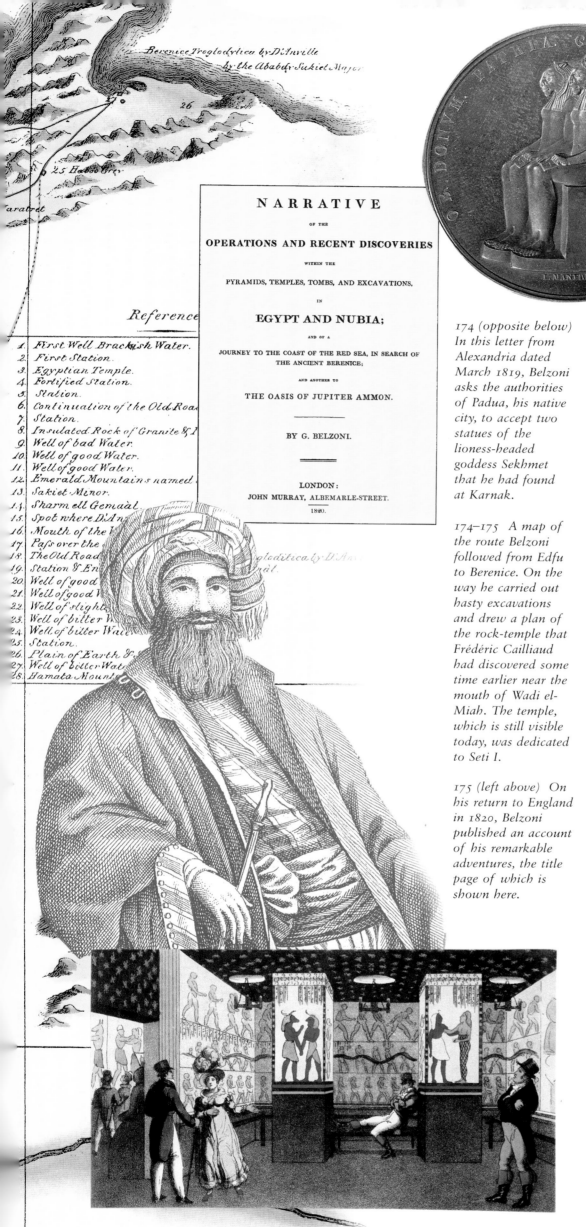

NARRATIVE

OF THE

OPERATIONS AND RECENT DISCOVERIES

WITHIN THE

PYRAMIDS, TEMPLES, TOMBS, AND EXCAVATIONS,

IN

EGYPT AND NUBIA;

AND OF A

JOURNEY TO THE COAST OF THE RED SEA, IN SEARCH OF
THE ANCIENT BERENICE;

AND ANOTHER TO

THE OASIS OF JUPITER AMMON.

BY G. BELZONI.

LONDON:
JOHN MURRAY, ALBEMARLE-STREET.
1820.

175 (left) The city of Padua struck this commemorative medal to celebrate Belzoni's gift of two statues of Sekhmet.

175 (centre left) This portrait of Belzoni in Arab costume is from the Italian edition of his book.

174 (opposite below) In this letter from Alexandria dated March 1819, Belzoni asks the authorities of Padua, his native city, to accept two statues of the lioness-headed goddess Sekhmet that he had found at Karnak.

174–175 A map of the route Belzoni followed from Edfu to Berenice. On the way he carried out hasty excavations and drew a plan of the rock-temple that Frédéric Cailliaud had discovered some time earlier near the mouth of Wadi el-Miah. The temple, which is still visible today, was dedicated to Seti I.

175 (left above) On his return to England in 1820, Belzoni published an account of his remarkable adventures, the title page of which is shown here.

After Padua, Belzoni returned to London. Here he mounted a splendid exhibition at the Egyptian Hall in Piccadilly, presenting to the public the antiquities he had collected in his four-year stay in Egypt. Included in the display were the drawings and casts of the tomb of Seti I, the two finest rooms of which were reconstructed. Gas lamps, still a novelty at that time, were employed for the illumination, their soft light recreating the atmosphere of the tombs. The exhibition was then transferred to Paris, at the very time when Champollion was writing his celebrated *Lettre à M. Dacier* in which he unveiled the mystery of the decipherment of hieroglyphs.

Belzoni died the following year, on 3 December 1823, in a small village near the mouth of the River Benin en route to Timbuktu. He had gone to Africa with the aim of discovering the source of the Niger. He was buried six feet beneath a large tree, but all trace of his grave was subsequently lost. In *Who Was Who in Egyptology*, published by the *Egypt Exploration Society*, the entry for Belzoni comments:

[Belzoni] cannot be judged by the standards of later excavators, such as Petrie, or even Mariette, but must be seen in the context of the period before decipherment [of hieroglyphs]; at the start of his career he was neither better nor worse than other contemporary figures, but he later evolved techniques for his work and acquired knowledge that raised him above the general level....

175 (left) For the exhibition that Belzoni staged in the Egyptian Hall in Piccadilly, London, two of the finest chambers in the tomb of Seti I were reconstructed, *including the hall with four pillars, which he called the antechamber. On the opening day, 28 April 1821, Belzoni unwrapped a mummy in front of a large audience.*

176 In 1820 a Prussian general, Baron Heinrich Carl Menu von Minutoli, was sent on a mission to Egypt by the government of his country. He headed a large expedition to the oasis of Siwa in the Libyan Desert in October 1820 and assembled a sizeable collection of antiquities. Most were lost, however, when the ship carrying them to Europe sank. In this painting of 1823 by Louis Faure, in the State Museum in Berlin, Minutoli is portrayed resting in his tent at the oasis of Siwa.

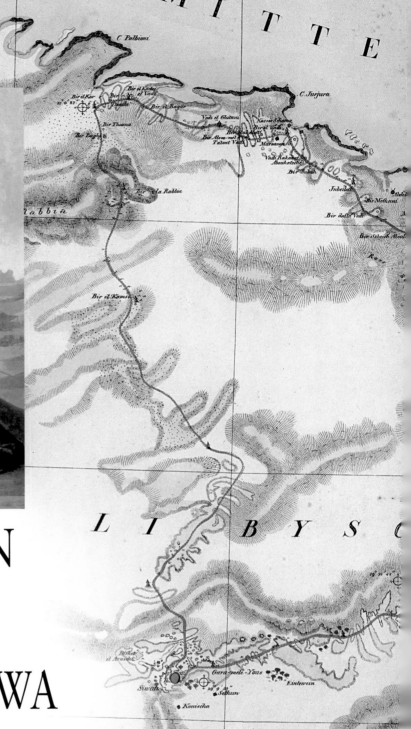

THE EXPEDITION OF BARON VON MINUTOLI TO THE OASIS OF SIWA

176 (left) Von Minutoli carried out excavations at the site of the Graeco-Roman city of Hermopolis Magna (now called el-Ashmunein) and at Saqqara, where the work was continued on his behalf by Girolamo Segato, who concentrated in particular on the Step Pyramid of Djoser.

176–177 Von Minutoli's map shows the route he took to the oasis of Siwa. He followed in the footsteps of other Europeans, most recently Frédéric Cailliaud and Bernardino Drovetti. The latter had accompanied the military expedition of Hassan Bey that in 1820 conquered Siwa on the orders of Muhammad Ali.

177 (right) The inhabitants of Siwa were not Muslim and spoke a local dialect deriving from Berber. Initially hostile to Western travellers, it was only after Hassan Bey's expedition that they moderated their warlike ways. Thus, von Minutoli, who arrived in Siwa some months after its conquest, could visit

The pictures reproduced in this section are from Reise zum Tempel des Jupiter Ammon in der Libyschen Wüste und nach Ober-Aegypten in den Jahren 1820 und 1821, by Heinrich Von Minutoli (Berlin, 1824).

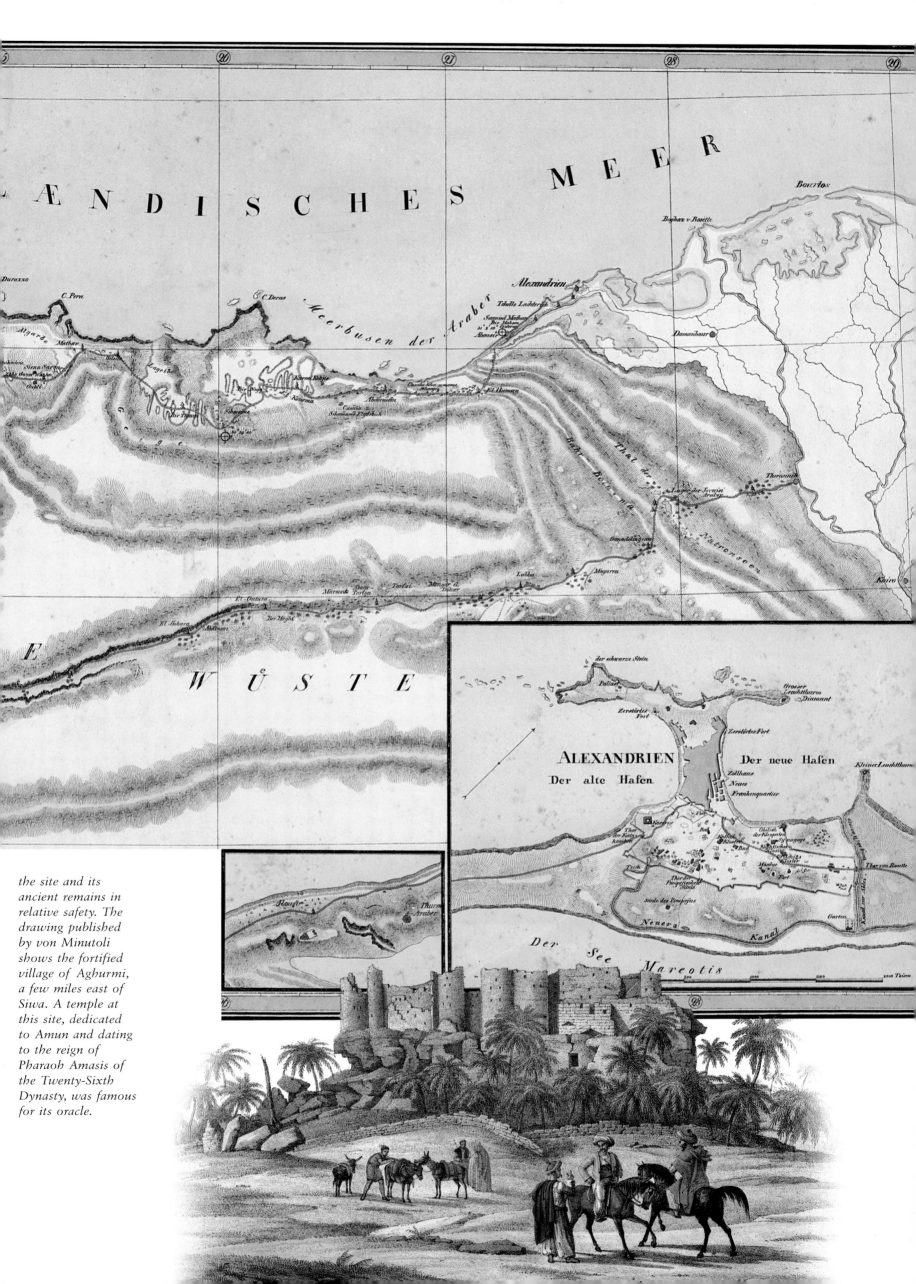

the site and its ancient remains in relative safety. The drawing published by von Minutoli shows the fortified village of Aghurmi, a few miles east of Siwa. A temple at this site, dedicated to Amun and dating to the reign of Pharaoh Amasis of the Twenty-Sixth Dynasty, was famous for its oracle.

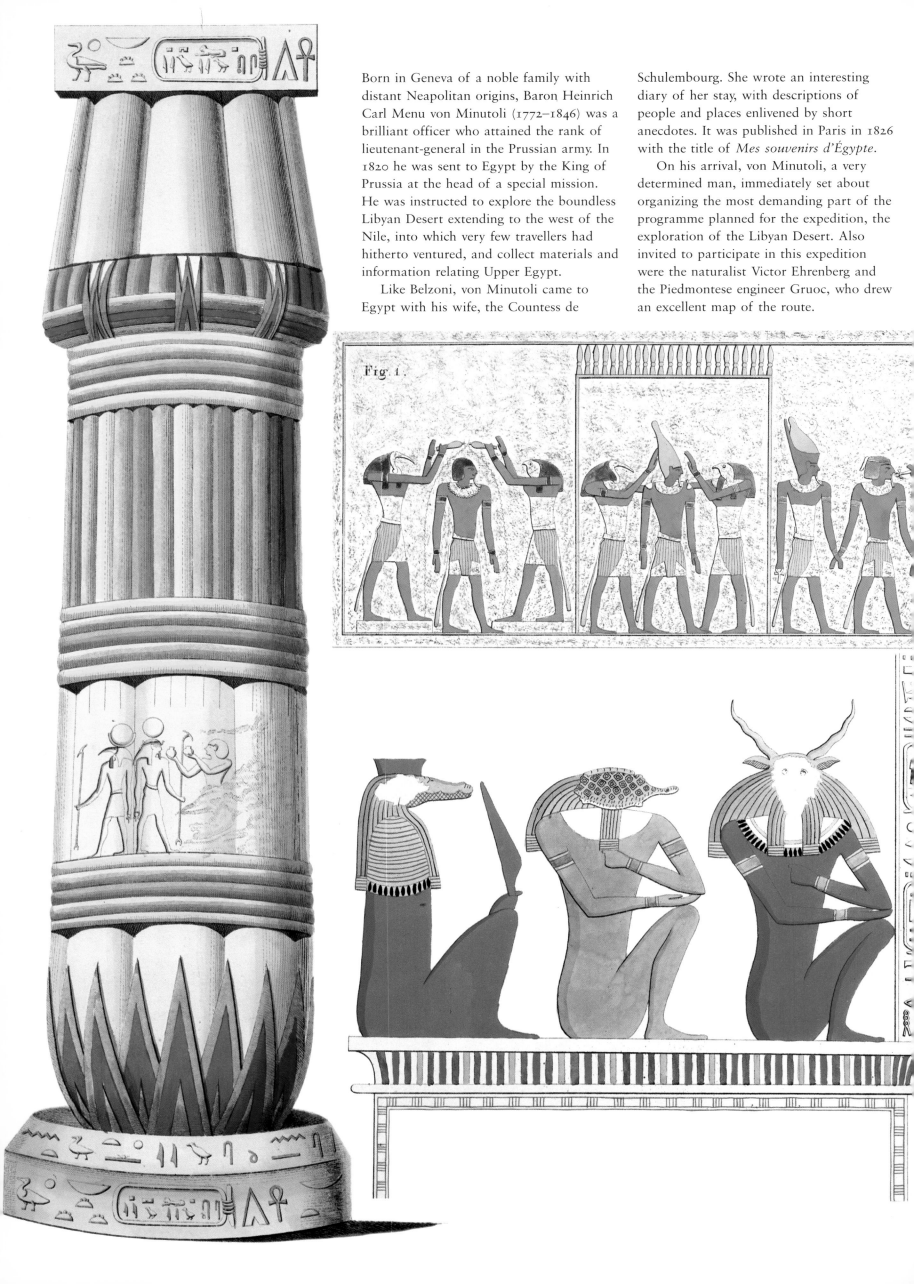

Born in Geneva of a noble family with distant Neapolitan origins, Baron Heinrich Carl Menu von Minutoli (1772–1846) was a brilliant officer who attained the rank of lieutenant-general in the Prussian army. In 1820 he was sent to Egypt by the King of Prussia at the head of a special mission. He was instructed to explore the boundless Libyan Desert extending to the west of the Nile, into which very few travellers had hitherto ventured, and collect materials and information relating Upper Egypt.

Like Belzoni, von Minutoli came to Egypt with his wife, the Countess de Schulembourg. She wrote an interesting diary of her stay, with descriptions of people and places enlivened by short anecdotes. It was published in Paris in 1826 with the title of *Mes souvenirs d'Égypte*.

On his arrival, von Minutoli, a very determined man, immediately set about organizing the most demanding part of the programme planned for the expedition, the exploration of the Libyan Desert. Also invited to participate in this expedition were the naturalist Victor Ehrenberg and the Piedmontese engineer Gruoc, who drew an excellent map of the route.

Fig. 1.

178 (opposite left)
This elegant papyriform column with a papyrus bud capital and painted decoration was once part of a temple dedicated to Thoth, dating from the reign of Philip Arrhidaeus. It stood among the ruins of Hermopolis Magna (modern el-Ashmunein), but nothing now remains of it.

178 (opposite right)
In the small chapel of Philip Arrhidaeus at Karnak reliefs depict the purification and coronation of the pharaoh. Below, three genii guard one of the gates of the kingdom of Osiris in one of the tombs discovered by Belzoni in the Valley of the Kings.

179 A deceased pharaoh holds the attributes of the god Osiris, a nekhakha (flail) and a heqa (sceptre), while the remains of an elaborate hemhem crown (three atef-crowns surmounted by sun disks) can be seen on his head.

179

After beginning excavations at Saqqara, von Minutoli set out for Siwa, known in antiquity as the 'oasis of Jupiter Ammon', on 5 October 1820. He took twenty days to reach the oasis, and was the fifth European to arrive there: he was preceded by an Englishman, William George Browne, who was the first to visit it in 1792; followed in turn by a German, Frederik Hornemann, in 1798; a Frenchman, Frédéric Cailliaud, in 1819; and the French consul, Bernardino Drovetti, in 1820.

Von Minutoli explored the oasis, making drawings and plans of the main monuments, before, on 12 November, he began his return journey. When he got back to Alexandria, however, he realized that the expedition drawings of Siwa were of poor quality and that many of the notes relating to the journey had been lost due to the sudden death of Gruoc. Thus von Minutoli charged Girolamo Segato, from Belluno in northern Italy, with the task of returning to Siwa to complete the documentation. Segato set out on this arduous journey, which took him nearly two months, in late September 1821.

Meanwhile, von Minutoli had decided to return to Europe and embarked on the Austrian ship *Cleopatra*. He took with him on board the objects he acquired in Egypt. Accumulated with the assistance of both Segato and Drovetti, this sizeable collection of ancient Egyptian antiquities filled no fewer than ninety cases.

Von Minutoli and his wife, together with their precious cargo of antiquities, arrived safely in Livorno after a voyage of

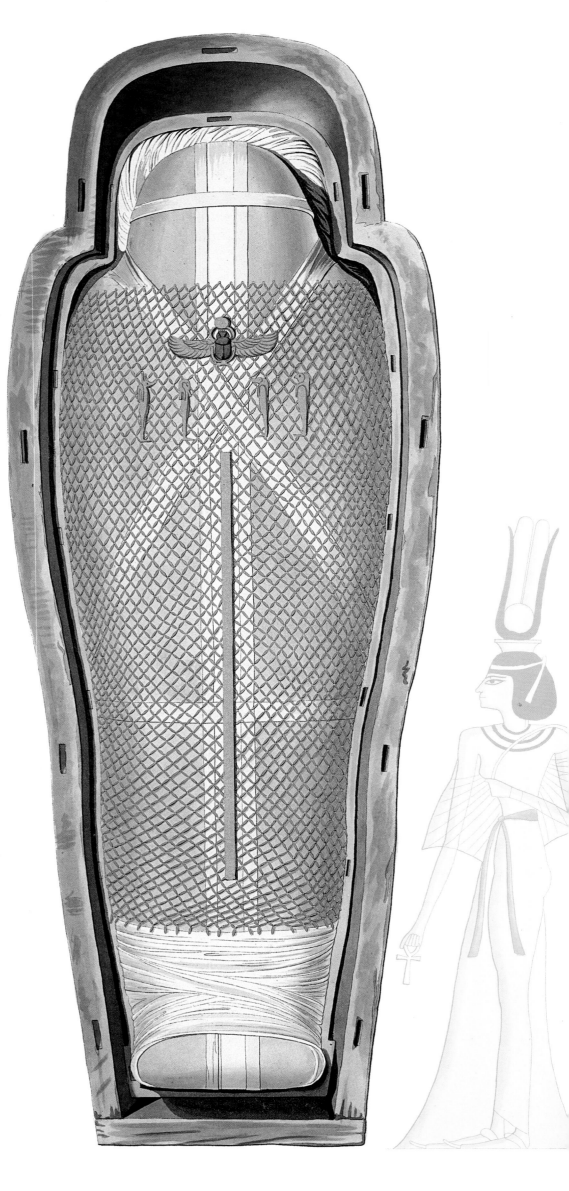

180 and 181 (opposite right) Among the ancient Egyptian artifacts collected by von Minutoli were numerous coffins and mummies. This anthropoid coffin, seen here in a drawing by a German artist, Dälhing, was given to the King of Prussia by the French collector, the comte James de Pourtalés-Gorgier. Inside the sarcophagus, the mummy was in a perfect state of preservation, still covered with a net of semiprecious stones intended to ensure its protection. Over the net were a number of amulets, representing a winged solar scarab and the four sons of Horus, the protective deities of the canopic jars containing the internal organs of the deceased. The drawing was published in von Minutoli's own account of his journey and was also reproduced by Girolamo Segato.

thirty-nine days. From here von Minutoli
travelled overland to Berlin, taking only
twenty cases with him. The largest and
heaviest ones continued their journey by
sea but never reached their destination
because the ship carrying them was
wrecked and all the antiquities, including
numerous sarcophagi and mummies, were
lost for ever.

In 1824 von Minutoli published a
monumental account of his journey,
entitled *Reise zum Tempel des Jupiter
Ammon in der Libyschen Wüste und nach
Ober-Aegypten…* (*Journey to the Temple
of Jupiter Ammon in the Libyan Desert
and to Upper Egypt*). It included an atlas
illustrated with 38 plates, containing a
total of 234 drawings, 41 of which were by
Segato, 54 by von Minutoli himself and 29
by the Siennese physician Alessandro Ricci,
who had accompanied Belzoni on his
journeys. Part of what survived of von
Minutoli's collection was sold in Paris; the
other part was assigned to the Berlin
Museum, which, on the orders of Frederick
William IV of Prussia, also acquired the
important collection of Giuseppe
Passalacqua, an antiquarian and collector
from Trieste, who was subsequently
appointed as curator of the museum.

*181 (below) Von
Minutoli's drawing
of a relief from the
Small Temple at Abu
Simbel depicting
Queen Nefertari
dressed in a long
tunic and holding
a sistrum in her left
hand. She is followed
by the goddess
Hathor, who is
wearing her
distinctive crown
with two feathers
and horns in the
form of a lyre
framing a solar disc.*

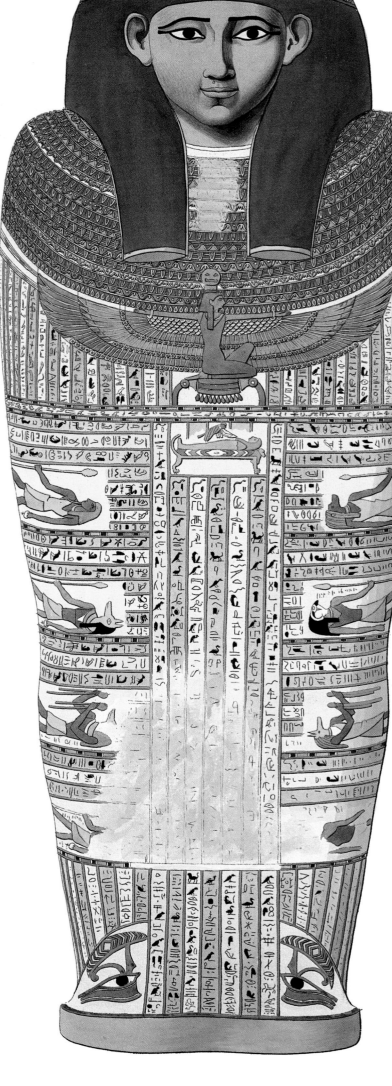

The pictures reproduced in this section are taken from Atlante del Basso e Alto Egitto, by Girolamo Segato (Florence, 1835).

Like many other travellers of his day, Girolamo Segato (1792–1836) came to Egypt almost by chance. This remarkable draughtsman, naturalist and chemist was born at Vedana, near Belluno, in Veneto (northern Italy), in 1792. Looking for work, Segato went to Venice, where he was presented to Annibale de Rossetti, who offered him a job in the large trading firm managed by his family in Cairo. So it was that in 1818 Segato sailed on the brigantine *Arpocrate* to Egypt, where he remained for five years, staying until 1823.

When Segato reached Cairo, the Paduan adventurer Giovanni Battista Belzoni had already carried out his remarkable exploits, but there is no record of them ever having met. Like his more famous countryman, Segato was immediately fascinated by the

GIROLAMO SEGATO: EXPLORING THE STEP PYRAMID OF DJOSER

182 (above) Girolamo Segato was a naturalist, draughtsman and traveller. He arrived in Egypt in 1818, where he worked as a map-maker for the Pasha and undertook adventurous journeys to the Nubian and Libyan Deserts. His most remarkable achievement was entering the Step Pyramid of Djoser at Saqqara in 1821.

182 (right) During his travels in Upper Egypt, Segato visited the temple of Hathor at Dendera, where he reworked drawings published both by Denon in his Voyage and also in the Description de l'Égypte.

*183 (above)
An excellent
cartographer, Segato
drew a plan of the
monuments at
Thebes, which
appeared in his atlas
published in 1837, a
year after his death.*

*183 (right) Segato's
fine drawing of a
Hathor-headed
column with brightly
coloured reliefs from
the temple of
Dendera is an almost
identical copy of
one published in the
fourth volume of
the Description de
l'Égypte.*

ancient and still largely unexplored world of the pharaohs. But he did not join in the general search for ancient artifacts and precious objects that at that time occupied most travellers, antiquarians and adventurers working on behalf of the European countries wanting to establish museums of Egyptian antiquities. Segato instead devoted himself – at least initially – to map-making. He received commissions from Muhammad Ali's son, Ismail Pasha, to draw maps and plans of the capital. Segato then extended his interests to the great monuments of ancient Egyptian civilization and, in 1819, went on his first journey to Upper Egypt.

In 1820, Segato had the opportunity to visit the rest of the country and the upper Nile Valley. Together with two other Italians, the traveller Enegildo Frediani and the engineer Lorenzo Masi, he joined the great military expedition to the Sudan. This had been set up by Muhammad Ali to subjugate the region and was led by his son Ismail Pasha. Preceding the expedition, Segato left Cairo on 6 May, reaching Aswan on 17 May. A month later he was at the Second Cataract. From here he set out alone across the desert after he had been excluded from the expedition, probably due to intrigues though the exact circumstances are not known.

In his solitary exploration of the Nubian Desert, Segato walked for forty days to reach a large settlement of the people who lived in this hot and inhospitable land. Calling it the 'kingdom of Chiollo', he described it in his notes, which, unfortunately, were later accidentally destroyed. After staying for a week in this area, Segato began the return journey. He first reached Wadi Halfa and then sailed back down the Nile, breaking his journey at the main archaeological sites en route.

With his sheets of paper, pencils, paints and, as a guide, a copy of Denon's *Voyage*, Segato made countless drawings,

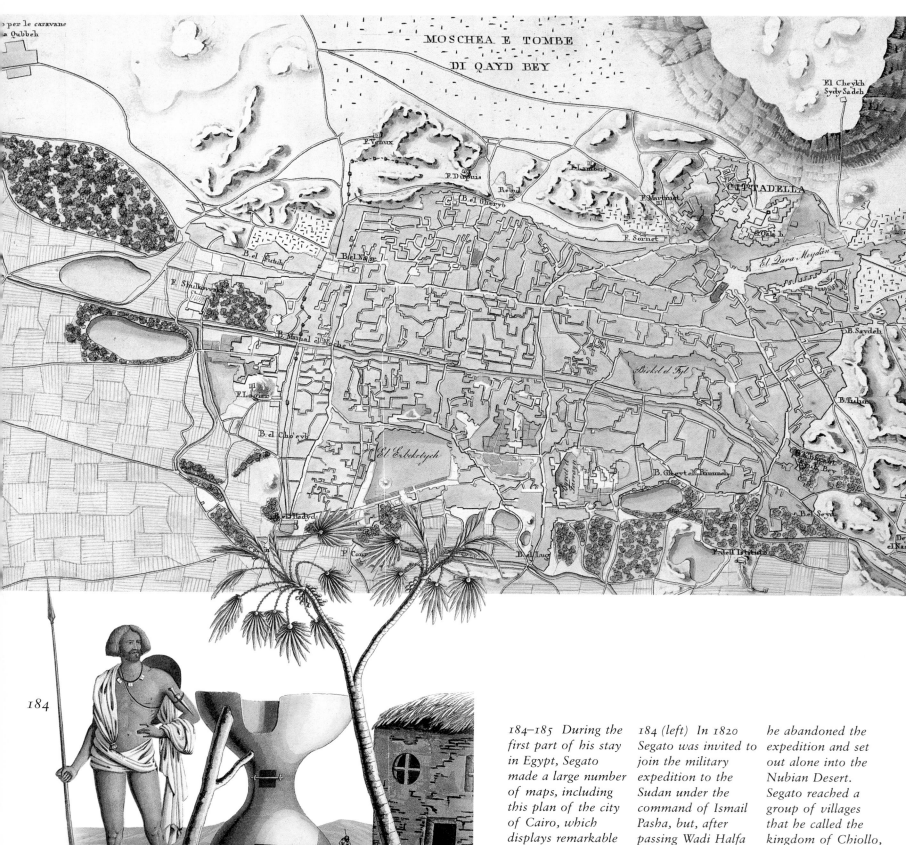

184

184–185 During the first part of his stay in Egypt, Segato made a large number of maps, including this plan of the city of Cairo, which displays remarkable technical skill combined with admirable precision.

184 (left) In 1820 Segato was invited to join the military expedition to the Sudan under the command of Ismail Pasha, but, after passing Wadi Halfa and the Second Cataract, for reasons that are still unclear,

he abandoned the expedition and set out alone into the Nubian Desert. Segato reached a group of villages that he called the kingdom of Chiollo, the exact location of which has never been identified.

comparing Denon's illustrations – on which his watercolours were often based – with his own observations. On occasion, he even corrected the Frenchman's work when he thought it was incomplete or imprecise.

At the great Ptolemaic temple dedicated to the goddess Hathor at Dendera, Segato made new plans and a drawing of the famous zodiac, which is now in the Louvre. When Segato returned to Cairo, completely exhausted, on 29 November 1820, he had produced an enormous quantity of drawings that formed an extremely useful addition to the documentation existing at the time. Segato left a vivid record of his first remarkable encounter with Egypt in

a long letter written to his brother Vincenzo, dated 26 December 1820:

I visited thirty ruins of magnificent cities…. I visited the fountain of the sun, the sacred island of Philae…. I was the first to ascend the First Cataract, hauled against the current by two hundred men…. I visited another sixteen magnificent temples, especially the one of Ebsambul [Abu Simbel], excavated like numerous others in the side of the mountain, but more splendid than all those of its kind…. I crossed the Coloicombo, I climbed the interminable Troglodytic chain, dividing Nubia from the great desert of the Abadi, which I penetrated in an east-south-easterly

185

185 Segato visited the oasis of Siwa in September 1821 at the request of von Minutoli in order to complete the drawings of its monuments. While there, he drew the reliefs of the temple of Amun at Aghurmi, which were then published in von Minutoli's monumental account of his journey.

186 (below) 'The Influence of the Moon on the Soul' is the fanciful title that Segato gave to this drawing he made of a stela he found in the funerary chambers of the pyramid of Djoser. In fact it depicts the revivifying powers of the sun's rays on the deceased, who is represented as Osiris with his face painted green, the colour of resurrection.

186 (right) At Thebes Segato drew the hieroglyphs on the obelisks of the temple of Luxor, which were then published in von Minutoli's account of his journey.

187 (opposite) The spectacular zodiac in the temple at Dendera was first discovered and drawn by Denon, in 1798. Segato, inspired by the work of his predecessor, drew it again in 1820. In 1821 a French engineer, Jean Baptiste Lelorrain removed it from the ceiling of the temple and transported it to France, where it is now in the Louvre.

direction…. Many a time I thought of how different things were from when I was in Italy, in the bosom of our family and surrounded by friends, with the comforts of life in a temperate climate, and compared it with life in the endless desert amidst naked, savage blacks, where all desires are limited to that for water….

It was in Cairo that Segato made the acquaintance of Baron von Minutoli, who had just returned from the oasis of Siwa. Impressed by the skill and precision of his drawings, von Minutoli asked him to undertake the exploration of the archaeological area of Saqqara, a task that he began in early 1821.

The Step Pyramid of Djoser was the first pyramid to be built in Egypt, and it immediately attracted Segato's attention. Just as Belzoni had done at the pyramid of Khafre at Giza, Segato concentrated on discovering its entrance. Taking a scientific approach, Segato first of all surveyed the exterior of the pyramid, then, with a team of workmen, he removed the debris surrounding the base and thus discovered a shaft leading to the main entrance of the pyramid, which was situated at a depth of fifteen metres.

After clearing the shaft and freeing the entrance, Segato – the first person to do so in modern times – entered the pyramid. Unfortunately, it had already been violated in ancient times by tomb-robbers, who spared none of the great pyramids. In three days of continuous work in the narrow passages, where the lack of ventilation and the smoke from the torches made breathing and moving difficult, Segato explored and surveyed the extremely complex internal structure of the pyramid, drawing and planning it in detail. Through a labyrinth of corridors he reached the burial chamber, made of red granite, which was very impressive but now empty.

Meanwhile, after his return from the oasis of Siwa, von Minutoli had been able to study the drawings made during the expedition more carefully and realized that they were incomplete and of poor quality. He thus asked Segato to go to Siwa and to make new drawings, which the Italian willingly agreed to do. Segato set out for Siwa in late September 1821, returning to Cairo three months later, having successfully carried out the mission with which he had been entrusted.

In the following months, Segato devoted himself to assembling a collection of antiquities on von Minutoli's behalf, and made accurate drawings of two cubit measures (the basic unit of measurement of the ancient Egyptians), one of which had been found by Baron Giuseppe di Nizzoli, chancellor of the Austrian Consulate in Egypt, and the other by the French Consul, Bernardino Drovetti. As far as is known, this was the final period of Segato's archaeological activity in Egypt, since, in the remainder of his stay in the country, he seems to have devoted himself to other kinds of studies, related to botany and chemistry and the processes of mummification and petrifaction, which became the main focus of his interest after his return to Italy in April 1823.

It is difficult to assess Segato's achievements in Egypt today because he was continuously beset by ill fortune. Almost all his documents, drawings and notes, which he had left for safe keeping at de Rossetti's house in Cairo before returning to Italy, were destroyed by fire in August 1823. A sad fate also awaited the majority of his collection of antiquities, which he had helped to assemble on von Minutoli's behalf and which was destined for the Berlin Museum. Packed in ninety cases and loaded on to the ship also carrying von Minutoli back to Europe, the objects reached Livorno, where von Minutoli decided to travel overland to Berlin with about twenty cases. These were thus saved, but the rest were lost when the ship carrying them sank in a storm.

A disappointed and embittered man, Segato settled in Florence, where, with the collaboration of Lorenzo Masi, he began to put together a large work, of which only the first volume was published, in 1827, entitled *Saggi pittorici, geografici, statistici, catastali sull'Egitto (Pictorial, Geographical, Statistical and Cadastral Essays on Egypt)*. Subsequently, in 1833, he began to prepare another work; entitled *Atlante monumentale dell'Alto e Basso Egitto (Atlas of Upper and Lower Egypt)* and illustrated by Domenico Valeriano, this was finally published in 1837, a year after Segato's death. Even taking into account the fact that a number of other drawings and paintings by Segato were published in the account by Baron von Minutoli of his expedition, it is clear that only a small part of Segato's work has survived to the present day.

Although we can only judge his work on the basis of the extant documents, these are sufficient to throw light on his essential characteristics. An attentive traveller, an explorer of the course of the Nile and the eastern part of the Nubian Desert, an indefatigable and keen observer, a skilled draughtsman and map-maker whose work heralded the age of the scientific plan and accurate scale drawing, he was a talented and versatile person who was the first to enter and carry out a systematic study of Djoser's Step Pyramid at Saqqara. While the bad luck that dogged him in his Egyptian adventures means that it is not possible to form a complete picture of his contribution to the development of Egyptology, there is no doubt that he was one of the most outstanding explorers of the country in the last century.

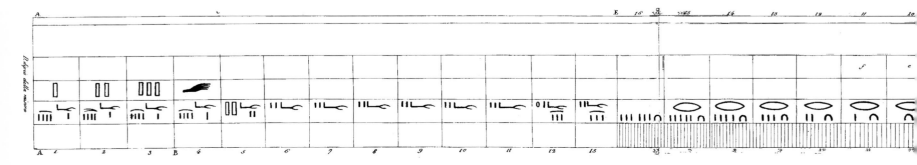

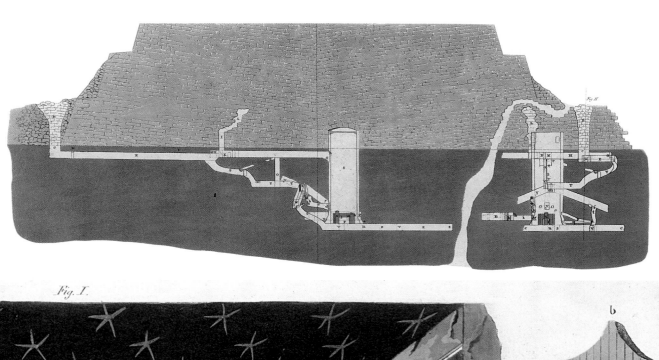

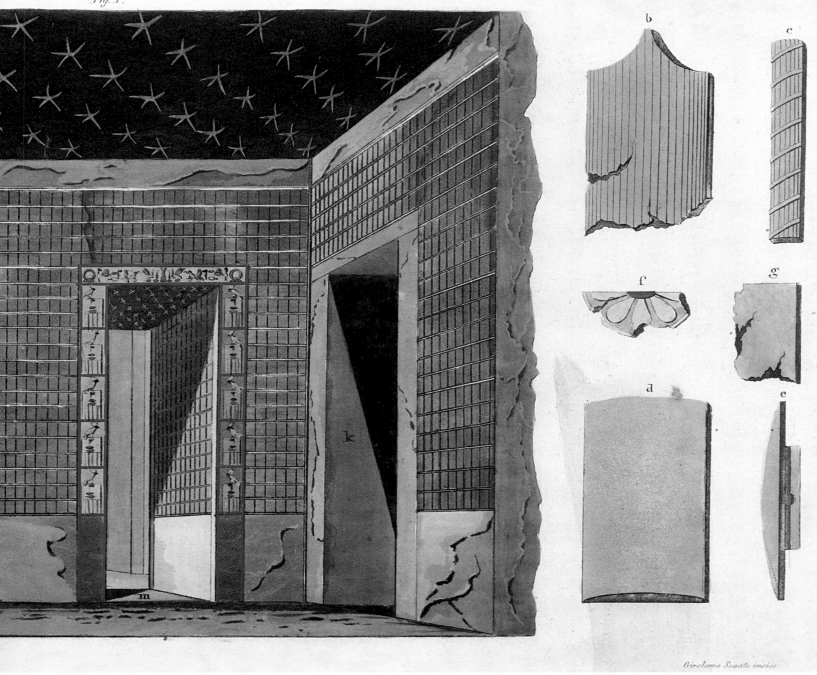

Girolamo Segato incise.

188–189 (left) In 1822 the French Consul Bernardino Drovetti and the chancellor of the Austrian consulate Giuseppe di Nizzoli both acquired rare examples of the royal cubit, the unit of measurement used by the ancient Egyptians, equal to 52.5 cm and subdivided into 28 digits. Segato made drawings of the two cubits, one made of wood and the other of quartzite, that are now in museums in Turin and Florence respectively. This drawing is of the cubit in the Drovetti collection; it originally belonged to a New Kingdom dignitary called Amenemope.

189 (top) Segato drew the first north–south cross-section of Djoser's Step Pyramid, highlighting the complexity of the funerary apartments that were built for the king's afterlife.

190 (left) As part of their work in the Valley of the Kings, members of the Franco-Tuscan expedition copied the reliefs and inscriptions in sixteen tombs. For the first time for many centuries the hieroglyphs were not merely seen as ornamental designs or mysterious symbols, but were able to convey their original intended meaning and the royal tombs could be attributed to their owners. This drawing shows a relief in the hall with four pillars in the tomb of Seti I, depicting the fourth gate and the beginning of the fifth hour in the Book of Gates, with the god Horus.

190 (below) The grand-duke Leopoldo II of Tuscany, together with the King of France, Charles X, was a supporter of the joint Franco-Tuscan expedition. In July 1827 he approved the setting up of two joint committees: the Tuscan one directed by Ippolito Rosellini and the French one directed by Jean François Champollion.

CHAMPOLLION AND THE FRANCO-TUSCAN EXPEDITION

190–191 In this painting by Giuseppe Angelelli, the members of the Franco-Tuscan expedition are shown in front of the temple of Luxor. Seated in the centre is Champollion. Ippolito Rosellini stands nearby, with his brother Gaetano on his left. Salvatore Cherubini is in front, holding a painting, while behind is the naturalist Giuseppe Raddi and the artist Albert Bertin. On the far left are the artist Alessandro Ricci, seen from behind and wearing a red tunic, and the painter Alexandre Duchesne and the draughtsmen Nestor L'Hôte and Pierre Lehoux. In the shadows is Angelelli himself with an open drawing-book.

In July 1799, while his men were busy building the fort of St Julien to defend the town of Rashid, better known as Rosetta, Pierre Bouchard, an officer in the Napoleonic army, noticed a strange dark stela protruding from the ground. Made of basalt and little more than a metre in height, it bore a long inscription divided into three parts, each written in different characters: hieroglyphic, demotic (both in the Egyptian language) and Greek. Captain Bouchard immediately gave orders to dig it up and he then sent it to General Menou, the commander of the expeditionary force. In his turn, Menou submitted it to the specialists of the Commission des Arts et des Sciences. They, perhaps without fully appreciating its importance, copied the texts and made casts of the stone. Two years later, after the defeat of the French army, the British took possession of the

find and immediately sent it to the British Museum, where it is still on display in the large hall devoted to Egyptian statuary.

A few years later, in 1808, a young Frenchman, Jean François Champollion (1790–1832), began to study one of these casts. Born in Figeac, a small town in southwest France, Champollion, encouraged by his elder brother Jacques Joseph (who later assumed the name of Champollion-Figeac), became interested in languages and Oriental studies at an early age. Champollion first attended the lycée at Grenoble and, subsequently, the Collège de France and the École Pratique des Langues Orientales in Paris, where he went to live in 1806. His knowledge of numerous languages (at the age of sixteen he spoke about ten) and, above all, his command of Coptic, were of great help to him in the decipherment of hieroglyphs, a puzzle to

which many other scholars at the time – such as Thomas Young, Johan David Åkerblad and Georg Zoëga – were attempting to discover the solution.

After being appointed professor at the University of Grenoble at the precocious age of eighteen, Champollion spent no less than fourteen years on the study of hieroglyphs. He based his successful method of decipherment on three brilliant pieces of intuition. The first was that Coptic, a well-known language, was simply the final stage in the evolution of ancient Egyptian; the second was that hieroglyphs had two values – that is, they were both ideograms and phonetic signs; and the third was that the hieroglyphs enclosed in the cartouches were phonetic transcriptions of the names of pharaohs.

From the study of the Greek text on the stela, it became clear that it was a decree

191

192 (left) The crucial object in Champollion's decipherment of hieroglyphs, the Rosetta Stone bears an inscription in two languages but three scripts. The same text, a decree issued in 196 BC by Ptolemy V Epiphanes, is written in hieroglyphs and demotic characters, both Egyptian, with a translation in Greek. Found by the French in July 1799 it had to be handed over to the British when the French army left Egypt. It is now in the British Museum.

from the reign of Ptolemy V Epiphanes (second century BC). Furthermore, the last part of the inscription in Greek specified that the text of the decree was to be transcribed into demotic (the writing used in Egypt at the time) as well as hieroglyphs. Champollion immediately realized that he now possessed the key to understanding the principles underlying hieroglyphic writing.

Postulating that each hieroglyphic sign corresponded to an alphabetic symbol, Champollion managed to read the signs transcribing the name *Ptolmys*. Subsequently, in 1821, he analysed the bilingual text (Greek and hieroglyphic) on the obelisk from Philae removed from its original site by Giovanni Battista Belzoni in 1819 on behalf of the British antiquarian William John Bankes. Bankes then erected it in the garden of his house at Kingston Lacy, in Dorset, where it remains to this

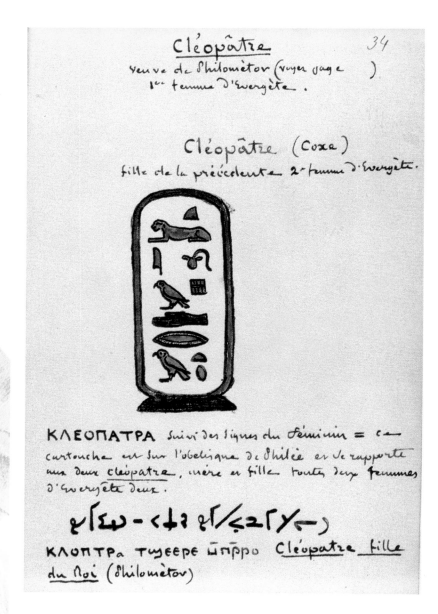

192 (left) This portrait of Champollion wearing Bedouin-style dress was painted in Egypt and is attributed to Giuseppe Angelelli. Champollion was thirty-two years old

when he deciphered hieroglyphs in September 1822, working from a reproduction of the Rosetta Stone made by the printers Marcel and Galland in Cairo before it fell into British hands.

192 (above) By assuming that the cartouches contained pharaohs' names, Champollion read the name of Ptolemy on the Rosetta Stone and that of Cleopatra on the obelisk of Philae.

day. Champollion was able to read the name Cleopatra and in this way discovered the alphabetic values of twelve hieroglyphic signs. By extending the method to other cartouches, Champollion managed to obtain the values of many other signs and, on 22 September 1822, he presented his discovery to the academic world with the celebrated *Lettre à M. Dacier...*, which was followed in 1824 by a book entitled *Précis du système hiéroglyphique*, in which he expounded the fundamental concepts of the system of hieroglyphic writing.

In order to test his method on new texts, Champollion next made various journeys – especially to the Museo Egizio in Turin, where there was what was then probably the largest collection of Egyptian antiquities in the world. The importance of this museum to the French scholar is demonstrated by his famous aphorism 'La route pour Memphis et Thèbes passe par

Turin' ('The road to Memphis and Thebes passes through Turin'). In Turin, where he worked for a number of months until February 1825, Champollion was able to examine a vast quantity of material, which he classified in chronological order in his *Lettres à M. le Duc de Blacas d'Aulps*. He then went to Rome and Florence, where he met a young professor, Ippolito Rosellini (1800–43), who immediately became his friend and disciple.

Rosellini, who is considered the founder of Egyptology in Italy, was born in Pisa in 1800 and, after graduating in theology, studied Oriental languages in Bologna at Giuseppe Mezzofanti's school, where he was later offered the chair in this subject. In 1827 he went to Paris for a year in order to improve his knowledge of the method of decipherment proposed by Champollion. The two philologists decided to organize an expedition to Egypt to confirm the

validity of the discovery. Headed by Champollion, who was assisted by Ippolito Rosellini, the mission was known as the Franco-Tuscan Expedition, and was made possible by the support of the grand-duke of Tuscany, Leopoldo II, and the King of France, Charles X.

On 21 July 1828, the fourteen members of the expedition boarded the ship the *Eglé* at Toulon and set sail for Egypt, where they would work for the next year. Among them was a physician and draughtsman from Sienna in Italy, Alessandro Ricci. He had already worked in Egypt with Belzoni ten years previously, making magnificent drawings of the paintings decorating the tomb of Pharaoh Seti I, which Belzoni had just discovered in the Valley of the Kings. The group also comprised the painter, Giuseppe Angelelli; the draughtsmen Nestor L'Hôte, Salvatore Cherubini, Alexandre Duchesne, Albert Bertin and

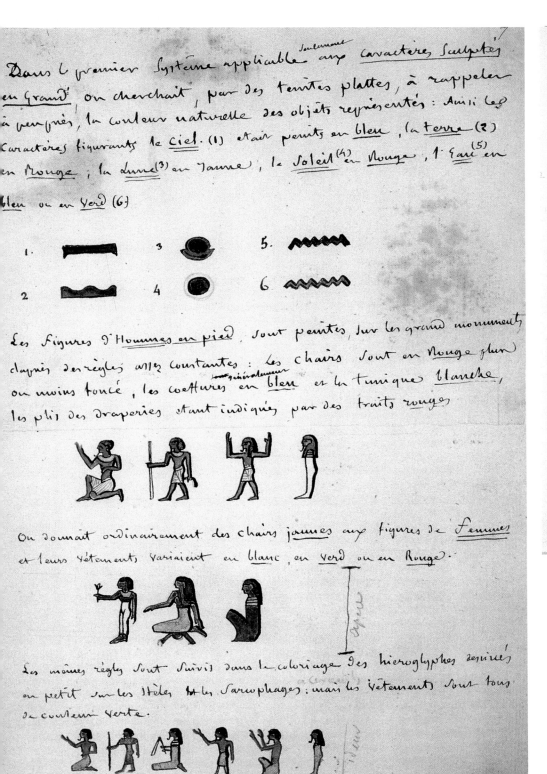

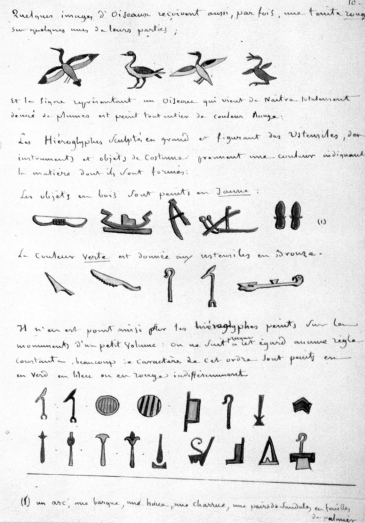

193 (left) One of Champollion's great insights was that hieroglyphs had a double value, both phonetic and ideographic: some signs simply corresponded to sounds while others were the graphic representation of concepts.

193 (above) Later, Champollion also managed to attribute a meaning to other signs used to transcribe the Egyptian language, and he wrote the first grammar of hieroglyphs, a page from the manuscript of which can be seen here.

Pierre Lehoux; a historian, Charles Lenormant; two architects, Antoine Bibent and Gaetano Rosellini (Ippolito's brother); and the naturalist Giuseppe Raddi, accompanied by his assistant Gaetano Galastri.

For the first time for many centuries, people came to Egypt who could read the inscriptions written on the walls of the temples and tombs and on the obelisks of the ancient Egyptians. It was thanks to these scholars that the monuments were able to recount their history and that of the remarkable civilization that had conceived and built them.

At first, however, the official permit needed to carry out excavations and archaeological research in the country – which had to be obtained directly from the Pasha, Muhammad Ali – was not forthcoming. The delay was caused by the Pasha's unwillingness to grant such authorization to two mere scholars, when it was normally only granted to consuls – that is, official representatives of the foreign powers. It is also quite likely that the antiquarians and powerful dealers in works of art opposed the issuing of new permits because they did not welcome the arrival of possible competitors.

194 (centre) On 22 September 1822, in his celebrated Lettre à M. Dacier…, *Champollion announced that he had deciphered hieroglyphs and explained the basic elements.*

194–195 (below) In the course of the expedition, the painter Salvatore Cherubini – whose sister Zenobia was Ippolito Rosellini's wife – made sketches of the landscape in this note-book.

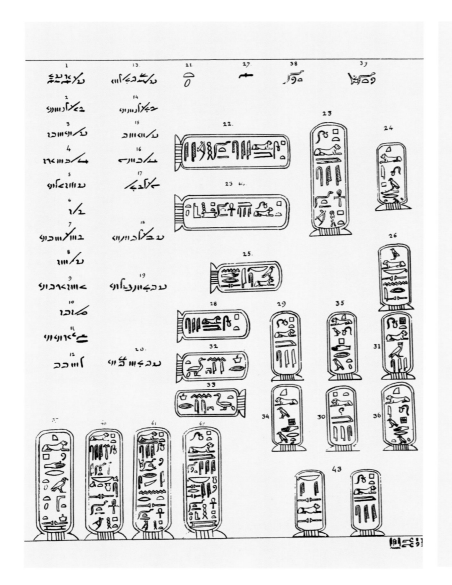

LETTRE
A M. DACIER,
SECRÉTAIRE PERPÉTUEL DE L'ACADÉMIE ROYALE
DES INSCRIPTIONS ET BELLES-LETTRES,

RELATIVE A L'ALPHABET
DES HIÉROGLYPHES PHONÉTIQUES
EMPLOYÉS PAR LES ÉGYPTIENS POUR INSCRIRE SUR LEURS MONUMENTS LES TITRES, LES NOMS ET LES SURNOMS DES SOUVERAINS GRECS ET ROMAINS;

PAR M. CHAMPOLLION LE JEUNE.

A PARIS,
CHEZ FIRMIN DIDOT PÈRE ET FILS,
LIBRAIRES, RUE JACOB, N° 24.

M. DCCC. XXII.

On 18 August, after a voyage of twenty-nine days, the *Eglé* docked at Alexandria, where Champollion and Rosellini were welcomed by Bernardino Drovetti and Carlo de Rossetti, respectively the consuls of France and Tuscany, who provided them with accommodation for about a month while they attended to the bureaucratic formalities and planned the expedition down to the smallest detail. Although the organization of the journey was a complex matter and they had numerous official and social engagements during their stay in Alexandria, Champollion and Rosellini managed to find time to study the city's monuments, especially the celebrated ones: Pompey's Pillar and Cleopatra's Needle.

195 (right) This drawing by André Bertin shows a painting from the tomb of Seti 1 depicting Libyans with blue eyes and dressed in long tunics.

195 (centre) Champollion, portrayed at Thebes in July 1829, in a drawing by Salvatore Cherubini. Three years earlier, on 15 May 1826, Champollion was appointed keeper of the new section of the Louvre devoted to Egyptian antiquities, opened under the auspices of King Charles X.

In order to facilitate the expedition's departure as soon as possible, Drovetti and his colleague Giovanni Anastasi, the Consul of Sweden and Norway, lent their permits to Champollion and Rosellini with the Pasha's approval. So it was that, after hiring two sailing boats named *Isis* and *Athyr*, the members of the expedition left Alexandria on 14 September 1828, and began to sail up the Nile, heading for the most important archaeological sites of the country. Before leaving, the rules and regulations governing the expedition were drawn up, and the roles and tasks of each member were specified: Champollion was the commander-in-chief, Rosellini the second-in-command, while the position of inspector-general was assigned to Lenormant.

It took them five days to pass through the Delta, with a halt at San el-Hagar, the site of the ancient city of Sais. The expedition then reached Cairo, where, as guests of the Tuscan vice-consul, they stayed for about ten days. On 3 October the expedition continued along the Nile for about ten kilometres, reaching the village of Mit Rahina where there are the ruins of Memphis, the great capital of Egypt during the Old Kingdom.

195 (left) This painting by Leon Cogniet, dated 1831, has become the official portrait of Champollion, despite the fact that, according to his contemporaries, it hardly resembled him, as can be seen by comparing it with the previous portrait on this page. In fact, Cogniet painted the portrait in 1834, two years after Champollion's death on 4 March 1832.

After a short visit to the site, where very little remained of the ancient city, the members of the expedition travelled overland a few kilometres to the archaeological sites of Saqqara, the main cemetery area of Memphis, and the huge cemetery region of Giza, where they stayed for a few days.

On 12 October the expedition set off once more up the Nile and, after a voyage of eight days, reached the necropolis of Beni Hasan, where they stayed for a fortnight to draw and survey the interesting rock-cut tombs, dating from the Middle

Kingdom, in the sides of the mountain. This was the first important task of the Franco-Tuscan expedition in Egypt, and before they left the site its members had made about four hundred drawings, almost all in colour, recording the majority of the reliefs decorating the tombs.

After visiting the remains of Antinoöpolis, the city built on the banks of the Nile by Emperor Hadrian, the city of Asyut and the temple of Dendera, on 20 November Champollion and Rosellini arrived at Luxor, the site of the ancient city of Thebes, the religious centre of Egypt

during the New Kingdom. Their stay at what is probably still considered the largest and most important archaeological site in Egypt was very brief because it was necessary to take advantage of the favourable climatic conditions to continue the journey southwards to Nubia.

On 26 November the expedition left Luxor for Aswan – the town on the southern border of Egypt, known in ancient times as Syene – which they reached on 4 December. Here the members of the expedition had to leave the large boats that had carried them up to this

point because the craft were not able to pass the First Cataract, immediately above Aswan, where the tumultuous waters of the Nile formed a great obstacle and a danger to river traffic.

After unloading their equipment and baggage, the members of the expedition decided to go round the cataract by land and stay on the island of Philae. This was the site of important monuments from the Ptolemaic and Roman periods, such as the magnificent temple of Isis and the so-called Kiosk of Trajan, which they wanted to study and draw. The expedition's camp was

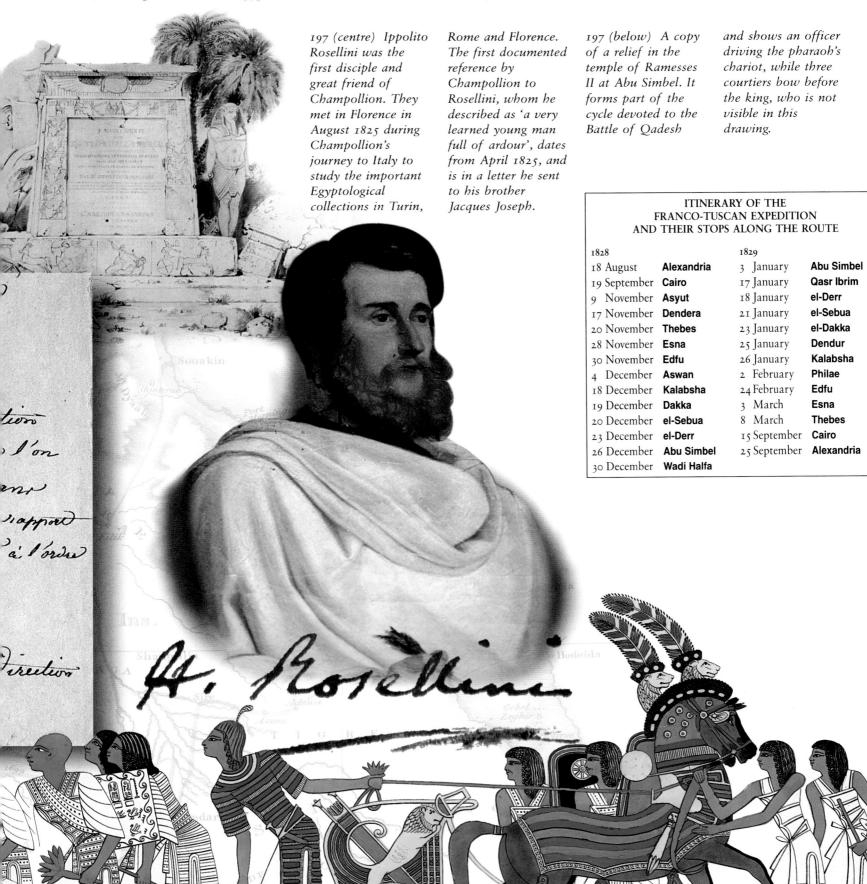

197 (centre) Ippolito Rosellini was the first disciple and great friend of Champollion. They met in Florence in August 1825 during Champollion's journey to Italy to study the important Egyptological collections in Turin,

Rome and Florence. The first documented reference by Champollion to Rosellini, whom he described as 'a very learned young man full of ardour', dates from April 1825, and is in a letter he sent to his brother Jacques Joseph.

197 (below) A copy of a relief in the temple of Ramesses II at Abu Simbel. It forms part of the cycle devoted to the Battle of Qadesh

and shows an officer driving the pharaoh's chariot, while three courtiers bow before the king, who is not visible in this drawing.

ITINERARY OF THE FRANCO-TUSCAN EXPEDITION AND THEIR STOPS ALONG THE ROUTE			
1828		**1829**	
18 August	**Alexandria**	3 January	**Abu Simbel**
19 September	**Cairo**	17 January	**Qasr Ibrim**
9 November	**Asyut**	18 January	**el-Derr**
17 November	**Dendera**	21 January	**el-Sebua**
20 November	**Thebes**	23 January	**el-Dakka**
28 November	**Esna**	25 January	**Dendur**
30 November	**Edfu**	26 January	**Kalabsha**
4 December	**Aswan**	2 February	**Philae**
18 December	**Kalabsha**	24 February	**Edfu**
19 December	**Dakka**	3 March	**Esna**
20 December	**el-Sebua**	8 March	**Thebes**
23 December	**el-Derr**	15 September	**Cairo**
26 December	**Abu Simbel**	25 September	**Alexandria**
30 December	**Wadi Halfa**		

198 (right) Nestor L'Hôte was twenty-four years old at the time of the expedition. He is portrayed here in a sketch by Alexandre Duchesne at Thebes in March 1829. L'Hôte produced over six hundred pencil drawings and watercolours, depicting not only monuments and inscriptions but also the landscape of Egypt. He also wrote a large number of letters and a travel journal, which he published in 1833. After two more journeys to Egypt in 1838–39 and 1840–41, he died in 1842, at the age of thirty-eight.

set up inside the Kiosk of Trajan, while the nearby *mammisi* – the small temples, typical of the Ptolemaic period, that were built adjacent to a main temple to celebrate the mythological birth of the god to whom the temple was dedicated – served as their kitchen and larder.

After staying in Philae for twelve days, the expedition set off again southwards towards the temples of Abu Simbel. This was the toughest part of the journey, partly because it had to be undertaken in small boats since the larger ones could not go beyond the cataract, and also because it was here that the true desert began. The

Nile now flowed through a sandy, inhospitable wilderness where the heat became increasingly intense.

On 26 December the expedition reached Abu Simbel, the site of the Great Temple of Ramesses II, rediscovered by Johann Ludwig Burckhardt in 1813 and opened up by Belzoni in 1817, although it was still largely covered by desert sand. It took the hard toil of sixty men to make even a small opening in the mass of sand that obstructed the entrance, allowing the members of the expedition to enter the monument and gaze in astonishment at its splendour.

The stay in Abu Simbel was also very brief, and on 28 December the members of the expedition set off for Wadi Halfa, at the Second Cataract. This was the final destination of their journey, where they found and removed a stela of Ramesses I. They had thus travelled along the whole of the Egyptian section of the Nile Valley from north to south. It was now time to think of the return journey, which began on 1 January 1829.

Normally the journey from south to north was easier and faster because the current was favourable, but, in this case, their progress was hindered by contrary

winds blowing from the north and north-north-west. During the outward journey, when these would have helped to overcome the resistance of the current, they were almost entirely absent. Champollion and Rosellini decided, therefore, to stop again at Abu Simbel, where they remained for twelve days. The task they set themselves was enormous in view of the complexity and size of the monument, but for the first time after the opening of the temple the vast numbers of reliefs and inscriptions were studied and drawn.

On 16 January the members of the expedition reluctantly left the site and, after visiting and surveying the temples of el-Sebua and Kalabsha, they continued back to Philae, which they reached on 1 February 1829. After passing the cataract they reached Aswan and then continued northwards, stopping on the way to explore the temples of Kom Ombo, the sites of Gebel Silsila and el-Kab, and the temple of Esna, and reached Luxor once more on 8 February.

This was probably the most important archaeological area of the whole journey and there was a huge amount to see and study. It was therefore decided to stay in this remarkable area for a long period – six months. During this stay the expedition members carefully explored the great tombs of the Valley of the Kings, the Tombs of the Nobles, the Ramesseum and the temples of Medinet Habu, Karnak and Luxor. Detailed drawings were made of the reliefs and, for the first time, it was possible to decipher the inscriptions and the names of the pharaohs.

The results of the period spent in Thebes were astonishing: the scholars visited over three hundred tombs, while numerous important artifacts were discovered or purchased and hundreds of drawings and plans were made.

On 4 September, the members of the expedition set out again for Cairo, which they reached rapidly after a voyage of only eleven days. In the few days they then spent in the capital, Champollion and Rosellini were received on numerous occasions by Muhammad Ali. The two scholars and their companions then continued to Alexandria, where they arrived on 25 September. Here the whole group had to wait for a lengthy period for the arrival of the *Eglé*, the ship that had brought them all to Egypt and was now to take them back to Europe.

This long wait, however, at least allowed the members of the expedition to sort out their travel notes and the approximately fourteen hundred drawings they had made, and also pack their precious artifacts ready for the voyage. But since the *Eglé* still failed to arrive, the members of the expedition decided to leave Egypt without further delay in order to avoid having to cross the Mediterranean in the winter months, when the weather conditions were often unfavourable.

The first to leave the land of the pharaohs were Rosellini and his Tuscan friends, who set sail on 17 October on the *Aristide* for Livorno. Champollion and the other remaining members left on 6 December for Toulon, where they landed on 25 December 1829.

Thus the Franco-Tuscan expedition had been a complete success. Champollion and Rosellini were now left with the laborious task of examining and arranging the material collected during the many months of hard work, anxiety, risks and hardship. The result of their labours was an

200–201 Nestor L'Hôte painted this marvellous watercolour of the Second Cataract, and described it in his diary: 'In its vast expanse, the plain occupied by the river contains nothing but an infinity of islands and rocks between which the roaring river flows'.

201 (above) The Kiosk of Trajan on the island of Philae was depicted by L'Hôte in a fresh way. Next to the monument is visible one of the tents used by the expedition during their stay on the island in December 1828 and again from 1 to 7 February 1829.

imposing publication entitled *Monumenti dell'Egitto e della Nubia* (*Monuments of Egypt and Nubia*), which is still of great value for the study of ancient Egypt.

In the hope of gaining his support, Rosellini sent a letter to the grand-duke of Tuscany, Leopoldo II, in December 1830, containing an outline of his projected book. With the assistance of his brother, Gaetano, and Alessandro Ricci, he had already prepared the material – the drawings and notes – that had been collected during the expedition. Since the Tuscan government was willing only to grant him a loan to help him in his venture

Rosellini decided to finance the publication himself. Thus, on 15 January 1831, he published a prospectus – essential to attract support and orders – in which the features of the work were explained in detail.

In order to raise the necessary funds Rosellini sent his friend and collaborator Ricci to Germany and England to sell copies in advance of publication, the proceeds of which would allow him to begin paying the printers. A few months earlier, on 6 October 1830, Rosellini had sent a long letter to his mentor and travelling companion Champollion, asking him to collaborate in writing the work.

The French scholar, who was presumably very busy preparing his grammar of hieroglyphs, delayed a long time before replying to Rosellini in a letter dated 18 May 1831. He invited the Italian to Paris for a meeting that took place in the second half of July. Despite some minor differences, Champollion and Rosellini reached an agreement, and the latter was able to return satisfied to Pisa in September to finish writing *Monumenti dell'Egitto e della Nubia*. This was the last meeting between Champollion and his pupil; a few months later, on 4 March 1832, the French scholar died prematurely of a stroke.

Thus the final version of Rosellini's work was edited with the assistance of Champollion's brother, Jacques Joseph Champollion-Figeac. But relations between the two soon became strained, and were brusquely broken off when the Frenchman demanded that he should become the sole editor of the work. At this point Rosellini and the grand-duke of Tuscany agreed to proceed with the publication of the work independently, and before the end of 1832 the Pisan printer Nicolò Capurro & Co. had already begun to bring out the first instalments. Giuseppe Angelelli, a painter who had himself been a member of the Franco-Tuscan expedition, was responsible for selecting the illustrations for this remarkable publication.

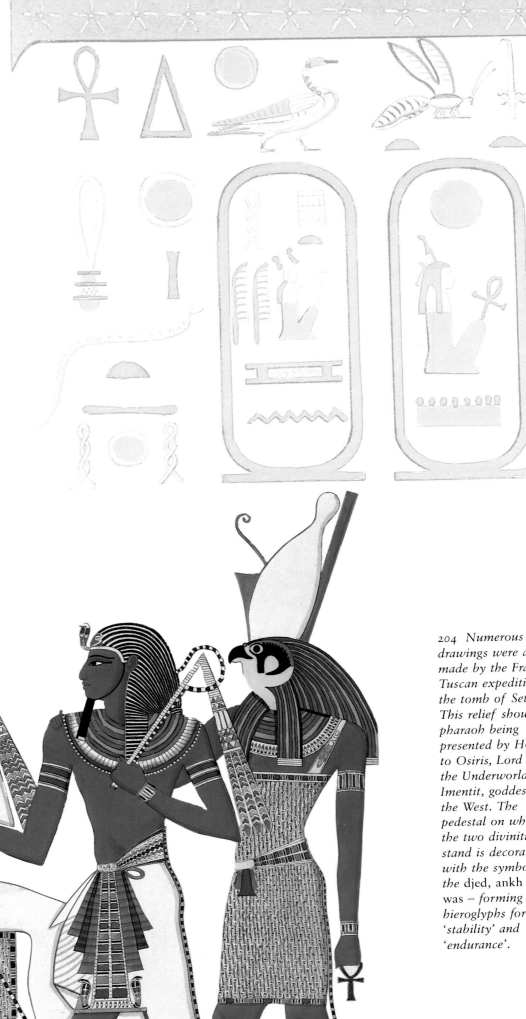

204

204 *Numerous drawings were also made by the Franco-Tuscan expedition in the tomb of Seti I. This relief shows the pharaoh being presented by Horus to Osiris, Lord of the Underworld, and Imentit, goddess of the West. The pedestal on which the two divinities stand is decorated with the symbols of the* djed, ankh *and* was – *forming the hieroglyphs for 'life', 'stability' and 'endurance'.*

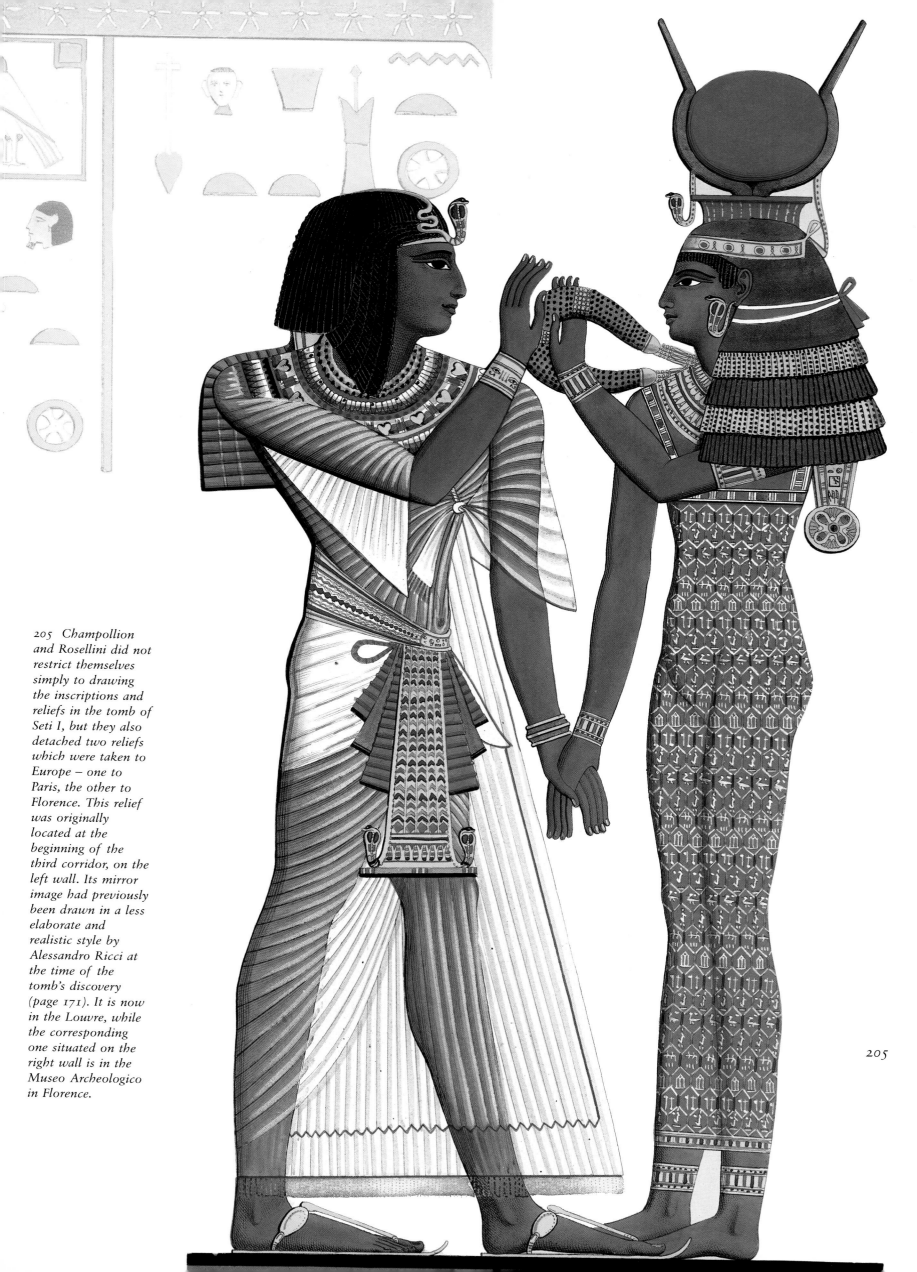

205 Champollion
and Rosellini did not
restrict themselves
simply to drawing
the inscriptions and
reliefs in the tomb of
Seti I, but they also
detached two reliefs
which were taken to
Europe – one to
Paris, the other to
Florence. This relief
was originally
located at the
beginning of the
third corridor, on the
left wall. Its mirror
image had previously
been drawn in a less
elaborate and
realistic style by
Alessandro Ricci at
the time of the
tomb's discovery
(page 171). It is now
in the Louvre, while
the corresponding
one situated on the
right wall is in the
Museo Archeologico
in Florence.

205

206–207 The private tombs of the Theban necropolis – the so-called Tombs of the Nobles – were also studied by the members of the Franco-Tuscan expedition. They faithfully reproduced the most interesting paintings decorating certain tombs, such as that belonging to the vizier Rekhmire of the Eighteenth Dynasty. Here we see scenes of Nubians offering tribute consisting of elephants' tusks, incense and African animals, including felines, an elephant and a giraffe with a monkey climbing up its neck. In the tombs at Thebes the animals are depicted realistically, but in the tombs of the Middle Kingdom in the cemetery at Beni Hasan wholly imaginary beasts are represented, which were also copied by the expedition's artists.

208–209 The task confronting the Franco-Tuscan expedition in the Great Temple of Ramesses II at Abu Simbel was enormous. Opened only eleven years previously by Belzoni, the temple's reliefs had never before been studied and drawn. Here, Ramesses II is shown presenting Nubian and Ethiopian prisoners to the supreme god of the Theban pantheon, Amun-Re, and his consort Mut. Ramesses is depicted in deified form between Amun-Re and Mut. The columns of text contain invocations and prayers to the three divinities.

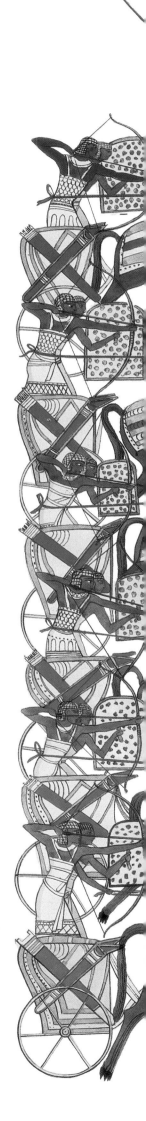

210 (above) In this famous relief on the southern wall of the hall of the Great Temple of Abu Simbel, Ramesses II is about to impale a Libyan enemy with his spear – shown somewhat unrealistically behind his head in order not to cover his face – while he tramples on another enemy who has already been killed.

210 (left) The decoration of the large hall of the temple of Abu Simbel depicts episodes in the war Ramesses II waged against the Hittites; this concluded with famous Battle of Qadesh, fought near the River Orontes in Syria in c. 1274 BC. Here a Syrian fortress is under attack from the army of Ramesses: its defenders are pierced by the arrows of the pharaoh.

211 (opposite) Egyptian chariots (left) confront Syrian ones (right) in the Battle of Qadesh. Maintaining perfect order, the Egyptian archers shoot arrows that transfix and kill their enemies and their horses.

212–213 Ramesses II, in his war chariot drawn by a pair of fiery horses adorned with elegant trappings, is about to shoot an arrow against the Syrian fortress shown in the previous drawing; to leave his hands free for his bow, he has tied the reins around his waist.

In the following four years, eight volumes were published in octavo and two, forming an atlas, in folio; a ninth volume in octavo and a third volume of the atlas were added in 1844, a year after the death of Rosellini on 4 June 1843. The work was subdivided into three main sections: ancient monuments; civil monuments; and religious monuments. The nine volumes of text comprised no less than 3,300 pages, while the atlas contained 390 large plates (by the artists and draughtsmen Giuseppe Angelelli, Salvatore Cherubini, Nestor L'Hôte and Gaetano Rosellini), 110 of which were coloured under the supervision of Angelelli.

Meanwhile, between 1835 and 1847, Champollion-Figeac published his version of the work with the title *Monuments de l'Égypte et de la Nubie…* (*Monuments of Egypt and Nubia…*), followed by two volumes in which the majority of the plates and drawings already published by Rosellini were reproduced.

214–215 Ramesses II depicted in the act of sacrificing a group of prisoners of various races, indicated by the different colours of their skin, as an offering to Amun-Re, who in turn presents the khepesh sword to the pharaoh. Behind the pharaoh is his Horus name.

215 The final plates in the section of Rosellini's work devoted to the ancient monuments of Egypt reproduce reliefs from the tombs of Seti I and Ramesses III. These depict the various foreign peoples that the Egyptians were in contact with, showing their distinctive characteristics and costumes. On the left is a Libyan, with a sidelock of hair, while on the right is an Asiatic, aamu, with an aquiline nose and thick black pointed beard.

216 (opposite above)
Two Syrians
portrayed with their
distinctive reddish-
blond beards.

216 (opposite centre
and below)
Rosellini's copies
of depictions of
a Libyan and a
Nubian, with their
typical hairstyles
and ornaments.

217 The figure on
the right, copied
from the decorations
at Abu Simbel, is
part of the group of
Asiatic prisoners
shown being killed
by Ramesses II. In
the centre and below,
also copied from the
decorative cycle of
the Great Temple of
Abu Simbel, are two
Asiatic soldiers in
the Hittite army
defending the fortress
of Qadesh; it is
noticeable that both
have blue eyes.

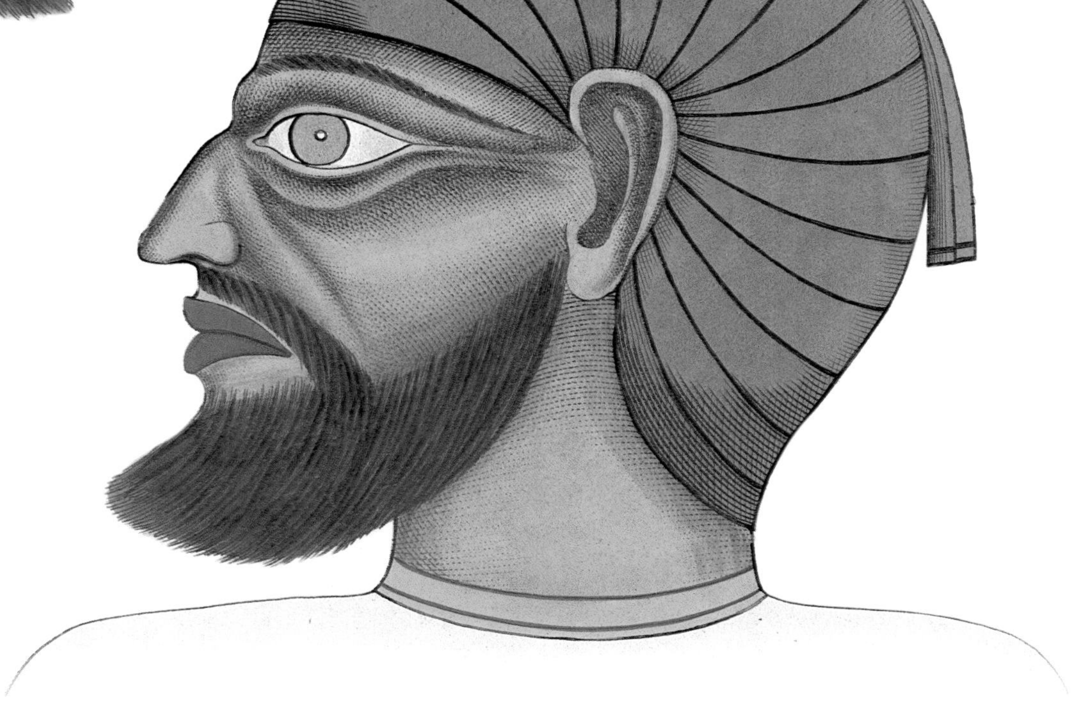

JOHN GARDNER WILKINSON
THE FOUNDER OF EGYPTOLOGY IN GREAT BRITAIN

A PLAN OF
THEBES
P-AMEN, NO AMON
(DIOSPOLIS)

Reduced from Wilkinson's Survey.

Scale of English Feet.

218 (left) John Gardner Wilkinson worked for over twelve years at Thebes. He was the first scholar to study the material culture and daily life of ancient Egypt. The author of various publications, he left copious notes, plans and drawings, as yet unpublished, that are kept at the Bodleian Library in Oxford in fifty-six volumes.

218 (above left) Wilkinson made numerous paintings in the tombs and temples of Thebes: this is Seti I in his war chariot in a battle scene from the large hypostyle hall in the temple of Karnak. Wilkinson, who was an excellent draughtsman, was able to make this reconstruction of a war chariot on the basis of two reliefs.

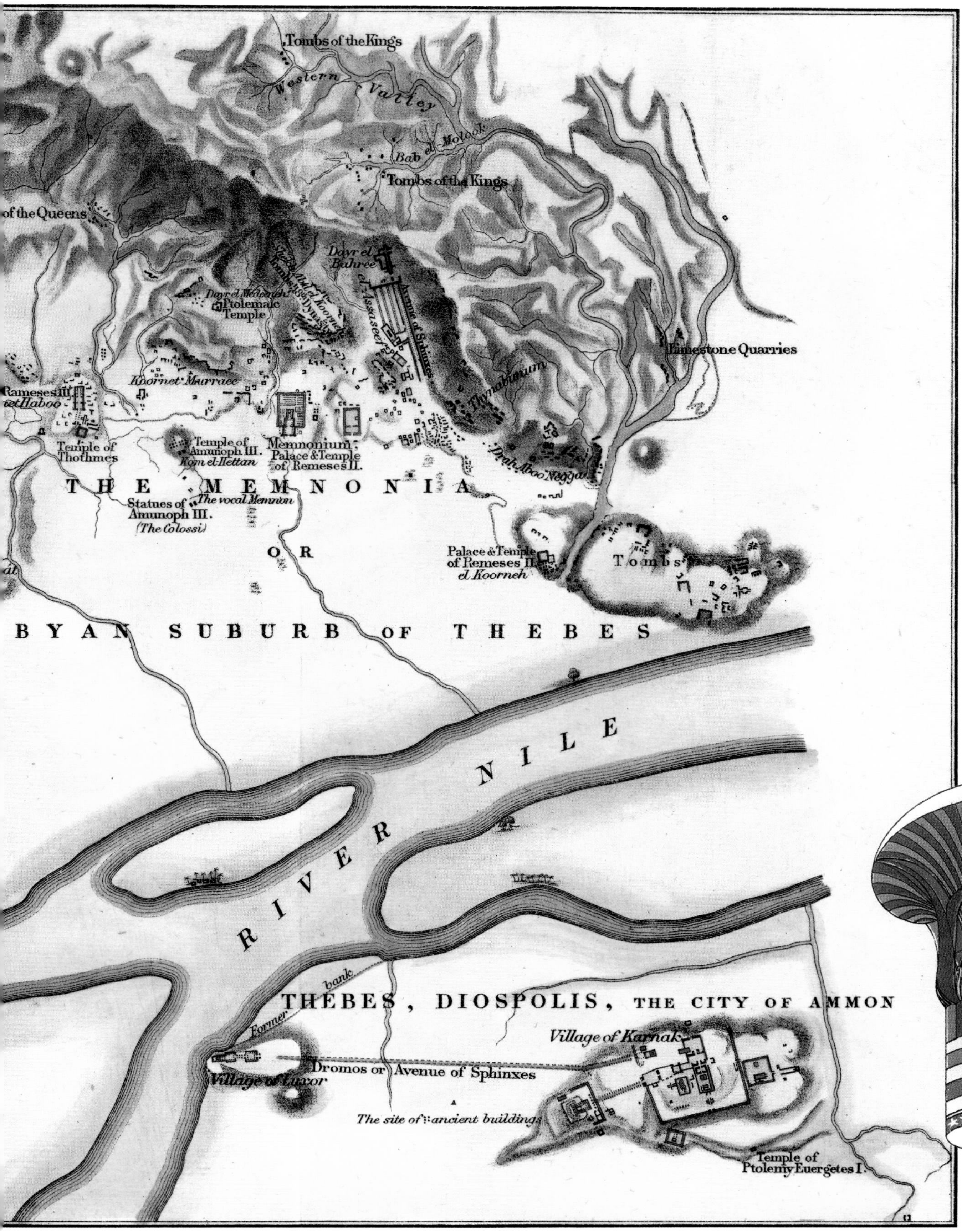

Tombs of the Kings
Western Valley
Bab el Molook
Tombs of the Kings
of the Queens
Dayr el Bahree
Ptolemaic Temple
Limestone Quarries
Koornet Murraee
Rameses III
Temple of Thothmes
Temple of Amunoph III. Kom el Hettan
Memnonium; Palace & Temple of Remeses II.
THE MEMNONIA
Statues of Amunoph III. (The Colossi)
The vocal Memnon
OR
Drah Aboo Negga
Palace & Temple of Remeses II. el Koorneh
Tombs
BYAN SUBURB OF THEBES
RIVER NILE
Former bank
THEBES, DIOSPOLIS, THE CITY OF AMMON
Village of Karnak
Dromos or Avenue of Sphinxes
Village of Luxor
The site of ancient buildings
Temple of Ptolemy Euergetes I.

218–219 Wilkinson drew the first accurate map of the Theban region, on which he showed the exact position of all the major monuments. He was also the first to assign a logical system of numbers to the tombs of the Valley of the Kings, which is used today.

219 (below) The architecture of the Egyptian temples was carefully studied by Wilkinson, who classified the various types of columns and capitals; this illustration shows a papyriform column with a papyrus bud capital.

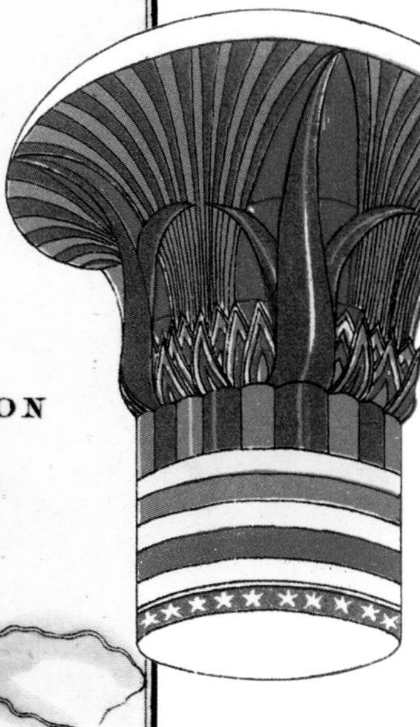

John Gardner Wilkinson (1797–1875) was educated at Harrow and then Oxford University, but abandoned his studies without graduating, after only two years. He then intended to embark on a military career as an officer in His Majesty's army, but, before enlisting, he decided to travel to Europe and Egypt.

In 1820, while in Italy, he went to Naples where he met Sir William Gell, an antiquarian. Gell persuaded him to renounce his plans for a career as a soldier and devote himself instead to the study of Egyptian archaeology. The following year, Wilkinson, who was only twenty-four years old, arrived in Egypt, seven years before Champollion and Rosellini.

Over the next twelve years Wilkinson visited all the monuments and sites of the country, travelling up the Nile as far as the Second Cataract. He was the first to study in detail the paintings and reliefs adorning the tombs of el-Amarna and Beni Hasan, and to identify the site of the 'Labyrinth' of the Classical authors at Hawara in the Faiyum. He was also the first to write, unassisted, a historical and chronological survey of Egyptian antiquities. In 1824 the young British Egyptologist visited Thebes, where he made his home in an undecorated pillared tomb (TT83) on the west bank of the Nile, belonging to a dignitary of the Eighteenth Dynasty called Amethu. This is still clearly visible today, on the hill of Sheikh Abd el-Qurna, where there is one of the largest and most important of all the Theban private cemeteries. In a letter addressed to his cousin, Wilkinson describes his unusual dwelling – with which he was most satisfied:

I am now living in a grotto at Thebes and much inclined to give the Troglodytes my praise for their good sense in choosing these abodes which present a uniform and unvaried temperature both in summer and in winter.

Wilkinson was not the only European to live in the necropolis at Qurna: a few years earlier Belzoni had also stayed here, and Wilkinson now found himself in the company of other Europeans, including the

220 (below left) In Wilkinson's day tomb robberies were very frequent because the local people, noting the growing interest of the Europeans in Egyptian antiquities, attempted to increase their meagre earnings by selling whatever they could find. In this watercolour by Wilkinson, a woman is searching for precious objects among the mummies in a Theban tomb.

220 (below) During the long period he spent at Thebes, Wilkinson found the head of a mummy in an excellent state of preservation, and he rapidly made this accurate drawing of it to record its state.

220–221 Wilkinson was the first systematically to study the private tombs of Thebes, also known as the 'Tombs of the Nobles'. In his book he reproduced this large scene adorning a wall of the tomb of the royal scribe Horemheb (TT78), who lived during the reigns of Thutmose IV and Amenhotep III, in the Eighteenth Dynasty. In the upper register the sarcophagus of the deceased is being transported to the tomb, followed by his funeral furnishings in the middle registers. In the lower one, the ritual pilgrimage to Abydos is depicted.

221 (opposite above, right) The ancient Egyptians believed that this small stela representing Horus of the crocodiles had magical powers and could avert danger; Wilkinson's drawing reproduces the object in beautifully precise detail.

agents of the consuls Salt and Drovetti, such as Piccinini (his first name is unknown) from Lucca, in Italy, and the Greeks Giovanni D'Athanasi (called Yanni) and George Triantaphyllos.

Unlike the consuls and their agents, however, Wilkinson had neither sufficient personal resources nor the financial backing to carry out excavations and instead copied the drawings and inscriptions in the tombs with immense patience and skill. He was the first scholar to focus his attention on the material culture and daily life of ancient Egypt. His unpublished notes, drawings and copies of inscriptions, forming a corpus of fifty-six volumes held in the Bodleian Library in Oxford, are still considered to be of great value to students of Egyptology today.

Wilkinson was also interested in hieroglyphic writing, the rudiments of which he had learnt before leaving England. He had studied the theories of Thomas Young, whose method of decipherment was reasonably correct, at least as far as the interpretation of many alphabetic signs was concerned. Thus the

young Egyptologist, who later adopted Champollion's method, had gained sufficient knowledge to read, at least approximately, names and royal cartouches. While he was at Thebes he decided systematically to study the tombs of Biban el-Muluk (as it was still known at that time – it was only later called the Valley of the Kings) which were not far away from his dwelling. Wilkinson believed that this would enable him to establish a precise chronology of the New Kingdom – in other words, of the kings who reigned in Thebes at the time when the Egyptian empire was at the height of its splendour and power.

Pococke and Bruce had already made sketches and drawn plans of some of the royal tombs, but without any order; Belzoni had discovered splendid new ones of great importance; James Burton, who began to work at Thebes in 1820, had drawn the first fairly accurate plans. But none of these explorers had studied the tombs methodically; still less had they classified them chronologically. Wilkinson was the first to read the

222–223 (above) Wilkinson copied this scene from the decoration of a wall in the vestibule of the tomb of Rekhmire (TT100), vizier of Thutmose III and Amenhotep II (Eighteenth Dynasty). It depicts the offering of tribute by Nubians, Asiatics and Libyans, consisting of African animals, elephants' tusks, skins of felines, gold in the form of ingots and dust, and pottery.

222–223 (below) Wilkinson carefully copied this scene in the tomb of the royal scribe Neferhotep (TT49), who lived during the reign of Pharaoh Ay (Eighteenth Dynasty). It shows the procession of boats transporting the deceased to his tomb, accompanied by weeping women and bearers of the tomb furnishings. In the first boat (on the left), a sem-priest, dressed in a leopard skin, burns incense. Often these drawings are the only records of scenes that have since been ruined or lost and so would otherwise be unknown today.

cartouches in the tombs, which were then correctly attributed to their owners.

In 1827, the British Egyptologist, working alone, had the inspired idea of assigning numbers to the tombs in the Valley of the Kings, based on the topography of the area – his system is still in use today. He painted the number of each tomb near its entrance, beginning with those in the lower part of the main valley and continuing with those located towards the end and in the side valleys.

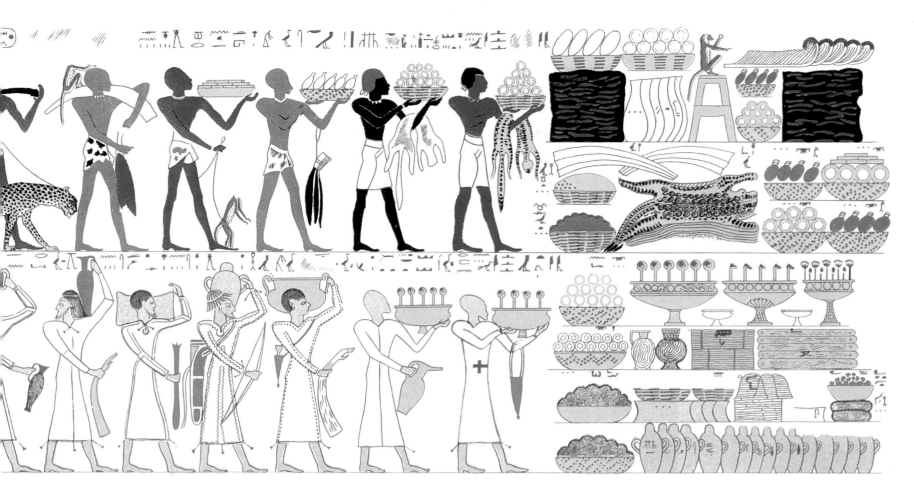

The twenty-one tombs in the Valley of the Kings numbered by Wilkinson were shown on his map entitled *Topographical Survey of Thebes*, which he made in 1830. When he returned to London in 1833, Wilkinson published his magnum opus, *Manners and Customs of the Ancient Egyptians, Including their Private Life, Government, Laws, Arts, Manufactures, Religion and Early History...*, which, for many years, was the most important study available on the society and material culture of ancient Egypt. Thanks to this work Wilkinson achieved great fame and was awarded a knighthood, although this hardly compensated for the fact that, unlike Champollion, Lepsius and other scholars, he had never received financial support from his country for his studies and researches.

Wilkinson returned to Egypt for the last time in the winter of 1855–56, and in the latter year he married, at the age of fifty-nine. After returning to England he remained there for the rest of his days. Having received great honours, he continued his Egyptological studies and published numerous books and articles until his death in 1875.

He is described in the prestigious publication *Who Was Who in Egyptology* as 'the real founder of Egyptology in Great Britain'.

Line of Original Casing

VYSE AND PERRING
THE LAST SECRETS OF THE GREAT PYRAMIDS

LEVE

GRE
VERTICAL SE
THROUGH PAS

The pyramids of Giza were much visited by travellers both in the Middle Ages and in the seventeenth century. It was only in the later period, however, that the first methodical studies and measurements were made, first by the Oxford astronomer John Greaves and then the French consul Benoît de Maillet. The leading travellers of the eighteenth century, such as the French Jesuit Claude Sicard, Captain Frederik Norden and the Reverend Richard Pococke all drew the pyramids, and, in 1765, a British diplomat, Nathaniel Davison, together with a French merchant called Meynard, explored the pyramid of Khufu, discovering the first of the five stress-relieving chambers above the burial chamber. But no true excavations were carried out until the nineteenth century. Even the scholars and engineers of the Napoleonic expedition, who studied the site of Giza meticulously, examining the internal structure of the pyramid of Khufu and making an accurate plan of the whole archaeological area, did not carry out excavations. Instead, they limited themselves to attempting to dismantle the westernmost of the three secondary or queens' pyramids next to the pyramid of Menkaure in 1801.

The first excavations at Giza were carried out by a Genoese naval captain, Giovanni Battista Caviglia, who began to work on the site in 1816 on behalf of the British Consul-General, Henry Salt. He first investigated the pyramid of Khufu, freeing the Descending Corridor from debris and discovering the unfinished subterranean chamber situated below the base of the pyramid.

Caviglia then carried out excavations around the Sphinx, where he uncovered the great stela of Thutmose IV – known as the 'Dream Stela' – between the forepaws of the monument, and large fragments of the ritual beard that originally adorned the chin of the colossus.

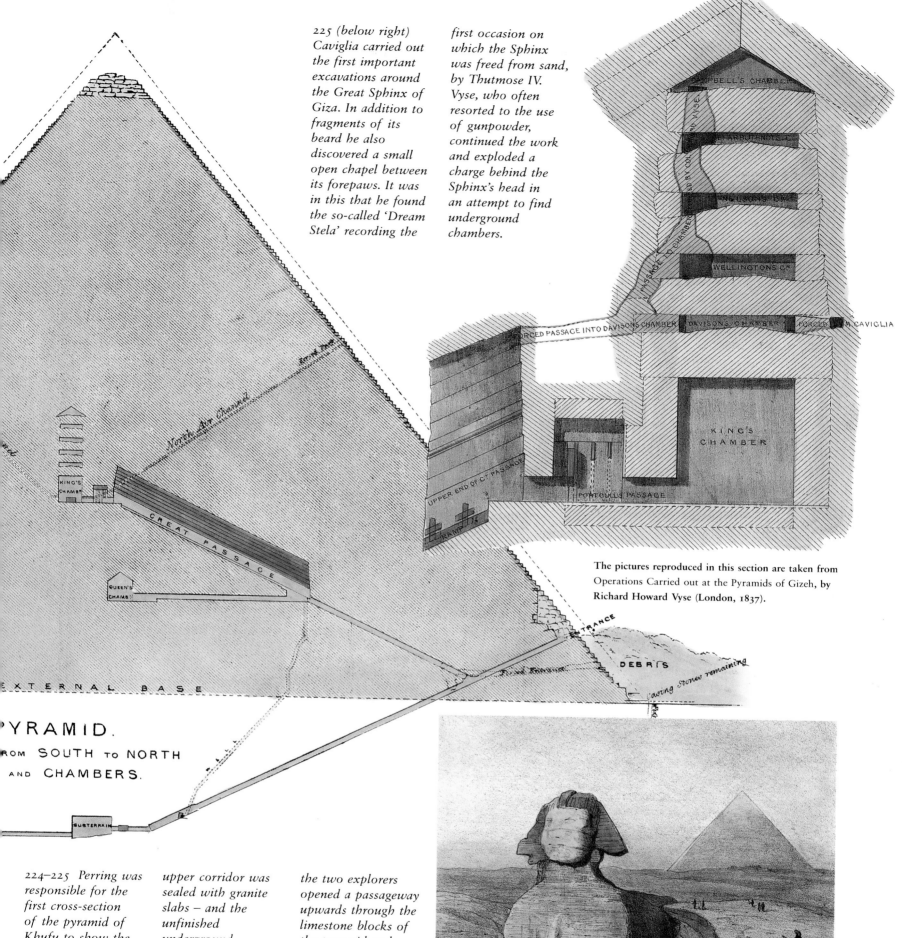

225 (below right) Caviglia carried out the first important excavations around the Great Sphinx of Giza. In addition to fragments of its beard he also discovered a small open chapel between its forepaws. It was in this that he found the so-called 'Dream Stela' recording the first occasion on which the Sphinx was freed from sand, by Thutmose IV. Vyse, who often resorted to the use of gunpowder, continued the work and exploded a charge behind the Sphinx's head in an attempt to find underground chambers.

CAMPBELL'S CHAMBER

ARBUTHNOT'S C.

NELSON'S CH.

WELLINGTONS C.

FORCED PASSAGE INTO DAVISONS CHAMBER   DAVISONS CHAMBER   FORCED BY M. CAVIGLIA

KING'S CHAMBER

UPPER END OF GT PASSAGE

PORTCULLIS PASSAGE

RAMP

PYRAMID.
FROM SOUTH TO NORTH
AND CHAMBERS.

North Air Channel

Forced Pass.

KING'S CHAMBER

GREAT PASSAGE

QUEEN'S CHAMB.

EXTERNAL BASE

ENTRANCE

DEBRIS

Casing Stones remaining

SUBTERRAIN

The pictures reproduced in this section are taken from Operations Carried out at the Pyramids of Gizeh, by Richard Howard Vyse (London, 1837).

224–225 Perring was responsible for the first cross-section of the pyramid of Khufu to show the complete details of the internal structure, which Vyse later reproduced in his book. Compared with earlier cross-sections, the new features are the stress-relieving chambers, the passage linking the Ascending Corridor with the Descending Corridor – probably used by workers to escape after the upper corridor was sealed with granite slabs – and the unfinished underground chamber. The last two structures had been discovered in 1817 by Caviglia.

225 (above right) Vyse and Perring focused their attention on the structures above Khufu's burial chamber where, in 1765, Davison had discovered an empty space. Starting from Davison's chamber, the two explorers opened a passageway upwards through the limestone blocks of the pyramid and discovered another four voids, named by them 'Wellington's chamber', 'Nelson's chamber', 'Lady Arbuthnot's chamber' and 'Campbell's chamber'. These 'stress relieving chambers' were designed to reduce the weight of the structure pressing down on the burial chamber.

225

Two years later, in 1818, the Paduan adventurer Giovanni Battista Belzoni made a sensational discovery, when he entered the pyramid of Khafre. Nevertheless, the first systematic excavations in the area of Giza were only carried out about twenty years later by two Englishmen, Colonel Richard Howard Vyse (1784–1853) and the engineer John Shae Perring (1813–1869).

On his arrival in Egypt in 1835, Vyse hired Caviglia, whom he instructed to begin excavations at Giza in 1836. However, Vyse was soon dissatisfied with Caviglia's methods, which he considered to be unproductive and disorganized. The following year Vyse began to work with Perring, an extremely methodical man, a good topographer and a skilled draughtsman, who had already worked in Egypt as the director of public works for the Pasha Muhammad Ali. Vyse first

located the lower entrance of the pyramid of Khafre, which Belzoni had overlooked, and he then carried out excavations inside the pyramid of Khufu, creating a passage up through the body of the monument from 'Davison's chamber' (named after its discoverer). He found four other voids above, which he named 'Wellington's chamber' (II), 'Nelson's chamber' (III), 'Lady Arbuthnot's chamber' (IV, named after the wife of a senior British officer), and 'Campbell's chamber' (V, named in honour of the British Consul-General in Egypt). On the walls of the last two Vyse and Perring found hieroglyphs painted in red and the cartouche of Khufu, the ancient name of the king who was better known by the Greek name 'Cheops'. This was a very significant discovery: for the first time the Great Pyramid could be firmly attributed to this pharaoh.

226 (centre left) Vyse paid particular attention to the pyramid of Menkaure, the only one of the Giza pyramids to which the entrance had not been found. On its north side is the huge breach made in 1196 by Abd el-Aziz Othman, son of Saladin, in his attempt to enter the pyramid.

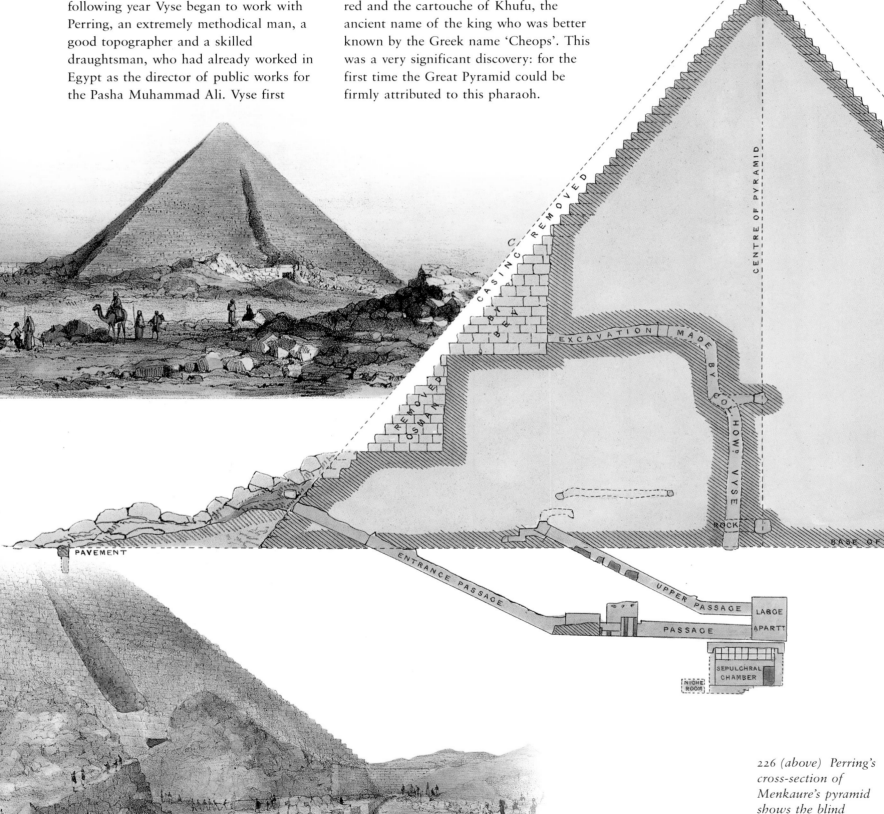

226 (above) Perring's cross-section of Menkaure's pyramid shows the blind passage that Vyse dug in vain, and reveals the complex structure of the funerary apartments.

226 (opposite below, left) Vyse began to excavate the north face of Menkaure's pyramid, near the existing large breach. He opened a passage that allowed him to reach the pyramid's centre, but not the funeral apartments. It was only after the debris had been removed from the pyramid's base that Vyse came upon the entrance to the descending corridor leading to the burial chamber.

C

REMOVED

20   30   40   60   100 ft.

In order to create an opening in the mass of limestone blocks that formed the pyramid – something that even Caviglia had been unable to do, although he had attempted to excavate on the south side of 'Davison's chamber' – Vyse had resorted to using explosives. He used gunpowder again on the Sphinx, in an attempt to ascertain whether there was a cavity inside it.

But it was the pyramid of Menkaure that produced the most rewarding results for Vyse and Perring. They first excavated one of the three secondary, or queens', pyramids (the central one, now labelled GIIIb), opening up a passage that took them to the interior of the burial chamber. Here they found a granite sarcophagus containing the skeleton of a woman, as well as inscriptions attesting, for the first time, that the third great pyramid of Giza did indeed belong to Menkaure.

227 (below) On 1 August 1837 Vyse and Perring entered the burial chamber of the pyramid of Menkaure, which contained a large sarcophagus against one of the granite walls. In this drawing Edward Andrews, an artist working with Vyse, depicts the moment of the discovery.

227 (top) Inside Menkaure's pyramid, in the antechamber preceding the burial chamber, Vyse and Perring found an incomplete wooden anthropoid coffin and fragments of a human body. Although the coffin bore the name of Mycerinus (Menkaure), it was in a style typical of the Twenty-Sixth (Saite) Dynasty, and was therefore about twenty centuries too recent, while the bones dated from the Islamic era. This chronological discrepancy suggests that these were later reburials.

227 (centre right) The most important find in the pyramid was the royal sarcophagus made of basalt and decorated with a palace-façade motif. After it had been removed with great difficulty, the sarcophagus was loaded on to a ship, the Beatrice, to be taken back to England. It never arrived, however, because the vessel sank during a storm.

227

228 (above) Vyse and Perring also carried out surveys at Saqqara, where some years previously Girolamo Segato had entered the Step Pyramid of Djoser, although they did not undertake any excavations in this area.

Vyse then attempted to enter the interior of the king's pyramid, the only one to which the entrance had not yet been found. Starting at the large breach visible in the centre of its north side – which had been made at the end of the twelfth century by Abd el-Aziz Othman, son of the famous Saladin – Vyse dug a long tunnel. This initially took a horizontal direction, to reach the centre of the pyramid, and then became a vertical shaft, arriving at the base of the monument.

This laborious effort turned out to be fruitless, however, and the operation had to be abandoned. Vyse and Perring then decided to remove the debris from the northern side of the pyramid, where they finally found the original passage leading to the burial chambers. In his book *Operations Carried on at the Pyramids of Gizeh...*, Vyse wrote:

As soon as they [the workers] were dismissed, Mr. Andrews and myself returned full of expectation to the mysterious entrance, impatient to examine what had excited the curiosity, and had hitherto been supposed to have eluded the researches of all explorers....

Vyse, accompanied by a painter, Edward J. Andrews, finally managed to enter the pyramid of Menkaure on 1 August 1837 – the last pyramid at Giza to be re-entered in modern times. Sadly, as had had been the case when Belzoni entered Khafre's pyramid, Vyse found Arabic inscriptions revealing that this pyramid too had already been violated.

A basalt sarcophagus still stood in the interior of the burial chamber. Decorated with the palace-façade motif typical of the Old Kingdom, the sarcophagus was empty and lacking its lid. This was the only example of a decorated sarcophagus found in the pyramids of Giza. The lid was discovered in an upper chamber in pieces, together with fragments of a human body and an incomplete wooden anthropoid coffin in a style typical of the much later Twenty-Sixth, Saite, Dynasty (seventh and sixth centuries BC). An inscription on the coffin stated that it belonged to 'Osiris Menkaure', the name of the pharaoh transcribed as Mycerinus by the Greeks. Radiocarbon dating of the bones, however, has revealed that they are much more recent – after the start of the Islamic era.

The sarcophagus was sent to the British Museum, but never arrived because the ship that was carrying it sank in a storm off the Tuscan coast. The other finds, however, arrived safely at the museum, as they were transported on the ship that took Vyse back to England late in 1837.

228

HIEROGLYPHICS FOUND IN G.T PYRAMID.
DRAWN ½ REAL SIZE.

Fig.1.

FORMER HEIGHT 327.10.

SECTION THROUGH CENTRE (LOOKING W.)

BASE OF PYRAMID

ROOF

ENTRANCE & PASSAGE

SUPPOSED SITUATION OF PASSAGE

RUBBLE MASONRY

LOOSE STONES & RUBBISH

Fig. 4.

BASALT   BASALT

PAVEMENT

MASONRY

SECTION OF S.ᴿᴺ

Fig. 3.

PROBABLE EXTENT OF APART

CENTRE OF PYRAMID

Fig. 2.

PASSAGE
PLAN

Scale of   10   20   30   40   50   100 F.ᵗ

229 (above) At Abusir, between Giza and Saqqara, Perring drew a cross-section of the pyramid of the Fifth-Dynasty pharaoh Neferirkare.

The funerary apartments inside the pyramid were covered with inscriptions, which Perring copied very precisely.

228 (below) and 229 (centre) At Dahshur, south of Saqqara, Vyse and Perring visited the pyramid of Amenemhet III (Twelfth Dynasty) built of mud-brick; at that time it was in a much better condition than it is today. They also studied the Bent Pyramid of Sneferu, founder of the Fourth Dynasty.

229 The pyramid of Meidum, a few miles south of Dahshur, was built during Sneferu's reign and may be regarded as the transitional stage between the step pyramid and the true pyramid. Perring drew the monument at the time of the annual Nile flood, when the waters of the river almost reached its base.

229

230 (below) On 15 October 1842, the nine members of the Prussian expedition celebrated the birthday of the King of Prussia on the top of Khufu's pyramid:

Lepsius, on the left in a light suit, is waving his hat in the air. The scene was drawn by Johann Jacob Frey, a painter who took part in the expedition.

231 (opposite) Lepsius visited the great archaeological sites of Upper Nubia (present-day Sudan) such as Gebel Barkal (1), Napata (2), Meroë (3) and Naqa (4). The route followed by the

Prussian expedition and all the sites visited in Upper Nubia are highlighted in this detail taken from the map of the Nile drawn by the German astronomer Güfsefeld.

231 (opposite, below right) Richard Lepsius as a young man (left), and after his second journey to Egypt in 1866 (right). It was on the later visit that he discovered at Tanis the famous Canopus Decree, a bilingual stela which confirmed once and for all the validity of Champollion's method of decipherment.

THE PRUSSIAN EXPEDITION OF RICHARD LEPSIUS

230 (right) Having made plans and drawings of the archaeological sites of Lower Egypt and the cemetery at Memphis, Lepsius and the members of his expedition set sail from Beni Suef on 23 August 1843 for Upper Egypt. After the usual visit to Thebes, they arrived at Esna, where they admired the great Ptolemaic temple dedicated to the god Khnum, 'the divine potter', who modelled living creatures and was the guardian of the First Cataract. The temple was still half-buried and to reach the hypostyle hall it was necessary to descend by the steps visible here.

In July 1833, a brilliant twenty-three-year-old Prussian Orientalist, a pupil of the diplomat and archaeologist Christian Josias von Bunsen and the famous naturalist and explorer Alexander von Humboldt, arrived in Paris. He was there to complete the philological studies that he had begun at the universities of Leipzig and Göttingen and to attend the lectures given by the archaeologist and historian Jean Antoine Letronne. His name was Karl Richard Lepsius (1810–1884) and within a few years he had earned the title 'the German Champollion'.

Champollion had died the year before Lepsius arrived in Paris, leaving the task of continuing his study of hieroglyphs to his pupils: Ippolito Rosellini, who taught at the University of Pisa and was his natural and most qualified successor; Francesco Salvolini, a controversial figure who was accused of having stolen some important notes from his mentor and publishing them in his own name; two Frenchmen, Charles Lenormant and Nestor L'Hôte, who had both accompanied Champollion on the

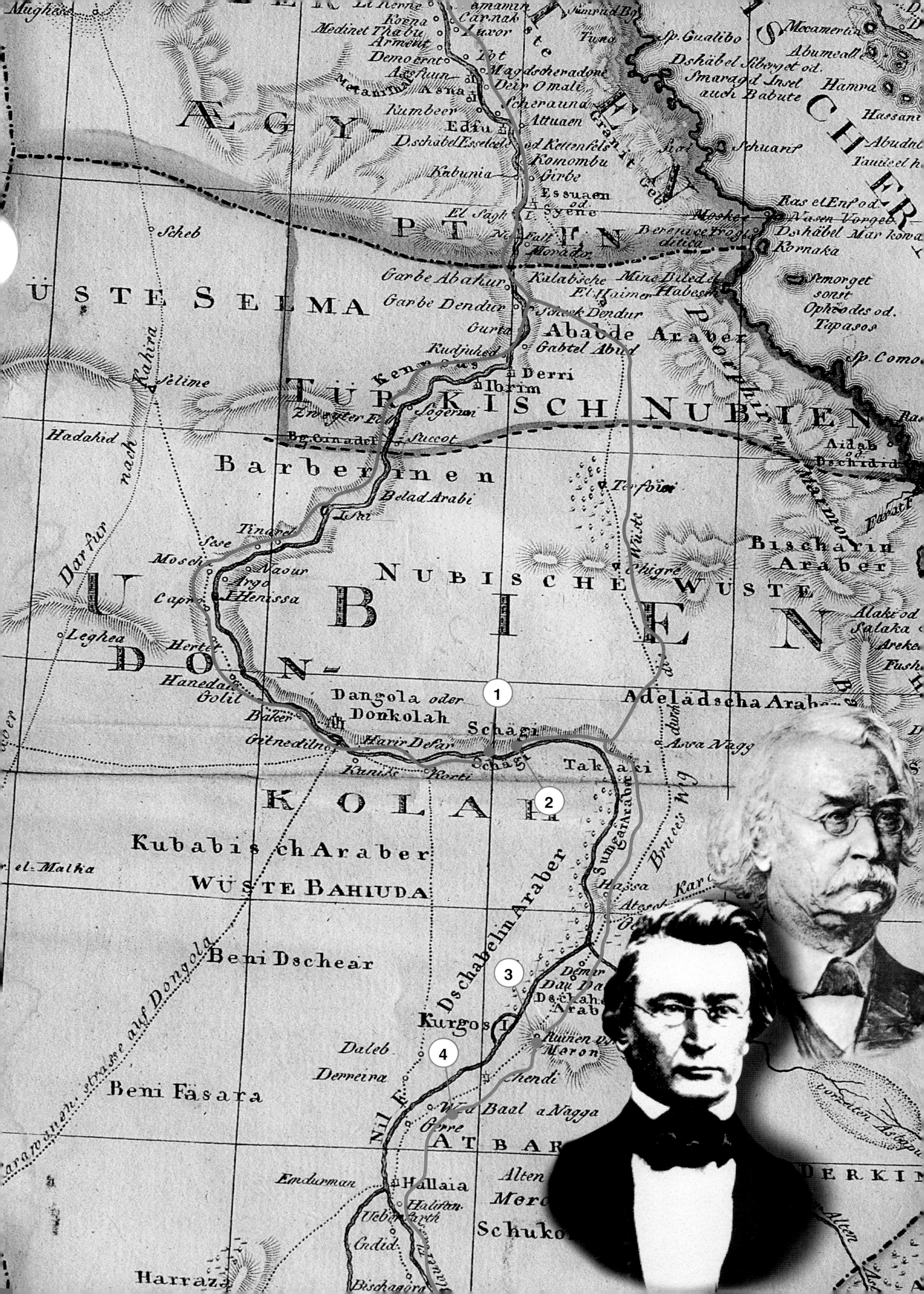

Mughara

ÆGY-

Medinet Thabu
Medinet Habu
Armênt
Demoerat
Agetun
Metanthis Aswa
Kumbeer
Edfu
Dschabel Esselede od Kettenfels
Kabunia
El Sagh
Garbe Abahur
Garbe Dendur
Guria
Rudjuhee
Keneus
ÜSTE SELMA

Scheb

Hadahid

Kahira

Seline

nach

Belad Arabi

Tinarel
Sase
Moschu
Argo
Capra
Herter
Hanedan
Golil
Baker
Octnedilho

Leghea

Dangola oder
Donkolah

Hanir Defar
Kanits
Korti

KOLAH

Kubabis ch Araber
WÜSTE BAHIUDA

el Malka

Beni Dschear

Beni Fasara

Daleb
Derreina

Harraza
Bischagora

ÆGY-PTIEN

Carnak
Luxor
Lot
Magdscheradone
Deir Omali
Scherauna
Attuaen
Komombu
Girbe
Essuaen
L. Syene
Neball
Monador

Kulabsche
El Haimer
Schech Dendur
Abade Araber
Gabtel Abud
Derri
Ibrim
Jogerin
Succot

TÜR-KISCH NUBIEN

Terfoisi

NUBISCHE WÜSTE

Tschigre

Schägi
Schägi
Takaki
Awa Nagg

Adelädscha Araber

Dschabelin Araber

Hassa

Demir
Dau Dau
Dschaha Araber

Ruinen von
Meroe

Wa Baal a Nagga
Gerre
ATBARA

Emdurman
Hallaia
Halfan
Ueber Garth
Gidid

Schukor

Alten
Mero

DON-

Kurgos I.

Nil F.

Tuno

Sp. Gualibo
Mecamertin
Abumealli
Dshäbel Siberget od
Smaragd Insel
auch Babute
Hamra
Hassani
Abudul
Tauisel h

CHER

Ras et Enf od
Nasen Vorgeb
Dshäbel Mar kowa
Kornaka

Moskee
Berenice Trogle
ditica

Semorget
sonst
Ophro des od
Tipasos

Sp. Como

Mine Biled el
Habesch

Aidab od
Dschidid

Bischariu
Araber

Alaki od
Salaka
Areke
Fush

DERKIN

Franco-Tuscan expedition; an Englishman, John Gardner Wilkinson; and a Dutchman, Conradus Leemans.

Prompted by Bunsen and Humboldt, Lepsius soon decided to abandon the study of other Oriental languages in order to devote himself to Egyptology. In 1836 he arrived in Italy to study the Egyptian collections, first in Turin and then in Rome, where he stayed for three years, working as a secretary at the German Archaeological Institute. In Italy he became acquainted with Salvolini and became a pupil of Ippolito Rosellini, adopting Champollion's method of decipherment, which he began to perfect by applying to hieroglyphic writing the rigorous methodology typical of German scholars.

Lepsius soon suggested a number of improvements on the method of interpretation devised by Champollion, as can be seen from his *Lettre à M. le Professeur H. Rosellini sur l'alphabet hiéroglyphique* of 1837. In this he explained the function of the alphabetical signs contained in hieroglyphic writing and demonstrated that they were used not only for writing proper nouns, but also as a guide to the pronunciation of the signs made up of a number of consonants.

While he was waiting to fulfil his dream of travelling to Egypt, Lepsius patiently copied many important hieroglyphic texts, and visited England and the Netherlands to examine the main Egyptian collections in those countries. In 1839 he returned to Germany, hoping to obtain a chair of Egyptology, and three years later, in 1842, he was appointed temporary professor of Egyptology at Berlin University. At the suggestion of Bunsen and Humboldt, the

232 (opposite above) Lepsius carefully studied and copied the texts and wall paintings of the private tombs in the great cemetery at Giza. This drawing shows a dignitary seated on a wooden stool, dressed in the classic attire of the Old Kingdom, with an accompanying text in vertical columns.

232 (opposite below) This unusual view of the pyramid of Khufu was drawn from the top of the pyramid of Khafre. On the left are the numerous rows of mastaba tombs of the western cemetery. Lepsius proposed a theory, now discredited, according to which the size of each pyramid varied in relation to the length of the reign of the pharaoh for whom it was built.

232–233 At the time of the visit by the Prussian expedition, some remains of Amenemhet III's immense mortuary temple still survived next to his pyramid at Hawara, in the Faiyum. Said to have contained over three thousand rooms, this structure was called the 'Labyrinth' by Classical authors. Today, this huge temple made of mud-brick has completely disappeared.

King of Prussia, Frederick William IV – who was particularly interested in Egyptian antiquities and had already purchased the collection of Giuseppe Passalacqua – entrusted Lepsius with the direction of a great expedition to Egypt. Its aim was to collect artifacts for the future Berlin Museum and document the monuments of ancient Egypt as thoroughly as possible.

Lepsius, who was then thirty-two years old, began to organize this journey of a lifetime, inviting nine members to take part in the expedition – for which the king had allocated the notable sum of 34,600 thalers. The other members included the well-known engravers Ernest and Max Weidenbach, the Swiss painter Johann Jacob Frey, the Reverend Heinrich Johann Abeken, the British draughtsman Joseph Bonomi and his fellow countryman, the architect James William Wild. It was the most important and best organized scholarly expedition ever to visit Egypt.

King Frederick William contacted the Pasha of Egypt personally, asking him to ensure that the Egyptian authorities provided support and protection for the expedition. Not only was this request granted but permission was also given to carry out excavations anywhere in the country and in addition to export all objects found.

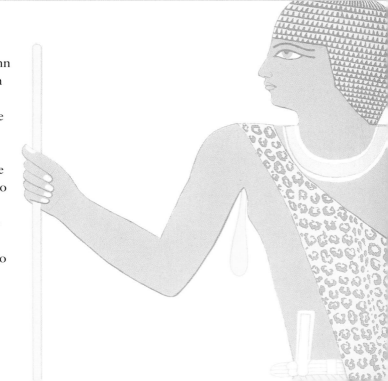

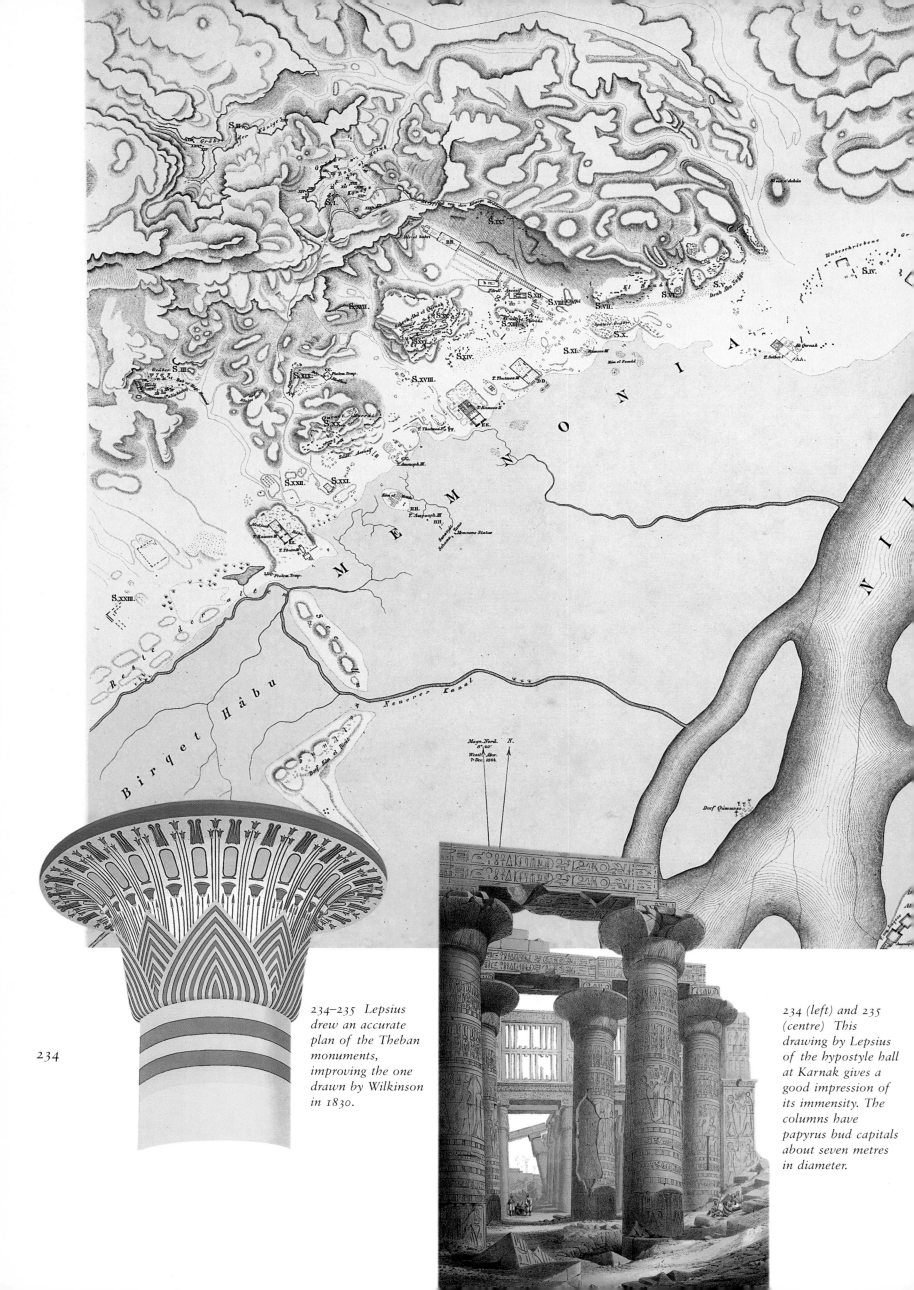

234–235 Lepsius
drew an accurate
plan of the Theban
monuments,
improving the one
drawn by Wilkinson
in 1830.

234 (left) and 235
(centre) This
drawing by Lepsius
of the hypostyle hall
at Karnak gives a
good impression of
its immensity. The
columns have
papyrus bud capitals
about seven metres
in diameter.

234

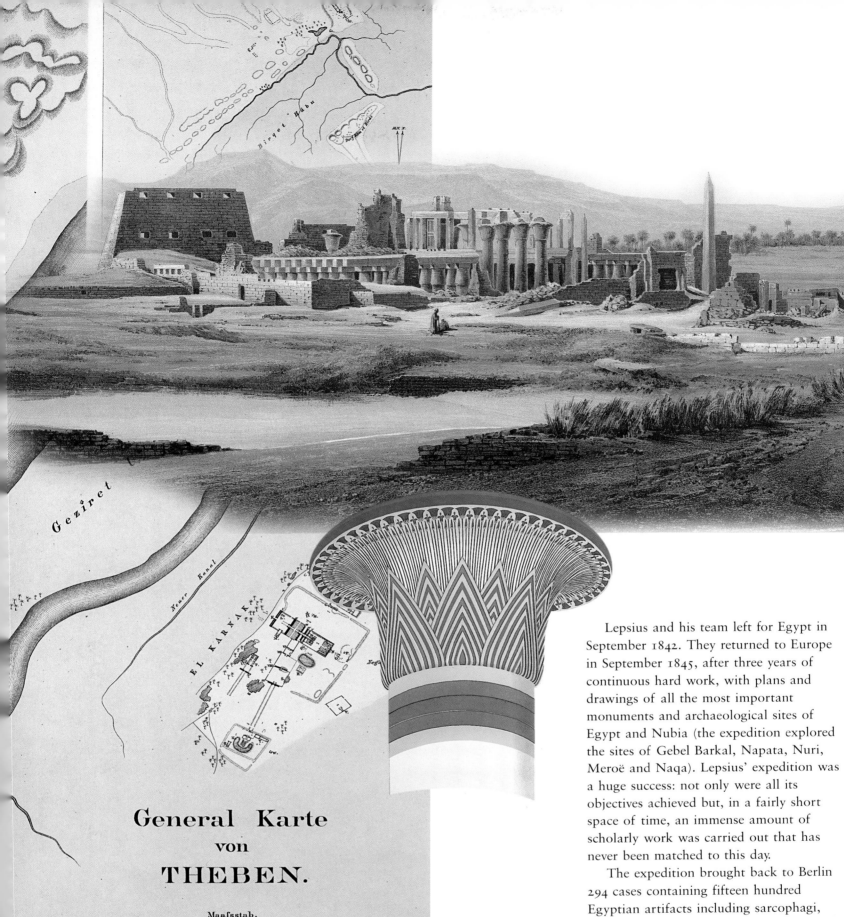

General Karte
von
THEBEN.

Maafsstab.

Lepsius and his team left for Egypt in September 1842. They returned to Europe in September 1845, after three years of continuous hard work, with plans and drawings of all the most important monuments and archaeological sites of Egypt and Nubia (the expedition explored the sites of Gebel Barkal, Napata, Nuri, Meroë and Naqa). Lepsius' expedition was a huge success: not only were all its objectives achieved but, in a fairly short space of time, an immense amount of scholarly work was carried out that has never been matched to this day.

The expedition brought back to Berlin 294 cases containing fifteen hundred Egyptian artifacts including sarcophagi, mummies, an obelisk and three complete burial chambers removed from Saqqara. The scholars also returned with thousands of drawings, copies of inscriptions and plans of archaeological sites and monuments that were published between 1849 and 1859 in an immense work entitled *Denkmäler aus Ägypten und Äthiopien* (*Monuments of Egypt and Ethiopia* – the term Ethiopia was used by the Germans to refer to Nubia).

In size and importance the *Denkmäler* can only be paralleled by the *Description de l'Égypte*. It consisted of twelve enormous folio volumes containing 894 plates that are still of fundamental importance to Egyptology today. This colossal work would not have been

235

234 (opposite below) Lepsius worked at Thebes on three separate occasions: first in October 1843, when he spent only about ten days there; then from November 1844 to February 1845, when he carried out a thorough investigation of the site; and, finally, when he returned for the last time in April 1845. This drawing is of the large hypostyle hall of the temple of Amun at Karnak, which Lepsius studied systematically for the first time, looking in particular at its inscriptions.

235 (above) At Karnak Lepsius hoped to obtain some precious reliefs for the Berlin Museum: the famous 'Table of Kings' of Thutmose III. These depict the pharaoh paying homage to sixty-one of his predecessors and are very important for the study of Egyptian chronology. Lepsius searched in vain among the ruins of the temple; but, shortly before, the French architect Émile Prisse d'Avennes had removed the reliefs at night and in great secrecy, and had sent them to Cairo. From there they were taken to France.

possible, however, without the previous publication by Champollion and Rosellini of the *Monumenti dell'Egitto e della Nubia*, which was used by Lepsius for comparing, correcting and improving his plans and drawings. In some respects, indeed, the *Denkmäler* may be considered as a complement to Champollion and Rosellini's work, especially with regard to its coverage of the monuments of the Old Kingdom, which were largely ignored by the Franco-Tuscan expedition.

After he had rearranged all the material he had brought back from Egypt, Lepsius began to teach Egyptology at Berlin University. In 1855 he was appointed co-director, together with Giuseppe Passalacqua – who had built up the original nucleus of its collection – of the new Egyptological museum in Berlin, where the objects found during the expedition were displayed.

In 1866, twenty years after the end of his expedition, Lepsius returned to Egypt to explore the Suez area and the eastern part of the Delta. Here he made another important discovery: a bilingual stela, known as the 'Canopus Decree', which once again confirmed the validity of the method of decipherment discovered by Champollion and perfected by his pupil, Rosellini.

Lepsius returned to Egypt once more in 1869, to attend the opening ceremony of the Suez Canal. He died in Berlin in 1884 at the age of seventy-four. In his long and brilliant career the 'German Champollion' was the author of 142 publications, but these did not include the text that should have accompanied his magnum opus, the *Denkmäler*.

At his death, this text was still in the form of notes, many on loose sheets. All the material was collected together in five volumes that were published later, between 1897 and 1913, by the Egyptologists Édouard Naville, Ludwig Borchardt and Kurt Sethe.

236–237 The mortuary temple of Seti I near the village of Qurna (West Thebes) is one of the few monuments that still appears today much as it did in the nineteenth century.

In the background is the peak of el-Qurn, with its pyramidal form towering over the royal and private cemeteries, while to the left the waters of the Nile in flood are just visible.

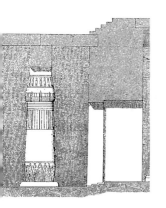

238 (opposite above and centre) Having carefully studied the remains of its original structure, Lepsius drew these reconstructions of the Ramesseum.

238 (opposite below) When in flood, the waters of the Nile lapped at the feet of the Colossi of Memnon; these once stood in front of the mortuary temple of Amenhotep III, which, because it was built of mud-brick, had been eroded by the river.

239 (centre) Lepsius worked in the Valley of the Kings in the winter of 1844–45. He examined no fewer than twenty-five tombs and cleared and cleaned the tombs of Ramesses II (KV7), Merneptah (KV8) and queen Hatshepsut (KV20).

239 (right) The reliefs adorning the columns and architraves of the hypostyle hall of the Ramesseum at West Thebes retained much of their original colouring when they were drawn by Lepsius, and still do today.

239

240 (left) Lepsius was assisted by the British draughtsman Joseph Bonomi in drawing the most outstanding reliefs of the Theban temples, such as these elegant depictions of a king and his royal spouse of the Eighteenth Dynasty. Bonomi had already worked at Thebes with Robert Hay.

240 (below left) and 241 (opposite, below right) Lepsius copied these texts and images taken from the Book of Gates in the chamber with four pillars in the tomb of Seti I. Unfortunately, he also removed part of a beautifully decorated pillar, damaging it irreparably.

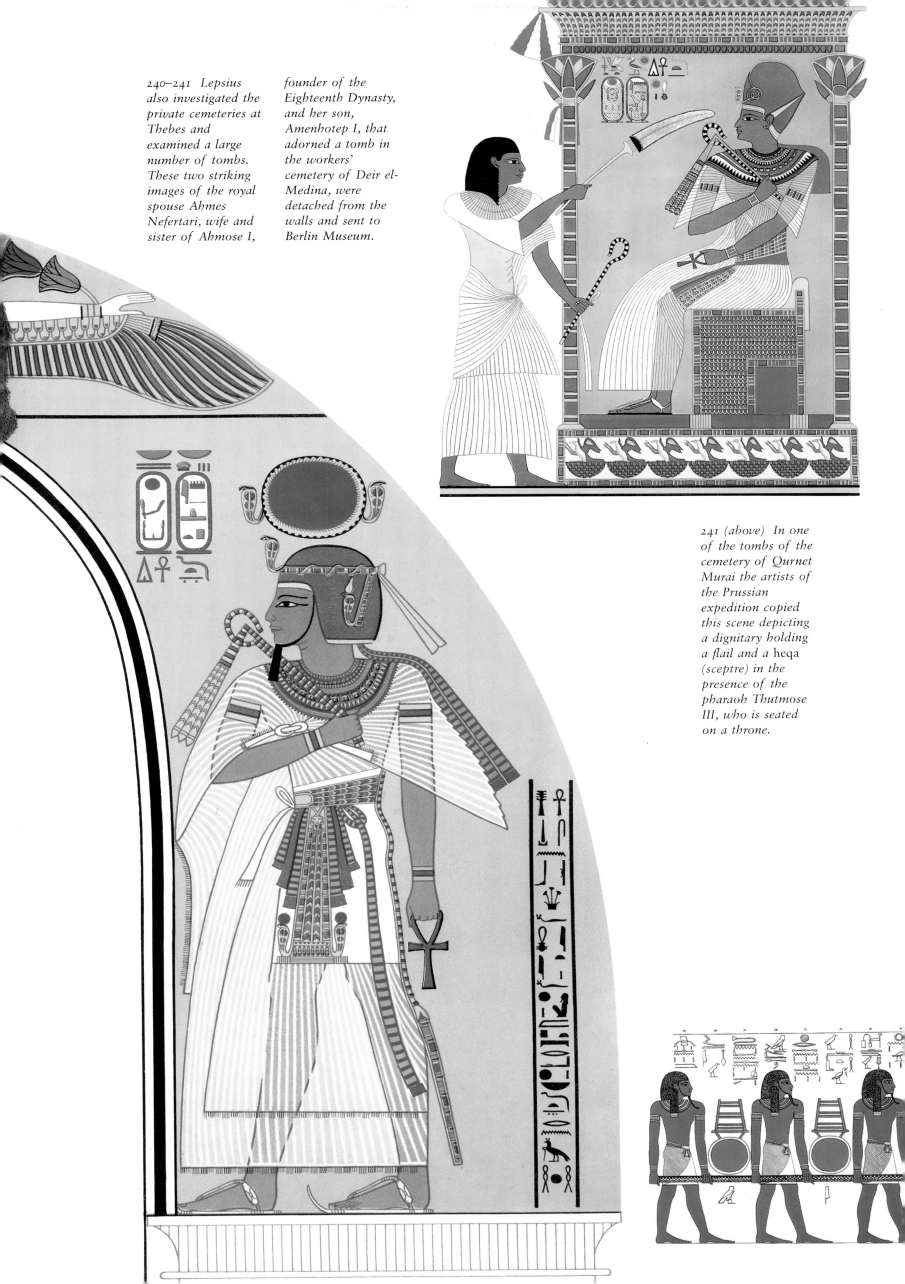

240–241 Lepsius also investigated the private cemeteries at Thebes and examined a large number of tombs. These two striking images of the royal spouse Ahmes Nefertari, wife and sister of Ahmose I, founder of the Eighteenth Dynasty, and her son, Amenhotep I, that adorned a tomb in the workers' cemetery of Deir el-Medina, were detached from the walls and sent to Berlin Museum.

241 (above) In one of the tombs of the cemetery of Qurnet Murai the artists of the Prussian expedition copied this scene depicting a dignitary holding a flail and a heqa (sceptre) in the presence of the pharaoh Thutmose III, who is seated on a throne.

242 and 243
The artists of the
Prussian expedition
were highly
accomplished and
produced many
beautiful drawings:
(left) a copy of relief
of a young prince of
the Twentieth

Dynasty with his
distinctive sidelock
of hair held in place
by gold ornaments;
and (right) a profile
of pharaoh Seti I,
lightly sketched in
charcoal in an
unfinished room in
his tomb.

244–245 One of the
most magnificent
Theban tombs
belonged to
Amenhotep, called
Huy – viceroy of
Kush in the reigns of
Amenhotep IV and
Tutankhamun – in
the cemetery of

Qurnet Murai
(TT40). Lepsius
drew one of the
most interesting
scenes with great
precision and
attention to detail.
The deceased is
depicted receiving
tributes from his

subjects (princes,
princesses and
Nubian dignitaries),
arranged in three
registers. In the
fourth register (the
lowest one),
Egyptian men and
women acclaim the
deceased.

242

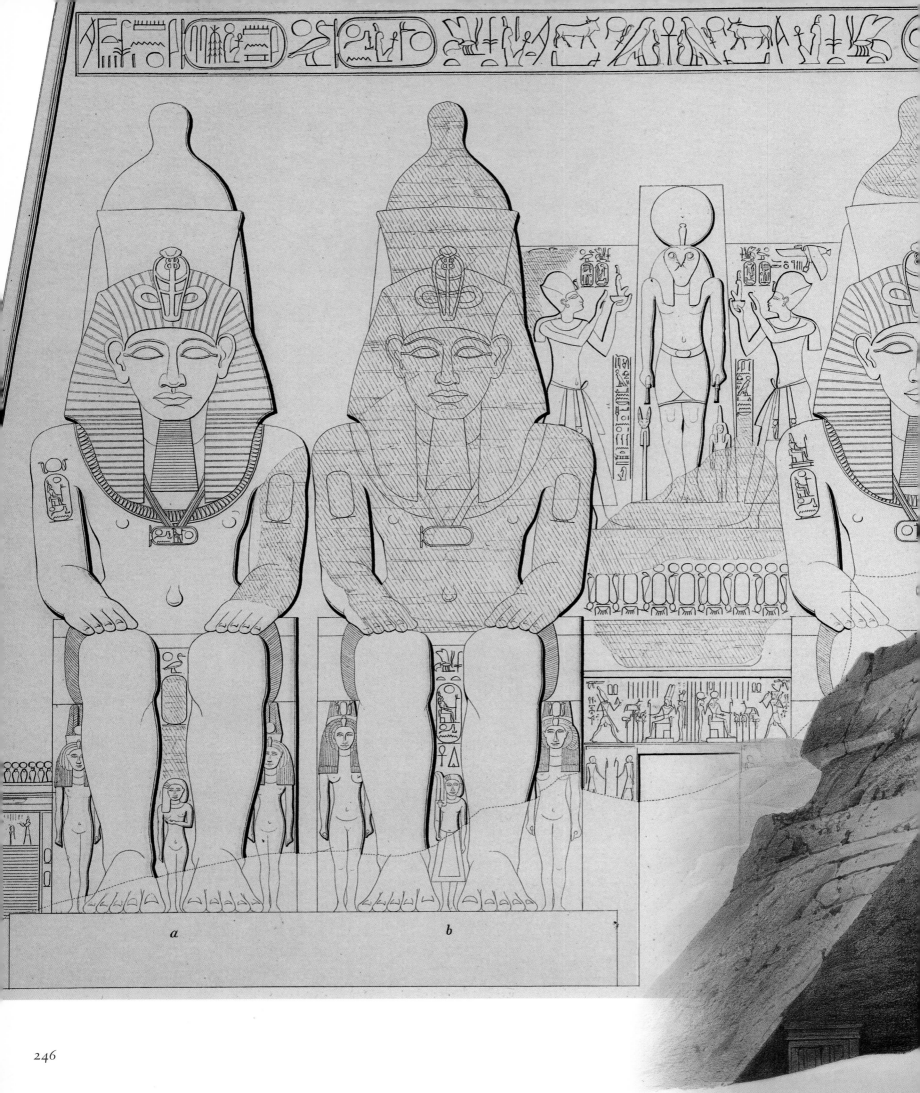

a

b

246

246 Lepsius drew a
reconstruction of the
façade of the Great
Temple of Ramesses
II at Abu Simbel as
it must have
appeared at the time
of its inauguration.

It is probable that
the head of the first
colossus to the south
fell during Ramesses'
reign, due either to
an earthquake or
fissuring of the
sandstone.

247 Lepsius arrived at Abu Simbel with his expedition in December 1843. He returned there on 2 August of the following year, after he had explored the archaeological sites of the Sudan. He then stayed at the site for nine days, to copy texts and reliefs. At that time the façade was still partially covered with sand, almost up to the level of the chin of the northern colossus. Lepsius and his companions had to clean a large part of the temple's external structure in order to copy the inscriptions and stelae on the north and south sides.

248–249 Inside the temple of Ramesses II at Abu Simbel, the large hypostyle hall had not changed since Belzoni had first seen it on 1 August 1817. A layer of sand reached up to the knees of the eight Osirian colossi adorning the internal faces of the pillars.

250 (left) In order to
reach the sites of the
Sudan more quickly,
Lepsius, like many
other travellers at the
time, preferred to
leave the Nile at
Korosko. He then
continued across the
Nubian Desert on a
camel, thus reaching
the village of Abu
Hamed directly and
avoiding the large
loop that the river
described in the
region of Dongola.

250–251 During his
return journey,
Lepsius and his
companions stopped
at Semna, a village
to the south of the
Second Cataract on
the narrows formed
by the Nile at this
point. He was able
to visit two temples
on the east and west
banks of the river
that are now in the
Archaeological
Museum in
Khartoum.

251 *Ramesses II and his wife Nefertari as depicted in reliefs at the Small Temple of Abu Simbel. The royal couple made a journey to Nubia on the occasion of the inauguration of the temple, in c. 1225* BC.

252 (above left) Lepsius and his companions ventured as far as Naqa, near the Sixth Cataract, about three hundred kilometres southwest of Meroë, where there were the remains of an important Meroitic city with two temples. One was dedicated to the Nubian lion god Apedemak and the other to Amun. From here they continued to Sennar, before beginning their return journey back up the Nile.

252 (below left) Amun was also worshipped in Nubia, above all in the form with a ram's head.

252 (opposite below, right) Napata, close to Gebel Barkal, was the political centre of a Nubian state some centuries before the heyday of Meroë. It rapidly developed in the eighth century BC and imposed its kings on Egypt until the mid-seventh century BC. Imitating Egyptian funerary customs of the Old and Middle Kingdoms, the kings of Napata, among them Taharqa, built their tombs in the form of pyramids, especially at Nuri.

252–253 (above) At the foot of Gebel Barkal, the 'sacred mountain' situated downstream from the Fourth Cataract, the Prussian expedition visited the temple of Amun. Here Lepsius took possession of a huge statue of Amun with a ram's head, which he removed with the assistance of a team of ninety-two Nubians; the sculpture was then transported to the Berlin Museum, where it can still be seen today.

253 (below) On 28 January 1844 the Prussian expedition reached the ruins of Meroë, capital of a vast kingdom that flourished between the fifth century BC and the third century AD as far north as the First Cataract. This site had been rediscovered by Frédéric Cailliaud in 1821, and was badly damaged in 1834 by Giuseppe Ferlini. He removed the tops of many of the pyramids in the royal cemetery in his search for treasure.

254 (left) In 1838 Maximilian Joseph, the Duke of Bavaria, undertook a journey to Egypt and the Near East in the company of friends and artists. The group included a painter, Heinrich von Mayr, who made numerous drawings of places, landscapes and people. These were published in two volumes; the frontispiece of the second is reproduced here.

254 (below) In the nineteenth century, Alexandria was the most important trading centre in the eastern Mediterranean, always crowded with ships carrying goods from the East to Europe. Goods from India and the Far East arrived at Suez by sea and were then either carried overland, or taken to the Nile and loaded on to boats for Alexandria.

255 (opposite) On his arrival in Egypt, Maximilian of Bavaria was officially received by the Pasha, Muhammad Ali. At that time the 'lord of Egypt' was sixty-nine years old, while the young German duke was only twenty-seven.

MAXIMILIAN OF BAVARIA
A JOURNEY TO NUBIA

One of the many travellers who journeyed up the Nile to Upper Egypt and Nubia in the first half of the nineteenth century was Maximilian Joseph, the Duke of Bavaria and son of King Ludwig I of Bavaria, who ascended the throne in 1848 as Maximilian II. Born in Munich in 1811, Maximilian displayed a deep interest in the arts, architecture and literature, and travelled to Italy and Greece. His small court welcomed artists, philosophers and men of letters, with whom the duke, who was particularly attracted by the humanities, engaged in long discussions.

In 1838 Maximilian undertook a long journey to the Near East, during which he visited Egypt, Palestine, Syria and Malta.

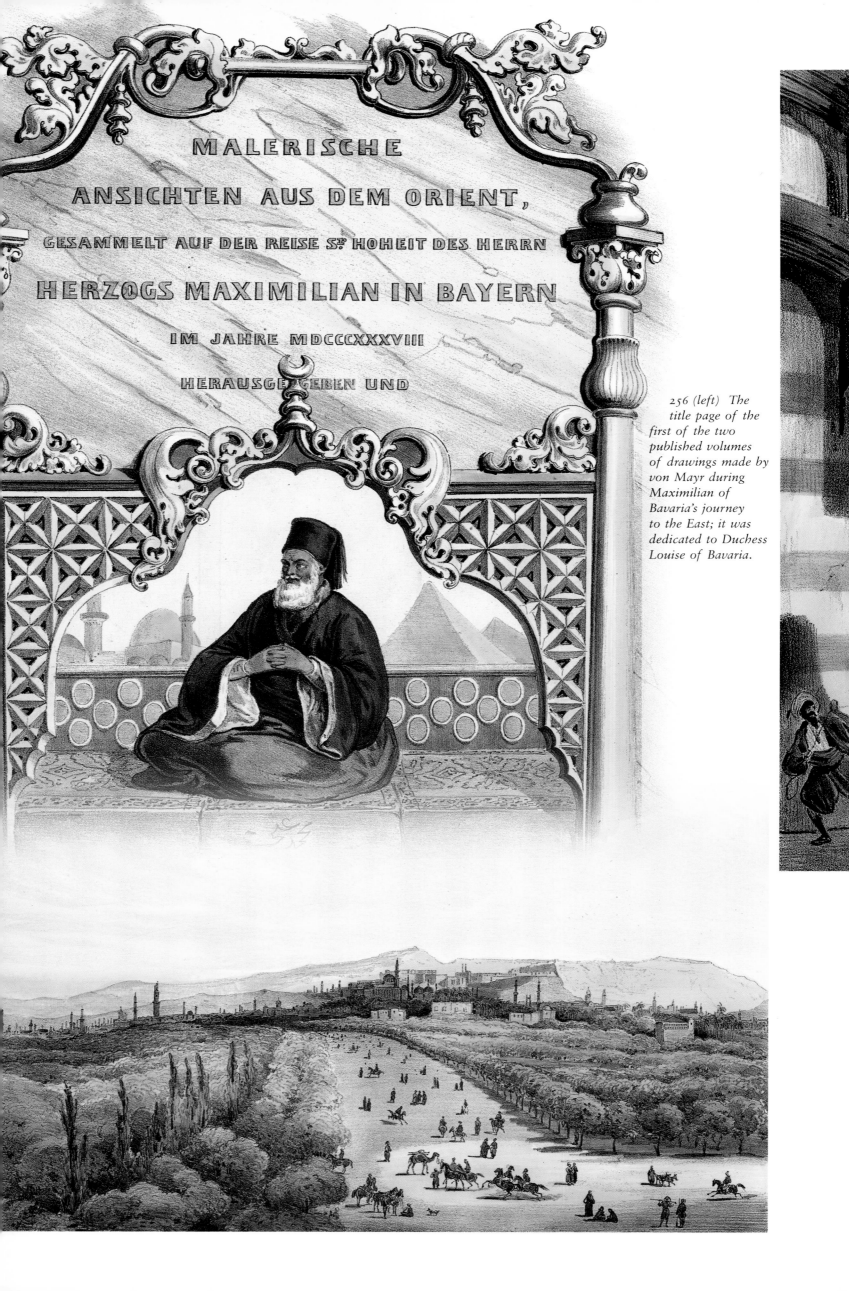

MALERISCHE

ANSICHTEN AUS DEM ORIENT,

GESAMMELT AUF DER REISE Sr. HOHEIT DES HERRN

HERZOGS MAXIMILIAN IN BAYERN

IM JAHRE MDCCCXXXVIII

HERAUSGEGEBEN UND

256 (left) The title page of the first of the two published volumes of drawings made by von Mayr during Maximilian of Bavaria's journey to the East; it was dedicated to Duchess Louise of Bavaria.

256 (opposite below) This view of Cairo seen from the residence of Ibrahim Pasha (one of Muhammad Ali's sons) – situated outside the city walls – shows the wide avenue leading into the city across the huge park surrounding the palace. In the distance, the Moqattam Hills and the fortress known as the Citadel are visible.

257 'None of the cities of the East can rival with Cairo for variety and interest', wrote Heinrich von Mayr. This is a view of one of the busiest streets of the suq, the city's market area. The crowds of merchants, traders and craftsmen thronging the streets were so large that the artist had to be escorted by a bodyguard to keep onlookers at a distance while he made this drawing.

He set out with a group of friends and a number of artists, including the painter and illustrator Heinrich von Mayr. After visiting Cairo, Maximilian sailed up the Nile, firstly to Thebes and then to Aswan. Having passed the First Cataract he arrived at Abu Simbel on 29 March 1838; he then ventured as far as the Second Cataract.

Maximilian was greatly impressed by the majesty of the Great Temple of Ramesses II, which von Mayr described as 'the greatest and most magnificent masterpiece of antiquity'. The entrance had been opened twenty-one years previously thanks to the efforts of Belzoni, but it was still 'so low that it was only possible to enter on all fours'. Next to the signature of another German nobleman, Prince Hermann von Pückler-Muskau, who had visited the site the previous year, the Duke

of Bavaria had his name and the date engraved (MAXIMILIAN HERZOG IN BAYERN - 29.3.1838), together with the ducal crown, on the breast of one of the four colossal statues representing the enthroned pharaoh that dominate the façade of the temple.

On his return to Europe, Maximilian published an account of his journey in a book entitled *Wanderung nach Oriente* (*Journey to the Orient*). And Heinrich von Mayr published a splendid collection of engravings entitled *Malerische Ansichten aus dem Oriente... (Picturesque Views of the Orient...).*

A large section of this work, which is of the highest artistic quality, is devoted to the Nubian part of Maximilian's journey. Illustrations depict the customs of the inhabitants of the area, who are described as 'robust and handsome, with a graceful

258 A harem – a word that has always fired the imagination of Western visitors – was the part of a palace reserved for the use of wives and concubines and their maidservants. Eunuchs were the only other men allowed into this area apart from the owner. The women spent their time listening to music, playing musical instruments, dancing, conversing and eating.

259 (opposite above) In the great palaces of Cairo the baths were divided into two separate areas, one for women and the other for men. They formed important centres of domestic life.

259 (opposite below) Egyptian women were often elegantly attired and very accomplished. This painting depicts a woman in an exquisite silk dress, bedecked with numerous jewels.

carriage, armed with a spear and a shield made out of crocodile skin and a knife enclosed in a sheath and carried attached to the upper part of the right arm'. The temples of Abu Simbel and the other lesser Nubian temples, such as Amada and el-Derr, el-Sebua, el-Maharraqa, el-Dakka, Dendur, Kalabasha and Gerf Hussein, are also depicted.

The illustrations of Gerf Hussein, described as 'very imposing, with colossal caryatids and the vestibule constructed with huge stones…', are particularly interesting: not only are they the first depictions of this site, but they are now also the best record of it. Gerf Hussein is one of the monuments that, at the time of the Nubian Rescue Campaign co-ordinated by UNESCO, it was unfortunately not possible to save from submersion under the rising waters of the Nile due to the construction of the Aswan High Dam. Today, its ruins lie at a depth of around sixty metres below the surface of the enormous lake, Lake Nasser, that formed behind the dam.

Eight years later, in 1846, the first collection of engravings was followed by another one, entitled *Genre-Bilder aus dem Oriente* (*Genre Pictures from the Orient*), also illustrated by Mayr, but accompanied by a text written by the physician and naturalist Sebastian Fischer, director of the hospital of Qasr el-Ain in Cairo and a keen Orientalist.

This work was mainly concerned with the customs and daily lives of the people of Egypt at the time of Muhammad Ali. With an almost ethnographic interest, the plates depicted typical subjects of the day, such as military uniforms, including those of the cavalry; mosques with their minarets and the *muezzin* calling the faithful to prayer; *harems*; peasants; pilgrims on their way to Mecca; Koranic schools; and other themes that recall – although they are different in style – the drawings of the English traveller Richard Dalton a century earlier.

260–261 A group of female musicians and dancers entertains some elegantly dressed women, who are seated on cushions, smoking and drinking coffee.

261 When the rich Bedouins journeyed with their harems, the wives travelled under a canopy on the back of a camel, protected from prying eyes by curtains.

262 (below)
'Numerous pylons, columns and ruins of temples covered the part of Thebes known as Karnak' – this how von Mayr described the great complex at Thebes. His drawing shows the southern part of the temple of Amun, with the magnificent portal of Ptolemy III Euergetes and the temple of the god Khonsu, the starting-point of processional avenue lined with ram-headed sphinxes, most of which were already headless, leading to the temple of Luxor.

262–263 For von Mayr, the great temple of Amun at Karnak 'for its size, its style and its magnificence, surpassed all the other monuments of the country'. This drawing shows the second pylon and the columns of the hypostyle hall, with their huge capitals that still retained their original bright colours. On the right is a column from the kiosk of the Nubian pharaoh Taharqa (Twenty-Fifth Dynasty), while in the background the obelisk of Thutmose I is just visible.

263 (below) At the time of Maximilian's journey, the temple of Luxor was still half-buried in sand and used as a dwelling-place by the local people. The western obelisk had already been removed and sent to France; part of the ditch dug to remove it can be seen on the extreme right of the drawing.

264 (centre) Maximilian of Bavaria and his companions visited all the Nubian temples. This drawing of Gerf Hussein is of particular interest since the temple is now submerged beneath Lake Nasser; at that time it stood on the west bank of the Nile. Constructed by the viceroy of Kush, Setau, during the reign of Ramesses II, the temple had a rock-cut section, the vestibule of which is seen here. The pillars were decorated with colossal statues of the pharaoh.

264 (below) The Romano-Ptolemaic temple of el-Dakka has a pylon detached from the central body of the building. Between 1962 and 1968 the temple was dismantled and rebuilt, with its original orientation, at its present site at Wadi es-Sebua.

265 (above) Maximilian of Bavaria's caravan resting during the long journey across the Nubian Desert.

265 (below) To commemorate his visit to Abu Simbel, Maximilian had his name, the ducal crown and the date carved on the façade of the temple. It is still visible today on the breast of one of the colossi of the king, situated to the north of the entrance. The painter von Mayr carved his name on the same colossus.

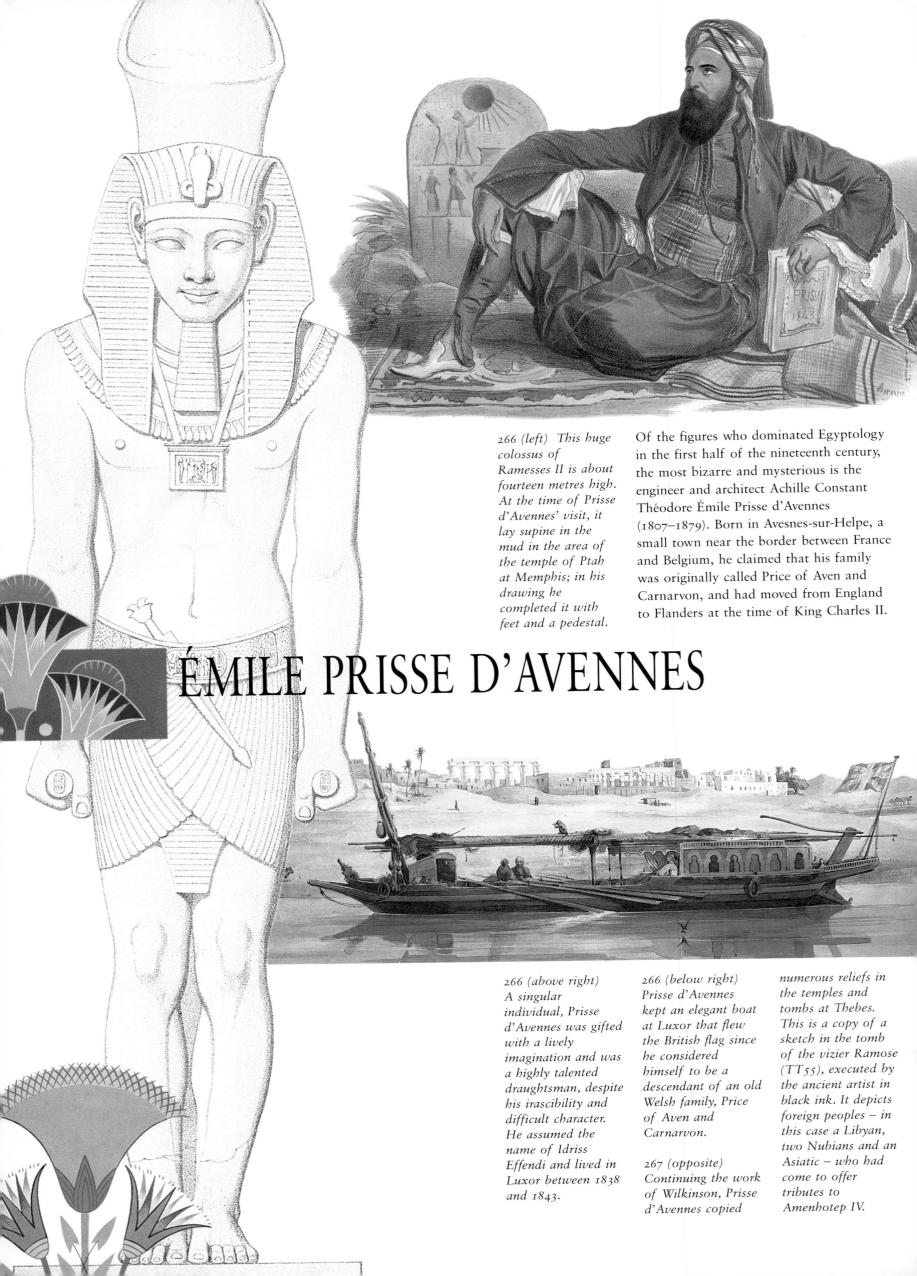

ÉMILE PRISSE D'AVENNES

266 (left) This huge colossus of Ramesses II is about fourteen metres high. At the time of Prisse d'Avennes' visit, it lay supine in the mud in the area of the temple of Ptah at Memphis; in his drawing he completed it with feet and a pedestal.

Of the figures who dominated Egyptology in the first half of the nineteenth century, the most bizarre and mysterious is the engineer and architect Achille Constant Théodore Émile Prisse d'Avennes (1807–1879). Born in Avesnes-sur-Helpe, a small town near the border between France and Belgium, he claimed that his family was originally called Price of Aven and Carnarvon, and had moved from England to Flanders at the time of King Charles II.

266 (above right) A singular individual, Prisse d'Avennes was gifted with a lively imagination and was a highly talented draughtsman, despite his irascibility and difficult character. He assumed the name of Idriss Effendi and lived in Luxor between 1838 and 1843.

266 (below right) Prisse d'Avennes kept an elegant boat at Luxor that flew the British flag since he considered himself to be a descendant of an old Welsh family, Price of Aven and Carnarvon.

267 (opposite) Continuing the work of Wilkinson, Prisse d'Avennes copied numerous reliefs in the temples and tombs at Thebes. This is a copy of a sketch in the tomb of the vizier Ramose (TT55), executed by the ancient artist in black ink. It depicts foreign peoples – in this case a Libyan, two Nubians and an Asiatic – who had come to offer tributes to Amenhotep IV.

After participating in the Greek war of independence from Turkish rule, Prisse d'Avennes went to Egypt in 1827. Here he was offered a position by Muhammad Ali as a civil engineer and professor of topography at the military academy for training the staff officers of the Egyptian army. Intelligent, dynamic, gifted with a highly developed artistic sense and exceptional skill as a draughtsman, but extremely irascible, Prisse d'Avennes' difficult character soon got him into trouble. An argument with the commander of the academy resulted in a transfer to the infantry school at Damietta, in the Delta, where Prisse d'Avennes began to examine and draw the ancient monuments. He learnt perfect Arabic and, by studying the works of Champollion, he was able to acquire a fairly sound knowledge of hieroglyphic writing.

Prisse d'Avennes found the duties associated with teaching increasingly burdensome, and in 1836 he resigned his post, leaving the Delta region and setting out for Upper Egypt. He stayed first at Aswan and Abu Simbel, and then in 1838 he settled in Luxor, where he bought a comfortable house. Like many other travellers and Orientalists at the time, Prisse d'Avennes abandoned Western clothes and wore Arab dress, adopting the name Idriss Effendi.

268 (opposite) Before devoting himself to the study of archaeology, Prisse d'Avennes had already spent nearly ten years in Egypt learning Arabic. He took a particular interest in the customs and habits of the Egyptians, portraying them with great sensitivity. On the left are two women near a Theban temple; below, next to the child, is the large water pipe, called a shisha *in Egypt, still used today.*

269 These two rich sheikhs belonging to the tribe of the Maaza (left) and the Suwarka (right), in the Suez area, display their elegant and elaborate costumes. This drawing was made by George Lloyd, a botanist and traveller who was a close friend and assistant of Prisse d'Avennes. Lloyd, who published a series of drawings of Egypt in a volume entitled The Valley of the Nile, *died tragically at Thebes in 1843 at the age of twenty-eight, when he accidentally shot himself with his own gun. The death of his friend was probably one of the reasons why Prisse d'Avennes decided to leave Luxor shortly afterwards.*

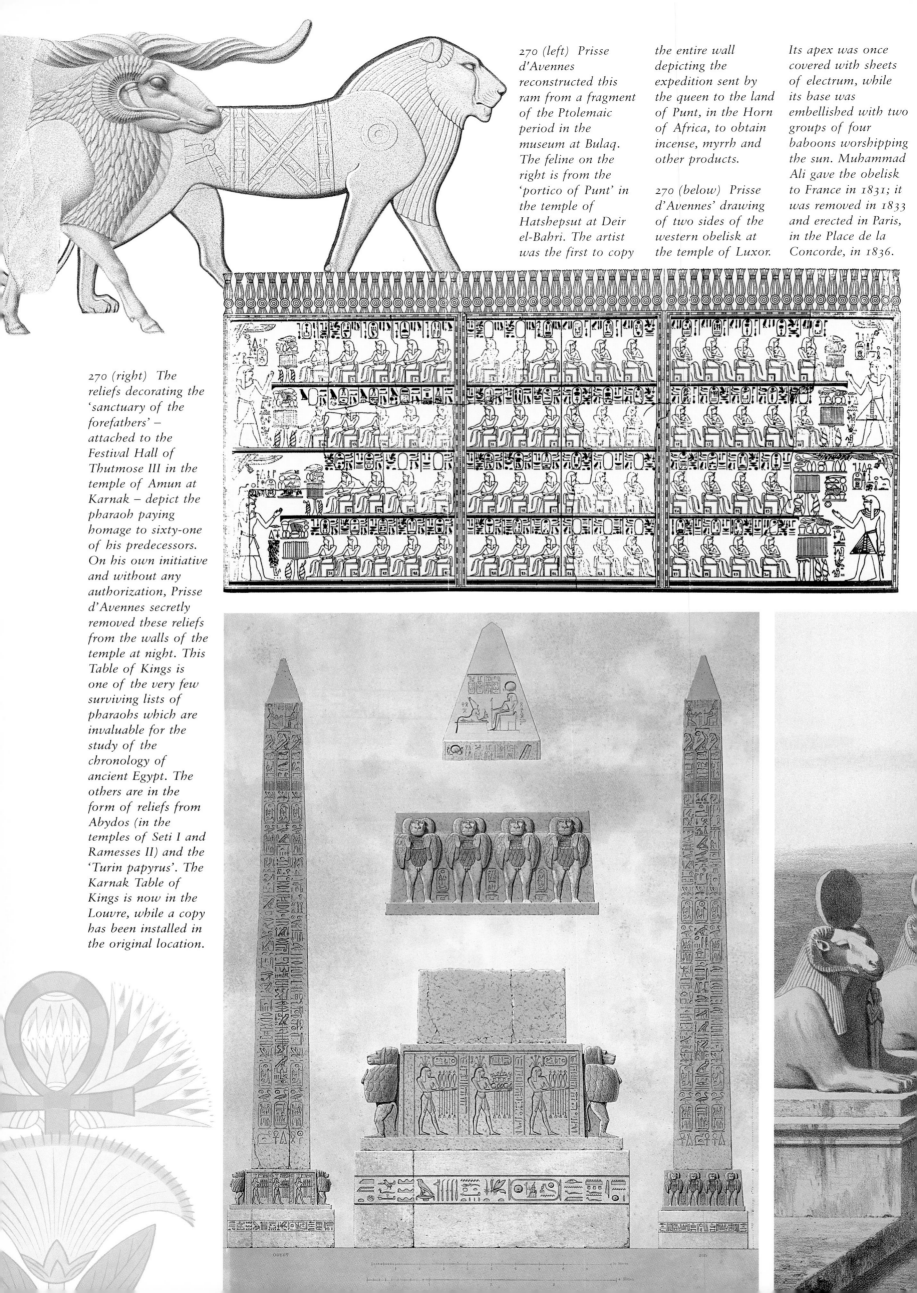

270 (left) Prisse d'Avennes reconstructed this ram from a fragment of the Ptolemaic period in the museum at Bulaq. The feline on the right is from the 'portico of Punt' in the temple of Hatshepsut at Deir el-Bahri. The artist was the first to copy the entire wall depicting the expedition sent by the queen to the land of Punt, in the Horn of Africa, to obtain incense, myrrh and other products.

270 (below) Prisse d'Avennes' drawing of two sides of the western obelisk at the temple of Luxor. Its apex was once covered with sheets of electrum, while its base was embellished with two groups of four baboons worshipping the sun. Muhammad Ali gave the obelisk to France in 1831; it was removed in 1833 and erected in Paris, in the Place de la Concorde, in 1836.

270 (right) The reliefs decorating the 'sanctuary of the forefathers' – attached to the Festival Hall of Thutmose III in the temple of Amun at Karnak – depict the pharaoh paying homage to sixty-one of his predecessors. On his own initiative and without any authorization, Prisse d'Avennes secretly removed these reliefs from the walls of the temple at night. This Table of Kings is one of the very few surviving lists of pharaohs which are invaluable for the study of the chronology of ancient Egypt. The others are in the form of reliefs from Abydos (in the temples of Seti I and Ramesses II) and the 'Turin papyrus'. The Karnak Table of Kings is now in the Louvre, while a copy has been installed in the original location.

270–271 (below)
This is how Prisse d'Avennes imaginatively reconstructed the original appearance of the avenue of ram-headed sphinxes linking the first pylon of the temple of Amun at Karnak to the landing stage for the procession of sacred barques of the Theban triad of Amun, Mut and Khonsu.

271 (right)
When Prisse d'Avennes drew his map of the area of the pyramids of Giza, based on the one by Napoleon's scholars, Auguste Mariette had only recently discovered the valley temple of the pyramid of Khafre. It is shown here correctly for the first time.

During his residence in Thebes, Prisse d'Avennes took a special interest in the temple of Karnak, studying the buildings in depth and making copies of many reliefs. This was especially at the request of the British Egyptologist John Gardner Wilkinson, who feared for the future of these masterpieces. Moreover, it was Prisse d'Avennes who drew the attention of the members of the academic world – and Wilkinson in particular – to the *talatats*, the marvellous rectangular stone blocks with polychrome decoration from structures built by Amenhotep IV, better known as Akhenaten. The buildings of this heretic pharaoh had been demolished after his death and some of the blocks reused in the construction of the ninth pylon of the temple of Karnak. This, in turn, was then used as a source of building materials in the nineteenth century.

A few years later, in 1843, a meeting occurred between the German Egyptologist Karl Richard Lepsius, who was heading towards Thebes with his expedition, and Prisse d'Avennes, who was coming down the Nile, near Beni Hasan. The Frenchman received Lepsius on board his boat, amicably offering him a cup of coffee. During the conversation, Lepsius explained that he had an important task to carry out

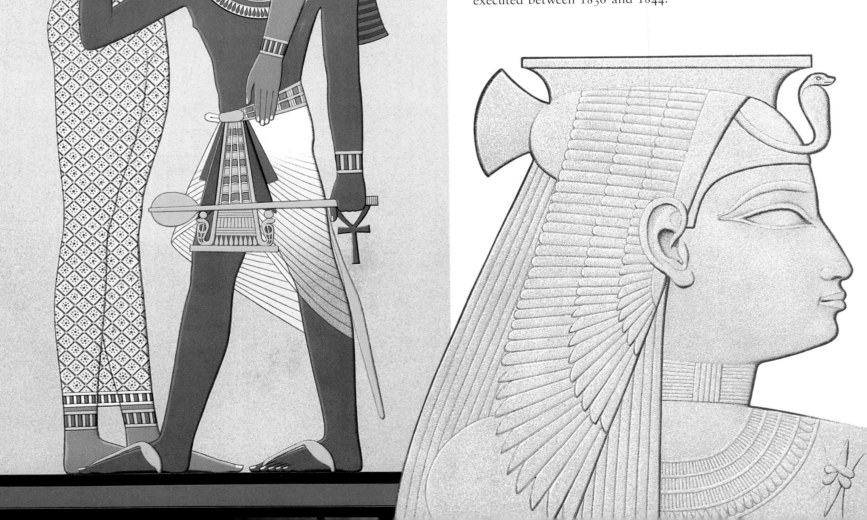

in the temple of Karnak: he had to remove and transport to Berlin the reliefs decorating the 'sanctuary of the forefathers', also known as the 'chamber of the king', dating from the reign of Thutmose III. Its name derives from the fact that its walls were decorated with the cartouches of all the kings who had enlarged and embellished the temple. Prisse d'Avennes listened attentively and wished Lepsius good luck in his venture. What he omitted to mention, however, was that the reliefs in question were actually in the cases on which they were both seated as they sipped their coffee.

Prisse d'Avennes had, in fact, already suspected that these masterpieces of Egyptian art would attract the attention of the Prussian expedition, about which he had been informed. Therefore, in order to secure the reliefs, although he had no authorization to do so, he detached them from the walls, working by night or during the hottest period of the day when no one ventured out from their homes.

Unfortunately, due to an accident during this operation in which two of his workers were injured, the Frenchman found himself in trouble with the authorities, who wanted to confiscate his precious cases. If necessary, Prisse d'Avennes was prepared to resort to the use of arms to defend the reliefs, but, after lengthy negotiations and with the aid of suitable gifts, he was given permission to keep them, providing he left Thebes by night. So it was that Lepsius, having arrived at Karnak furnished with all the requisite official permits, searched for the 'sanctuary of the forefathers' in vain – it had been dismantled eighteen days previously. Meanwhile, Prisse d'Avennes had reached Cairo, where he had various problems to solve – first and foremost those resulting from his illegal removal of the reliefs from Karnak.

The following year, 1844, Prisse d'Avennes managed by some stratagem to load his reliefs on to a ship bound for France. The precious objects were contained in twenty-six cases, each one bearing the label: 'Natural history objects for the Paris Museum'. He himself also left Egypt in the same year with all the countless drawings and plans that he had executed between 1836 and 1844.

272 (left) Anuket – 'She who loves the flood' – the goddess of the First Cataract, suckles the infant Ramesses II: a drawing of a relief in the small rock-cut temple of Beit el-Wali, near Kalabsha.

273 (opposite) Prisse d'Avennes copied this tender scene from a relief in the tomb of a Theban dignitary Kenamun (TT93), who lived during the reign of Amenhotep II. The mother of the deceased, the royal wet-nurse Amenemopet, holds the young pharaoh in her arms.

274 (opposite) Prisse d'Avennes copied this relief in the tomb of Ramesses III (KVII) in the Valley of the Kings. It shows the pharaoh magnificently attired and crowned with a headdress decorated with uraei. Behind the king are two cartouches with his throne-name and name, accompanied by an epithet: Usermaatre Meryamun – Ramses Heqaiunu.

275 Two women in a Theban tomb bear offerings of fruit (figs and grapes) and lotus flowers for the deceased.

These plans and drawings were later published in his most outstanding work, *L'Atlas de l'Histoire de l'Art Égyptien...* (*Atlas of the History of Egyptian Art...*). Another object Prisse d'Avennes took back to France was one of the oldest papyri found in Egypt. Purchased at Thebes at the cemetery of Dra Abu el-Naga and dating from the Middle Kingdom, it is now known as the Prisse Papyrus and is in the Bibliothèque Nationale in Paris. The papyrus contains the complete text of the 'Instruction of Ptahhotep' – who was the vizier of king Isesi of the Fifth Dynasty – which consists of a series of considerations on old age and the conduct suitable for all the various circumstances of life. It also has the final part of a second text called

heady days of unauthorized excavations were but a distant memory. Auguste Mariette had founded the Egyptian Antiquities Service, of which he himself became director, and he had managed to enforce the severe laws made for the protection of ancient monuments. Thus Prisse d'Avennes obtained a permit that allowed him only to visit the monuments and draw them, but he did not have permission to carry out excavations or collect antiquities.

During his stay in Cairo which lasted almost a year he made plans and drawings of the most important monuments built during the Arab domination of Egypt – which were later published in a work entitled *Art arabe d'après les monuments*

du Caire depuis le VII siècle jusqu'à la fin du XVIII siècle (*Arab Art from the Monuments of Cairo from the Seventh Century to the End of the Eighteenth Century*). Then, on 6 June 1859, he set sail up the Nile accompanied by Jarrot, Testas and the American traveller Edwin Smith. Having visited all the major archaeological sites of the Nile Valley the party reached Abu Simbel.

On the return journey, Prisse d'Avennes stopped in Luxor, where he returned to 'the scene of the crime' in the temple of Karnak and made plans and drawings of the royal and private tombs in the cemeteries at Thebes. He continued to be astonished by the changes: everywhere he saw new excavations carried out on the

the 'Instruction for Kagemni' written by a vizier of King Huni, the last ruler of the Third Dynasty.

Prisse d'Avennes returned to Egypt in June 1858 at the head of a small official expedition supported by the French ministry of education. On this occasion he was accompanied by a Dutch draughtsman, Willem de Famars Testas, and a young man by the name of Jarrot who practised a new craft that was just beginning to become popular – photography.

In the fourteen years of his absence the country had changed a great deal, and the

276 (opposite) In this copy of one of the reliefs of the portico of Punt at Deir el-Bahri, an African is shown transporting incense on a donkey. This precious gum was used during religious ceremonies and was the most important of the products from the land of Punt.

277 Prisse d'Avennes, like Wilkinson, was attracted by the scenes of everyday life found in the private tombs at Thebes. This relief, copied from the tomb of the vizier Rekhmire (TT100),

shows a number of servants carrying products of the various regions under the jurisdiction of the deceased – bundles of papyrus, jars of oil and amphorae containing wine – to his storerooms.

277

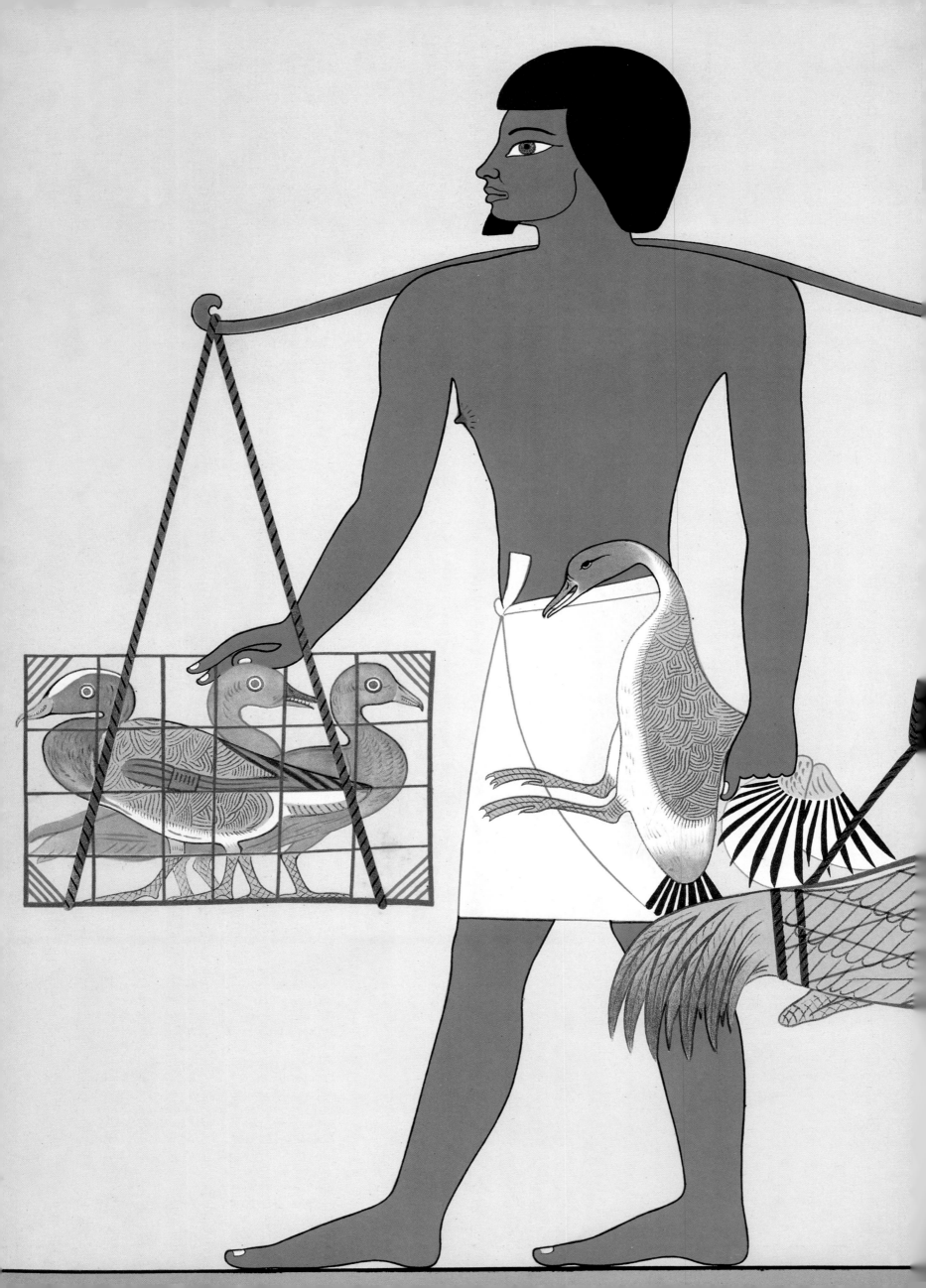

orders of Mariette, whom he unjustly – and somewhat inconsistently – held in contempt. Many of the reliefs that had adorned the walls of tombs and temples, which he had drawn only a few years previously, had disappeared, while new ones had come to light, especially at Deir el-Bahri and Medinet Habu. He spent some time at these sites supervising excavations on behalf of Mariette, before returning to Cairo in April 1860.

After staying at Mariette's house at Saqqara as his guest until June 1860, Prisse d'Avennes set sail for France. This time he took with him not Egyptian antiquities, but a rich collection of material including 300 drawings, 150 photographs and numerous casts.

278 (opposite) Prisse d'Avennes also drew some of the most beautiful scenes decorating the tombs in the Middle Kingdom cemetery at Beni Hasan. The reliefs of the tomb of Khnumhotep include this one of a hunter returning from the marshes, laden with birds for his master: three pigeons, two cranes and a goose.

279 Hunting is also the theme of this relief that Prisse d'Avennes copied in a tomb of the Eighteenth Dynasty during his first stay in Thebes. When the French artist returned to Thebes fifteen years later, in 1859, no trace of this splendid scene remained.

280 In the tomb of Ramose (TT55), Prisse d'Avennes copied this scene that was simply sketched out on the wall. It depicts a Nubian, two Asiatics and an Egyptian prostrating themselves before Amenhotep IV. The original drawing was executed using red ochre which was later corrected with black ink.

281 (opposite) In the Theban tomb of Kenamun (TT93) this elegant maid is depicted playing the lute for the royal wet-nurse Amenemopet, the mother of the deceased. The musician is portrayed in a realistic and unusual style that Prisse d'Avennes stresses in his copy.

By the time Napoleon's army left Egypt, four years after it had arrived, the country had undergone a radical change. The reforms carried out by Napoleon, together with the fact that Europeans – called 'Franks' regardless of their nationality – were now a familiar sight, had transformed the outlook of the inhabitants of the Nile Valley. Besides, not all the Europeans had left: some, who were called 'French Mamelukes', chose to remain in Egypt in the service of the Pasha; others were the diplomatic representatives of the European powers or the travellers who began to arrive in increasingly large numbers.

In Europe, too, after the publication of Dominique Vivant Denon's *Voyage* and the *Description de l'Égypte*, public perception of Egypt – which had previously been known mainly through the drawings of Frederik Ludwig Norden, Reverend Richard

282 (below) Luigi Mayer was a German painter about whom very little is known, though we do know he completed his artistic training in Rome, in the studio of the engraver Giovanni Battista Piranesi. Mayer's drawings of the monuments of ancient Egypt were immediately very popular and are still used today to illustrate books. This drawing shows the Sphinx as it was at the end of the eighteenth century, when it was still almost completely covered with sand.

ARTISTS AND TRAVELLERS ON THE NILE
EGYPT: AN INEXHAUSTIBLE SOURCE OF INSPIRATION

282–283 (above) Mayer drew this view of the top of the pyramid of Khufu: at that time, nearly every traveller to Egypt attempted to climb the pyramid. At the summit is a square platform, originally occupied by the capping pyramid known as a pyramidion, where many of those who reached it carved their names.

283 (right) The French architect Jean Nicolas Huyot (1780–1840), who designed the Arc de Triomphe in Paris, was a great friend of Champollion. During his visit to Egypt in 1818 and 1819, when he met the comte de Forbin and the traveller Édouard de Montulé, Huyot executed many drawings, which he then put at Champollion's disposal. This one demonstrates the artist's theory of how an obelisk was erected in front of a temple.

283

Pococke and Louis François Cassas – had changed. Egypt had become fashionable: in the salons where society people and intellectuals assembled it was the main topic of conversation; artists drew inspiration from the world of the pharaohs and the Arabs; pyramids, temples, *harems*, caravanserai and Mamelukes captivated the public – and as a result everyone wanted to see this fascinating country for themselves.

The first significant wave of travellers thus set out from Europe. Among them were antiquarians and collectors in search of ancient artifacts, archaeologists and scientists, explorers, artists, writers and ordinary tourists. An entire group of painters, known as 'Orientalists', were inspired by the Arab world of the Maghreb and the Near East. A number of exponents

of this genre painted magnificent works which took Egypt as their theme: they included David Roberts (1796–1864), Eugène Delacroix (1798–1863), Léon Cogniet (1794–1880), Horace Vernet (1789–1863), Alexandre Gabriel Decamps (1803–60), Prosper Marilhat (1811–47) and Eugène Fromentin (1820–76). Fromentin was a remarkable writer and artist who attended the opening of the Suez Canal in 1869. He then sailed on the cruise to Upper Egypt organized for the guests at the celebration by the viceroy Ismail under the direction of Auguste Mariette, founder of the Egyptian Museum of Cairo and the Egyptian Antiquities Service.

Europeans arriving in Cairo found a country that was no longer hostile and difficult to enter, but one that was open

284 (above left) In 1822 the Reverend Cooper Willyams published his drawings of his journey to the Near East. In addition to Egypt, he also visited Rhodes, Italy and Minorca. Like the artist Richard Dalton in the eighteenth century, Willyams depicted the popular procession of the 'sacred camel' through the streets of Cairo.

The Arabic text visible on the ceremonial palanquin:

ان الله والنفس الاهوم تزل عياتك اله
السد . و . مبد ها ب باسم نسمه وانزل السو
رلاه . والا حمل ؛ ن بنون ومى الوسى

284 (opposite below) The French architect Hector Horeau, who made a long journey to Egypt and Nubia in 1839, painted a number of bird's-eye views that are a very typical feature of his work. He also depicted the streets, monuments and other sights of Cairo: this is his view of the great slave market, one of the favourite subjects of nineteenth-century artists on the lookout for exotic or unusual themes. The market was visited by rich Arabs from all the surrounding regions, and by emissaries of the sultan of Constantinople, in search of women for their harems.

284–285 Adorned with feathers and plumes, the 'sacred camel' – depicted here by Willyams – made its way through the crowds with a tent on its back. Inside were textiles for the sanctuaries of Mecca and Medina. The exterior was decorated with fabrics embroidered in gold with passages from the Koran.

285 (right) Willyams also drew this view of Old Cairo on the banks of one of the branches of the Nile forming the island of Rodah. In this part of the city were the gardens and holiday homes of the wealthy, used during the summer when the river was in flood.

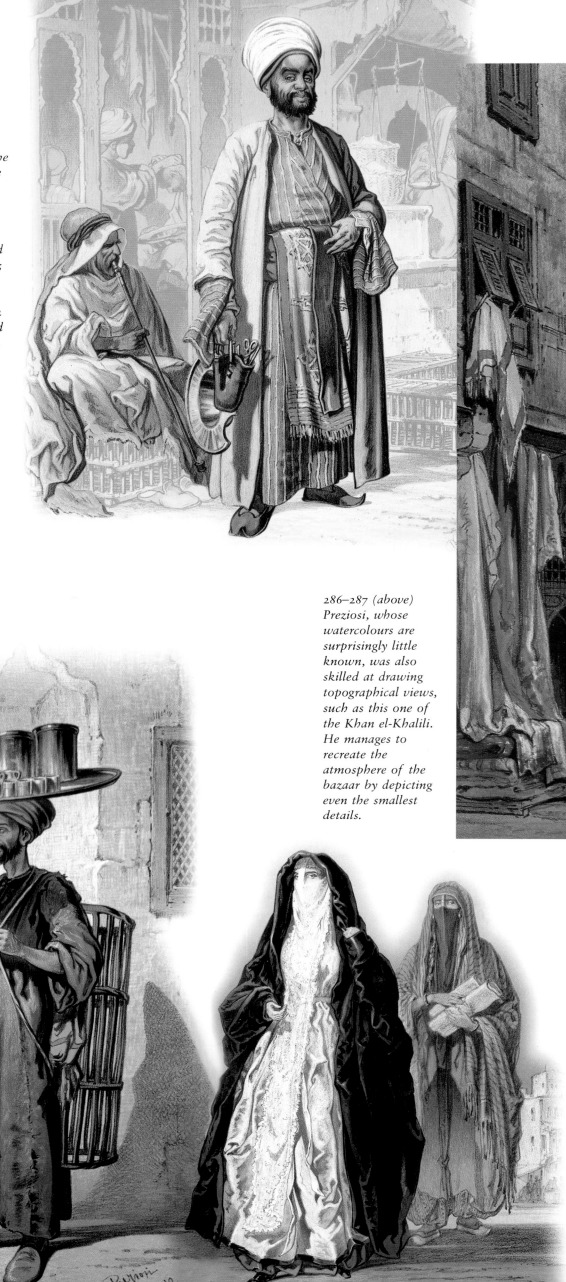

286 and 287 (below) Amedeo Preziosi was a Maltese artist who had settled in Constantinople. During his travels to Egypt he painted numerous watercolours of the costumes of local people, which were his favourite subject. Here we see some typical figures of the Khan el-Khalili, the great market in the centre of Cairo: a craftsman; two street-traders; a richly dressed veiled lady with her maid; and a soldier. Preziosi published these works in 1862 in a volume entitled Souvenirs du Caire.

286–287 (above) Preziosi, whose watercolours are surprisingly little known, was also skilled at drawing topographical views, such as this one of the Khan el-Khalili. He manages to recreate the atmosphere of the bazaar by depicting even the smallest details.

and welcomed visitors. And a voyage up the Nile was facilitated by the numerous dragomans (Europeans who had settled in the country and offered their services to foreign visitors as guides and interpreters).

In his *Itinéraire de Paris à Jérusalem*, François René Chateaubriand wrote:

Nothing was more amusing or singular than the sight of Abdallah of Toulouse taking the girdle of his caftan and using it to flick the faces of the Arabs or Albanians pestering him in order to open up a path for us through the crowds in the busiest streets. Besides, following Alexander's example, these kings in exile had adopted the costumes of the conquered peoples: they wore long silk tunics and splendid white turbans and bore superb arms; they had a harem, slaves and thoroughbreds — things that their parents certainly did not have in Gascony or Picardy....

These dragomans were not only French soldiers who had served in the Napoleonic army, but were also adventurers of other nationalities – principally Italians and Greeks – who had arrived in Egypt in the years immediately after the departure of the French army. They included Giovanni Finati, who accompanied William John Bankes and Giovanni Battista Belzoni on their journeys; Antonio Lebolo, who was in the service of the French Consul Bernardino Drovetti; Joseph Rosignani, who travelled with Frédéric Cailliaud; and the celebrated Giovanni d'Athanasi, known as Yanni.

The first tourists to arrive in Egypt were collectors of antiquities – rich British aristocrats attracted to the East by the opportunity to create their own collections with which to embellish their stately homes. The most famous of these, William

John Bankes, adorned the garden of his house at Kingston Lacy, in Dorset, with an obelisk that originally stood in front of the first pylon of the temple of Isis at Philae and was removed on his behalf by Belzoni.

Lord Algernon Percy, Duke of Northumberland, a naval officer, travelled to Egypt in the company of a major in the British army, Orlando Felix. He ventured as far as Nubia, where he met Champollion

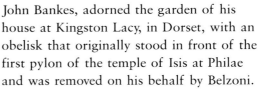

288 (below) Roberts produced a great number of paintings of Cairo, where he arrived in 1838, including views of the city, its mosques and the most picturesque streets.

in 1828, and managed to acquire a collection of antiquities comprising over two thousand items, which was sold to the University of Durham in 1950. Ten years previously, Somerset Lowry-Corry, Lord Belmore, had sailed to Egypt and the East in his yacht, journeying up the Nile as far as the Second Cataract. He, too, managed to accumulate a rich collection of antiquities, including numerous stelae and important papyri, most of which were purchased by the British Museum in 1843.

In February 1818 the comte de Forbin was at Thebes, a site that had become very fashionable and was much frequented by Europeans. Other visitors at that time included the British Consul-General Henry Salt and Frédéric Cailliaud, who had just discovered the emerald mines of the pharaohs in the Arabian Desert. De Forbin described the arrival of Lord Belmore, who stayed in Thebes before returning to Cairo:

An English family had just arrived at Thebes, on their return from the Cataracts. Lord and Lady Belmour had been visiting a part of Nubia, indulging themselves in all the pomp, parade, and grandeur, of luxurious speculation. Four large bateaux were in the train of the one which conveyed them; husbands, wives, young children, chaplains, surgeons, nurses, cooks, all in various phrases, were anxiously talking of Elephantina. But with me now the illusion had vanished....

288 (above) The Scottish painter David Roberts is the best-known of the European artists working in Egypt in the nineteenth century. The popularity his lithographs enjoyed at that time still endures today. Although he showed a preference for landscapes and architectural subjects, Roberts nearly always included human figures in his views.

289 (opposite) Pascal Coste, an architect from Marseille who was employed in the service of Muhammad Ali from 1817 to 1827, was a skilled draughtsman. His are some of the best drawings of the Islamic monuments of Cairo and he received special permission to work inside the great mosques of the city.

290–291 In this view of the hypostyle hall of the temple of Isis at Philae, David Roberts displays his skill in representing the monuments of ancient Egypt. He uses the human figure not so much to animate the scene or simply to add a note of colour, but rather to give an impression of the scale of the building and to reinforce the perspective of the painting.

288

292 and 293 (below) Robert Hay, a remarkable artist, archaeologist and traveller, lived for over five years at Qurna, sharing his home, a tomb in the side of the mountain, with John

Gardner Wilkinson. Hay drew a number of views of Cairo and its monuments, his only published works. These two views of Bulaq, the city's river port, are in fact part of the same drawing.

were led to extend far beyond the original design. Curiosity at first, and an increasing admiration of antiquities as they advanced, carried them at length through several parts of the Levant, which have been little visited by modern travellers, and gave them more than four years of continued employment.

Many other Europeans, famous for other reasons, also explored Egypt. They included Sir Charles Barry (1795–1860), the British architect who designed the Houses of Parliament, who travelled up the Nile in 1819 to the Second Cataract, making numerous plans and drawings of the temples and tombs; Joseph Bonomi (1796–1878), a sculptor of Italian origin and an accomplished draughtsman who worked for many great Egyptologists, including Rosellini and Wilkinson and ascended the Nile as far as Dongola;

A few months later, in December 1818, the comte Édouard de Montulé, a great traveller and collector of antiquities, also arrived at Thebes in the company of the Roman antiquarian Silvestro Guidi. He was one of the first to admire the tomb of Seti I that Belzoni had only just discovered.

Charles Irby (1789–1845) and James Mangles (1786–1867), two British naval officers, also visited Egypt during a journey to the Near East. In 1817 they participated in the expedition to Nubia of Belzoni and Salt, and were present at the opening up of the Great Temple of Abu Simbel. In the introduction to their travel diary, which was published in a private edition for their friends and acquaintances, they rather modestly explained why they had decided to travel to the East:

On the 14th August, 1816, the Hon. Charles Leonard Irby and James Mangles, Commanders in the Royal Navy, left England with the intention of making a tour on the continent. This journey they

Thomas Legh (1793–1857), one of the first travellers to reach Nubia between 1812 and 1814; Giuseppe Forni, a chemist and naturalist from Milan, in Italy, who explored the Arabian Desert, the mines of Gebel Zabara and Gebel Sikeit, ascending the Nile in 1819 to the region of Sennar; Giovan Battista Brocchi, a naturalist from Bassano del Grappa, in Italy, who studied the flora of Egypt, venturing as far as Sennar and Khartoum, where he fell ill and died in 1825; an architect, Joseph John Scoles (1798–1863), who travelled up the Nile as far as the Second Cataract with Frederick Catherwood and Henry Westcar (1798–1868) who himself became well-known due to a papyrus that still bears his name today; Edward William Lane (1801–76), a great Orientalist, draughtsman and writer, who worked with Wilkinson; Francis Arundale (1807–53), an architect and draughtsman who worked with Robert Hay at Qurna in 1832; the artist and poet Edward Lear (1812–88), who travelled in

292–293 View of the
Nile, *by the French
painter and writer
Eugène Fromentin.
A keen Orientalist,
Fromentin painted
numerous pictures
inspired by Algeria,
a country that he
visited on three
occasions. He went*
*to Egypt in 1869
with the French
delegation to the
opening ceremony of
the Suez Canal and
made numerous
sketches and
drawings, some of
which he used later
as the basis for
several paintings.*

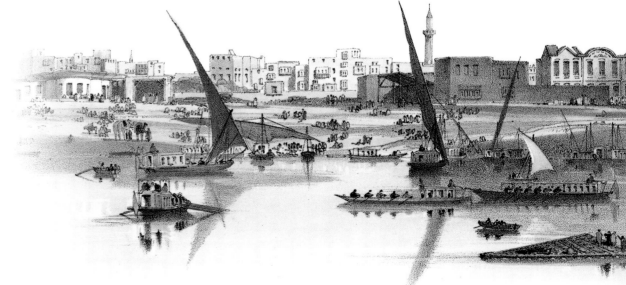

294–295 Henry de Montaut, a French artist, depicted the life, people and costumes of Egypt in a lively – if often stereotyped – style. He taught map-making and architecture at the military school of the Citadel and published a collection of pictures entitled Égypte moderne. It included this watercolour of Western tourists visiting the mosque of Sultan Hassan.

294 (right) The whirling dervishes, the subject of this watercolour by Henry de Montaut, are the devotees of a religious sect who reach a state of ecstasy by spinning rapidly. Their costume consists of a wide tunic in white cotton, the hem of which contains lead weights, and a tall conical felt cap.

Egypt and Nubia in 1849, making numerous drawings; and Amedeo Preziosi, a traveller and artist with Maltese nationality (although his family came from Rome), who executed a splendid series of drawings of an essentially ethnographic nature portraying the customs and lifestyle of the inhabitants of the country.

This influx of European travellers, who studied the antiquities or sought to obtain them, soon had a marked effect on the local population. In 1826, Linant de Bellefonds, in the Aswan area, wrote:

[The inhabitants] are now the shrewdest people in Egypt and Nubia and sell everything at four times its real value... and this happens thanks to the Europeans who come here....

The number of people travelling to Egypt increased continuously throughout the nineteenth century. As the first companies organizing cruises on the Nile were being established and the earliest guides to the country were being published, the old-style travellers disappeared, making way for the true tourists.

295 (below) Here de Montaut depicts the procession of the sheikh of the Saadyeh dervishes (one of the various orders of this sect) going to pay homage to Sheikh el-Bekry, the spiritual leader of all the dervishes of Egypt, during a religious feast.

295 (right) In this watercolour, de Montaut has portrayed a scene in a harem of a group of female dancers and musicians. The artist based his picture on the account of his mother, who was permitted to visit the royal harem in 1859.

Luigi Mayer

296 (above) A view of the pyramids of Khufu and Khafre at Giza by Luigi Mayer, a German artist who visited Egypt in 1792. During his time in Egypt Mayer made numerous drawings of the greatest monuments both of ancient Egypt and the Islamic period.

Luigi Mayer was a gifted artist about whom, inexplicably, we have only very scant biographical information. There is little doubt that his drawings are, second only to the famous paintings by David Roberts, the ones most frequently used today to illustrate the theme of Egypt in the nineteenth century.

Although his wonderful colour illustrations depicting the great monuments of ancient Egypt, executed in his unique style, are well known, the artist's life and career are shrouded in mystery. All that is known about this great draughtsman, painter and engraver is that he was born in Germany and lived for some time in Rome, where he belonged to the studio of the famous engraver Giovanni Battista Piranesi, one of the most outstanding artists of his day (it was here that Mayer acquired the name Luigi). In 1792 Mayer travelled to Asia Minor and the Near East in the entourage of Sir Robert Ainslie, the British ambassador to the Ottoman Empire. Among the various countries he visited were Palestine and Egypt.

296 (opposite, below left) The people of Egypt noticed European interest in mummies and other antiquities from the Middle Ages on, but increasingly so in the eighteenth and early nineteenth centuries. They therefore searched tombs for objects to sell at the markets in Cairo. This drawing shows a number of men removing stone blocks in order to enter one of the numerous private tombs at Giza.

296 (opposite, below right) In the burial chamber of the pyramid of Khufu, known as the 'King's Chamber', stands a granite sarcophagus that must have originally contained the royal mummy. However, despite all the precautions taken by the pharaoh's architects, the tomb had already been violated in antiquity, and from the Middle Ages had become in effect a tourist attraction.

297 One of Mayer's most famous drawings, this shows the beginning of the Grand Gallery of the pyramid of Khufu which leads up to the burial chamber. At the bottom is the entrance to the corridor leading to the so-called Queen's Chamber.

On his return to Europe with Ainslie, Mayer entrusted his drawings to an engraver, Thomas Milton, who prepared the magnificent plates depicting the monuments of Egypt that appeared in a folio volume entitled *Views in Egypt, from the Original Drawings in the possession of Sir Robert Ainslie,...*, published in London in 1801. This was followed by another volume in 1803, devoted to Asia Minor and the Ottoman Empire, although this was less successful.

In 1814 the French writer Jean Baptiste Breton de la Martinière published a work in six volumes entitled *L'Égypte et la Syrie, ou Moeurs, Usages et Monuments des Égyptiens, des Arabes et des Syriens* (Egypt and Syria, or Customs, Habits and Monuments of the Egyptians, Arabs and Syrians) that was largely illustrated with Mayer's drawings. He was the first of a long series of authors – which continues to this day – who have used Mayer's plates to enrich their works.

298–299 A view of the main square in Cairo, with Murad Bey's palace. Although Mayer is mainly known for his drawings of ancient Egyptian monuments, he also depicted the various districts and the most important mosques of Cairo.

299 (top) Mayer painted this military drill in the palace of Murad Bey, the principal Mameluke leader who was defeated a few years later by Napoleon in the Battle of the Pyramids.

299 (centre) An excellent landscape artist, Mayer painted this view of Old Cairo, with its houses built on the banks of the river which is animated by the passing boats.

299 (right) Mayer also accurately recorded the details of the costumes of the people of Egypt. This painting shows a bey, the title given to the most important dignitaries of the Ottoman Empire, who is wearing a sumptuous robe and an elaborate turban indicating his status.

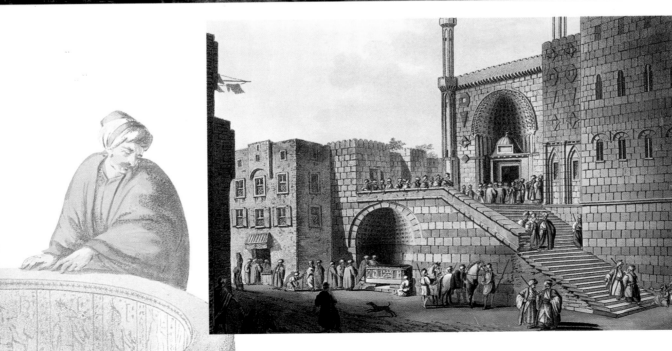

300–301 (above)
In the fortress now
known as the
Citadel, Mayer drew
this large columned
hall, at that time
called 'Joseph's
Hall', from which
there was a splendid
view over the city to
the pyramids.

300 (below) and 301
From ancient times
the level of the
waters of the Nile
had been measured
by special structures
called Nilometers,
such as this one,
drawn by Mayer in

Cairo on the island
of Rodah. The water
flowing from it ran
into a granite
sarcophagus. This
curious monument,
known as the 'lovers'
fountain', was next
to a mosque.

301

302 (below) Louis Maurice Adolphe Linant de Bellefonds made his first journey to Upper Egypt in November 1818. At the tender age of nineteen he was a draughtsman on the expedition to the First Cataract organized by the antiquarian and traveller William Bankes and headed by Giovanni Battista Belzoni. They travelled up the Nile to Abu Simbel, where the temple of Ramesses II, opened by Belzoni in 1817, was still deeply buried in sand.

L.M.A. Linant de Bellefonds and Léon de Laborde

302 (left) Linant de Bellefonds arrived in Egypt in 1817 and spent the rest of his long life there. He made various journeys, including two to the Sudan to explore the Blue Nile and the White Nile. A talented artist, explorer, geographer and engineer, he held prestigious public posts under Muhammad Ali: he was appointed minister of public works and received the titles of bey and pasha. This official photograph shows Linant de Bellefonds at the height of his brilliant career in the service of the Egyptian government.

302–303 Linant de Bellefonds made numerous pencil drawings of the colossi dominating the façade of the Great Temple of Abu Simbel, where the expedition led by Belzoni stopped from 25 January to 18 February 1819.

302 (above) This is Linant de Bellefonds' reconstruction of the original appearance of a relief in the temple at Abu Simbel.

303 (opposite right) Only one colossus of the temple at Abu Simbel was wholly free from sand.

In 1818 Giovanni Battista Belzoni led a small expedition to Upper Egypt. One of its aims was to retrieve the obelisk of Philae in order to transport it back to England on behalf of William John Bankes. Other members of the party included the British Consul-General Henry Salt, the Siennese physician and draughtsman Alessandro Ricci, and a young French draughtsman who was just nineteen years old. His name was Louis Maurice Adolphe Linant de Bellefonds (1799–1883).

It was only by chance that Linant de Bellefonds, a talented draughtsman gifted with a lively intelligence, came to Egypt. The son of a Breton naval officer, he began to travel with his father at the age of fourteen, visiting the United States and Canada. Later he, too, joined the navy and embarked on the frigate *Cléopatre*. This was taking an expedition of artists and scientists, headed by Auguste de Forbin, on a voyage in the Mediterranean, visiting

Greece, Turkey, Syria, Palestine and Egypt, where they arrived in 1818. The young midshipman decided to remain in Egypt.

During the voyage, Linant de Bellefonds had replaced one of the members of the expedition who had died suddenly, and, since he was too young to aspire to a post in the civil service, he decided to travel through the country in order to get to know it better. Then, in 1820, thanks to the support of Bankes, Linant de Bellefonds managed to get permission to accompany the military expedition sent by Muhammad Ali to the oasis of Siwa in the Libyan Desert, under the command of Hassan Bey, to assert Egyptian authority over the area. This expedition also included other Europeans such as the French Consul Drovetti, Alessandro Ricci and Enegildo Frediani, the unfortunate traveller who during Ismail Pasha's expedition to the Sudan, was overtaken by madness and died, partially insane, in Cairo in 1823.

After he had returned from the Libyan Desert, Linant de Bellefonds set out once again in early September on a journey to the Sinai. This was followed in June 1821 by his first expedition to the Sudan, undertaken on behalf of Bankes. This area, politically unstable and badly governed by the local potentates, was believed to be rich in gold deposits. It had therefore attracted the attention of Muhammad Ali, who set out to conquer it by sending troops under the command of his son Ismail Pasha.

On this occasion, however, Linant de Bellefonds did not join the military expedition – in which other Europeans such as the geologist Frédéric Cailliaud and Enegildo Frediani took part – as he had when he went to Siwa. Instead, he decided to travel independently with just a few other people, including the faithful Ricci, to carry out his task of studying the geology of the area and its archaeological remains.

303

304 (left) Ramesses II in the act of killing a Hittite, in a relief from one of the walls of the pharaoh's temple at Abu Simbel. This relief was copied by Champollion and Rosellini, and also by Lepsius.

304 (below) An unpublished watercolour by Linant de Bellefonds, showing African prisoners: those with darker skin are Nubians, while the others belong to tribes of the Barabra.

304–305 Linant de Bellefonds drew the expedition's boat, called a kanja, as it sailed, propelled by a strong favourable wind, near the site of Qasr Ibrim.

This journey, which lasted for over a year and took Linant de Bellefonds as far as Meroë and the Sennar region in southern Sudan, can be viewed as the prelude to a second expedition to the same area four years later. Linant de Bellefonds continued his studies, spending a few months in the Arabian Desert to the east of the Nile, in 1823, and beginning a study of the area of the Isthmus of Suez in 1825.

His next journey was to London, where he was entrusted with an official mission for the first time. The Association for Promoting the Discovery of the Interior Parts of Africa had already financed the journeys of the Swiss Orientalist Johann Ludwig Burckhardt and was now eager to contribute to the advance of geographical knowledge of the Upper Nile. The Society therefore entrusted Linant de Bellefonds –

with whom a formal contract was drawn up – with the preparation of an expedition to explore the course of the White Nile, from the point of its confluence with the Blue Nile in Khartoum to its source. Backed by the wealth and prestige of the Association, Linant de Bellefonds was able to organize his first true expedition, with adequate resources at his disposal.

The journey lasted over a year, from March 1826 to September 1827. The first eight months were spent ascending the Nile as far as Khartoum. From here the Frenchman made his first reconnaissance of the area towards the River Atbara, but the difficulties encountered in this region, which was infested with marauding bands and tropical fevers, as well as the hostility of some of the tribes, compelled him to give up. After seeking in vain for local

backing to enable him to continue his exploration of the White Nile, Linant de Bellefonds was obliged to return to Cairo, which he reached on 27 September 1827.

In Cairo in the following year Linant de Bellefonds met a nineteen-year-old Parisian, Léon de Laborde. The son of a prominent French politician and diplomat, de Laborde had considerable financial resources at his disposal, thanks to his family fortune, and had received a sound liberal education; he was also an excellent draughtsman. His aim at this time was to organize a journey to the city of Petra, which, following its discovery in 1812 by Burckhardt, had subsequently been visited by very few travellers. Linant de Bellefonds felt an immediate bond of sympathy with the enterprising and gifted young man, and decided to set out with him for the remote

305 The island of Philae was the final objective of the expedition organized by Bankes in 1818, in which Linant de Bellefonds took part. Bankes had entrusted Belzoni with the task of retrieving the obelisk which stood in front of the temple of Isis so that it could be transported back to England. Belzoni, having successfully completed his task, returned to Thebes, while Bankes, Salt and Linant de Bellefonds continued to Abu Simbel.

306 In February 1828 Léon de Laborde set out with Linant de Bellefonds for the city of Petra (in present-day Jordan), which had been discovered by the Swiss Orientalist Johann Ludwig Burckhardt. De Laborde, who was twenty-one, wears Bedouin costume.

307 (opposite) The two French explorers crossed the Sinai peninsula in sixteen days to reach Aqaba on the Red Sea, the last important stopping-place before Petra. During their march across the desert of the Sinai, Linant de Bellefonds and de Laborde took every opportunity to draw the monuments and inhabitants of the area, such as these Bedouins involved in a skirmish.

Léon de

site which he had long dreamed of visiting. With his thorough knowledge of both the language and the area, acquired during the ten years he had spent in Egypt, he made an invaluable contribution to the voyage.

On 23 February 1828, Linant de Bellefonds and de Laborde left Cairo, dressed as Arabs, at the head of their expedition. As they crossed the Sinai they stopped to make a number of drawings at Serabit el-Khadim, where there was a large Middle Kingdom temple dedicated to the goddess Hathor, 'Mistress of Turquoise'.

The temple was built near some of the ancient turquoise mines.

The two young explorers then reached Aqaba, on the Red Sea, and, after a week spent obtaining the necessary permits and awaiting guides, they set out for Petra. Here, amazingly, they managed to achieve what had been impossible even for the great Burckhardt – they were able to remain several days at the site. The local Bedouin, convinced that the monuments contained splendid treasures and that the Europeans came with the express purpose of stealing them, discouraged visitors.

Hence the drawings made by Linant de Bellefonds and de Laborde revealed the magnificence of the ancient Nabataean capital to Europe for the first time.

With the expedition over, de Laborde left to return to Europe, while Linant de Bellefonds began to study the problems and techniques of hydraulic engineering, in order, as he later wrote, 'to acquire the scientific knowledge that I lacked so that I could enter the service of the Egyptian government as an engineer'. Wishing to devote himself entirely to his studies, he decided to live alone for over a year in a valley in the Sinai, the location of which is uncertain (thought it was probably Wadi Feiran). In 1831 Linant de Bellefonds was appointed engineer-in-chief of public works for Upper Egypt, thus beginning a long and successful career as a government official.

Laborde.

He did, however, undertake a final journey to the then unknown region of Etbaye (in the Nubian Desert to the east of the Dongola loop), inhabited by the Bisharin tribe. This voyage marked the conclusion of the first phase of Linant de Bellefonds' life – a period devoted to exploration – which had occupied him for thirteen years.

After promotion to engineer-in-chief of canals, bridges and roads for the whole of Egypt, Linant de Bellefonds subsequently became director-general, and then minister, of public works, as well as privy counsellor to the Pasha. He was responsible for major hydraulic works, the creation of a modern irrigation system and the preliminary survey for a canal between the Mediterranean and the Red Sea, which, in 1844, was submitted to Ferdinand de Lesseps, who went on to direct the construction of the Suez Canal.

Linant de Bellefonds received the title of Bey in 1837 and retired from office in 1869, the year the Suez Canal was opened. He spent his retirement years writing his memoirs. After being awarded the title of Pasha – the highest honorary title of the Ottoman Empire – Linant de Bellefonds died in Cairo in 1883, leaving a huge quantity of manuscripts and drawings that have yet to be published. They are now kept partly in the Louvre and partly in England, at Kingston Lacy, the home of William John Bankes.

308 (above) In the first part of their journey, Linant de Bellefonds and de Laborde crossed the Isthmus of Suez. This corresponds to the biblical land of Goshen, where the encounter between Joseph and his father Jacob took place, as represented here.

308 (below) In the northern part of the Sinai the explorers visited the temple of Serabit el-Khadim, dating from the Middle Kingdom. It was dedicated to Hathor, 'Mistress of Turquoise', and was near mines exploited by the Egyptians from the Old Kingdom on.

309 (opposite above) Linant de Bellefonds and de Laborde had agreed that on their return each would publish an account of their journey. Only de Laborde succeeded in this, however. Linant de Bellefonds was too taken up with his commitments to find time to have his diary printed, and it

is still largely unpublished. De Laborde's volume, published in 1830, contained sixty-nine plates, fourteen of which were by Linant de Bellefonds. The author dedicated the work William II of Hesse as a token of appreciation for the period he had spent at Göttingen university.

A SON ALTESSE ROYALE

GUILLAUME II,

ÉLECTEUR ET LANDGRAVE SOUVERAIN DE LA HESSE, GRAND DUC DE FULDE,

PRINCE DE HERSFELD, HANAU, FRITZLAR, ET ISENBURG,

COMTE DE CATZENELENBOGEN, DIETZ, ZIEGENHAYN, NIDDA, ET SCHAUMBURG, ETC., ETC.

309 Sitting on the top of a mountain in the Sinai, Léon de Laborde draws the surrounding landscape. After visiting Petra the two explorers returned to Aqaba, from where they began the journey across the Sinai together. They separated on 20 April 1829 because Linant de Bellefonds wanted to return to Cairo quickly – he reached the city after a forced march of under five days – while de Laborde stayed in the area.

310 (below)
Elegantly dressed in
a white shirt and a
long dark frock coat,
and surrounded by
his servants, the
comte Édouard de
Montulé crosses the
desert on a camel.
This French traveller
visited Egypt in 1818
and 1819 and can be
considered one of
the first true tourists.

Édouard de Montulé

310 (above right) In
de Montulé's book
about his travels in
America, Italy and
Egypt the section on
Egypt is illustrated

with a few drawings,
including some of
the ancient
monuments, which
are depicted rather
inaccurately.

310 (above) De
Montulé also took
part in the few social
events that a journey
to Egypt offered.

Here, accompanied
by a servant, he pays
a visit to the village
authorities to drink
the customary tea.

Édouard de Montulé is one of the many
people who, in the nineteenth century,
travelled purely for pleasure and may be
seen as the forerunners of the tourists of
today. Until the end of the eighteenth
century, all Western visitors to Egypt can
be regarded as explorers rather than
tourists – a journey to Middle and Upper
Egypt was difficult and often even
dangerous. It was only after the
Napoleonic expedition that things began to
change: a voyage up the Nile became less
hazardous and the monuments of Egypt
became more widely familiar to the public
thanks to the illustrations published in
Denon's *Voyage dans la Basse et la Haute
Égypte* and the *Description de l'Égypte*.
Reports of further discoveries encouraged
all those who had the means, the time and
the desire to do so to set out for Egypt.

One such person was Lord Belmore,
who ventured as far as Nubia with his
family. He was accompanied by Carlo
Vidua di Conzano – who carved his name
on the façade of the temple at Abu Simbel
in the following words: 'Carlo Vidua
italiano qui venne dalla Laponia' ('The
Italian Carlo Vidua came here from
Lapland') – and the comte Édouard de
Montulé. De Montulé was a keen traveller
and collector of antiquities who visited
Egypt between October 1818 and early
March 1819.

A contemporary of Auguste de Forbin, who was director-general of the museums of France and André de Marcellus, a young diplomat, Édouard de Montulé held no official positions. His journey from Cairo to Aswan took place between those of de Forbin and de Marcellus, and his book *Voyage en Amerique, en Italie, en Sicile et en Égypte…* (*A Journey to America, Italy, Sicily and Egypt…*) is interesting because it contains a detailed account of the period when the large collections of Egyptian antiquities were being built up and acquired by the museums of Europe.

This work was a reasonably priced volume written with the general public in mind. It was intended to provide a picture of the country for those who could not afford to go there, or purchase or have access to more detailed and expensive books. The part devoted to Egypt, which was translated into English and published with the title *Travels in Egypt during 1818 and 1819*, gives a first-hand account of the precise roles of main protagonists of the notorious 'war of the consuls' – Belzoni, Salt, Drovetti and Rifaud – about whom de Montulé wrote:

I firmly believe that Messrs. Drovetti, Salt and Belzoni are not to blame, but their Agents, who are frequently rewarded in proportion to the value of the discoveries which they make, and consequently nurture mutual animosity against one another.

After reaching the Valley of the Kings on 29 December 1818, de Montulé, accompanied by Belzoni himself, was one of the first to enter the tomb of Seti I, discovered just a couple of months earlier by the Paduan adventurer. This is how de Montulé described this fascinating experience:

At the extremity of the valley we perceived the baggage and the encampment of M. Belzoni, who, with his wife, inhabits the entrance of the tomb; he gave me a very cordial reception and tendered refreshments, of which we stood in great need, for the heat was suffocating, and he himself conducted us into the sepulchre which he had discovered, and whereof he had full possession; for those gentlemen who undertake excavations in Egypt appear to have entered into a secret treaty, which renders them absolute masters of what they have the good fortune to find.

The French traveller was greatly impressed by the magnificent wall decorations of the tomb – which he described at length and in considerable detail, with numerous quotations from Belzoni's *Narrative*. He wondered if any tombs remained to be found intact, adding:

If any perfect ones still exist, I sincerely wish they may escape the research of the curious antiquary; to them the learned are become objects as much to be dreaded as Cambyses, for the sarcophaguses and mummies which they contained would inevitably take the road to London or Paris.

In conclusion, de Montulé suggested that there should be greater control over the archaeological excavations by the Pasha, who allowed all manner of objects to be exported from the country, and he hoped that a major museum would be set up in Cairo or Alexandria. Two months later, on 2 March 1819, de Montulé sailed on the *Pyrrhus* for Europe. In his baggage was the mummy of a woman wrapped in linen bandages and contained in a double sarcophagus decorated with paintings in an excellent state of preservation.

ARCHITECTURE ARABE

Pascal Coste

MONUMENS DU CAIRE

In 1817, at almost the same moment as Linant de Bellefonds, another Frenchman arrived in Egypt. Pascal Coste was an architect from Marseille who had been commissioned by Mohammed Ali to build a factory for the manufacture of saltpetre, the chief constituent of gunpowder. This was to be in the area of Mit Rahina, not far from the ruins of Memphis. Coste, who worked in the service of the Pasha for ten years, until 1827, was also charged with the construction of a powder magazine on Rodah, one of the two large islands in the Nile as it flows through Cairo.

Muhammad Ali also had recourse to the skills of Coste in an attempt to conclude the building of the Mahmudiyyah

313 (left) In his usual pleasing style, Coste drew this splendid view of the fourteenth century madrasah of Sultan Hassan.

313 (below) A view of Khourbaryeh Street, with the mosque of the Amir Aqsunqur, also called the mosque of Ibrahim Aga.

312 (opposite) Pascal Coste, an architect from Marseille and a contemporary of Linant de Bellefonds, was the first great expert on Islamic architecture. He published a useful *study on the subject, illustrated with thirty informative hand-coloured lithographs, depicting the mosques, minarets and most interesting streets and monuments of the city of Cairo.*

Canal, an important watercourse that was to link Cairo and Alexandria. Work on the canal had begun some time previously, but as no precise plan had been worked out in advance and no preliminary survey made of the route, Coste had to join together the various sections that had already been constructed, each of which went in a different direction.

Coste somehow managed to solve this problem successfully and the canal, on which over four hundred thousand people had worked, was opened in 1821. This allowed the architect to devote himself to other tasks, including the restoration of Muhammad Ali's residence at Shubra – now a densely populated area near the

centre of Cairo but at that time on the outskirts of the city – and the construction of a new pavilion for the Pasha's palace in Alexandria.

Coste, who, together with Linant de Bellefonds, was one of the leading figures in Muhammad Ali's programme of modernization of the country, also founded the first school in Egypt to train the technicians and managerial staff required to carry out the public works planned by the Pasha. In addition, he also set up a system of optical signals that allowed messages to be transmitted between Cairo and Alexandria – cities that are over two hundred kilometres apart – in just forty-five minutes.

314 (above) The great courtyard of the mosque of Muayyad Shaykh, near the monumental gate known as Bab Zuwaylah. The central open space is surrounded by a covered walk, its roof supported by numerous elegant columns.

315 (opposite) The lofty entrance portal of the mosque of Muayyad Shaykh opens on to the el-Sukkariyyah bazaar. The mosque, one of the most impressive of the Circassian Mameluke period, is enriched with bronze doors taken from the mosque of Sultan Hassan and is considered the most beautiful in Cairo.

During the long period he spent in Egypt, Coste travelled all over the country, meeting many of the numerous Europeans who came to the Nile Valley to see the ancient monuments or to acquire collections of archaeological finds, such as the comte de Forbin, the comte de Marcellus – who was also responsible for purchasing the Venus de Milo for the Louvre – and Giovanni Battista Belzoni. It was Coste, moreover, who presented Colonel Joseph Sève, a former officer in the Napoleonic army, to Muhammad Ali. Sève later became the celebrated Soliman Pasha, a major-general in the Egyptian army.

While he was working as Muhammad Ali's official architect, the dynamic Coste not only concerned himself with completing the works that he had been commissioned to carry out, but he also took an interest in Islamic art and architecture and made many plans and drawings of the monuments of Cairo. Taking advantage of his official assignments and the high esteem in which he was held by Muhammad Ali, Coste managed to obtain a special permit

316 (opposite left)
The Sultan Qalaun
mosque, built in
1285, comprises a
mausoleum with a
minaret, a madrasah
(Muslim college)
and a hospital. It
is one of Cairo's
most imposing
monuments.

316 (opposite right)
Coste drew and
studied the many
caravanserai of
Cairo, which are
often very interesting
architecturally. These

buildings, like that
built by Qayt Bey
shown here, provided
accommodation for
the caravans and
storage for their
merchandise.

316–317
Muhammad Ali, in
whose service Pascal
Coste worked, had a
luxurious palace
with a large garden
at Shubra, now a
densely populated
district of Cairo.

allowing him to work and draw inside the mosques – a privilege not accorded to other Europeans. Coste was making his drawings and plans about ten years before Prisse d'Avennes, who arrived in Egypt in the same year that Coste returned to France, and who in a sense can be regarded as his heir.

The results of Coste's immense, patient work were collected in a massive volume entitled *Architecture Arabe ou Monuments du Caire…* (*Arab Architecture or the Monuments of Cairo…*). Published in Paris in 1839, after his return to France, it was illustrated with thirty glorious hand-coloured lithographs depicting the mosques, minarets and most interesting streets in Cairo from an architectural point of view, with great precision and in inordinate detail. Many of the Islamic monuments in the city depicted by Coste had never previously been described or treated in this way, highlighting the purity of their lines and their geometrical perfection. This study can be considered to be the first accurate record of Islamic architecture and it aroused a great deal of interest at the time.

318–319 The el-Khalih el-Nasir canal, built by the sultan Melek el-Nasir, son of sultan Qalaun, crossed the entire city of Cairo and was filled with the waters of the Nile during the flood in August. The rich inhabitants of the city had elegant second homes here that were used from August to November. In the parts of the houses reserved for the women there were finely wrought grilles covering the windows, known as musharabiye *in Arabic.*

320–321 A view of the aqueduct, over five kilometres long, that supplied the Citadel with water from the Nile. The intake tower at one end, still visible today, stands opposite the island of Rodah.

320 (below left) Hay shared the home of John Gardner Wilkinson at Qurna – an Eighteenth Dynasty tomb in the side of the Theban cliffs. This view is of the verandah built in front of their unconventional dwelling. After Hay's arrival it became a meeting-place for the many Europeans staying in the area. Standing in the doorway is Kalitza, the young Cretan woman that Hay married in 1828.

320 (below right) Robert Hay of Linplum, a rich traveller and collector and a keen archaeologist, lived in Egypt from 1824 to 1834, working mainly at West Thebes. He surrounded himself with numerous, skilled collaborators, including the draughtsman Joseph Bonomi, the artist Frederick Catherwood, the Orientalist Edward William Lane and the traveller George Hoskins. Although he did not publish an archaeological account of his discoveries, Hay left a large number of manuscripts and documents, as yet unpublished, now in forty-nine volumes in the British Library, London.

Robert Hay

321 (opposite, below left) Robert Hay was one of the first to carry out excavations in the Valley of the Queens, where he surveyed and drew a number of tombs, including those dating to the reign of Ramesses II: Nebtawy (QV60), Tuya (QV80), Meritamun (QV68) and Bentanta (QV71).

321 (opposite, below right) A plan and cross-section of the tomb of Queen Titi (QV52), drawn with great precision by Hay; this tomb can still be visited.

321 Hay also excavated and surveyed in the Valley of the Kings, where he lived in the tomb of Ramesses IV (KV2). This is his watercolour of a relief in the tomb of Ramesses III: the pharaoh, wearing a hemhem-crown, stands before the god Re-Harakhty.

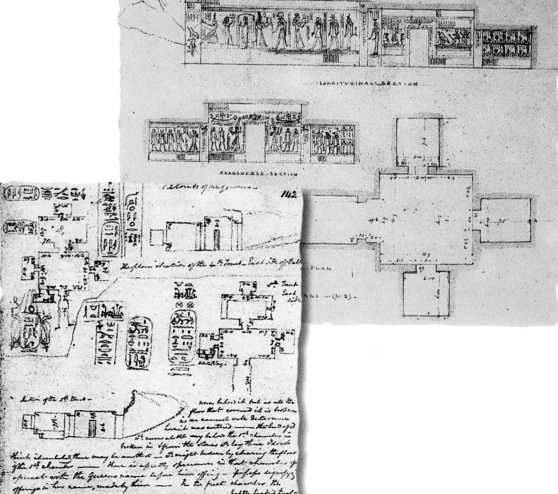

Robert Hay of Linplum (1799–1863) was a young nobleman fond of travel, adventure and the East. Born in the castle of Duns in Scotland, he inherited the family estate at Linplum from his brother. After a brief interlude in the Royal Navy and stimulated by Belzoni's account of his journey, Hay decided to set out for Egypt and the Near East in 1824. He broke his journey in Rome, where he worked for a brief period in Joseph Bonomi's studio.

Hay stopped again in Malta – where he met Frederick Catherwood and Henry Parke, who were returning home after visiting Upper Egypt and Nubia – and arrived in Alexandria in November 1824. After a stay in Cairo, Hay visited the main archaeological sites of the country, and stopped for a while in the Thebes area at Qurna, where James Burton and John Gardner Wilkinson were already at work. Wilkinson lived in a tomb of the Eighteenth Dynasty and, when he visited him at the end of July 1827, Hay was deeply impressed by this unusual, but comfortable, home.

In 1828 Hay went to Malta, where he married a beautiful Cretan girl, Kalitza Psaraki, whom he had rescued from the slave market of Cairo. He subsequently returned to Qurna, where he lived in the tomb used as a dwelling by Wilkinson. Hay stayed in the area until 1834, making plans and drawings of sixteen tombs in the Valley of the Queens and twenty-three tombs in the Valley of the Kings, where he also remained for a time, using the tomb of Ramesses IV (KV2) as his home.

Hay was fond of the company of artists and architects, and frequently worked in collaboration with them – for instance, the draughtsman Joseph Bonomi, his first assistant in 1824, and the British Orientalist Edward William Lane. Lane later became well known for his English translation of the *Arabian Nights* as well as being the author of the first scientific ethnographic work on Egypt, entitled *An Account of the Manners and Customs of the Modern Egyptians*. He was, furthermore, the first artist in Egypt to use the camera lucida. This equipment allowed the objects and monuments observed to be drawn directly on to a sheet of paper with great precision.

In 1832 Francis Arundale came to stay at Qurna and worked with Hay. In the same year, Frederick Catherwood returned to Egypt and, with George Hoskins, undertook a journey of exploration with Hay to Kharga Oasis in late 1832 and early 1833. In 1834, the same year as James Burton, Hay decided to leave Egypt and return to Britain, where, a few years later, in 1840, he published a series of views of Cairo entitled *Illustrations of Cairo*. But the most important part of his work in Egypt, consisting of thousands of drawings, plans of monuments and copies of inscriptions – contained in no fewer than forty-nine volumes in the British Library in London – is still unpublished today and has only been partially studied.

Hay also made a large number of plaster casts of reliefs, most of which were acquired by the British Museum, which also bought many of the artifacts found by Hay during the years he spent in Egypt. The rest of his collection was purchased by the Museum of Fine Arts in Boston.

322 (opposite left) Hay's view of the Birket el-Fil, in Cairo. This was a large reservoir, formerly situated between Bab Zuwaylah and the mosque of Hassan Pasha (an officer in Muhammad Ali's army), that was drained in the nineteenth century.

322–323 Robert Hay's only published work was a book entitled Illustrations of Cairo, with numerous drawings. Many of these were by his friend and collaborator Owen Browne Carter, but this one, showing the fortress of Qalat el-Kebsh, is by Hay.

324 *The fountain of Tussun Pasha, built at the time of Muhammad Ali, is one of the most remarkable in Cairo.*

The drawing by Owen Browne Carter is from the volume illustrating the monuments of Cairo published by Hay.

325 *Carter also drew the fountain of Nafisa Bayda. Nafisa was a very intelligent and cultured woman who played a role as an intermediary between Murad Bey and Napoleon; she is the only woman to whom a monument has been dedicated in the area of the Bab Zuwaylah, in what was considered to be the most important street in Cairo.*

326 (right) On the back pillar of the Colossi of Memnon are three vertical columns of hieroglyphs forming a dedication to Amenhotep III.

326 (below left) The thrones on which the two colossi of the king are seated are decorated with the allegorical representation of the union of Upper and Lower Egypt. Two forms of the god of the Nile inundation, Hapy, tie the lotus and papyrus, the symbolic plants of the two areas.

326 (below right) Catherwood visited Egypt twice, in 1823 and 1832. During his second visit he worked at Thebes with the collector and archaeologist Robert Hay and made the first systematic survey and excavation of the Colossi of Memnon.

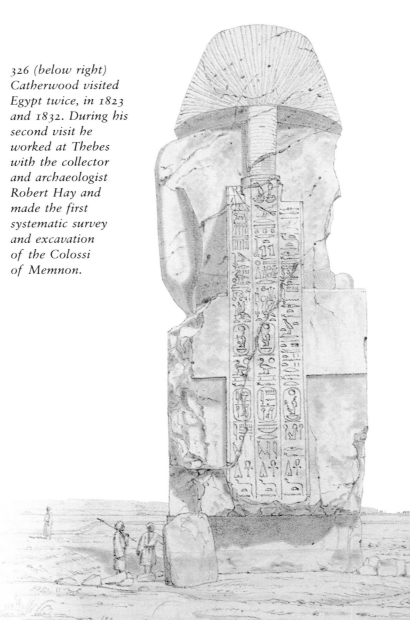

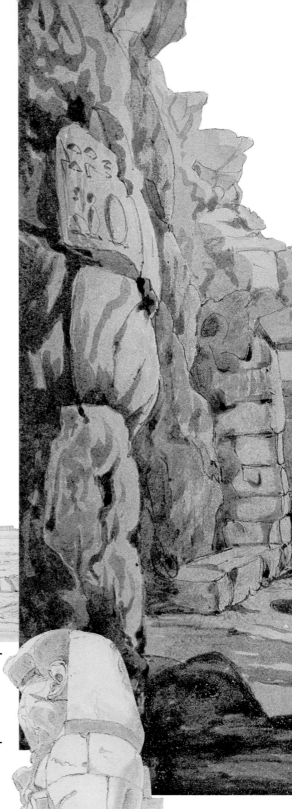

Frederick Catherwood

326–327 *During his first visit to Egypt, Catherwood, in the company of the architects Joseph John Scholes and Henry Parke, and the antiquarian Henry Westcar, ventured as far as the Second Cataract, visiting various monuments including the temple of Gerf Hussein, where he made this drawing.*

Anyone with an interest in Mesoamerican archaeology, especially the ruins of Maya cities and monuments, is familiar with the marvellous drawings of Frederick Catherwood (1799–1855). But few perhaps are aware that this talented artist, born in London, had previously worked for some time in Egypt.

To complete his artistic training Catherwood went to Rome in 1822 – at that time the city was considered to be an essential part of any grand tour undertaken by young artists, lovers of antiquity and aristocratic Englishmen. In Rome he became acquainted with the great draughtsman Joseph Bonomi, who left two years later for Egypt. Bonomi stayed in Egypt for about ten years, working with numerous Egyptologists and participating in Richard Lepsius' Prussian Expedition. He made an enormous quantity of drawings of archaeological finds, including the alabaster sarcophagus of Seti I that

Belzoni sent to England, and prepared the illustrations for John Gardner Wilkinson's most famous work, *Manners and Customs of the Ancient Egyptians*. Bonomi was also responsible for the cataloguing and pictorial documentation of many collections of ancient Egyptian antiquities, including a selection of objects in the British Museum that he published in collaboration with the architect Francis Arundale in a volume called *Gallery of Antiquities Selected from the British Museum*.

Bonomi introduced the architects Henry Parke (1792–1835) and Joseph John Scholes, from London, to Catherwood, and the three set out for Egypt in the following year. Having been joined by Henry Westcar (1798–1868), a collector and antiquarian, the party travelled up the Nile as far as the Second Cataract. On this journey Parke drew the first detailed map of the monuments of Nubia.

Catherwood returned to England in 1824, but eight years later, in 1832, he left for a second visit to Egypt. In Luxor he met his old friend Bonomi again, who by now had been in the country for nine years. This time Bonomi recommended him to a remarkable individual with whom he had been working: Robert Hay, the archaeologist, draughtsman and collector whom Catherwood had met briefly in Malta in 1824 when returning from his first visit to Egypt. Thus Catherwood began to work with Hay – who, like Wilkinson, had chosen to live at Qurna on the slopes of the Theban mountain, making his home in a tomb – and undertook the first systematic survey and excavation of the Colossi of Memnon. These two huge statues representing the pharaoh Amenhotep III originally stood in front of the first pylon of the pharaoh's mortuary temple, of which nothing now remains. Because the temple was situated too close

327

328–329
Catherwood
travelled as far as
Abu Simbel and the
Second Cataract: his
drawing of the
temple of Ramesses
II, probably rapidly
executed on the spot,
is a fresh, almost
impressionistic
rendering of the
subject.

328 (below) On his
journey to Nubia,
Catherwood stopped
at Wadi es-Sebua,
where he made this
drawing of the pylon
of the temple built
by Ramesses II.

to the river, it had been completely eroded by the waters of the Nile during the annual floods.

Catherwood also drew a detailed plan of the monuments in West Thebes and the temple of Karnak, and, together with the artist George Hoskins, took part in the expedition that Hay made to Kharga Oasis. In 1833, after he had finished his work in Thebes, Catherwood went on another journey, this time with Bonomi and the architect Francis Arundale, to the Sinai,

Palestine, Jordan, Syria and Lebanon, before returning to London. Here, his plans and drawings contributed to the creation of a giant panorama of the temple of Karnak that the painter Robert Burford displayed in Leicester Square.

It was on this occasion that Catherwood met the architect and explorer John Lloyd Stephens, his future companion in the jungles of the Yucatán and the neighbouring areas of Mexico, Guatemala, Honduras and present-day Belize.

Catherwood died in 1854 when the steamship on which he was travelling from Liverpool to New York sank.

Unlike other explorers of his day, Catherwood was a reluctant writer, and little is known about his private life and the details of his visits to Egypt. Many of his numerous drawings have been lost, while many others are kept in the British Museum together with Hay's manuscripts, and they have yet to be fully studied and published.

330 *George Alexander Hoskins, seen here at work while a servant shields him from the sun with an umbrella, was an amateur artist who arrived in Egypt in 1832 and worked with Robert Hay at Qurna.*

George Alexander Hoskins (1802–1863) was an amateur artist who was fascinated by ancient monuments and artifacts, as well as by travel and the East. He arrived in Egypt in 1832, when he was thirty years old. At Qurna he met Robert Hay, who was living comfortably in an ancient tomb, which had become a genial meeting place for European travellers visiting the area. This is how Hoskins described the experience:

On Thursday evenings also the artists and travellers at Thebes used to assemble in his house, or rather tomb I should call it; but never was the habitation of death witness to gayer scenes. Though we wore the costume, we did not always preserve the gravity of Turks, and the saloon, although formerly a sepulchre, threw no gloom over our mirth.

Hoskins began to work with Hay, but his passion for travel was stronger than his interest in archaeology, and he decided to set out for Nubia to visit the cataracts, venturing as far as the Dongola area in the Sudan. Subsequently, Hoskins, together with Hay and Catherwood, explored the Kharga Oasis. During this adventurous journey he made numerous drawings that were later collected in three volumes, now kept in the Griffith Institute in Oxford.

330 (below) In 1832 and 1833 Hoskins undertook a journey to Nubia, visiting all the main archaeological sites. This drawing is of the cemetery at Nuri, opposite Gebel Barkal, on the west bank of the Nile. Just as the Theban kings were buried in the Valley of the Kings on the west bank of the river opposite Karnak, Taharqa, the third king of the Twenty-Fifth Dynasty, chose to be buried at Nuri, where he had a pyramid built. His example was then followed by the other kings until the founding of the Meroitic kingdom.

George Alexander Hoskins

330–331 At the time of Hoskins' visit, the pyramids of Meroë were still intact, but two years later their tops were removed systematically by Giuseppe Ferlini, an Italian traveller, in his search for precious objects. Ferlini, an unscrupulous but fortunate adventurer, managed to uncover the treasure of queen Amanishakheto (first century BC), which is now in museums in Munich and Berlin.

When he returned to England, Hoskins published an account of his journeys in two books entitled *Travels in Ethiopia* and *Visit to the Great Oasis of the Libyan Desert*, the latter containing a detailed description of his adventures in the desert. After he became secretary of the White Nile Association, which was set up to promote the study and exploration of this section of the great river, Hoskins abandoned his Egyptological interests in order to devote himself to the social sciences, in particular the study of prisons. After undertaking a final journey to Egypt in 1860 and 1861, he died in Rome in 1863.

331 (above) A drawing by Hoskins of the temple of Taharqa at Gebel Barkal, the sacred mountain believed to be the dwelling-place of Amun. In the sanctuary built by Taharqa were a number of columns adorned with figures of the god Bes, the only example of this type of decoration found in either Egyptian or Nubian architecture.

331 (right) Hoskins participated in Robert Hay's expedition to the Kharga Oasis during which he made numerous drawings. This one is of the large temple of Amun, the most important monument in the oasis.

332 (below) Owen
Jones visited Egypt
in 1832 during his
journey to Greece
and the Near East.
This drawing is of
the temple of Amun

at Karnak, seen from
the southeast, with
the obelisks of
Hatshepsut and
Thutmose I. In the
foreground is the
Sacred Lake.

332 (below right)
In 1843 Jones
published a large-
format volume
entitled Views on the
Nile from Cairo to
the Second Cataract.
With an introduction

by the famous
Egyptologist Samuel
Birch, it contained
thirty lithographs
accurately
reproducing the
architectural details
of the monuments.

Owen Jones

333 (opposite) This
view of a colonnade
in the temple of
Karnak shows the
attention to detail
typical of Jones's
style; the British
architect was
particularly
interested in the
brightly coloured
decoration of the
monuments of
ancient Egypt.

A brilliant engineer and draughtsman,
Owen Jones (1809–74) may be considered
the British counterpart to the French
architect Hector Horeau. Like the
Frenchman, Jones, who was born in
London in 1809, was apprenticed to an
architect before setting out, in 1832, on his
only journey to Greece and the Near East.
During this he met up with Jules Goury,
and together they visited Egypt. After he
had returned to London, Jones drew the
frontispiece of the only work published by
Robert Hay, *Illustrations of Cairo*, in 1840.
Then, in 1843, Jones published his own
large-format volume containing a collection
of thirty lithographs made by the engraver
George Moore after his original drawings
executed at the main archaeological sites
of Egypt. Each plate was accompanied by
a long and learned historical annotation.

In his drawings, Owen Jones faithfully
reproduced the architectural details of the
monuments and showed a particular
interest in their original, brightly coloured,
painted decoration. The book, entitled
*Views on the Nile from Cairo to the
Second Cataract*, contained a preface by

334 (above) At the time of Jones's journey, the temple of Kom Ombo was still half-buried in sand. This was only cleared in 1893 during the first excavation and restoration of the monument. The temple is dedicated to the crocodile god Sobek and Haroeris, one of the forms of the god Horus called 'Horus the Elder'.

334–335 (right) The elegant Kiosk of Trajan at Philae, surrounded by a group of palms, was one of the most picturesque spots on the island and was the usual landing-place for boats. It was also the preferred spot for travellers to stay when they visited the island, and it was here that Jones pitched his small tent, visible in this drawing.

335 (opposite above) The first pylon of the temple of Isis, the most imposing monument on the island of Philae, is flanked on its east and west sides by two long colonnades. In the foreground Jones portrayed a number of Nubians who lived at the site, using a device that was favoured also by David Roberts, giving a clear impression of the size of the monument and, at the same time, adding a note of local colour.

the famous Egyptologist Samuel Birch (1813–55). Birch, who was the main advocate and champion in Britain of the method of deciphering hieroglyphs proposed by Champollion, later became keeper of the Department of Oriental Antiquities at the British Museum. In his preface he wrote:

In drawing up the accompanying descriptions, the author has availed himself of the labours of those writers who have shed, by means of their hieroglyphical and other researches, so much new light upon the monuments of ancient Aegypt, a country pre-eminently distinguished for the early development of art and civilization. The grandeur of her monuments, which still survive the wreck of empires, is unequalled by those of any other people; and the discoveries of this age have invested with a reality and a name, her history, her religion and her art, till now seen through the dim mist of traditions of travelling Greeks. Of all the nations her monuments are avowedly the most ancient, and the brilliancy of their art increases as it recedes from the time she fell under the

335

power of the Greeks and the Romans into dimness of those ages called, in the story of other nations, heroic and mythic....

In 1854 Jones wrote another book on ancient Egypt, entitled *A Description of the Egyptian Court*, in collaboration with Joseph Bonomi and Samuel Sharpe, a rich banker who was particularly fond of archaeology and Bible studies. After this he devoted himself exclusively to his career as an architect. Examples of Egyptian styles and motifs were included in his most famous work, *The Grammar of Ornament*.

336–337 (above) Jones and Goury ascended the Nile as far as the Second Cataract, making the customary stops in the journey to visit the Nubian temples. This drawing by Jones is of the temple of Ramesses II at Gerf Hussein, now submerged by the waters of the Nile because a lack of time meant it could not be saved during the famous Nubian Rescue

Campaign. One of the colossi of the king was saved, however, and is now displayed in the new museum of Aswan.

336–337 (below) The Second Cataract has now also been submerged by the waters of Lake Nasser. Beginning some miles south of the village of Wadi Halfa, which marks the border between Egypt and the Sudan, it was known

to the local people by the curious name of Batn el-Haggar ('belly of stone'). This cataract was about ten miles long and flowed faster than that at Aswan. It was formed of a series of rapids with a multitude of boulders and rocky towers. One of these was known as the Abusir Rock and it was the custom for travellers to carve their names and the date on it.

338 (left) Dressed in Arab clothes, with an easel and drawing paper at hand, David Roberts is seen at work, helped by an assistant, in the small Ptolemaic temple of Deir el-Medina. This is one of his rare self-portraits.

David Roberts

On descending into the splendid hall, over the sand which again almost reaches to the top of the door, a double row is seen of colossal figures, representing Remeses the Great, attached to square pillars ... the placid expression of these statues is still finer than that of the colossi without.... The walls and pillars are covered with the most interesting sculptured representations ... painted in vivid colours.

This description of the interior of Abu Simbel is by David Roberts (1796–1864), the most famous and popular of all the artists who depicted the monuments of ancient Egypt and the landscapes of the Nile Valley. For him, Abu Simbel surpassed all the other temples in Egypt.

Born at Stockbridge, now a suburb of Edinburgh, in 1796, Roberts was a talented decorator who specialized in painting scenery for the theatre. After a very successful period of work at the Royal

338 (left) The great Scottish painter David Roberts, portrayed here in Arab dress by Robert Scott Laundler in 1840, arrived in Egypt in 1838, a few years after Owen Jones. Roberts was a prolific artist and executed hundreds of drawings and watercolours during his travels in Egypt and the Near East, that, on his return to London, were made into lithographs by Louis Haghe and published in several volumes.

339 (bottom)
Roberts was received
by the Pasha
Muhammad Ali in
Alexandria on 16
May 1839, shortly

before his return to
Britain. This drawing
shows the Pasha,
reclining on a divan
with a water pipe,
while seated opposite

him are Colonel
Campbell, the
British Consul
in Alexandria,
Lieutenant Waghorn
and David Roberts.

The meeting lasted
for about twenty
minutes and the
scene was drawn
from memory by
the Scottish artist.

338–339 One of
Roberts' most
renowned
watercolours is
Approach of the
Simoon, Desert of
Gizeh. Beneath a
fiery sky a group
of Arabs on camels
seeks shelter from
the clouds of sand
raised by the simoon
– a hot desert wind
– in the shadow of
the Sphinx, where
other members of

the caravan have
already stopped. This
scene, probably
painted after Roberts
had returned to
Britain, is sufficiently
dramatic to excuse
some artistic licence:
in the painting the
Sphinx is oriented
to the west, not the
east as it should be,
and by Roberts' day
it had already been
freed from sand
by Caviglia.

Theatre in Glasgow in 1819, Roberts moved to London in 1822 to avail himself of the greater opportunities the city offered young artists trying to make a name for themselves.

Here the enterprising painter began to work at the Covent Garden Theatre, where he was held in high esteem for his ability. He showed his works at the Royal Academy and the Society of British Artists. After being elected president of the latter in 1831, Roberts became acquainted with the leading figures of the London cultural scene, such as the writer Charles Dickens and the great landscape painter J.M.W. Turner, who, together with Roberts' friend

John Wilkie, had a marked influence on the artist. It was Turner, in fact, who managed to persuade him to abandon scene painting and devote himself to becoming a true artist. As a result, Roberts undertook journeys abroad to widen his artistic horizons. After travelling to Spain and Morocco, where he came into contact with Arab art for the first time, Roberts set sail for Egypt on 31 August 1838 with the intention of producing drawings that he could later use as the basis for paintings and lithographs to sell to the public. Egypt was very much in vogue at this time, and travellers, collectors and lovers of antiquities were very keen to buy works

depicting the great monuments of ancient Egypt or inspired by the East.

Roberts, whose fame had already begun to spread, landed at Alexandria on 24 September and presented himself to the British Consul Robert Thurburn, who helped him to obtain the permits necessary for him to travel freely around the country and execute his drawings undisturbed. Roberts left almost immediately for Cairo, though not before he had drawn some of the most famous monuments of Alexandria, including one of the two obelisks of Thutmose III, known as Cleopatra's Needle, and Pompey's Pillar. When he reached Cairo on 30 September, the Scottish artist could finally see for himself the fascinating world that he had previously known only through the illustrations by Frederik Norden, Richard Pococke, Dominique Vivant Denon, Luigi Mayer, Giovanni Battista Belzoni and John Gardner Wilkinson.

Roberts sought to adapt himself as much as possible to the culture and customs of the country and, like many other travellers of the period, immediately abandoned Western dress in favour of the long Arab *jellabah* and a turban. Thus

340–341 (left) A panoramic view of Cairo looking east, over the district of al-Sayyidah Zeinab. In the background on the left is the great mosque of Sultan Hassan and on the right the *fortress known as the Citadel. The sight of the many minarets, veiled by the wind-blown sand and towering over the multitudes below, made a deep impression on Roberts.*

341 (below) Roberts drew this view of the pyramids of Giza seen from the Nile in January 1839, during his second visit to the site after he had returned from his journey to Upper Egypt. He noted in his diary: 'Before these titanic monuments I cannot express my feelings'.

attired, he was able to immerse himself in the hustle and bustle of Cairo, a city which, a few years later Maxime Du Camp, Flaubert's travelling companion, described:

Cairo is the meeting place of all the peoples living in Egypt or for all those coming there for trade, and it is above all in the bazaar that it is possible to admire the variety of the costumes and people....

Roberts drew not only the Islamic mosques and monuments but also the most picturesque streets, the inhabitants and the bustling markets, subjects that also occupied Pascal Coste and Prisse d'Avennes, who visited in Egypt in the same period. He also managed to obtain,

as a particular favour, permission to draw the interior of the mosques, as Coste had already done, and a bodyguard.

Roberts was also busy organizing his voyage up the Nile. After making some inquiries, he managed to find a boat – which would have to serve as both a means of transport and a home – that met his requirements, hiring it for three months, the time that he had calculated his river cruise would take. He set out in the company of a certain Captain Nelley and two other travellers, one of whom was called Vanderhorst, while the other was simply referred to as Mr A. The small party was also accompanied by an Italian

342 (below) A detail of a lithograph from Roberts' book Holy Land, Syria, Idumea, Arabia, Egypt and Nubia, showing a group of Egyptians in the temple of Seti I at Thebes. In the centre, an official of the Pasha sits in front of a water pipe; he has arrived in the region to collect taxes and settle any disputes. On his right is the local village sheikh, accompanied by an attendant.

342 (above) Roberts emphasizes the size of the columns of the hypostyle hall of the temple of Karnak by including human figures. He has also attempted to reproduce the original colours of the reliefs.

342 (above right) Roberts stopped at Dendera at the beginning of December 1838, on his return from Abu Simbel; he stayed for a few days and made numerous drawings. The magnificence of the temple of Hathor, so perfectly preserved, made such an impression on him that he painted four watercolours and a large oil painting, now in the City Art Gallery in Bristol. This view of the hypostyle hall shows its large, Hathor-headed capitals.

cook and a Maltese servant. The travellers left Cairo on 6 October on board two boats. By the evening of 18 October they were already near the temple of Dendera, and on 21 October were within sight of the ruins of Thebes, where they stayed for three days before leaving for Esna, Edfu, Kom Ombo and Aswan. On 30 October Roberts disembarked to pass around the First Cataract on the back of a donkey and visit the island of Philae, which he described as a paradise in the middle of a desolate landscape.

For Roberts, the monuments on this island were the most picturesque of all those he had seen up till then. He first drew the so-called Kiosk of Trajan, which he called the 'hypaethral temple' because it lacked a roof. This monument – which the locals referred to as 'pharaoh's bed' because of a legend that the pharaohs slept there when they visited the temples on the island – excited the admiration of the artist, who was impressed by its elegance and perfect state of preservation. In fact, Roberts noted that

The details of the decorations are so clear as to suggest that the stone cutters have only just finished work. I can hardly convince myself that I have seen a 2,000-year-old monument.

On 8 November 1838, Roberts and his companions reached Abu Simbel, where they stayed for almost a week. In order to gain access to draw the interior of the Great Temple, Roberts was obliged to free the entrance once more from the sand that, after the most recent excavation carried out by Robert Hay in June 1831, had again accumulated in front of the monument's façade. The writer William Brockedon, who wrote a commentary on Roberts' illustrations, based on the artist's notes, explained:

For the latest excavations here, as well as for many important discoveries in Egypt and Nubia, the public are indebted to Mr. Hay; he had the sand so far removed as to disclose entirely the two colossi on the south side of the door, together with the doorway down to its base, and now nine or ten Nubians can remove the sand in a few hours which may fall in, and give ready access to the temple, of which the whole height of the facade is shewn. In doing this, he also exposed to view a curious Greek inscription....

343 (above) The watercolours Roberts painted on his travels were made into lithographs for publication by Louis Haghe. This one is of the spectacular ruins of the temple of Luxor, which particularly impressed the artist.

343 (right) It had become a custom for artists visiting Egypt to draw the colossal statue of Ramesses II, lying on the ground in the second courtyard of the Ramesseum at West Thebes. Known also as the 'tomb of Ozymandias', it inspired Shelley to write his sonnet 'Ozymandias'.

Roberts produced numerous drawings and watercolours of the two temples, for which he felt a deep admiration and respect. He analysed their every detail and lamented the behaviour of the tourists of the day who, on occasion, did not hesitate to disfigure them irreparably, as Brockedon noted in his comments:

Roberts in his Journal complains indignantly of the way in which "Cockney tourists and Yankee travellers" have knocked off a toe or a finger of these magnificent statues. "The hand," he says, "of the finest of them has been destroyed …by these contemptible relic-hunters, who have also been led by their vanity to smear their vulgar names on the very forehead of the Egyptian deities."

After spending a few days at Abu Simbel Roberts began the return journey, during which he visited the other Nubian temples. He also stopped at Edfu and Thebes, where he remained for about ten days before heading back to Cairo, reaching the capital on 21 December.

On 6 February of the following year Roberts, who had taken nearly a month to sort out all his material and then make the necessary preparations for another journey, left Cairo once more. This time he was in the company of two travellers he had recently met, John Pell and John Kinnear, and a young Egyptian called Ismael Effendi, who spoke fluent English and acted as interpreter. Roberts and his new companions first visited the Sinai, staying

344 (opposite) After Edfu, Roberts visited the Ptolemaic temple of Khnum at Esna, which he reached at dawn on 25 November after sailing downriver through the night. Although the hypostyle hall was free from sand, its floor was several metres below the level of the surrounding land. In order to enter the hall, it was therefore necessary to descend the steps visible on the left. While at work, the artist was surrounded by a group of Copts who were very happy to allow him to include them.

344–345 This view of the Ptolemaic temple of Horus at Edfu shows part of the first hypostyle hall, the colonnaded courtyard and the first pylon. Like the temples at Dendera and Esna, Edfu was perfectly preserved but still half-buried in sand. Roberts arrived there on 22 November 1838 and stayed for two days, fascinated by the elegance and the proportions of this monument, which is second only to the temple of Amun at Karnak in size.

345 (left) The first stop after Roberts' departure from Philae was the temple of Kom Ombo. Built on a rocky spur overlooking the Nile (the Arabic word kom means 'hill' or 'mound'), its construction began under Ptolemy VI in the third century BC and continued for nearly a century until the reign of Ptolemy XIII, while other additions were made in Roman times.

at St Catherine's monastery, which they reached on 18 February 1839, before continuing to Aqaba on the Red Sea. On 6 March they arrived at the site of Petra. From here they carried on to Hebron, Gaza, Jaffa, Jerusalem, Nazareth, Acre, Tyre, Sidon and Baalbek, returning by sea to Alexandria, where, on 16 May 1839, Roberts was received by Muhammad Ali.

On his return to London, Roberts devoted himself to the task of putting the finishing touches to his drawings and watercolours. Having been made a member of the Royal Academy, he presented the

works he had produced during his journey to Egypt and the Holy Land to the public in London. They were shown in two very successful exhibitions that were also put on in Glasgow and Edinburgh.

His wonderful illustrations were published in various editions, including six large-format volumes, between 1842 and 1849, entitled *The Holy Land, Syria, Idumea, Arabia, Egypt and Nubia*. These volumes contained 247 lithographs prepared by the engraver Louis Haghe, of which 124 were of Egypt. The work was reprinted from 1846 to 1850 in a smaller,

less expensive format with a commentary by William Brockedon, which brought worldwide fame to Roberts that has lasted until the present day.

In the following years the artist enjoyed the fruits of his success. After he had received an award at the international exhibition of Paris in 1855, he travelled at length in France, Belgium, the Netherlands and Italy. He died in London on 25 November 1864. His travel journal, which is full of lively anecdotes and observations, is kept in the National Library of Scotland and has yet to be fully published.

347 (above) As the frontispiece for one of the editions of his book, Roberts chose his drawing of the entrance to the temple of Abu Simbel. The large statue of the falcon-headed god Re holding a user-sceptre and an ostrich feather, symbol of Maat, the goddess of cosmic order, is a cryptogram for one of the names of pharaoh Ramesses II: Usermaatre.

347 (below) Roberts particularly admired the Kiosk of Trajan at Philae, calling it the 'hypaethral temple' because it lacked a roof. It was also known as 'pharaoh's bed' because, according to legend, the pharaohs slept there when they visited the temples on the island.

346–347 On 9 November 1838 Roberts reached Abu Simbel, where he stayed for almost a week, impressed by the size and majesty of the temple of Ramesses II. To gain access to the interior of the temple, the artist had to clear away the sand from façade that had accumulated since the previous time it had been removed by Robert Hay in 1831.

348 During his
ascent of the Nile,
Roberts stopped for
a day at the temple
of Ramesses II,
Amun-Re and Re-
Harakhty at el-
Sebua, before
continuing to Abu
Simbel. Roberts
made several
drawings of the
temple, including
this one of the two
colossal statues of
Ramesses II in front
of the pylon (one
lying on the ground).
The temple has been
moved to a new site,
but one of the
statues can be seen
in the same position
as Roberts drew it.
348–349 (right) In
November 1838, on
his return journey
down the Nile to
Cairo after visiting
Abu Simbel, Roberts
stopped in his boat,
visible here, near
Qasr Ibrim. He
visited the ruins of
an ancient fortress
originally founded in
the Eighteenth
Dynasty, which at
the time of his visit
was situated on the
high promontory
overlooking the river.
Thanks to this
elevated position,
the site – in Roman
times an important
military post known
as Primis – escaped
being drowned by
the waters of the
Nile after the Aswan
High Dam was built.

349 *At a village on the banks of the Nile below Qasr Ibrim, near the temple of el-Dakka, Roberts drew this group of young Nubian women gracefully carrying water pitchers.*

349

Hector Horeau

350 (left) As a result of the huge surge of interest in Egypt in the early nineteenth century, Hector Horeau decided to organize a visit to the country. During his adventure, between 1837 and 1839, he ascended the Nile as far as Abu Simbel and visited all the main archaeological sites of the area. In his drawings he paid particular attention to the architectural and decorative details of the buildings. This aquatint is of the interior of the temple of Khnum at Esna.

351 (left)
Undoubtedly one of
Horeau's most
famous works, this
illustration may be
regarded as a typical
example of the
imaginative power
and romantic taste
of artists in the early
nineteenth century.

An imaginary bird's-
eye view of Egypt, it
shows the Nile valley
from Alexandria to
the temples of Abu
Simbel and the
Second Cataract,
with the main
monuments clearly
represented on both
banks of the river.

350–351 After his
return to France,
Horeau set about
producing aquatints
from the large
number of sketches
and drawings he had
made during his
wanderings along the
Nile and in Cairo.

With the assistance
of Pierre Gustave
Joly de Lotbinière, a
photographer friend,
Horeau published
Panorama d'Égypte
et de Nubie in 1841.
It immediately
excited great interest
among the public,

who were eager for
what were regarded
as exotic pictures.
In his views, such
as this one of the
temple of Edfu,
Horeau shows an
impressive
descriptive skill, if
a rather naive style.

When, in 1826, Frédéric Cailliaud decided
to publish an account of his second
journey to Nubia, entitled *Voyage à
Meroé*, he chose a young architect who
had recently graduated from the École des
Beaux Arts to draw the illustrations for the
book. This was Hector Horeau (1801–72).
Horeau, who was born in Versailles, made
his own first journey to Egypt and Nubia
in 1837. Immediately fascinated by the Nile
and the ancient monuments, he hired a
boat and, on 1 April 1837, began his
voyage towards Thebes. While in Cairo,
he had made a number of drawings of the
most picturesque streets, various mosques,
the slave market and, naturally, the
pyramids of Giza and the Sphinx. Horeau
reported the latter monument had a door
in its base that gave access to a system of
tunnels excavated in the rock leading to the
Great Pyramid (the pyramid of Khufu). In
his diary he describes the preparations for
his journey:

*I left Cairo on a boat of medium size
that I hired for a hundred and fifty francs a
month, with the captain and a crew of six
men, who had to keep themselves. As a
precaution, I ordered that the boat should
be submerged for twenty-four hours so as
to kill all the insects that normally infest
the boats sailing on the Nile. My
provisions consisted of rice, biscuits, dried
fruit, cheese, sugar, a little alcohol and a
small medicine case.... I also had a permit
issued by the French consul and I wore
Arab clothes so that I would feel more at
ease and be treated with greater respect. I
left alone, without any companions,
although I had a little servant who lorded
it over my boat more than any king would
in his kingdom.*

Horeau ascended the Nile, stopping
off at the sites of archaeological interest,
following the itinerary that had already
become standard by this time and is still
followed by tour operators today. It
included the tombs of Beni Hasan, Asyut,

352 (right) Like many other European travellers of his day, Horeau was particularly impressed by the temple of Luxor, which he depicted from different angles. In this painting the artist has shown the entrance pylon, with the two colossi of Ramesses II and the eastern obelisk.

352 (centre) In the first decades of the nineteenth century a visit to the Valley of the Kings was still something of an adventure: the last resting-place of the pharaohs was difficult to reach, dangerous due the frequent landslides and was infested with robbers. None the less, the thrill of seeing the beautiful decorations emerge from the darkness was considered sufficient reward.

Dendera – where the artist was particularly moved by the splendour of the great temple of Hathor – and Luxor, the site of the ruins of the ancient city of Thebes, which Horeau drew from the Nile as his boat drew near to the temple of Luxor.

At that time Luxor was a village with a population of around a thousand people, living in houses around the temple and even in its interior. Horeau found the site pleasant and the village 'cheaper than Cairo, with lower prices'. He painted two watercolours of the first pylon of the temple of Luxor, built during the reign of Ramesses II. At the time of his visit, as can be seen in his paintings, the two colossi representing the pharaoh situated in front of the pylon were still buried in sand up to the waist and the western obelisk, given to France by Muhammad Ali, had already been transported to Paris where it was erected in the Place de la Concorde.

Horeau also drew the temple complex of Karnak, of which he painted an imaginary, but remarkable, reconstruction – with great wooden flagpoles anchored to the pylons from which the standards with the colours of Amun and Upper and Lower

352 (opposite below) Paying particular attention to the wall decorations, Horeau depicted the burial chamber of the tomb of Ramesses IV, one of the royal tombs in the Valley of the Kings. Conditions in the tomb must have been extremely difficult, with the artist having to work by flickering torchlight in a confined and poorly ventilated space.

353 It was Champollion, the decipherer of hieroglyphs, who gave the name of the Ramesseum to the imposing mortuary temple built by Ramesses II on the west bank of the Nile at Thebes. It was a huge, perfectly proportioned building, and Horeau drew the surviving columns of the hypostyle hall, which still bore traces of their original polychrome decorations. Behind them are the ruins of the two pylons and the colossal statue of the pharaoh, lying on the ground.

354 (opposite above) Like Roberts, Horeau was especially fascinated by Philae and painted a number of watercolours of it. This is a view of the small Kiosk of Nectanebo I, at the end of the large colonnade leading up to the first pylon of the temple of Isis.

354–355 Horeau painted this panoramic view of Philae from the top of the nearby island of Biga. Following the construction of the first Aswan Dam Philae's monuments

were half covered by the Nile for part of the year and they were threatened with complete submersion by the building of the High Dam. Between 1974 and 1979, therefore, the

buildings of Philae were cut up into 45,000 blocks and rebuilt on the island of Agilqiyyah. Biga is now to the south of Philae, not to the west as it was in Horeau's day.

355 (centre) From the island of Biga the artist painted the west side of Philae, with the great colonnade, the Kiosk of Trajan and the temple of Isis.

355 (below) In front of the temple of el-Sebua, reached by an avenue of lion-headed sphinxes, stood two colossal statues of Ramesses II. A comparison with the human figures gives an idea of their true size.

Egypt fluttered. Other monuments situated on the east bank, such as Medinet Habu, the Ramesseum and the tombs of the Valley of the Kings were also painted by Horeau. He then continued his journey towards Nubia, and after passing Esna, Edfu, Kom Ombo and Gebel Silsila, he arrived at Aswan, where he was greatly impressed by the magnificence of the monuments on the island of Philae. From here, Horeau carried on up the Nile, drawing all the Nubian temples south of the First Cataract and venturing as far as Abu Simbel, where he painted a large number of splendid watercolours.

After returning to France, Horeau reworked the numerous drawings and

sketches he had executed on the spot. For this purpose he found the daguerreotype technique of Pierre Gustave de Lotbinière, a photographer friend of his, very useful. In 1841 Horeau published a volume entitled *Panorama d'Égypte et de Nubie* that immediately made him famous.

For the rest of his life Horeau devoted himself to his career as an architect and town planner, specializing in the design and construction of iron structures. In 1856 he moved to England, where he lived for a number of years. He did visit Egypt once more, in 1869, only three years before his death in Paris in 1872.

The fame of Horeau, who was an undistinguished traveller but an outstanding

illustrator, is closely linked to some of his most remarkable drawings, especially his well-known bird's-eye view of the Nile from Alexandria as far as the temples of Abu Simbel and the Second Cataract. A collection of forty-five sketches and watercolours produced by Horeau at the main archaeological sites in Egypt was acquired by the Griffith Institute in Oxford in 1967.

356 (opposite above) In this bird's-eye view of the Nile valley, similar to the one above (page 351), the perspective is reversed: in the foreground are the foaming waters of the Second Cataract and the rock-temples of Abu Simbel, then come the Nubian temples and the island of Philae, then Karnak and Luxor and finally, on the horizon, are the pyramids of Giza and the Delta.

356–357 The boat hired by Horeau for his voyage up the Nile is seen here moored in front of the Small Temple of Abu Simbel, not far from the Great Temple. The façade of this rock-temple is decorated with two groups of sculptures carved out of the living rock on both sides of the entrance. Each represents the queen Nefertari between two statues of Ramesses II. Unique in Egyptian art, the statue of the royal wife is the same size as those of her husband, the pharaoh, not merely as high as his knee as was customary.

357 (above) In Horeau's day, the four colossi of Ramesses II adorning the façade of the Great Temple of Abu Simbel were still half buried in sand. Using artistic licence, the artist has shown the face of the broken statue in the sand below, though in fact it was completely missing.

357

358 (below) By the time Bartlett, an artist and traveller from London, made his journey up the Nile in 1845, the great era of the rediscovery of Egypt, that had begun in the early eighteenth century and lasted until the first few decades of the nineteenth, was drawing to a close. Exploration had turned into tourism. Although written as an account of his journey, Bartlett's book, The Nile Boat, may be regarded as the first tourist guide to the Nile valley. The great attention to detail typical of his work is evident in this drawing of the first pylon of the temple of Luxor.

William Henry Bartlett (1809–54) combined an innate artistic talent with the precision of the topographer, the spirit of observation of the ethnographer and a passion for exploration and adventure. Born in London in 1809, Bartlett entered the service of the architect John Britton at the tender age of fourteen and worked in his office as an illustrator. But the young artist did not feel suited to a desk-bound existence and, after his apprenticeship, he decided to set out on a grand tour of Europe, America, the Near East and Turkey. This provided him with the material for the publication in 1839 of his first book, *The Beauties of the Bosphorus*, which became his best-known work.

Bartlett arrived in Egypt in 1845 and made the standard journey to Upper Egypt and the Sudan; then, at the head of a small expedition, he went to Petra, after crossing the whole of the Sinai. He published his diaries of these journeys, and his observations on them, in two works, *Forty Days in the Desert, on the Track of the Israelites* and *The Nile Boat or Glimpses of the Land of Egypt*, which were very

William Henry Bartlett

successful. Their popularity was due not only to the text, which was very interesting and well-documented from a historical point of view, but also to the numerous illustrations, which reproduced the sights extremely realistically and in very accurate detail. *The Nile Boat* was more than just an account of the journey – it contained

such a large quantity of information that it could in effect be used as a guide book by those visiting Egypt.

Bartlett, who set sail from Marseille in June 1845, landed at Alexandria and, after the obligatory visit to the city, continued to Cairo using the new canal that Muhammad Ali had been able to finish thanks to the assistance of Pascal Coste. Linking the Egyptian capital to its port, it allowed the journey to be completed in just thirteen hours – much less than the time taken by boats following the Nile.

Having spent some time visiting the monuments of Cairo and the nearby pyramids, Bartlett boarded a *kanja*, a special type of wide river craft suitable for

cruising. He sailed to Luxor, after stopping at Beni Hasan to visit the tombs of the Middle Kingdom and also at Dendera. After a long and thorough inspection of the monuments on the west bank of the Nile, the description of which occupies most of his travel diary, Bartlett continued his journey southwards, passing the First Cataract and venturing as far as Abu Simbel where 'the great rock temples… terminate the most remarkable of the monuments on the Nile'.

Bartlett's journey can be seen as marking the end of an adventurous and romantic era: the age of intrepid exploration was over, supplanted by that of the tourist cruise.

358 (opposite below) Bartlett reached the great temple of Amun at Karnak when the sun had almost set and the shadows were lengthening amidst the forest of 134 columns of the hypostyle hall. The last rays of light caught their papyriform capitals and the reliefs decorating them.

358–359 After passing the cataract and leaving behind the roar of its waters, Bartlett came into sight of the island of Philae 'its temples of mysterious sanctity half-hidden by sheltering groves of palms, and reflected far down into the broad, silent, and glassy river'.

359

SELECT BIBLIOGRAPHY

ÅKERBLAD, Johan David (1763–1819), *Lettre à M. de Sacy*, Paris, 1802.

ALPINUS, Prosper (1553–1616), *Rerum Aegyptiarum Libri IV*, Leiden, 1735.

ALPINUS, Prosper, *De Medicina Aegyptiorum Libri IV*, Venice, 1591.

ALPINUS, Prosper, *De Plantis Aegypti*, Venice, 1592.

ANONIMO VENEZIANO, *Viagio che ò fato l'anno 1589 dal Caiero in Ebrin navigando su per el Nillo*, ms. II, VII 15, Biblioteca Nazionale, Florence.

ATHANASI, Giovanni d' (1798–1854), *A Brief Account of researches and discoveries in Upper Egypt made under the direction of Henry Salt Esq.*, London, 1836.

BANKES, William John (1786–1855), *Geometrical elevation of an Obelisk... from the Island of Philae, together with the pedestal... first discovered there by W.J.B.*, London, 1821.

BANKES, William John, *Narrative of the Life and Adventures of Giovanni Finati*, London, 1830.

BARTLETT, William Henry (1809–54), *Forty Days in the Desert, on the track of the Israelites; or, a Journey from Cairo... to Mount Sinai and Petra*, London, 1848.

BARTLETT, William Henry, *The Nile Boat*, London, 1850.

BELON, Pierre (1517–65), *Les Observations des plusieurs singularitez et choses mémorables trouvés en Grèce, Judée, Égypte, Arabie et autres pays étranges*, Paris, 1553–58.

BELZONI, Giovanni Battista (1778–1823), *Narrative of the Operations and Recent Discoveries within the Pyramids, Temples, Tombs, and Excavations, in Egypt and Nubia; and of a Journey to the Coast of the Red Sea, in search of the ancient Berenice; and another to the Oasis of Jupiter Ammon*, London, 1820.

BELZONI, Giovanni Battista, *Plates illustrative of the Researches and Operations of G. Belzoni in Egypt and Nubia*, London, 1820.

BELZONI, Giovanni Battista, *Hierogliphics found in the Tomb of Psammis, discovered by G. Belzoni*, London, 1822.

BOURGUIGNON D'ANVILLE, Jean Baptiste (1697–1782), *Mémoire sur l'Égypte ancienne et moderne suivis d'une description du Golfe arabique ou de la Mer Rouge*, Paris, 1766.

BRETON DE LA MARTINIÈRE, Jean-Baptiste, *L'Égypte et la Syrie, ou moeurs, usages, costumes et monumens des Égyptiens...*, Paris, 1814.

BROWNE, W.G. (1768–1813), *Travels in Africa, Egypt and Syria from the year 1792 to 1798*, London, 1799.

BROWNE, W.G., *Nouveau voyage dans la Haute et Basse Égypte, la Syrie, le Dar-Four, trad. de l'anglais sur la 2e édition, par J. Castéra*, Paris, 1800.

BRUCE, James (1730–94), *Travels to Discover the Source of the Nile in the years 1768, 1769, 1770, 1771, 1772 & 1773*, Edinburgh, 1790.

BRUCE, James, *Voyage en Nubie et en Abyssinie (1768–1773) trad. par J. Castéra*, Paris, 1790–1792.

BURCKHARDT, Johann Ludwig (1784–1817), *Travels in Nubia*, London, 1819.

BURCKHARDT, Johann Ludwig, *Travels in Syria and the Holy Land*, London, 1822.

CAILLIAUD, Frédéric (1787–1869), *Voyage à l'Oasis de Thèbes et dans les déserts situés à l'orient et à l'occident de la Thébaïde fait pendant les années 1815, 1816, 1817 et 1818*, Paris, 1821.

CAILLIAUD, Frédéric, 'Lettres à M. Jomard', *Bulletin de Société Géographie*, Paris, 1822.

CAILLIAUD, Frédéric, *Voyage à Méroé, au Fleuve Blanc, au delà de Fâzoql, dans le midi du royaume de Sennar...*, Paris, 1826.

CAILLIAUD, Frédéric, *Recherches sur les arts et métiers, les usages de la vie civile et domestique des anciens peuples de l'Égypte, de la Nubie et de l'Éthiopie, suivies de détails sur les moeurs des peuples modernes de ces contrées*, Paris, 1831–37.

CASSAS, Louis François (1756–1827), *Voyage Pittoresque de la Syrie, de la Phénicie, de la Palestine et de la Basse Égypte*, Paris, 1795.

CHAMPOLLION, Jean François (1790–1832), *Introduction à l'Égypte sous les Pharaons*, Paris, 1811.

CHAMPOLLION, Jean François, *L'Égypte sous les Pharaons ou Recherches sur la géographie, la religion, la langue, les écritures et l'histoire de l'Égypte avant l'invasion de Cambyse*, Paris, 1814.

CHAMPOLLION, Jean François, *De l'écriture hiératique des anciens Égyptiens*, Paris, 1821.

CHAMPOLLION, Jean François, *Lettre à M. Dacier...*, Paris, 1822.

CHAMPOLLION, Jean François, *Panthéon égyptien, collection des personnages mythologiques de l'ancienne Égypte*, Paris, 1823.

CHAMPOLLION, Jean François, *Précis du système hiéroglyphique des anciens Égyptiens ou Recherches sur les éléments premiers de cette écriture sacrée, sur leurs diverses combinaisons et sur les rapports de ce système avec les autres méthodes graphiques égyptiens avec un volume de planches*, Paris, 1824.

CHAMPOLLION, Jean François, *Précis du système hiérogliphique augmenté de la lettre à M. Dacier*, Paris, 1824.

CHAMPOLLION, Jean François, *Lettres à M. le duc de Blacas d'Aulps, relatives au Musée royal égyptien de Turin*, Paris, 1824–26.

CHAMPOLLION, Jean François, *Précis du système hiéroglyphique des anciens Égyptiens ou Recherches sur les éléments premiers de cette écriture sacrée...*, Paris, 1827–28.

CHAMPOLLION, Jean François, *Notice descriptive des momuments égyptiens du Musée Charles X*, Paris, 1827.

CHAMPOLLION, Jean François, *Lettres écrites d'Égypte et de Nubie en 1828 et 1829*, Paris, 1833.

CHAMPOLLION, Jean François, *Monuments de l'Égypte et de la Nubie d'après les dessins exécutés sur les lieux, sous la direction de Champollion le jeune*, Paris, 1835–47.

CHAMPOLLION, Jean François, *Grammaire égyptienne, ou Principes généraux de l'écriture sacrée égyptienne appliqués à la représentation de la langue parlée*, Paris, 1836.

CHAMPOLLION, Jean François, *Grammaire égyptienne, ou Principes généraux de l'écriture sacrée égypienne appliqués à la représentation de la langue parlée. Publié sur le ms. autographe*, Paris, 1836–41.

CHAMPOLLION, Jean François, *Dictionnaire égyptien en écriture hiéroglyphe, publié par Champollion-Figeac d'après les mss. autographes; dessiné et écrit par Jules Feuquières*, Paris, 1841–44.

CHAMPOLLION, Jean François, *Notices descriptives conformes aux notices autographes rédigées sur les lieux par Champollion le jeune*, 2 vol., Paris, 1844–89.

CHAMPOLLION-FIGEAC, Jacques Joseph (1778–1867), *Lettre à M. Fourier sur l'inscription grecque du temple de Denderah en Égypte*, Paris, 1806.

CHAMPOLLION-FIGEAC, Jacques Joseph, *Annales des Lagides, ou Chronologie des rois grecs d'Égypte successeurs d'Alexandre le Grand*, Paris, 1819.

CHAMPOLLION-FIGEAC, Jacques Joseph, *Explication de la date égyptienne d'une inscription grecque tracée sur le colosse de Memnon à Thèbes d'Égypte*, Paris, 1819.

CHAMPOLLION-FIGEAC, Jacques Joseph, *Observations sur les coudées égyptiennes découvertes dans les ruines de Memphis*, Paris, 1824.

CHAMPOLLION-FIGEAC, Jacques Joseph, *L'Obélisque de Louqsor, transporté à Paris...*, Paris, 1833.

CHAMPOLLION-FIGEAC, Jacques Joseph, *Fourier et Napoléon, l'Égypte et les cents jours. Mémoires et documents inédits*, Paris, 1844.

CHAMPOLLION-FIGEAC, Jacques Joseph, *Des Dynasties égyptiennes, à l'occasion des ouvrages de MM. Baruchi et Bunsen, da Nouvelle Revue enc.*, Paris, 1847.

CHAMPOLLION-FIGEAC, Jacques Joseph, *Histoire des peuples anciens et modernes*, Paris, 1857.

CHAMPOLLION-FIGEAC, Jacques Joseph, *Égypte ancienne*, 1858.

CHAMPOLLION-FIGEAC, Aimé, *Les deux Champollion, leur vie et leurs oeuvres*, Grenoble, 1887.

COSTE, Xavier Pascal (1787–1879), *Architecture Arabe ou Monuments du Kaire, mesurés et dessinés de 1818 à 1825*, Paris, 1839.

COSTE, Xavier Pascal, *Mémoires d'un Artiste*, Paris, 1878.

DALTON, Richard (1715–91), *Antiquities and Views in Greece and Egypt*, London, 1791.

DAPPER, Olivier (1635–89), *Description de l'Afrique, contenant les noms, la situation et les confins de toutes les parties, ...avec des cartes des États, des Provinces et des Villes...*, Amsterdam, 1676.

D'ARVIEUX, Laurent, *Mémoires du Chevalier Laurent d'Arvieux contenant ses voyages de 1653 à 1683 à Constantinople, dans l'Asie, la Syrie, la Palestine, l'Égypte et la Barbarie, la description de ces pays, les religions, les moeurs...*, Paris, 1735.

DAWSON, Warren R. and UPHILL, Eric P., *Who was Who in Egyptology*, London, 1951.

DE LABORDE, Léon and LINANT DE BELLEFONDS, Louis Maurice Adolphe, *Voyage de l'Arabie Pétrée*, Paris, 1830.

DELLA VALLE, Pietro (1586–1652), *Viaggi*, Rome, 1650–58.

DELLA VALLE, Pietro, *Les fameux voyages de Pietro della Valle...*, Paris, 1663–70.

DE MAILLET, Benoît (1656–1738), *Description de l'Égypte,... Composée sur les mémoires de M. de Maillet, ancien Consul de France au Caire, par M. l'abbé Le Mascrier*, Paris, 1735.

DE MAILLET, Benoît, *Idée du gouvernement ancien et moderne de l'Égypte, avec la description d'une nouvelle pyramide et des nouvelles remarques sur les moeurs et les usages des habitants de ce païs*, Paris, 1743.

DE MONTAUT, Henry, *L'Egypte Moderne –Table de Moeurs Arabes*, Paris, 1869

DE MONTULÉ, Édouard, *Voyage en Amérique, en Italie, en Sicile et en Égypte pendant les années 1816, 1817, 1818 et 1819*, Paris, 1821.

DE MONTULÉ, Édouard, *Travels in Egypt in 1818 and 1819*, London, 1823.

DENON, Dominique Vivant (1747–1825), *Voyage dans la Basse et la Haute Égypte*, Paris, 1802.

DESGENETTES, Nicolas-René Dufriche (1762–1837), *Histoire medicale de l'armée d'Orient*, Paris, 1830.

DIODORUS SICULUS, *Bibliotheca Historica*, Book I.

DONATI, Vitaliano (1717–62), *Giornale del viaggio fatto in Levante d'ordine di S.M. dal medico Vitaliano Donati di Padova, Professore di Botanica nella Regia Università di Torino*, mss n.291, Biblioteca Reale, Turin.

DROVETTI, Bernardino (1776–1852), *Epistolario* (a cura di Silvio Curto e Laura Donatelli), Milan, 1985.

EBERS, George Moritz (1837–98), *Aegypten und die Bücher Mose's: sachlicher Commentar zu den aegyptischen Stellen in Genesis und Exodus*, Leipzig, 1868.

EBERS, George Moritz, *Papyros Ebers: das hermetische Buch über die Arzneimittel der Alten Ägypter in hieratischer Schrift*, Leipzig, 1875.

EBERS, George Moritz, *Durch Gosen aus Sinai: aus dem Wanderbuche und der Bibliothek*, Leipzig, 1881.

EBERS, George Moritz, *Papyrus Ebers: di Maasee und das Kapitel über die Augenkrankheiten; von G.E.*, Leipzig, 1889.

EDMONSTONE, Archibald (1795–1871), *Journey to two of the Oases of Upper Egypt*, London, 1822.

EDWARDS, Amelia Ann Blanford (1831–92), *A Thousand Miles up the Nile*, London, 1877.

EDWARDS, Amelia Ann Blanford, *Pharaohs, Fellahs and Explorers*, New York, 1891.

FINATI, Giovanni (1787–1829+), *Life and Adventures of Giovanni Finati*, ed. W.J. Bankes, London, 1830.

FORBIN, Louis Nicolas Philippe Auguste, comte de, (1777–1841), *Voyage dans le Levant*, Paris, 1819.

FOURMONT, Claude-Louis (1703–80), *Description historique et géographique des plaines d'Héliopolis et de Memphis*, Paris, 1755.

GAU, Franz Christian (1790–1853), *Antiquités de la Nubie, ou Monuments inédits des bords du Nil, entre la première et la deuxième cataracte*, Paris, 1824.

GRANGER, N. (? –1733) , *Relation d'un voyage fait en Égypte en l'année 1730, où l'on voit ce qu'il y a de plus remarquable, particulièrement sur l'histoire naturelle*, Paris, 1745.

GREAVES, John (1602–52), *Pyramidographia, or a description of the Pyramids in Aegypt*, London, 1646.

GREAVES, John, *Demonstratio Ortus Sini Heliaci pro parallelo inferioris Aegypti*, London, 1648.

GROBERT, Jacques François Louis, *Description des pyramides de Ghizé…*, Paris, 1800–1.

GUERIN DU ROCHER, Pierre-Marie-Stanislas, *Histoire véritable des temps fabuleux. Qui contient l'Histoire d'Égypte, depuis Chéops jusqu'à Amasis*, Paris, 1776–77.

HARTLEBEN, Hermine (1846–1918), *Champollion, sein Leben und sein Werk*, Berlin, 1906.

HARTLEBEN, Hermine, *Lettres et Journaux de Champollion le jeune*, Paris, 1909.

HASSELQUIST, Frederik (1722–52), *Voyage and travels in the Levant etc.*, London, 1766.

HASSELQUIST, Frederik, *Voyage dans le Levant, dans les années 1749, 1750, 1751 et 1752, trad. de l'allemand*, Paris, 1769.

HAY, Robert (1799–1863), *Illustrations of Cairo*, London, 1840.

HERODOTUS, *History*, Book II.

HOREAU, Hector (1801–72), *Panorama d'Égypte et de Nubie*, Paris, 1841.

HORAPOLLO, *The Hieroglyphics of Horapollo Nilous*, London, 1839.

HOSKINS, George Alexander (1802–63), *Travels in Ethiopia*, London, 1835.

HOSKINS, George Alexander, *Visit to the Great Oasis of the Libyan Desert*, London, 1837.

HOSKINS, George Alexander, *A Winter in Upper and Lower Egypt*, London, 1863.

IRBY, Charles Leonard (1789–1845) and MANGLES James (1786–1867), *Travels in Egypt, Nubia, Syria and Asia Minor in 1817 and 1818*, London, 1821.

IRWIN, Eyles (1751–1817), *Voyage à la mer Rouge, sur les côtes de l'Arabie, en Égypte et dans les déserts de la Thébaïde en 1777, suivi d'un autre de Venise à Bassorah par Latiqué, Alep, Les déserts, …, dans les années 1780 et 1781. Traduit sur la troisième édition anglaise par M. Parraud*, Paris, 1792.

JOLLOIS, Prosper, *Journal d'un ingénieur attaché à l'expédition d'Égypte (1798–1802)*, Paris, 1804.

JOMARD, Edmé François (1777–1862), *Voyage à l'Oasis de Syouah rédigé et publié par M. Jomard…*, Paris, 1823.

JOMARD, Edmé François, *Observations sur le voyage au Darfour*, Paris, 1845.

JONES, Owen (1809–74), *Views on the Nile from Cairo to the Second Cataract*, London, 1843.

KIRCHER, Athanasius (1602–80), *Prodromus Coptus sive Aegyptiacus*, Rome, 1636.

KIRCHER, Athanasius, *Lingua Aegyptiaca restituta*, Rome, 1643.

KIRCHER, Athanasius, *Oedipus Aegyptiacus*, Rome, 1652–54.

KIRCHER, Athanasius, *Obeliscus Aegyptiacus*, Rome, 1666.

LANE, Edward William (1801–76), *Manners and Customs of the Modern Egyptians*, London, 1836.

LEBAS, Jean Baptiste Apollinaire (1797–1873), *L'Obélisque de Luxor: histoire de sa translation à Paris…*, Paris, 1839.

LEGH, Thomas (1795–1857), *Narrative of a Journey in Egypt and the Country beyond the Cataracts*, London, 1817.

LE GOUZ DE LA BOULLAYE, François, (1610–69), *Les voyages et observations du Sieur Le Gouz de La Boullaye Gentil-Homme Angevin*, Paris, 1653.

LE MASCRIER, Jean-Baptiste, *Description de l'Égypte, contenant plusieurs remarques curieuses sur la géographie ancienne et moderne de ce Païs, sur ses monuments anciens, sur les Moeurs, les Coutumes & la Religion des Habitans, sur le Gouvernement & le Commerce, sur les Animaux, les Arbres, les Plantes &c., composée sur les Mémoires de m. de Maillet, ancien Consul de France au Caire*, Paris, 1735.

LENORMANT, Charles (1802–59), *Musée des antiquités égyptiennes*, Paris, 1842.

LEPSIUS, Karl Richard (1810–84), *Über die Anordnung und Verwandtschaft der semitischen, indischen, altägyptischen und äthiopischen Alphabete*, Berlin, 1835.

LEPSIUS, Karl Richard, *Lettre à M. le Professeur H. Rosellini sur l'alphabet hiéroglyphique*, Rome, 1837.

LEPSIUS, Karl Richard, *Auswahl der wichtigsten Urkunden des ägyptischen Alterthums, theils zum ersten Male, theils nach del Denkmälern berichtigt…*, Berlin, 1842.

LEPSIUS, Karl Richard, *Das Todtenbuch der Aegypter…*, Berlin, 1842.

LEPSIUS, Karl Richard, *Reise von Theben nach Halbinsel des Sinaï vom 4 März bis 14 April, 1845*, Berlin, 1845.

LEPSIUS, Karl Richard, *Lettre de M. le Dr R. Lepsius à M. Letronne…*, Berlin, 1847.

LEPSIUS, Karl Richard, *Denkmäler aus Aegypten und Aethiopien*, Berlin, 1848–59.

LEPSIUS, Karl Richard, *Die Chronologie der Aegypter*, Berlin, 1849.

LEPSIUS, Karl Richard, *Briefe aus Aegypten, Aethiopien und der Halbinsel des Sinaï, geschrieben, 1842–1845*, Berlin, 1852.

LEPSIUS, Karl Richard, *Königliche Museen. Abteilung der Aegyptischen Alterthümer. Die Wandgemälde*, Berlin, 1855.

LEPSIUS, Karl Richard, *Königsbuch der alten Aegypter*, Berlin, 1858.

LEPSIUS, Karl Richard, *Älteste Texte des Todtenbuchs nach Sarcophagen des altägyptischen Reichs im Berliner Museum*, Berlin, 1867.

LEPSIUS, Karl Richard, *Verzeichnis der ägyptischen Alterthümer und Gipsabgusse von R. Lepsius*, Berlin, 1871.

LEPSIUS, Karl Richard *Nubische Grammatik mit einer Einleitung über die Völker und Sprachen Afrikas*, Berlin, 1880.

LEPSIUS, Karl Richard, *Das bilingue Dekret von Kanopus in der Originalgrösse mit Übersetzung beider Texte*, Berlin, 1886.

LETRONNE, Jean Antoine (1787–1848), *Recherches… l'histoire de l'Egypt pendant la domination des Grecs et des Romains*, Paris, 1823.

LETRONNE, Jean Antoine, *Inscriptions Grecques et Latines du Colosse de Memnon restituées et expliquées*, Paris, 1832.

LETRONNE, Jean Antoine, *L'histoire du Christianisme en Egypt*, Paris, 1832.

LETRONNE, Jean Antoine, *Sur l'origine grecque des Zodiaques prétendus Égyptiens*, Paris, 1837.

LETRONNE, Jean Antoine, *Recueil des Inscriptions Grecques et Latines de l'Égypte étudiées dans leur rapport avec l'histoire politique…*, 1842–48.

LETRONNE, Jean Antoine, *Nouvelles recherches sur le calendrier des anciens Égyptiens, sa nature, son histoire et son origine*, Paris, 1863.

LETRONNE, Jean Antoine, *Oeuvres choisies: assemblées, mises en ordre et augmentées d'un index par E. Fagnan, I. Égypte Ancienne*, Paris, 1881.

L'HÔTE, Nestor (1804–42), *Notice Historique sur les Obélisques Égyptiens et en particulier sur l'Obélisque de Louqsor*, Paris, 1836.

L'HÔTE, Nestor, *Lettres écrites d'Égypte en 1838 et 1839*, Paris, 1840.

L'HÔTE, Nestor, *Lettres d'Égypte en 1840–41*, Paris, 1841.

LINANT DE BELLEFONDS, Louis Maurice Adolphe (1799–1883), *Account of a Journey into the Oases of Upper Egypt*, London, 1822.

LINANT DE BELLEFONDS, Louis Maurice Adolphe, *Journal d'un voyage à Méroé dans les années 1821 et 1822*, Khartoum, 1958.

LINANT DE BELLEFONDS, Louis Maurice Adolphe, *L'Etbaye, pays habité par les Arabes Bicharieh. Géographie, ethnologie, mines d'or*, Paris, 1832.

LINANT DE BELLEFONDS, Louis Maurice Adolphe, *Mémoires sur les principaux travaux d'utilité publique exécutés en Égypte depuis la plus haute Antiquité jusqu'à nos Jours. Accompagnés d'un Atlas renfermant neuf planches grand in-folio…*, 1872–73.

LUCAS, Paul (1664–1737), *Voyage…dans la Turquie, l'Asie, Sourie, Palestine, Haute et Basse-Égypte*, Paris, 1719.

MAYER, Luigi, *Views in Egypt…*, London, 1805.

MAYR, Heinrich von, *Malerische Ansichten aud dem Orient, gesammelt auf der Reise Sr. Hobeit des Herrn Herzogs Maximilian in Bayern nach Nubien, Aegypten, Palestina, Syrien, und Malta im Jahre MDCCCXXXVIII*, Munich, 1839.

MAYR, Heinrich von, *Genre-Bilder aus dem Oriente*, Stuttgart, 1846–50.

MAXIMILIAN OF BAVARIA, *Wanderung nach den Orient*, Munich, 1839–40.

MAXIMILIAN OF BAVARIA, *Bilder aus Orient*, Stuttgart, 1846.

MINUTOLI von, Heinrich Carl Menu (1772–1846), *Reise zum Tempel des Jupiter Ammon in der Libyschen Wüste und nach Ober-Aegypten in den Jahren 1820 und 1821. Mit einem Atlas von 38 Tafeln und einer Karte des Karavanenzuges*, Berlin, 1824.

NIEBHUR, Karsten (1733–1815), *Beschreibung von Arabien*, Copenhagen, 1772.

NIEBHUR, Karsten, *Reisenbeschreibung nach Arabien und andern umliegenden Ländern*, Copenhagen, 1744–78.

NIEBHUR, Karsten, *Voyage en Arabie et en d'autres païs circonvoisins (1761), traduit de l'allemand*, Paris 1776–80.

NORDEN, Frederik Ludwig (1708–42), *Voyages d'Égypte et de Nubie (1738) Ouvrage enrichi des cartes et figures dessinées sur les lieux, trad. du danois en français par des Roches de Parthenais*, Copenhagen 1751 and 1755.

NORDEN, Frederik Ludwig, *Travels in Egypt and Nubia*, London, 1757.

PALERNE, Jean (1557–92) *Pérégrination où il est traicté de plusieurs singularitéz et antiquités remarquées en provinces d'Égypte, Arabie déserte et pierreuse…*, Lyon, 1606.

PASSALACQUA, Giuseppe (1797–1865), *Catalogue raisonné et historique des antiquités découvertes en Égypte par J. Passalacqua*, Berlin, 1826.

PIGAFETTA, Filippo (1533–1604), *Relazione del Reame di Congo e delle circomvicine contrade…*, Rome, 1591.

PIGAFETTA, Filippo, *Viaggio da Creta in Egitto e al Sinai 1576–77*, Vicenza, 1984.

POCOCKE, Richard (1704–65), *A Description of the East, and Some other Countries*, London, 1743.

POCOCKE, Richard, *Voyage dans l'Égypte, l'Arabie, la Palestine, la Syrie, la Grèce, la Thrace, etc.*, contenant une description exacte de l'Orient et de plusieurs autres contrées ..., traduits de l'anglais sur la seconde édition [1771] par une société de gens de lettres, Paris, 1772–73.

PLUTARCH, *De Iside et Osiride*.

PREZIOSI, Amadeo, *Souvenir de Caire*, Paris, 1862

PRISSE D'AVENNES, Achille Constant Théodore Émile (1807–79), *Coup d'oeil sur la situation en Égypte*, Paris, 1831.

PRISSE D'AVENNES, Achille Constant Théodore Émile, *Excursion dans la partie orientale de la Basse–Égypte, Miscellanea Aegyptiaca*, Alexandria, Paris, 1842.

PRISSE D'AVENNES, Achille Constant Théodore Emile, *Excursion dans la partie orientale de la Basse-Égypte, Miscellanea Aegyptiaca*, Alexandria, 1842.

PRISSE D'AVENNES, Achille Constant Théodore Émile, 'Lettre sur l'archéologie égyptienne à M. Champollion-Figéac', 27 mai 1843, *Revue Archéologique*, 1844.

PRISSE D'AVENNES, Achille Constant Théodore Émile, *Les Monuments Égyptiens*, Paris, 1847.

PRISSE D'AVENNES, Achille Constant Théodore Émile, 'L'Égypte moderne,' *L'Univers*, Paris, 1848 and 1851.

PRISSE D'AVENNES, Achille Constant Théodore Émile, *Oriental Album*, London, 1848–51.

PRISSE D'AVENNES, Achille Constant Théodore Émile, *Miroir de l'Orient, ou tableau historique des croyances, moeurs, usages, sciences et arts de l'Orient Mussulman et Chrétien, ouvrage rédigé et illustré d'après des documents inédits et authentiques par une société d'orientalistes, d'artistes, sous la direction de M. Prisse d'Avennes*, Paris, 1852.

PRISSE D'AVENNES, Achille Constant Théodore Émile, *Les tribus nomades de l'Égypte. Les Ababdeh. Revue Orientale*, 1853.

PRISSE D'AVENNES, Achille Constant Théodore Émile, *L'Art arabe...*, Paris, 1877.

PRISSE D'AVENNES, Achille Constant Théodore Émile, *L'Histoire de l'Art Égyptien...*, Paris, 1878.

PRISSE D'AVENNES, Émile, fils, *Notice biographique sur É. Prisse d'Avennes, voyageur français, archéologue, égyptologue et publiciste*, Paris, 1894 and 1896.

PRISSE D'AVENNES, Émile, fils, *Prisse d'Avennes, explorateur français, égyptologue, archéologue et publiciste*. Mémoires de la Société archéologique de l'arrondissement d'Avesnes, 1904.

PRISSE D'AVENNES, Émile, fils, *Deux papyrus égyptiens hiératiques et figuratifs*. Mémoires de la Société archéologique de l'arrondissement d'Avesnes, 1912.

PRISSE D'AVENNES, Émile, fils, *Le Papyrus à l'époque pharaonique*, Avesnes, 1926.

PTOLEMAEUS, Claudius, *La geografia di Claudio Ptolemeo alessandrino...*, Venice, 1548.

QUATREMERE, Étienne-Marc (1782–1857), *Recherches critiques et historiques sur la langue et la littérature de l'Égypte*, Paris, 1808.

QUATREMERE, Étienne-Marc, *Mémoires géographiques et historiques sur l'Égypte et sur quelques contrées voisines*, Paris, 1811.

RAMUSIO, Giovan Battista, *Della Navigationi et Viaggi ...*, Venice, 1550.

RIFAUD, Jean Jacques (1786–c.1845), *Rapport faits par les diverses Académies et Sociétés savantes de France sur les ouvrages et collections rapportés de l'Égypte e de la Nubie*, Paris, 1829.

RIFAUD, Jean Jacques, *Tableau de l'Égypte, de la Nubie et des lieux cinconvoisins: ou itinéraire à l'usage des Voyageurs*, Paris, 1830.

RIFAUD, Jean Jacques, *Voyages en Égypte, en Nubie et lieux circonvoisins, depuis 1805 jusqu'en 1827*, Paris, 1830.

RIFAUD, Jean Jacques, 'Moeurs de l'Égypte et observations sur les Tantals', *Revue des Deux Mondes*, Paris, 1830.

ROBERTS, David (1796–1864), *The Holy Land, Syria, Egypt and Nubia*, London, 1842–49.

ROBERTS, David, *Egypt and Nubia*, London, 1846–50.

ROSELLINI, Ippolito (1800–43), *I Monumenti dell'Egitto e della Nubia*, Pisa, 1832–44.

ROSELLINI, Ippolito, *Tributo di riconoscenza e d'amore reso alla onorata memoria di G.F.Champollion il minore*, Pisa, 1832.

ROSELLINI, Ippolito, *Giornale della Spedizione letteraria toscana in Egitto negli anni 1828–29*, Rome, 1925.

SALT, Henry (1780–1827), *Twenty-four Views taken in St Helena, the Cape, India, Ceylon, Abyssinia and Egypt*, London, 1809.

SALT, Henry, *Account of a Voyage to Abyssinia and Travels into the Interior of that Country... in the years 1809 and 1810*, London, 1814.

SALT, Henry, *Essay on Dr. Young's and M. Champollion's Phonetic System of Hieroglyphics, with some additional discoveries*, London, 1825.

SAVARY, Claude Étienne (1750–88), *Lettres sur l'Égypte. Où l'on offre le parallèle des moeurs anciennes et modernes de ses habitants, où l'on décrit l'état, le commerce, l'agriculture, le gouvernement, l'ancienne religion du pays, et la descente de St. Louis a Damiette, tirée de Joniville et des auteurs arabes*, Paris, 1785–86.

SEGATO, Girolamo (1792–1836), *Saggi pittorici, geografici statistici e catastali dell'Egitto*, Florence, 1827.

SEGATO, Girolamo, *Atlante Monumentale del Basso e dell'Alto Egitto*, Florence, 1835.

SHAW, Thomas (1694–1751), *Travels or Observations relating to several parts of Barbary and the Levant*, Oxford, 1738.

SHAW, Thomas, *Voyages dans plusieurs provinces de la Barbarie et du Levant, contenant des observations géographiques, physiques, philologiques et mêlées sur les royaumes l'Alger et de Tunis, sur la Syrie, l'Égypte et l'Arabie Pétrée*, trad. de l'anglais, Le Haye 1743.

SICARD, Claude (1677–1726), *Lettre à Mgr le Compte de Toulouse, contenant une relation de ses trois voyages dans la Haute et Basse-Égypte, écrite en 1716*, Paris.

SICARD, Claude, 'Relation d'un voyage aux Cataractes et dans le Delta', in *Nouveaux Mémoires des Missions de la Compagnie de Jésus*, Paris, 1717.

SILVESTRE DE SACY, Antoine Isaac (1758–1838), *Chrestomathie arabe*, Paris, 1806.

SILVESTRE DE SACY, Antoine Isaac, *Grammaire arabe*, Paris, 1810.

SILVESTRE DE SACY, Antoine Isaac, *Journal Asiatique*, Paris, 1822.

SONNINI DE MANONCOUR, Charles Nicolas Sigisbert (1751–1812), *Voyage dans la Haute et Basse-Égypte, fait par ordre de l'ancien Gouvernement (de 1777 à 1780), et contenant des observations de tous genres*, Paris, 1799.

STRABO, *Geography*, Book XVII.

THEVENOT, Jean de (1633–67), *Relation d'un Voyage fait au Levant*, Paris, 1665–74–84.

THEVENOT, Jean de, *Voyages de M. Thévenot*, 1689.

THEVET, André (1504–92), *Cosmographie du Levant*, Lyon, 1554.

VALERIANO BOLZANIO, Giovanni Piero, *Hieroglyphica, sive De sacris Aegyptiorum, aliarumque gentium literis commentarii Ioannis Pierii Valeriani Bolzanii Bellunensis*, Basileae, 1567.

VANSLEB, Jean Michel (1635–79), *Nouvelle relation en forme de journal d'un voyage fait en Égypte en 1672 et 1673*, Paris, 1677.

VILLAMONT Jacques de (1558–1628), *Les voyages du sieur de Villamont, divisez en trois livres, ... Et au troisième est la description de Syrie, de Damas, Phénicie, Égypte, Damiette, du Grand Caire, de Babylone, des anciennes Pyramides et Mommies*, 1595.

VOLNEY, Constantin François Chassebeuf (1757–1820), *Voyages en Égypte et en Syrie pendant les années 1783, 1784 et 1785*, Paris, 1787.

VYSE, Richard William Howard (1784–1853), *Operations carried on at the pyramids of Gizeh in 1837*, London, 1840.

WALSH, Thomas, *Journal of the Late campaign in Egypt*, London, 1803.

WILKINSON, John Gardner (1797–1875), *Materia Hieroglyphica. Containing the Egyptian Pantheon and the Succession of the Pharaohs, from the earliest Times to the conquest by Alexander, and other Hieroglyphical Subjects*, London, 1828–30

WILKINSON, John Gardner, *Extracts from several Hieroglyphical Subjects found at Thebes and other parts of Egypt with remarks on the same*, London, 1830.

WILKINSON, John Gardner, *Topographical Survey of Thebes, Tape, Thaba of Diospolis Magna*, London, 1830.

WILKINSON, John Gardner, *Topography of Thebes, and general view of Egypt...*, London, 1835.

WILKINSON, John Gardner, *The Manners and Customs of the ancient Egyptians...*, London, 1837.

WILKINSON, John Gardner, *Modern Egypt and Thebes: being a description of Egypt, including the information required for travellers in that country*, London, 1843.

WILKINSON, John Gardner, *A Handbook for Egypt. Including Descriptions of the Course of the Nile to the Second Cataract, Alexandria, Cairo, the Pyramids, and Thebes, the Overland Transit to India, the Peninsula of Mount Sinai, the Oases...*, London, 1847.

WILKINSON, John Gardner, *The Architecture of Ancient Egypt: in which the Columns are arranged in Orders, and the Temples classified, with remarks on the early progress of Architecture...*, London, 1850.

WILKINSON, John Gardner, *The Egyptians in the Time of the Pharaohs. Being a Companion to the Crystal Palace Egyptian Collections. To which is added an Introduction to the Study of the Egyptian Hieroglyphs by Samuel Birch*, London, 1857.

WILKINSON, John Gardner, *The Fragments of the Hieratic Papyrus at Turin, containing the names of Egyptian Kings, with the Hieratic Inscription at the back*, London, 1851.

WILKINSON, John Gardner, *A Popular Account of the Ancient Egyptians, revised and abridged from his larger work*, London, 1854.

WILKINSON, John Gardner, *Desert Plants of Egypt. Illustrations with descriptions, by Wm Carruthers F.R.S.*, London, 1887.

YOUNG, Thomas (1773-1829), *Remarks on Egyptian Papyrus and on the Inscription of Rosetta*, London, 1815.

YOUNG, Thomas, *Account of some Thebaic Manuscripts written on leather. Legh's Narrative*, London, 1816.

YOUNG, Thomas, *An Account of Some Recent Discoveries in Hieroglyphical Literature and Egyptian Antiquities. Including the author's original alphabet as extended by M. Champollion*, London, 1823.

YOUNG, Thomas, *Hieroglyphics; collected by the Egyptian Society*, London, 1823.

ILLUSTRATION CREDITS

a = above; b = below; c = centre;
l = left; r = right

De Laborde and Linant de Bellefonds, *Voyage de l'Arabie Petrée*, Paris 1830. © Archivio White Star.

1-3 Louis François Cassas, *Voyage Pittoresque de la Syrie, de la Phénicie, de la Palestine et de la Basse Egypte*, Paris 1795. © Archivio White Star.
4-5 David Roberts, *Egypt and Nubia*, London 1846-49. © Library of Congress, Washington.
6-7 Karl Richard Lepsius, *Denkmaler Aus Aegypten und Aethiopen*, Berlin, 1848-59. © Archivio White Star.

INTRODUCTION
8a © Alberto Siliotti - Archivio Geodia.
8b Athanasius Kircher, *Oedipus Aegyptiacus*, Rome 1666. © Archivio White Star.
9 © Private collection.
9b © Alberto Siliotti - Archivio Geodia.
10a Dominique Vivant Denon, *Voyage dans la Basse et la Haute Egypte*, Paris 1802. © Archivio White Star.
10c Louis François Cassas, *Voyage Pittoresque de la Syrie, de la Phoenicie, de la Palestine et de la Basse Egypte*, Paris 1795. © Archivio White Star.
10-11 Frederick Ludwig Norden, *Voyage d'Egypte et de Nubie*, Copenhagen 1755. © Archivio White Star.
11a Richard Pococke, *A description of the East, and some other countries*, London 1743-45. © Archivio White Star.
12a Giovanni Battista Belzoni, *Egypt and Nubia*, London 1820. © Archivio White Star.
12bl © Private collection.
12-13 Émile Prisse d'Avennes, *L'Art Arabe*, Paris 1820. © Archivio White Star.
14 © Archivio White Star.
14-15 Luigi Mayer, *Views in Egypt*, London 1805. © Archivio White Star.

TOURISTS IN ANTIQUITY
16a © Alberto Siliotti - Archivio Geodia.
16b © Araldo De Luca, Museo Archeologico Nazionale, Naples.
16-17 © Archivio White Star.
17b © Archivio Scala, Museo Nazionale, Naples.
18-19 Österreichische National Bibliothek.
18b © Fotografica Foglia, Museo Nazionale, Naples.
19 bottom © Archivio Scala, Museo Nazionale, Naples.
20-21 © Michele Piccirillo.
22-23 © Giovanni Dagli Orti, Museo Prenestino Barberiniano, Palestrina.

EGYPTIAN TRAVELS FROM THE MIDDLE AGES TO MODERN TIMES
24al, 25l, 25br, 26l, 26br, 27, 29ar, 29l, 30, 32al and r, 34 © Alberto Siliotti - Archivio Geodia.
24ar © Archivio White Star.
24b © Biblioteca Nazionale, Florence.
25ar © Biblioteca Nazionale, Florence.
26-27 © Giovanni Dagli Orti, Biblioteca Marciana, Venice.
28a © Peter Whitfield - Wychwood Editions.
28b © Archivio Scala, Biblioteca Estense, Modena.
29br © Archivio Scala, Biblioteca Marciana, Venice.
31 © Civica Raccolta Stampe A. Bertarelli, Castello Sforzesco, Milan.
32bl and r, 33, 34-35 Athanasius Kircher, *Obeliscus Aegyptiacus*, Rome 1666. © Archivio White Star.

TRAVELLERS OF THE EIGHTEENTH CENTURY
36 Louis François Cassas, *Voyage*

Pittoresque de la Syrie, de la Phénicie, de la Palestine et de la Basse Egypte, Paris 1795. © Archivio White Star.
36-37 © Biblioteca Nazionale, Florence.
37b Frederick Ludwig Norden, *Voyage d'Egypte et de Nubie*, Copenhagen 1755. © Archivio White Star.
38a and b, 39 a and b Benoit de Maillett, *Description de l'Egypte*, Paris 1835. © Archivio White Star.
38-39 © Civica Raccolta Stampe A. Bertarelli, Castello Sforzesco, Milan.
40al © Archivio Scala, Galleria Sabauda.
40ar, 41 © Biblioteca Reale, Turin, Concessione del Ministero per i Beni culturali e Ambientali.
40br and l, © Alberto Siliotti - Archivio Geodia.
42, 43, 44, 45, 46, 47, 48, 49 Richard Pococke, *A description of the Egypt, and some other countries*, London 1743-45. © Archivio White Star.
50, 51, 52, 53, 54, 55 Frederick Ludwig Norden, *Voyage d'Egypte et de Nubie*, Copenhagen 1755. © Archivio White Star.
56, 57, 58, 59 James Bruce, *Travels to Discover the source of the Nile in the years 1768, 1769, 1770, 1771, 1772 and 1773*, London 1804. © Archivio White Star.
60, 61, 62, 63, 64, 65, 66, 67, 68, 69, 70, 71 Louis François Cassas, *Voyage Pittoresque de la Syrie, de la Phénicie, de la Palestine et de la Basse Egypte*, Paris 1795. © Archivio White Star.
72, 73, 74, 75, 76, 77 Richard Dalton, *Antiquities and views in Greece and Egypt*, London 1791. © Archivio White Star.
78, 79 Charles Nicolas Sonnini, *Travels in Upper and Lower Egypt*, London 1799. © Archivio White Star.

NAPOLEON AND THE EGYPTIAN EXPEDITION
80a, 80-81, 86, 88-89a and b, 90, 91, 92, 93, 94, 95, 96, 97, 98, 99 Dominique Vivant Denon, *Voyage dans la Basse et la Haute Egypte* Paris 1802. © Archivio White Star.
81b © Giovanni Dagli Orti, Château de Versailles.
82l *Description de l'Égypte* Paris 1809. © Archivio White Star.
82ar and b, 83, 87r © Photo R.M.N., Versailles and Trianon.
82-83 © The Bridgeman Art Library, Musée des Beaux Arts, Mulhouse.
84-85 © The National Maritime Museum, Greenwich.
86bl © Alberto Siliotti - Archivio Geodia.
86-87 © The Detroit Institute of Arts.
88l, 89a © Victoria & Albert Museum, London.
89b © Musée Denon, Châlon sur Saône.

THE DESCRIPTION DE L'ÉGYPTE
100, 101, 102-103, 102b, 103a, 104, 105, 106, 107, 108, 109, 110r, 112l, 112-113, 114, 115b, 116-117b, 118-119b, 119a, 120b, 121, 122, 123, 124, 125, 126, 127, 128, 129 *Description de l'Égypte*, Paris 1809. © Archivio White Star.
102a and bl, 103b, 110l © Biblioteca Nazionale, Florence.
111 © Photo R.M.N., Versailles and Trianon.
112-113a, 114-115a, 116, 116-117a, 118a, 118-119c, 120-121 © Photo R.M.N., Museé du Louvre, Paris.

THE 'WAR OF THE CONULS'
130a, 131 © Alberto Siliotti - Archivio Geodia.
130b, 132, 133, 148a and b, 148-149, 149a, 150, 151 L.N.P.A. de Forbin, *Voyage dans le Levant*, Paris 1819. © Archivio White Star.
134, 135, 136, 137, 138, 139, 140, 141,

142, 143, 144, 145 Jean Jacques Rifaud, *Voyages en Égypte, en Nubie*, Paris 1830. © Archivio White Star.
146, 147 Henry Salt, *Twenty-Four Views taken in St Helena, The Cape, India, Ceylon, Abyssinia and Egypt*, London 1809. © Archivio White Star.
146a © National Portrait Gallery, London.

FRÉDÉRIC CAILLIAUD
152l and ar, 159c and b © P. Jean - Museum d'Histoire Naturelle, Nantes.
152b, 152-153, 154, 155, 156, 157, 158-159, 159a, 160, 161 Frédéric Cailliaud, *Voyage à Méroé*, Paris 1826. © Archivio White Star.

GIOVANNI BATTISTA BELZONI
162, 163, 166, 173a, 174, 175 © Alberto Siliotti - Archivio Geodia.
164, 165, 166-167, 168-169, 170, 171, 172, 173, 174-175 Giovanni Battista Belzoni, *Egypt and Nubia*, London 1820. © Archivio White Star.
176a © Margarete Busing - Staatliche Museen zu Berlin - Preussischer Kulturbesitz Aegyptisches Museum.

THE EXPEDITION OF BARON VON MINUTOLI TO THE OASIS OF SIWA
176b, 176-177, 177b, 178, 179, 180, 181 Henrich Von Minutoli, *Reise zum Temple des Jupiter Ammon in der Libyschen Wùste und nach Ober-Aegypten*, Berlin 1824. © Archivio White Star.

GIROLAMO SEGATO EXPLORING THE STEP PYRAMID OF DJOSER
182a Alberto Siliotti - Achivio Geodia.
182-183, 183, 184, 185, 186, 187, 188, 189 Girolamo Segato, *Atlante del Basso e Alto Egitto*, Florence 1855. © Archivio White Star.

CHAMPOLLION AND THE FRANCO-TUSCAN EXPEDITON
190-191 © Archivio Scala, Museo Archeologico, Florence.
190, 192, 193, 194, 195, 196a and c, 197a and c, 198a © Alberto Siliotti - Archivio Geodia.
196-197b, 202, 203, 204, 205, 206, 207, 208, 209, 210, 211, 212, 213, 214, 215, 216, 217 Ippolito Rosellini, *I monumenti dell'Antico Egitto e della Nubia*, Pisa 1832. © Archivio White Star.
198b, 199, 201 © Photo R.M.N., Museé du Louvre, Paris.
200-201 © Edimedia, Paris.

JOHN GARDNER WILKINSON
218b © National Trust Photographic Library, Mike Williams.
218a, 219, 220-221b, 221a, 222-223 John Gardner Wilkinson, *The Manner and Customs of the Ancient Egyptians*, London 1878. © Archivio White Star.
220a © Biblioteca Nazionale, Florence.

VYSE AND PERRING
224, 225, 226, 227, 228, 229 Howard Vyse, *The Pyramids of Gizeh*, London 1837. © Archivio White Star.

THE PRUSSIAN EXPEDITION OF RICHARD LEPSIUS
230al and b, 231, 232a, 234, 235, 236-237, 238, 239, 240, 241, 242, 243, 244-245, 246, 247, 248-249, 250, 251, 252, 253 Karl Richard Lepsius, *Denkmaler Aus Aegypten und Aethiopien*, Berlin 1848-59. © Archivio White Star.
232b, 232-233 © Margarete Busing - Staatliche Museen zu Berlin - Preussischer Kulturbesitz Aegyptisches Museum und Papyrussammlung.

MAXIMILIAN OF BAVARIA
254, 255, 256, 257, 258, 259, 260, 261, 262, 263, 264, 265 Maximilian in Bayern, *Malerische Ansichten aus dem Orient*, 1838; *Bilder aus dem Orient*, Stuttgart 1846. © Archivio White Star.

ÉMILE PRISSE D'AVENNES
266l, 267, 274, 275, 276, 277, 278, 279, 280, 281 Émile Prisse d'Avennes, *Histoire de l'art Egyptien*, Paris 1878. © Private collection.
266a © Musée d'Annecy.
266b © Victoria & Albert Museum, London.
268, 269, 270a, 270b, 270-271, 271a Émile Prisse d'Avennes, *Oriental Album*, London 1846. © Archivio White Star.
270c © Alberto Siliotti - Archivio Geodia.

ARTISTS AND TRAVELLERS ON THE NILE
282b, 282-283 Luigi Mayer, *Views in Egypt*, London 1835. © Archivio White Star.
283b © École Nationale Superieure des Beaux Arts, Paris.
284a and b, 284-285, 285b Rev. C. Willyams, *Views in Egypt, Palestine, Rhodes, Italy, Minorca and Gibraltar*, London 1822. © Archivio White Star.
286, 287 Amadeo Preziosi, *Souvenir de Caire*, Paris 1862. © Archivio White Star.
288, 290-291 David Roberts, *Egypt and Nubia*, London 1846-49. © Library of Congress, Washington.
289, 312, 313, 314, 315, 316, 317, 318, 319 Pascal Coste, *Architecture Arabe ou Monuments du Caire*, Paris 1839. © Archivio White Star.
292, 293b, 320b, 320-321, 322, 323, 324-325 Robert Hay, *Views in Cairo*, London 1840. © Archivio White Star.
292-293 © Mathaf Gallery Ltd, London.
294, 295 Henry de Montaut, *L'Égypte Moderne, Tableau de Mouers Arabe*, Paris 1869. © Archivio White Star.
296, 297, 298, 299, 300, 301 Luigi Mayer, *Views in Egypt*, London 1805. © Archivio White Star.
302a, 304-305, 305bl, 326-327, 340, 341, 358-359 © Victoria & Albert Museum, London.
302bl © Archivio White Star.
302br, 302-303, 303l, 304, 305br, 321b, 323br, 325b © Alberto Siliotti - Archivio Geodia.
306, 307, 308, 309 De Laborde and Linant de Bellefonds, *Voyage de l'Arabie Petrée*, Paris 1830. © Archivio White Star.
310, 311 Édouard de Montulé, *Travels in Egypt*, London 1824. © Archivio White Star.
324bl, 326a, 326br, 328, 329 © The British Library, London.
330, 331 George Alexander Hoskins, *Travels in Ethiopia*, London 1835. © Private collection.
331 © The Griffith Institute, Ashmolean Museum.
332, 333, 334, 335, 336, 337 Owen Jones, *Views of the Nile*, London 1843. © Archivio White Star.
338, 339, 342b, 343, 344, 345, 346, 347, 348, 349 David Roberts, *Egypt and Nubia*, London 1846-49. © Library of Congress, Washington.
342al © City of Aberdeen Art Gallery & Museum Collections.
342ar © The Bowood Estate.
343a © Manchester City Art Galleries.
350, 351, 352, 353, 354, 355, 356, 357 H. Horeau, *Panorama d'Egypte et de Nubie* 1841. © Bibliothèque Publique Universitaire de Genève.
358 William Henry Bartlett, *The Nile Boat*, London 1858. © Archivio White Star.

INDEX

These pictures, taken from the book L'Histoire de l'Art Égyptien *by Émile Prisse d'Avennes, portray Prince Montuherkhepshef, the son of Ramesses II (left), and Queen Tiye, wife of Amenhotep III (right).*